WHERE THE TWO ROADS MEET

AMERICAN INDIAN CATHOLICS

CHRISTOPHER VECSEY

VOLUME III

Where the Two Roads Meet

WHERE THE TWO ROADS MEET

CHRISTOPHER VECSEY

UNIVERSITY OF NOTRE DAME PRESS

NOTRE DAME, INDIANA

Copyright 1999 by
University of Notre Dame Press
Notre Dame, IN 46556

Manufactured in the United States of America

Library of Congress Cataloging-in-Publication Data

Vecsey, Christopher,
    Where the two roads meet / Christopher Vecsey.
       p.   cm.—(American Indian Catholics ; v. 3)
    Includes bibliographical references and index.
    ISBN 0-268-01957-6 (alk. paper)
    1. Indians of North America—Religion. 2. Indians
of North America—Missions. 3. Indian Catholics—
North America—History. 4. Dakota Indians—Religion.
5. Dakota Indians—Missions. 6. Catholic Church—
Missions—North America—History. I. Title. II. Series:
Vecsey, Christopher. American Indian Catholics ; v. 3.
    E98.R3V446 1999
    282'.7'08997—dc21   99-22335

Book design by Will Powers
Set in Galliard CC
by Stanton Publication Services, Inc.

For my loved ones,
Carol Ann Lorenz and Christopher George Vecsey

Pima healer, Emmett White, blesses Pope John Paul II
at the annual Tekakwitha Conference, Phoenix, Arizona, 1987.

Photograph by James Baca.

CONTENTS

III

Catholic Indian Leadership

IV
Two Traditions, Meeting

MAPS

As we approach the end of the second millennium since Christ's birth and the formation of his Church on earth, there are close to a billion baptized Catholics in the world, somewhat less than a fifth of the human population. Sixty million of these are United States Catholics, a quarter of the U.S. population. Another twelve million are Canadian Catholics, close to one-half of Canada's population (Foy and Avato 1995: 368, 435, 337).

In the shadow of these substantial figures, the number of contemporary American Indian Catholics appears slight. Approximately 350,000 of the two million U.S. Indians are Catholics (ibid., 530; cf. McDonnell 1987: 19, Peterson, May 7, 1986). These statistics match the percentage of Catholics in the world population: 17 percent. In Canada about a quarter of the 900,000 Native peoples identify themselves as Catholics (Reddy 1993: 231; cf. Grant 1985: 242, Pouliot 1967: 402). This, after a half millennium of contact with Roman Catholicism.

I have found American Indian Catholicism well worth a decade and more of research and writing. In the first two volumes of *American Indian Catholics* I have described the means by which Native Americans over five centuries have become associated with Catholicism, and the ways in which Indians have adapted Catholic forms to their particular historical and cultural circumstances. I have traced the heritage of Spanish and French colonial missions throughout North America (but especially in the United States), observing their effects to the present day. I have observed regional, tribal, and individual patterns of Indian Catholic participation, and I have taken note of the often ambivalent relationship between American Indians and the Church.

On the Padres' Trail and *The Paths of Kateri's Kin* have both employed the imagery of the thoroughfare or the byway to depict the distinct cultural traditions—American Indian and Catholic, in all their variety—which have crossed and even come together over time. *Where the Two Roads Meet* carries on this metaphor by examining in depth the last century or so of interconnection between Native and Catholic ways. Informed and inspired by Carl F. Starkloff's (1991, 1995) missiological meditation upon the contrasting figures of speech, "Good

Fences Make Good Neighbors" and "The Meeting of the Two Rivers," this concluding volume asks how the two traditions continue to interact. More concretely, how have Indian Catholics tried to follow the route of two separable traditions, each with its own expectations, patterns, and identities?

We begin this volume by analyzing Lakota Catholics over the course of a century of contact with Holy Rosary Mission on the Pine Ridge Reservation in South Dakota. For many of these Catholic Sioux and their relatives across the northern plains, including catechists, deacons, seminarians, priests, and female religious, Catholic participation has been largely a matter of fulfilling the kinship obligations of their indigenous culture. These Lakota Catholics have often adopted the strategy of walking two alternating spiritual roads in a single life.

Our second section provides institutional context by recounting the development of Catholic evangelism among American Indians, from the founding of the United States, through the formation of the Bureau of Catholic Indian Missions, to the changes wrought by the Second Vatican Council. Contemporary exponents of Native American ministry, in urban as well as reservation locales, propose "inculturation"—making Christianity at home within indigenous cultural patterns—as their goal, a far cry from the often condemnatory exhortations of former times. The changing rhetoric and practice of Catholic missions have posed a mixed message to Indian Catholics in choosing the contour and direction of their spiritual roads.

Section three examines the lives of American Indian Catholics— priests, bishops, sisters, catechists, deacons, and other laypersons— who have been leaders in their communities and in the Church at large. How have these extraordinary men and women brought together their Indian and Catholic identities, sometimes accomplishing a cultural and religious syncretism within their personhood, and at what personal costs?

The final section scrutinizes two recent developments in Native American Catholic ministry. In certain situations Church personnel have engaged in interfaith dialogue with Indian religious authorities— as it were, a meeting of the two roads in serious conversation. Here we observe an extended example of such discussion, the Medicine Men and Clergy Meetings which took place on the Lakota Rosebud Reservation in the 1970s. Then we survey the last decade of a Church-sponsored organization, the National Tekakwitha Conference, whose stated goal is to foster American Indian Catholic inculturation, so that Catholic Indians may travel the two roads as if they were one. Finally, in the postscript we meditate upon the meeting of the two roads in northern California, among the Hoopa Indians.

The world has refused to sit still while I brought these three volumes of *American Indian Catholics* to conclusion. By committing myself to understanding the contemporary scene as well as the historical, I have sentenced myself to revisions of last year's conclusions—those of my sources as well as my own. New books have appeared, which would have improved my earlier volumes, had I been able to read them beforehand.

I wish that I had discovered Luis N. Rivera's *A Violent Evangelism* (1992) before completing my own appraisal of the Spanish colonial justifications for conquest and mission in the New World. Sylvia Rodríguez's (1996) study of the Matachine Dance in New Mexico, Eileen Oktavec's (1996) analysis of votive offerings in the Sonoran Desert, and Dana Salvo's (1997) photographs of home altars of Mexican Indians would have added to my portrayal of American Indian Catholic piety in the heritage of New Spain. Martha McCarthy (1995) and Raymond J. A. Huel (1996) have added to our knowledge of the Oblate missionaries of Canada and the Indians' responses to them. James D. White (1997) has provided the first, and no doubt definitive, inquiry into the history of Osage Catholicism in Oklahoma. Unfortunately, Joëlle Rostkowski's book, *La Conversion Inachevée: Les Indiens et le Christianisme* (1998) appeared after I had completed the writing of this third volume, as did a new study of Florida Indian missions (Hann and McEwan 1998).

No doubt there are more books I have missed. I know that the Marquette University Memorial Library, Department of Special Collections, Milwaukee, Wisconsin, has continued to accrue archival information, for example, regarding the recent history of the National Tekakwitha Conference. I also know that there are archives I have neglected (most notably the Jesuit Oregon Province Archives, Gonzaga University, Spokane, Washington), and there is one archive (the Diocese of Gallup, New Mexico), to which I was refused entry (Resendes, March 2, 1993). There is always more to learn; nonetheless, it is time for closure. I leave it to other researchers to correct my errors and offer their own interpretations.

ACKNOWLEDGMENTS

I proffer my thanks to Mark G. Thiel, Archivist, Marquette University Memorial Library, Department of Special Collections; Marina Ochoa, Archivist, Archdiocese of Santa Fe; Msgr. David W. Stinebrickner, Archivist, Diocese of Ogdensburg; Rev. Leo Cooper, Archivist, Archdiocese of Kansas City in Kansas; Dr. Josephine L. Harper, the State Historical Society of Wisconsin; and to the people who have shared their time and insight with me: Sister Marie Therese Archambault, O.S.F., Jeff Ballew, Dick Bancroft, Elizabeth Berkemeier, Benjamin Black Bear, Jr., Charlotte Black Elk, Eva Pierre Boudreaux, Joseph Norris Boudreaux, Msgr. Roland J. Boudreaux, Ron Boyer, Rev. Prof. Martin Brokenleg, Rev. Prof. Raymond Bucko, S.J., Leona Bull Bear, Rev. Camillus Cavagnaro, O.F.M., Most Rev. Charles Chaput, O.F.M. Cap., Sister Geraldine Clifford, O.S.F., Larry Cloud-Morgan, Prof. D. C. Cole, Harold Condon, Elaine Cook, Rev. Leo Cooper, Rev. John Cousins, O.F.M. Cap., Sister Therese Culhane, I.H.M., Sister Genevieve Cuny, O.S.F., Joan Dana, Sister Gloria Davis, S.B.S., Mercedes Degand, Rev. James M. Dixon, S.J., Lydia Gregoire Duthu, Ted Duthu, Sr., S.J., Chet Eagleman, the late Rev. Thomas F. Egan, S.J., Prof. Ross Enochs, the late Rev. Bernard Fagan, S.J., John Francis, Shirley Francis, Simon Francis, Rev. P. Michael Galvan, Doug George-Kanentiio, Cheryl Gillespie, Rev. Jim Green, S.J., Mary Gregoire, Prof. John A. Grim, Rev. John Hascall, O.F.M. Cap., Rev. Gilbert F. Hemauer, O.F.M. Cap., Sister José Hobday, Prof. Clyde Holler, Donna Holstein, Hilton Hostler, Rev. Ted Hottinger, S.J., Beverly Huhndorf, Max Huhndorf, Ursula Jacko, Eilleen Tibbits Jelovich, Rev. C. P. Jordan, Vivian Juan, Calvin Jumping Bull, Prof. Luis Kemnitzer, Sister Joan Lang, C.S.J., Msgr. Paul A. Lenz, Rev. Thomas Lequin, Rev. Charles Leute, O.P., Edsel Little Sky, Sister Lorraine Masters, O.L.V.M., the late Rev. Georges P. Mathieu, Prof. Michael David McNally, Sister Kateri Mitchell, S.S.A., Rev. John Mittelstadt, O.F.M., Rev. Ralph Monteiro, S.A., Rev. Roch Naquin, the late Rev. James F. O'Brien, S.J., Rev. Paul Ojibway, S.A., the late Prof. Alfonso Ortiz, Rev. Ralph Partida, the late Rev. Richard Pates, S.J., Sarah Patterson, Joan Paul, Most Rev. Donald E. Pelotte, S.S.S., Sister Mary Hugh Placilla, I.H.M.,

Prof. Marla N. Powers, Prof. William K. Powers, Rev. Prof. Francis Paul Prucha, S.J., Jane Puckkee, Sister Teresa Rigel, C.S.J., M. Grace Roderick, Chad Ronnander, Dolores Rousseau, Joseph Savilla, Peggy Cornelius Savilla, Rev. David Shields, S.J., Prof. Sarah Shillinger, Brother C. M. Simon, S.J., Rev. Carl F. Starkloff, S.J., Rev. Paul B. Steinmetz, S.J., Rev. Michael F. Steltenkamp, S.J., Mark Thiel, Sister Margaret Troy, S.S.M., Rev. Robert Two Bulls, Kirby Verret, Catherine Walsh, Rev. George M. White, O.M.I., Don Yellow, and Rev. Ted Zuern, S.J. Colgate University has provided generous grants of money to help defray research costs through the Division of the Humanities and the Faculty Research Council. Colgate's Case Library staff, particularly Emily Hutton, has been very helpful to my study. I appreciate the support. Finally, I thank Wanda Kelly and Beth Page for so ably typing portions of the index, and Julia Meyerson for creating the maps.

❋ I ❋

Sioux Catholicism

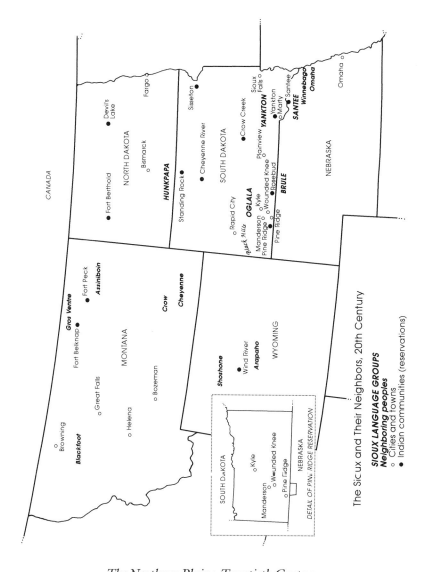

The Northern Plains, Twentieth Century

CANADA

NORTH DAKOTA

Fargo

Devil's Lake

Fort Berthold

Bismarck

HUNKPAPA

Standing Rock

Cheyenne River

Sisseton

SOUTH DAKOTA

Crow Creek

Sioux Falls

Rapid City

Black Hills

OGLALA

Kyle

Manderson

Wounded Knee

Pine Ridge

Pine Ridge

Rosebud

BRULE

Plainview

YANKTON

Yankton

Marty

Santee

SANTEE

Winnebago

Omaha

Omaha

NEBRASKA

Fort Peck

Assiniboin

Gros Ventre

Fort Belknap

Blackfoot

Browning

Great Falls

Helena

Bozeman

MONTANA

Crow

Cheyenne

Shoshone

Wind River

Arapaho

WYOMING

SIOUX LANGUAGE GROUPS
Neighboring peoples
o Cities and towns
● Indian communities (reservations)

The Sioux and Their Neighbors, 20th Century

DETAIL OF PINE RIDGE RESERVATION

SOUTH DAKOTA

Kyle

Manderson

Wounded Knee

Pine Ridge

NEBRASKA

In August 1988 the staff of Holy Rosary Mission–Red Cloud Indian School on the Pine Ridge Reservation in South Dakota arranged a centennial celebration for the institution. Situated in the rolling hills, several miles west of Pine Ridge town, the mission hosted hundreds of returning alumni, former staffers, and various guests for a four-day reunion. In the territory of the Oglala Lakota division of the Teton Sioux, the second largest Indian reservation in the United States, were camped the tents and trailers of the returnees and their families in the fields behind the red brick administration building—the original structure built a century ago, picturesque and isolated. The gymnasium, the classrooms, the cafeteria, and the chapel (which was later destroyed by fire on Good Friday, 1996) were filled with Indians, missionaries, scholastics, and teaching assistants, as well as anthropologists and foreign visitors, all marking a hundred years of Catholic-Indian relations.

They attended an art exhibition of Lakota works in the main building. They bought books and reminisced in the cafeteria over *wojapi*, a sweet cherry compote. They sat on the benches out front and visited relatives around the reservation. They watched a slide show featuring life at Holy Rosary. They shared public nostalgia of days in the Red Cloud Indian School. They attended a Sunday mass celebrated by Bishop Charles Chaput, the newly installed Potawatomi bishop of the Rapid City diocese. They enjoyed the Pine Ridge Days powwow, where Holy Rosary Mission donated a free supper to thousands of people as a public gesture of generosity. The Holy Rosary staff, including their Jesuit leaders, danced a number of Honor dances at the powwow. *The Lakota Times,* August 2, 1988, featured the reunion, and there were salutes to some of the Lakota graduates of Holy Rosary school: Tim Giago, editor and publisher of *The Lakota Times,* Chuck Cuny, principal at Red Cloud High School, Ed Little Sky, the movie actor, and others.

The Holy Rosary Mission centennial provides an opportunity to reflect upon a century of Lakota-Catholic relations at Pine Ridge, relations that are well documented in the archives at Marquette University, where most of the Holy Rosary records are stored. One can see the present relations as continuations of the past, and one can see that contemporary reflections upon those relations are also continuations of a century of changing consciousness. These are accumulated patterns of self-conscious relations with voluminous documentation, past and present.

TRADITIONAL SIOUX SPIRITUALITY

Before the Christians arrived, the Lakotas expressed their traditional forms of religiousness, holding much in common with the other Teton (western) Sioux such as the Brule and Hunkpapa, the Sioux further east (e.g., the Yankton and Santee), and the Assiniboin to the north. In general, Sioux religion was typical of the northern Plains Indian culture area and even bore similarities to the religion of their enemies, the Crows. The Lakotas held less in common with the Siouan Winnebagos of the Great Lakes and their more distant linguistic relatives to the south, the Osages.

For the Lakotas, religion constituted a means of making relatives; hence the term for prayer and kinship address was the same (*wacekiye*); both were means of "invoking relationship" (DeMallie 1984: 301). The Lakotas cared deeply and persistently about communicating with the mysterious, powerful, awe-inspiring holy realm of being, the *wakan* world. The *wakan* revealed itself in its many aspects through natural phenomena and permeated the whole cosmos. In their religiousness the Lakotas attempted to bind themselves as relatives to the *wakan* beings, and above all to the supreme class of *wakan* beings, *Wakantanka*. They smoked pipes of sacred symbolism, the smoke serving as a medium of communication with the divine, the natural, and the human realms. Among their many myths they told narratives of a particular sacred pipe's origin: how the White Buffalo Calf Woman delivered it as a moral instruction; how its ritual created a kinship of people.

The Lakotas made themselves clean and proper before the *wakan* beings through the purification ceremony of the sweat lodge. They bound themselves in the commonality of the ordeal, sweating, singing, and praying together, ever invoking the phrase "all my relations." In vision quests the Lakotas, particularly the men, sought direct communication with the holy ones under the guidance of trusted elders, in order to learn who they were and what they ought to become. These rites established lifelong personal relations with *wakan* beings and revealed something of the universe's structure and intent. Lakota girls came of age through the White Buffalo ceremony, which emphasized exchanges of gifts and the making of human relatives. Through this rite of passage young women bestowed the blessings of the *wakan* upon their communities.

In times of illness and other crises, the Lakotas elicited the help of the *wakan* beings through a conjuring ritual called Yuwipi, at which medicine men called upon the spirits to reveal hidden causes and future events; and Lowanpi, at which religious specialists sang to the spirits for cures and other forms of amelioration. Medicine men derived their healing prowess from the powers of *wakan*. The community members supported one another in order to persist as a people.

In the summer Sun Dance the Lakotas attemped the renewal of interrelations throughout the universe. They established a great lodge symbolic of the earth's central axis, joining this world with those above and below, and tried to orient themselves to this connective core of being. They fulfilled vows to the *wakan* beings and to each other, and made extended acts of generosity, suffering, and sacrifice, including rites of self-torture, so as to make themselves one with their fellow Lakotas and with their *wakan* ground of being. These rituals represented a greater matrix of ideas, images, behaviors, gestures, values, and relations, all designed at *wacekiye,* making Lakotas relatives to each other and to the cosmos as they knew it. This matrix of religiousness was still functioning fully in the late nineteenth century, despite many years of contact with Christians.

EARLY MIﬆIONARY PREﬆENCE

Although Holy Rosary did not commence its operation until 1888, Catholic missionary contact with the Sioux had taken place as early as the 1660s, when the Jesuits Claude Allouez and Jacques Marquette had met eastern Sioux in what is now Wisconsin, the former baptizing a dying Sioux child. Their confrere Gabriel Druillettes instructed a few Sioux in 1674; the Récollet Louis Hennepin smoked the pipe with Santee Sioux in 1680; and Father Joseph Marest served as itinerant missioner to the Sioux between 1689 and 1701. In the eighteenth century other Jesuits found the eastern Sioux a difficult audience, and it was not until the 1840s that a Catholic priest made sustained evangelical interchange with the western, Teton Sioux, when the Belgian Jesuit Pierre de Smet met them on his way to the Flatheads further west. He encountered the Oglala Lakotas for the first time in 1849, after they had just suffered a defeat from the Crows and were receptive to his spiritual powers. He baptized 239 Oglalas at the time, along with 280 Brules and 61 children of mixed descent.

Lakotas had already been in contact with Catholics for at least a century, through relations with fur traders, most of French extraction. Father August Ravoux noted in the 1840s that French, English, and Sioux were being spoken in the Dakota territory. Father de Smet became friendly with the new Lakota chief, Red Cloud, through the chief's French trader in-laws between 1865 and 1868. The fact that de Smet was a French-speaking holy man made him especially beloved to the Sioux, and he was savvy in making use of his French connections to mixed-bloods to further his appeal to the Indians. De Smet also employed astute technique in associating Native religious terminology with that of Christianity—as in using the expression "Great Spirit" as a translation for "God" when he prayed with the Sioux at the Council of Fort Rice in 1868 (Chittenden and Richardson 1905, 3:904–905). De Smet's fabulous reputation as a medicine man and his accommodationist liberality won many western Sioux to Catholic allegiance.

Nevertheless, when Pine Ridge Reservation was established in 1868, the U.S. government granted spiritual charge of the territory to Episcopalian authorities. In that same year some Sioux chiefs wrote to de Smet, saying that for seven years they had waited for a school, promised by government agents. These chiefs wanted to learn American language, Catholic religion, the ways of Whites, and in particular, they wanted de Smet. Notwithstanding, President Grant's Peace Policy of the 1870s did not permit a Catholic mission at Pine Ridge, even though Red Cloud and Spotted Tail persisted in requesting such, even traveling to Washington, D.C., to make their desires known.

In 1876 a Benedictine abbot, Martin M. Marty, arrived at Standing Rock Agency and found 159 Sioux Catholics. He was reputed among the Indians to have the power to cure smallpox with his prayers, and so he excited Sioux interest, even though most Sioux in the 1870s were either "completely indifferent" or "openly hostile" (Thiel 1989: 4) to Christian missions. In 1878 Marty met with Red Cloud, who had made a public appeal in 1876 for Catholic missions. Red Cloud stated that when God had sent His Son, Jesus, to the Whites, He had sent his daughter, Buffalo Calf Woman, to the Lakotas. The girl, Red Cloud said, had revealed that Indians would merge with Whites within the next ten generations; now it was time (Thompson 1953: 86). On a more mundane level, Red Cloud wanted priests and sisters to "teach our people how to read and write" (in Enochs 1993: 37) the English language. The chief recognized these skills as an adaptive "stratagem" (Powers 1987: 112) for his Lakota relatives. For him, Catholicism offered a means of enhancing his lineage organization, the traditional *tiyospaye*.

In 1879 Marty became Vicar Apostolic of Dakota Territory. At that time Jesuits exiled from Germany were starting schools and parishes in the Midwest. Marty had known the Jesuit de Smet from earlier days, so he asked the order to continue the Indian work begun by the Belgian priest. Preceding the Jesuits were pioneer priests such as J. A. Bushman, who baptized the first Pine Ridge Lakotas, including Red Cloud, in 1884; the colorful Rev. Francis M. Craft, who was photographed with feathers and peace pipe in the mid-1880s; and Rev. Meinrad McCarthy, who was barred from entering Pine Ridge by the U.S. agent in 1879, but set up a mission camp ("Meinrad's call") in nearby Nebraska. But the Jesuits with their reservation headquarters in Buffalo, New York, received government approval in 1884 to open St. Francis Mission at Rosebud in 1886. When Mother Katherine Drexel donated $60,000 in 1887 for a Lakota institution at Pine Ridge, the Jesuits led by John B. Jutz, S.J., arrived with the wherewithal to establish something that would last among the Oglalas.

The priests began a school, which at first they named after Drexel, and soon they had close to a hundred half-blood and Lakota students in grades 1–8, learning German, Latin, and later English. Some say that the Lakotas still speak English with a German accent, having learned it from German instructors. When the German Sisters of St. Francis of Penance and Christian Charity arrived in 1888, "The Indians called them Holy women, but asked if they were the four wives of the Blackrobe [Father Jutz]. The Sisters then explained to them that they were not and came only for the sake of the Indians" (Sisters of St. Francis: 1).

The goals of the first missionaries were clear to themselves, and have been well described for the past century. They came to make Christians of the Lakotas, by bringing to them not only the Good News of the Gospels, but also the institutions of Roman Catholicism. They meant to alter the fundamental conditions of Lakota existence: their family life, their economy, their spiritual orientation, their medicinal practices. Such was the basic "paradigm" of the early missionaries (Markowitz 1987). Father Florentine Digmann, one of the first Jesuits at Holy Rosary, criticized the habits of the Lakotas in the early years — "We had to do with little savages" who licked each other's plates (Digmann c. 1922: 4) — and he was determined to do away with the culture of Sioux savagery, God willing.

At the same time, the Jesuits found worthy elements in Lakota culture. Almost all of the German Jesuits — Fathers Eugene Buechel, Placidus Sialm, Emil Perrig, Louis J. Goll, Florentine Digmann, and others — spoke Lakota, and they investigated Lakota religious concepts and practices in order to graft Christianity upon them. They perceived monotheistic aspects of Lakota theology in the notion of a supreme class of *wakan,* named *Wakantanka,* and called the Christian God by that name. The priests taught about Catholic faith and institutions as if they were an outgrowth of Lakota religion: Eucharist was "holy food" *(yatapi wakan)*; a church was a "sacred house" *(tipi wakan)*; the devil was the evil mystery spirit *(wakansica).* The missionaries signified Catholicism as the "Black Robe prayer," using the traditional Lakota term, *wacekiye.* When the priests organized retreats for Lakota children, they referred to the meditative exercises as vision quests ("crying

for a vision": *hamble iciyope*). So whereas the Jesuits found fault with
many features of Lakota culture—what they considered the excesses of
self-torture in the Sun Dance, the devilish conjuring of spirits in
Yuwipi rituals, and the superstitious prestige of medicine men—and
thought condescendingly of the Indians as children in need of spiritual
correction, they condoned, approved of, and even encouraged specific
parts of traditional Lakota culture with which they were intimately familiar (see Enochs 1993: 135, 142–146, 154–159, 174–176, 190–197, 205).

The Jesuits established Sacred Heart Church in Pine Ridge Agency
in 1890, and by the 1930s there were more than thirty churches in various parishes throughout the various districts of Pine Ridge, all under
the Jesuit control at Holy Rosary. When Red Cloud died in 1909, he
received tribute from the missionaries: for inviting and protecting
them, for converting so thoroughly to their faith. Father Placidus F.
Sialm, S.J., one of the chroniclers of the mission in the 1930s, memorialized the chief:

> Red Cloud is by far the most noble character of all the Sioux Nation, a
> leader and a statesman, not a medicineman like Sitting Bull with a dou-
> ble mind. Red Cloud deserved a monument and he got a nice outstand-
> ing tombstone in the Catholic Graveyard of Holy Rosary Mission. He
> died as a Christian and a Catholic and was buried with all the rites of
> the Catholic Church by Father Eugene Buechel. (Sialm 1930s b: 83)

Sialm failed to record Red Cloud's abdication speech of 1903, in which
the chief vowed fidelity to the Sun *(Wi)* and his traditional religion in
general. He said:

> *Taku Skanskan* is familiar with my spirit *(nagi)* and when I die I will go
> with him. Then I will be with my forefathers. If this is not in the heaven
> of the white man, I shall be satisfied. *Wi* is my father. The *Wakan Tanka*
> of the white man has overcome him. But I shall remain true to him. (In
> Walker 1991: 140)

Notwithstanding, the Holy Rosary Mission School became known as
Red Cloud Indian School in 1911.

Although attendance figures at Red Cloud are not exact, there were
approximately 20,000 enrollees until 1958, when the boarding school
was turned into a day school, with perhaps another 10,000 since then.
In the late 1880s, about 7,000 Lakotas lived at Pine Ridge; within
twenty years a third of the Oglalas (c. 2,300) were baptized Catholics.
The priests baptized 7,500 in the first fifty years, marking half the

Indian population in the Catholic ranks. By 1963, seventy-five years after its founding, Holy Rosary had initiated over 13,000 Indians into Catholic life. In its first one hundred years Holy Rosary Mission has performed well over 20,000 baptisms, 2,000 marriages, and 1,500 funerals. Rapid City Diocese today includes five Sioux reservations, with 60,000 Sioux, a quarter to a third of whom are nominally Catholic. These 15,000 to 20,000 constitute almost half the Catholics in the diocese. At Pine Ridge almost half of the 20,000 Lakotas are baptized Catholics.

Before the Jesuits and Sisters of St. Francis arrived among the Sioux, there were already French, Irish, Canadian, and Mexican Catholics — traders, trappers, cowboys, "squawmen," and homesteaders — who introduced the Sioux to Catholic belief and ritual. By the 1880s many of these men who had been baptized and even received First Holy Communion in their youth had married Sioux and now had large families. "Through their children they came back to practice their religion, receiving here their second Communion and having their marriages revalidated" (Digmann c. 1922: 13). Throughout the middle of the nineteenth century, "The anxiety of the 'squawmen' to have their children baptized begot a desire for the 'saving waters' in the natives and prepared the way for the missionaries" (Duratschek 1943: 15). Some of these men were influential with certain tribal leaders, and once the missions arrived, these Catholic non-Indians served as translators, catechists, sponsors, and provided "religious continuity" (Thiel 1989: 3) in the absence of priests and sisters.

The Pouriers settled at Wounded Knee, the first coming from Missouri as a teenager with John Richard, the trader, in 1858. At the advice of an old French priest who gave him First Holy Communion before his journey, the elder Pourier would say his confession to a tree, once every spring, down on his knees: "I confessed to God before a tree many years when I could find no priest" (in Sialm 1930s a: 45). Richard and Pourier traded with Red Cloud's camp in 1858, and they came to Pine Ridge in 1878. Red Cloud adopted Baptist Pourier; he and his wife became full tribal members and got a section of land at Wounded Knee. The Pourier offspring numbered one hundred when he died in 1927, and he was buried at Holy Rosary Mission. The Richard family induced Father Henry I. Westropp to build a church in their area in 1890. Peter Richard married one of Red Cloud's daughters and over time there were many Richard branches; "the old good Catholic faith was found in most of the Richard families" (20).

The Mousseau founding father, Magloire by name, came from Canada. He was well educated, with three priests for brothers, even a bishop, it is said. He had two wives: a Cheyenne and an Oglala of Red

Cloud's Band. In 1878 the family came to Pine Ridge, and he insisted on having a Catholic school: "If my children cannot go to a Catholic school—they will stay with me at home" (in Sialm 1930s a: 2). In Kyle there was a Mexican settlement, including the Giago family, who would put up the priest when he came to their area. Another trader, Antoine Janis, advised the Indians to say: "'Black gowns, Black gowns!' . . . This was the Call of the Sioux Nation" (107).

The Cliffords were converted by Father Henry Grotegeers before 1914, evidence that some of the half-breeds became Catholic through contact with the Indians or with Holy Rosary. The Cliffords became the leading Catholic family at St. Barbara at Kyle: "Few families have so enlarged the number of Catholics as the Cliffords on Pine Ridge" (Sialm 1930s a: 10).

Chief Red Cloud was acquainted with many of these Catholic traders and half-bloods and he wanted them as allies and relatives. Thus, Red Cloud's love of Catholicism was partially a matter of relationship to the non-Indian families who wanted the presence of Catholic institutions for their offspring. Many of the first "converts" and "baptisms" came from these families, whose numbers comprised about 10 percent of the Pine Ridge populace in the late 1880s. Almost all the first pupils at the mission school were French or Mexican half-bloods; "the full-bloods were slow to come and when they did they were quick to leave" (Southall 1964: 44). The mixed-blood descendants were the first loyalists at Holy Rosary Mission. Today they are considered Sioux Indians, but they are of a special set of lineages—the Cliffords, the Cunys, the Tibbits, etc. They are no less "Sioux" than the Black Elk family or other full-blood lineages, or those families of other Indian national origin who entered the tribe in earlier centuries and whose family trees are accounted for at Buffalo Woman ceremonies (Black Elk, August 2, 1988).

The half-breeds were not the only ones to be baptized, and not the only ones to attend Holy Rosary Mission. At St. Cecelia's Church in Kyle District was an old man named Apple, one of the first full-blood Pine Ridge Lakotas baptized in 1884 by Rev. Bushman, before Holy Rosary began. His son John Apple went to Holy Rosary School and became a devout Catholic. Rosie Janis, one of the half-breeds, married him in 1906, converting in order to do it, and by the 1930s she was a "very good singer and a very good organist." Father Sialm wrote: "She has a good clean house and is a model Christian. Her children grew up into good deep faith" (1930s a: 7). Hence, the generations passed down the "faith" through marriage and through offspring. Catholicism became a family heritage at Pine Ridge, founded upon the first baptisms of a century ago.

Father Digmann spent time baptizing the young and dying. In January 1890 Two Calf went to be baptized. His child baptized two years ago had died of late.

"What did you call me for?"

"I go to see my child."

"Do you want to be baptized?"

"Yes." (Digmann c. 1922: 20)

So the priest instructed him and had him repeat an act of contrition. The man died and his family put his body near Digmann's room, "running and smelling strong," for burial.

Medicine men converted; husbands followed their wives; parents followed their offspring; children followed their guardians. Some sought baptism after long periods of resistance. Some sought the faith following dreams: "Many people saw visions of Jesus or the saints which confirmed them in their faith or prepared them for death" (Hatcher 1987: 83). In the 1930s one could still witness dramatic conversions, e.g., Mrs. Good Shell, who had resisted Catholicism for years. Before her death in 1932 she had a dream of a priest coming to pray for her. She asked Benjamin Black Elk (her nephew) to call a priest, from whom she received communion, or "holy food"—*yatapi wakan,* as she called it. Eating no more, she died ten days later, while songs to the Sacred Heart were sung over her (Red Cloud Indian School, Series 1/1, Box 1, Folder 5).

Some of these converts needed to alter their marriages in order to receive baptism or communion. For example, Joe Big Head sought baptism but could not hurt the feelings of one of his wives by dismissing her, which he would have to do before he became Catholic. Finally, he annulled his relation to the younger of the two, and all three of this ménage received baptism. In the following years he could be found making the stations of the cross at the mission five times a week (Westropp n.d.: 9–10).

Father Sialm witnessed a "Statement" written by Dick Red Bear on June 20, 1925:

> I Dick Red Bear, being very sick now and wishing to make my peace
> with God—declare that Maggie Romero is not my real wife. I believe

that my first marriage to Ema Little Moon was a true christian marriage
which cannot be broken.

I am sorry for my sin and wish to receive the last Sacraments to save
my soul. And I promise to live according to the Laws of the Catholic
Church.

I am thankful to Maggie if she nurses me, but she is not my wife before God. I am not really her man and if I get well, I shall not consider
her as my wife. (Local Sodalities)

On the same page Maggie Romero signed her agreement to the statement and promised to nurse him, but not as a wife.

If the Lakotas of the late nineteenth and early twentieth century
were willing even to change their familial life in order to receive baptism and other sacraments, what techniques did the missionaries use
to bring the Lakotas toward participation in Catholic life?

Father Digmann wrote that the Jesuits wanted the Lakotas to "forget 'camp life'" (c. 1922: 6), so they taught them to sing Christian
hymns in English (and Lakota) composed by Father Ravoux. Ravoux's
little bilingual catechism was the Jesuits' first textbook in learning
Sioux language, and the priests tried to impress the Indians by learning their language. In addition, "To attract them to Church on Sundays, we offered the following inducement," a magic lantern show
with colored biblical slides of Christ, the martyrs, but also some
"funny ones." Digmann suggested that "the scheme worked well" (6).

He and his fellow evangelists augmented songs and slides with the
use of an illustrative catechism, "The Road Picture," on which was vi-
sualized the rudiments of Catholic instruction: a road to heaven and a
road to the home of the devil. Along the two paths the Indians could
see God's creation, Adam and Eve, Noah, Abraham, Jesus, and the
Church with its commandments and liturgy, featuring mass on Sunday. There were illustrations of the seven capital sins, the seven sacraments, faith, hope, and love, the one, holy, universal and apostolic
Catholic Church, purgatory, the communion of saints, and Luther
leaving the good road for the bad one (see Grotegeers 1931). Hence,
the mission presented the Sioux with a Catholic worldview that set
forth clear choices regarding belief, behavior, and loyalties: which road
to take and which to eschew.

Concurrently, the missionaries worked with the United States government in undermining the traditional religion. They did not forbid
Indians their herbal medicines, but they "forbade them the use of the
drum, the flute, the pumpkin-shells and sacred dances and songs, to

which superhuman efficacy was ascribed" (Digmann c. 1922: 8). The priests confronted medicine men in the acts of curing: "We had a special eye on the sick, not to let them go without baptism. Several of these died soon after baptism, and the opinion was spread by the medicine man that pouring on of water had killed them." Digmann described a confrontation with medicine men conjuring over a dying child: Digmann and a sister threw the curers' medicine bags out of the lodge and would not leave the child until the conjurers yielded.

As an inducement toward conversion the missionaries provided food at Holy Rosary for those Lakotas interested in the Christian message, including sauerkraut, served for the first time on St. Valentine's Day, 1889. At first the Indians disdained the Germanic food, but upon encouragement they tried it, "and the ice was broken for the future" (16).

In order to establish their authority, the priests encouraged strict physical punishment of Lakota children. Lakota parents argued that they were not accustomed to doing such things; however, Digmann states that the "more sensible of them saw that our way was the right one" (19). When three girls tried to burn down Holy Rosary in 1893, and one of them escaped jail and sought asylum with her parents, Digmann "insisted on unconditional surrender," and she was brought back by force "like possessed by the devil" (38).

While establishing their authority, the missionaries and their secular allies tried to motivate the Lakotas toward culture change. At a Washington's Birthday celebration in 1893, the agent addressed the Holy Rosary pupils: "American citizenship was the highest they could strive for here on earth. . . . Any of the girls could become yet the mother of a President!" (39). At the same time, "The Jesuits never wanted the Lakota to adopt all the habits of white America, but rather they wanted them to become Catholic" (Enochs 1993: 217).

In order to make Catholic practices more meaningful to the Lakotas, the priests tried to use Lakota terms to describe some Catholic practices; e.g., Digmann used the phrase *hamble iciyope* (Digmann c. 1922: 58) to name retreats, referring to a Lakota practice of crying for a vision. This linguistic linkage led one convert to ask: "How is it about eating during the Retreat. The Indians do not eat during their recesses" (150). There was syncretism of terminology and belief at Pine Ridge around the turn of the century. For example, the Lakotas represented St. Nicholas at Christmas in his furs and winter garb, calling him *Waziya,* the traditional spirit of winter and the north. They referred to Christmas festivity as "the time when *Waziya* will come" (Walker 1991: 121).

The Indians may have been attracted by songs and pictures; they may have been lured by food or shelter. They were impressed by Christian charity and asceticism, and they perceived the Christian "God" as "Wakan Tanka" (MacGregor 1951: 92). It appears, however, that they were also motivated by fear regarding the afterlife. In a number of conversion episodes, the Sioux in the 1890s stated that they wished their souls to live after death, and they regarded baptism as a means of assuring life after death. The priests then performed burials, with pageantry and crosses over the graves, replacing the Lakota practice of scaffold burial. By the 1890s some Lakotas were requesting baptisms and burials for their dead.

Joseph F. Busch, bishop of the Diocese of Lead (forerunner of Rapid City), wrote a letter (c. 1910) to the "Catholic Indians" of his diocese, warning of three "spiritual dangers": drinking, dancing, and divorce. The bishop condemned each one by threatening the Indians with sorrow "in Hell forever," unable to enter "the kingdom of Heaven" (Red Cloud Indian School, Series 1/1, Box 1, Folder 3).

THE GHOST DANCE

The priests and sisters had no sooner arrived, bringing with them a Christian eschatology, when the Ghost Dance swept across western America, including the Dakota Territory. Short Bull and other Sioux brought the Ghost Dance from the prophet Wovoka in Nevada and adapted it to local contexts. Perhaps the missionaries' gospel of heavenly reward and Jesus' second coming was partially responsible for the Lakota participation in the Ghost Dance. Father Jutz, who was Holy Rosary Mission superior at the time, was an eyewitness to the dance. In his memoirs he described the economic, social, and political dissatisfaction of the Sioux in 1890, and the Ghost Dance's promises to eradicate Whites and restore the old cultural and natural environment. He and other priests portrayed the dance itself: its frenzied singing, its pushing and pulling, the ecstasy of the dancers. At a site four miles from Holy Rosary, he entered the whirling circle in his religious habit, and when various Indians fainted—or died, in the Ghost Dance ideology—and revived, he asked them what they had seen in their swoon. He even offered to pay $5 if they would tell him, but none would. Then he told them that there was no truth to their beliefs, that they were incapable of speaking with the dead through the medium of the dance. They would not heed him and resumed their dancing. During the Ghost Dance, the children at Holy Rosary "were just crazy over the Ghost Dance, and as soon as they thought they were not being observed, they danced it" (Jutz 1918a: 217). The sisters took these frenzied children into the sick room at the mission to keep them from the hysteria. (See Perrig 1886–1909 for a view of the dance from St. Francis mission.)

Jutz was not an observer at Wounded Knee, where Big Foot's band of dancers fell to cavalry assault; however, he related the aftermath to the dance and massacre, including the burning of squaw men's houses and Red Cloud's protection of Holy Rosary. In 1896 Father Digmann was at Short Bull's camp several miles from the mission, trying to convert the leader's band. The priest was mightily impressed with Short Bull's "electrifying influence over the Indians" (Digmann c. 1922: 54), and he could understand why they had followed such a charismatic personage into the Ghost Dance. He also found that the Ghost Dance prevented conversions to Christianity, providing Lakotas with confidence regarding their own Native afterlife. One Sioux told him:

> We know now for the past four years (since the ghost-dance) that the Indians after death go to heaven. They pass by Jesus, go up higher, come to a fork-road, take the longer one and come to their own people and relatives. The plume of an eagle on their head did the same service as baptism, and brings them direct to heaven. (54)

As a result, some Lakotas pulled blankets over their heads when Digmann approached them, and told him to go away. At the same time James Mooney (1973: 874) interviewed a Lakota man who explained his aversion to the 1890 Ghost Dance: "I had a little boy at the Drexel mission. He died and Father Jutz put a white stone over him. That is why I did not join the hostiles."

The emotions engendered by the Ghost Dance did not disappear with the slaughter at Wounded Knee, and the dance continued as competition with the Christian eschatology and ceremonialism. Father Sialm noted that forty years later many Lakotas still sang the most common Ghost Dance song:

> My mother, come here, come here.
> My little brother goes around crying.
> Father says so, Mother come here!
> (Sialm 1930s a: 81)

When a missionary sang these words as a joke, at hearing a little Lakota boy cry, the boy's mother went into a furious rage at the priest's sacrilegious mockery.

Over the century since the Wounded Knee massacre, the issues of Indian-White conflict have not disappeared. In 1973 American Indian Movement (AIM) militants took over the Catholic church at the massacre site and held a Holy Rosary priest hostage, and there were many charges of Church domination and exploitation of the Lakotas. If one travels the few miles from Holy Rosary to Wounded Knee, one finds that the mass graveyard of the massacre victims is still bedecked with yellow and red flags and sage sprigs, a custom that has persisted for years. The old church was destroyed in the AIM takeover, but there is a new log church just to the north of the site, where a priest says mass every Sunday morning.

PROTE/TANT RIVALRY

When the priests and sisters arrived in 1888, they were soon to contend with the Ghost Dance; however, their more chronic problem consisted of rival Christian proponents, particularly the Episcopalians who preceded the Catholics to Pine Ridge, who enjoyed governmental support, and who had already gained some Lakota loyalists. In the late nineteenth and early twentieth century, Episcopalians (White Gowns), Catholics (Black Robes), and Congregationalists (Short Coats) all jockeyed for favor with the Lakotas, slandering and insulting each other, trying to draw converts from one another's folds, and crowing over each success, all while denying any intention of interdenominational thievery. Sometimes the vying clergy sent their loyalists with arguments to their competitors. Captain George Sword, the Episcopalian catechist and policeman, challenged Digmann in 1893 regarding supposed Catholic errors concerning priestly celibacy, the kissing of a bishop's ring, and the authoritative role of oral tradition as well as the Bible. Between 1893 and 1896 Digmann and Sword carried out their interdenominational debate (Digmann c. 1922: 41–44).

Catholics and Protestants organized competing societies of their followers—Sodality of the Blessed Virgin versus YMCA, etc.—and attempted to keep their flocks from drifting off. Father Sialm wrote:

> There are some fallen away, but few. The protestants have their churches also and meetings and bigger Eats. So there is more attraction for people whose faith is in the belly rather than in the soul. . . . (1930s a: 90)

To his Episcopalian counterpart, Rev. Nevill Joyner of Pine Ridge, Father Sialm wrote in 1933:

> Some Indians told that a few bad Catholics have now joined your Episcopal church and were confirmed therein. I knew these unfortunate persons. I had repeatedly warned them of their public sins. But they don't understand their lost sin of apostasy. . . . If you can make them better Christians—we congratulate you. But will they not rather be confirmed in their sins by your confirmation? This is our fear for them. (Red Cloud Indian School, Series 1/1, Box 1, Folder 5)

When, four years later, Joyner informed the superior at Holy Rosary that a John White Cloud wanted his children removed from the mission, the father being Episcopalian, Father M. A. Schiltz, S. J., retorted that the children were baptized Catholic when their mother was sick in 1931. Now Schiltz would not give them up, nor let Joyner "destroy the Catholic faith of some of these Oglala Sioux." To Mr. White Cloud, Schiltz wrote that a father cannot "force them to abandon this Faith" (Red Cloud Indian School, Series 1/1, Box 1, Folder 7).

The Catholics attempted to prevent Lakota converts from marrying Protestants; however, they saw the impossibility of such prohibitions, and they absolved the Indians from excommunication for marrying before a Protestant minister or a justice of the peace, or contracting a mixed marriage. It is estimated that half of the Lakota marriages in the twentieth century have been mixed (Southall 1964: 92), and the fact of Lakota life has been what Arthur Amiotte calls "familial ecumenism: . . . After all, we're all Lakotas" (Two Roads Conference, August 4, 1988). During World War II, Episcopal and Catholic Lakota soldiers held joint services, and this practice continued on Pine Ridge for a short time after the war. In the past decade ecumenism has been revived, and today there are monthly interfaith meetings.

At present there are eight churches in Pine Ridge village itself and thirteen Christian church bodies on the reservation, and this denominational fractioning has undermined Lakota unity over the century. A Catholic priest admits that the "fierce rivalries" (Pates, August 5, 1988) have done great damage, even though today there is growing ecumenism on the reservation.

In reporting the early history of Holy Rosary, it is often difficult to find firsthand written documentation of Sioux motives for conversion or for denominational preferences. However, as an institution with financial security and stability, the Red Cloud Indian School attracted the interest of parents and other guardians, particularly in the 1930s, perhaps because of the economic hardships of the Depression. Numerous letters from Indians in the Red Cloud Indian School Records, especially in the 1930s, requested the superior to take children into the school. Julia Crazy Thunder wrote in the summer of 1937:

> I am sick and cannot take care of my orphan grandchildren. Will you please take them back at the mission *now*. The girls go to the mission

during school term. . . . Their father left us and I do not know where he is. Please help your schoolchildren as we have nothing to eat. (Series 1/1, Box 1, Folder 7)

Mrs. Hazel De Sersa wrote in 1938, asking if her five-year-old daughter could be admitted to Holy Rosary, since the mother was in a tuberculosis sanitarium in Rapid City and could not care for the girl. She attended Red Cloud herself and asked to be remembered to some of the sisters there (Box 2, Folder 1). A ninth-grade boy, Robert Stead, Jr., wrote in 1939, asking for school enrollment at the mission: "I'm a full blooded Indian, age 18, true Catholic." A week later Ora Standing Bear wrote from Wyoming, asking that her three baptized daughters be admitted to Holy Rosary to escape from their drunken father who refused to allow them Catholic sacraments, and who "abuses us" (Box 2, Folder 1).

Some of the children were only part Sioux. For example, Alice McBride, an orphan, was one-eighth Sioux, according to the principal at St. Paul's Indian Mission in South Dakota. St. Paul's was too near the girl's home, the principal wrote, and her guardians "want to place her in a Catholic school because they fear she will lose her faith in a Government institution" (Box 1, Folder 7). The mission thus became surrogate parent to many Indian children, as the priests and sisters attempted to feed and house generations of impoverished Lakotas and to train them for a more secure economic future.

PINE RIDGE CATHOLIC CULTURE

Red Cloud Indian School constituted the principal means by which Holy Rosary attracted Sioux children, and thus their families, to Catholic culture. The mission inculcated the thousands of Lakota children who attended Red Cloud with a pervasive Catholic spirituality. The mission sponsored Corpus Christi processions, retreats, rogation days, Christmas feasts and pageants, and Gregorian masses with singing in the Sioux language. There were baptisms, holy communions, burials, and the sayings of rosaries, as the Indians learned the liturgical forms of Catholicism. A mother superior wrote:

> At Easter, 1906, many Indians came to see the first communion celebration of 46 children for the first time. They brought all their belongings and erected their tents where they would live for the next eight days. It looked like an entire village arose in one night. (*The Lakota Times*: 3)

They attended the Catholic rite of passage as if it were a Lakota ritual, with full family participation.

The missionaries attempted to deepen the faith of the initiated children with various methods of spiritual training. There was an attempt to present Catholic theology and spiritual experience unadulterated, and if we look at "A Retreat for Our Indian Children" (in Lakota) conducted by Eugene Buechel in 1917, it is identical to retreat discourses delivered to non-Indians in Youngstown and Cleveland in 1907. Buechel emphasized the elevation of the soul over the body, the types of sins we commit, the sacraments that save us, the judgment that comes after death, the horrors of hell: its smells, sights, sounds are all horrible, but most horribly, it lasts forever; therefore, beware, use your time judiciously. He ended the retreat with a lesson upon the Prodigal Son, and reminded the children of our chance for forgiveness, God's love for us sinners, our hope, the Good News of the gospel. He told the Lakotas of a boy almost killed by snakes and reminded them that we are all close to death, and perhaps to hell: "We are not rocks, not bugs, not birds, not coyotes, not horses—we are men. Animals live & die & that's the end of them" (Buechel 1917). We owe our lives to God, he said, belong to Him, are his property, and we must do his will, as if he were our employer and owner. In his many sermons Buechel emphasized the necessity of work; it was for him the means to compensate for our human sinfulness. It was our Christian penance and our duty to work, he told the Lakota children.

The school spirituality focused upon death, particularly the death of young role models. Father Otto J. Moorman wrote obituaries in 1924 for two Sioux sisters, Esther and Grace Clifford, who died in 1922 and 1924, respectively, both at the age of twenty. Esther wanted to die and go to Jesus, and she persuaded her mother to release her to Him: "Esther, I told Jesus that I wish to keep you, dear, but that if He really wanted you He should take you now. I give you up to Him, Esther" (in Moorman 1924a). Moorman commented: "When she spoke of her dreams of the Blessed Virgin, of the Angels, of the Child Jesus, whom the Blessed Mother had placed in her arms to caress for a 'long while' . . . I realized that here was truly a lily, a lily of the Sioux" (Moorman 1924a). Her sister Grace received communion daily, was saintly, and always kept her soul white. The priest recalled her possessing ruddy good cheer, "red with a thirst for martyrdom" (Moorman 1924b). To this day, some Lakota Catholics keep the memory of these pious women.

To organize the pupils at Red Cloud into spiritual cadres, the missionaries formed a Young Women Society in the 1920s, a Holy Rosary Society in the 1930s, a Sacred Heart League in the 1940s, and members of these and other societies pledged to keep themselves "Right and Holy":

> With God's help I promise to do all I can to save my soul. I wish to obey the Laws of God and of His Holy Catholic Church. Especially do I promise to Marry Right and Holy before the Catholic priest. I hate to think about a mixed marriage. And I strictly object against marrying in any other Church. So help me God and his Holy Gospel. (Local Sodalities, 1923)

But even at these sodality meetings, there could be subterfuge of the mission goals. Father Sialm wrote in the 1920s that sodality meetings were not necessarily spiritual in their purpose. The Indians used them for socializing, for staying up late and missing Sunday masses. He noted that the membership rarely met the rules for membership; even Protestants would show up! Indeed, he said, the meetings leaned toward Protestantism: "They dodge the priest. . . . Smart gangs don't like the priest so that they may do as they please in these meetings"

(Local Sodalities). The history of Red Cloud was a struggle for control over the behavior of Lakota youths.

In the church the priests made rules for the Lakotas who became altar boys: "No *slouchy* position *in Church*. . . . *Hands & face* clean. . . . *Hand* should be *joined* folded *before breast*. . . . Movements on altar *not too fast*" (Red Cloud Indian School, Series 1/1, Box 2, Folder 1), as the Lakotas boys had to learn a new spiritual language of gesture and posture.

At the golden jubilee of Holy Rosary Mission in 1938, the students performed a play, "The Princess of the Mohawks," in the mission auditorium, portraying the life of Kateri Tekakwitha. As early as 1931 a mission committee had organized on her behalf, and in 1935 a petition was sent to Pope Pius XI to advance her cause toward sainthood. Lakota girls had acted in "Coaina: The Indian Rose" in 1931, portraying a pious Algonquin Catholic girl. The play promoted devotion to the Virgin Mary and discouraged marriages between Catholics and traditionalists. Two years later the Holy Rosary students performed the life of Tekakwitha on Easter Sunday, and again in 1935 they put on another devotional drama about Tekakwitha, "Lily of the Mohawks." These thespian endeavors led to the 1938 production. The play, written by Joseph P. Clancy, told of the pure princess resisting her stubborn pagan uncle's desire to marry her to a fierce medicine man, who prayed to the god of war. Kateri was saved by the blackrobe and taken off to the Christian reserve, Caughnawaga. Father Zimmerman wrote of the Tekakwitha pageant:

> Every feature was Indian, the cast of mission pupils, stage scenery painted by an Indian, Indian saint, Indian band playing Indian airs under its Indian leader, . . . and costumes of old tribal paraphernalia borrowed from our Indian homes. It is doubtful if this display of authentic regalia could be duplicated. (Scott 1963: n.p.)

Nevertheless, a non-Indian produced the script, and the missionaries prompted the performance, which served the purpose of socializing the Lakota children and their families. They were meant to identify with the Christian Kateri and to condemn the pagan medicine man, the war ceremony, indeed, all of traditional Mohawk religion. Through such pageants the mission personnel attempted to create an "authentic" Indian history with which contemporary Lakotas could identify on their journey toward Catholic American life. It was a fitting way to mark the first half century of progress at Holy Rosary.

Taking stock at the half century, Catholic publicists of the mission made the assessment that "Catholic education has been a success with the once war-like Sioux. . . . Who knows how many uprisings were prevented by educating the Indians?" (Zens 1936: 56; cf. Thompson 1953: 84). Rev. Louis J. Goll wrote in 1940 of the baptized Sioux: "They are not all saints. . . . But they are not a trifle less good than the average Catholic elsewhere . . . in the reception of the sacraments they surpass their white brethren. Four out of five who attend Mass also receive Holy Communion." He continued:

> A careful study of parish records reveals the fact that during all these fifty years and more, only five per cent of the Catholic Indians gave up the faith in which they were instructed, to return to the old pagan superstitions of the medicine man or to embrace pagan cults of recent origin. Certainly not more than one per cent joined another Christian sect. (Goll 1940: 69)

In the first fifty years the mission personnel had combined education and christianization in the same process, as expressed by Father William J. Fitzgerald, S.J., Red Cloud Indian School superintendent, in the early 1940s:

> We can teach them Christ, and the sacraments and the law of God, but we teach them in English. And if they don't know English, they'll never learn them. . . . So we teach them English that they may learn what it means to be Christian. That's why we are out here. (In Smith 1985: 16)

During the 1940s and 1950s the learning process continued with Forty Hours Devotions, May Day Crownings, sodality conventions, and special devotions to the Sacred Heart of Jesus. In 1949 Brother Francis Michalowski received a "spiritual Bouquet" of 259 holy masses, 259 holy communions, 259 rosaries, and 25,900 ejaculations from "your Grateful Freshman & Sophomore Girls," offering him a speedy recovery from an illness.

Red Cloud students also worked in the gardens, played basketball, performed in glee clubs, enjoyed picnics, watched approved films, and looked forward to fresh buns from the mission bakery, served up by Brother William Siehr, S.J. They joined sodalities, band, choir, and performed their course work. They took needlework, home economics, and shop. There are thousands of photographs of them over the century: at Catholic Congresses, praying at their bedsides, peeling potatoes, baking, butchering, singing, gardening, woodworking, shoemaking, cheerleading, attending Valentine's Day dances. Their hair and clothing styles were American, and changed as the American styles changed. The children in the photographs seem acculturated; however, as Marla Powers points out (August 3, 1988), the traditional culture did not disappear. Many Lakotas walked two roads simultaneously, Sioux and American, although the photographs did not picture the Sioux road. It is true that "many students did become Catholics, at least for a while" (Smith 1985: 16); however, they did not cease completely to be Lakotas in their cultural and religious orientation.

Edward J. Laskowski, S.J., commented in the 1940s that the Oglala boys at Red Cloud liked to eat the burnt skin of young dog, the spring buds of trees, pinegum, thorny cactus fruit, and wild roots caked with dirt. When he gave them hot dog buns, they carbonized them, in keeping with traditional Lakota taste (in *The Indian Sentinel,* March 1948: 45–47). No more in their religious than in their culinary tastes did the Lakotas cease to be themselves. Indeed, the Pine Ridge Sioux established patterns of "dual religious participation" (Powers 1987) during the first half century of Holy Rosary, and many have persisted in those patterns to the present day, speaking the languages of Catholicism and traditional Lakota religiousness in alternating, compartmentalized sequences, suitable to varying circumstances. Holy Rosary Lakotas were Catholics in some situations, and traditionalists at other times. Lakotas sent their children to the Catholic school because of its food, its security, its charity. Adult Lakotas attempted to appropriate the spiritual powers of the Church by participating in its rituals and structures. They did this, however, without necessarily foregoing aboriginal Sioux ways, especially since the Jesuits often characterized traditional Lakota faith as a primitive mode of Catholicism. Into the 1940s, Lakotas turned to Holy Rosary's Red Cloud School without necessarily turning away from their old ways.

The school was still crowded to capacity in the years following World War II. During the war one of the Sisters of St. Francis wrote:

> Although the terrible calamity of total war affects even remote corners of the world, it did but little to change the habits of prayer, work, study, and play of the inhabitants of Holy Rosary Mission, cloistered by hill and prairie. (Sisters of St. Francis, 1943)

In 1950 the Chronicles boasted: "Holy Rosary is to the Indian what Oxford is to the British Empire" (Sisters of St. Francis). In 1953 Father Harold A. Fuller, S.J., the superior at the mission, was quoted as saying that "great progress has been and will continue to be made in the as-similation of the Indians into our civilization" (Thompson 1953: 83–84).

Holy Rosary's core was its school; however, it also consisted of sev-eral dozen mission stations throughout Oglala country, through which the priests kept regular contact with the Indian communities. Father Zimmerman wrote in 1930 that he found the badland Lakotas "for the most part are very devout Catholics and go to the Sacraments each time the missionary goes there" (Scott 1963: 12). Zimmerman wrote circular letters to benefactors and friends through the 1930s and 1940s, depicting the spirituality of Lakotas, both in the school and around the reservation. His first fund-raising appeal described mid-night mass for Christmas, with Holy Rosary church crowded with In-dians "who had come from far and near with their hearts ready to re-ceive the Christ Child with love and joy" (Scott 1963: n.p.). Everywhere Zimmerman traveled, the Indians rejoiced at his coming and invited him to meal and bed. He heard confessions and witnessed the conver-sion of Lakota spirituality into Catholic spirituality. His letters were replete with heroic anecdotes: Sioux children begging for holy com-munion or baptism; last rites for old Catholic Indians on stormy nights, pious deaths with hands holding the relic bones of Kateri Tekakwitha; marriages of devout Lakotas; conversions from other Christian denominations. The colorful Lakota names—Silas Fills the Pipe, William Yellow Bear, Little Iron, Alvina Bear Saves Life, James Sweet Grass, Mercy Pipe on Head, Leroy Ten Fingers, Ora She Elk Voice—now belonged to devout Catholics: Lakota still, but now Christian, fifty years after the founding of Holy Rosary Mission.

Anecdotes in *The Indian Sentinel* in the 1930s and early 1940s em-phasized the manner in which "old customs have been transformed and transfigured into Christian customs with still a strong flavor of their Indian character," according to Father Sialm (in *The Indian Sen-tinel,* May 1937: 68). Thus Mary Kills Two's baptismal feast for her granddaughter at Pine Ridge celebrated her extended kinship relations in the old ritual way, only now in the Christian name. Pumpkin Seed's Lakota vision-seeking found "a lady in a white cloud, . . . wearing a white dress and blue cloak," with the words "Holy Mary, pray for us" (in ibid., May 1940: 79) at her feet. In the 1950s the Jesuits reported the attempt to transform Lakota attachment to deceased relatives "into something finer and nobler, Christian love" (in ibid., May 1956: 68).

The Church sponsored an "Indian Decoration Day," with an outdoor mass in the cemetery where Red Cloud and other Lakota worthies were buried. Priests led rosary prayers at the four-day mourning services held by the Indians. Lakota Catholics were drawing upon their two religious traditions for their spiritual sustenance and identity.

ST. JOSEPH AND ST. MARY SOCIETIES

By the early twentieth century most of the Lakotas belonged to one Christian denomination or another, with Catholic and Episcopal church organizations serving as the hubs of reservation neighborhood life, the *tiyospaye*. Government policy prohibited aboriginal rituals and social institutions. The Catholic missionaries encouraged Sioux adult participation in new rituals and institutions that were meant to replace the aboriginal forms and at the same time to bind the new converts to Christian church life. The most important of these were the St. Joseph and St. Mary Societies, which met not only locally throughout the year, but also in grand annual summer congresses. In this way a Lakota could join the Catholic church, become a member of a men's or women's society, and socialize with thousands of fellows at the summer encampments, all with the approval of the Holy Rosary authorities and government officials. Participation in these Christian institutions "was the source of the deepest solidarity and meaning of the Sioux people during the time that the 'reservation culture' flourished" (White 1965: 2), until World War II.

Rev. Francis M. Craft, the freelance missionary who served at Pine Ridge and Rosebud from 1883 to 1885, was inducted into the Omaha Society—a former warriors' society acquired from the Omaha Indians in the 1860s. Craft saw that the Omaha Society of his day emphasized righteous conduct rather than military prowess; generosity and brotherhood were its virtues. He saw these as counterparts to Christian virtues; hence, he attempted to modify them to fit Christian teaching and ritual. His efforts led the way to the official formation of the St. Joseph Society among the Sioux (see Thiel 1989: 6).

With the support of Bishop Marty, the first St. Joseph and St. Mary sodalities were officially sanctioned among the Devil's Lake Sioux, North Dakota, in 1884. They were structured similarly to traditional men's and women's sodalities, with doorkeepers, visitors of the sick, waiters, heralds, hair cutters, horse traders, etc.; however, membership was limited to Catholics married within the Church, who had received first communion. The members were known to observe the sabbath, catechize their brethren, and to avoid polygamy and drunkenness. They were designed to be adult models of Christian virtue (ibid., 8).

The members of these mutual aid societies eschewed participation in Native rituals abhorrent to Christianity. Instead, they spread the newly founded organizations to other Sioux communities in the 1880s. At each reservation those interested in joining applied to the local priests, and upon proving themselves worthy Catholics—having received baptism, having learned basic prayers and church precepts, receiving communion regularly and attending mass on Sundays and Holy Days of Obligation, respecting all church officials—the new members vowed to send their children to mission schools and to avoid Protestant services. The members performed corporal acts of mercy—visiting the sick, burying the dead, helping widows and orphans—and they abstained (or at least promised to abstain) from alcohol and superstitious customs.

In 1889 a Lakota asked Father Digmann for help in protecting the Omaha Dance and its brotherhood. The local agent was threatening to destroy it, charging that its nighttime dancing made the Indians unfit for "serious," steady work. Digmann replied:

> "Nobody blames your society for helping one another, keep that up but true friendships exist only among those who worship the Great Spirit, come to Church." Within myself I thought: "This pagan society may turn out a basis for a christian brotherhood (St. Joseph and Mary's Societies) and surely this was also Father Craft's idea. Go in with them in their door and lead them out to his." (C. 1922: 19)

The Catholic authorities thus aided in the formation of these sodalities, and held the first Sioux Congress of sodality members in 1891, on the Fourth of July. Sun Dances at the summer solstice had been banned; the U.S. government had tried to replace them with patriotic, mock military gatherings; now the Catholic missionaries were providing their own version of seasonal liturgy. Three thousand Indians journeyed to the Standing Rock Reservation, where the social functions of the banned Sun Dance—the gathering, the visiting, the feasting, the pledging, and even gambling—were celebrated. Abbot Marty had been reluctant at first to give too much room to the new sodalities of the 1880s, with their lay initiative; however, he wanted to rid Sioux reservations of the Sun Dances, and he saw Sioux Catholic congresses as direct replacements. Marty gave sermons about Jesus' hanging from a tree, in order to show the Sioux that the sacrifice of the mass was a higher form of Sun Dance self-torture, with Jesus providing the salvific sacrifice for all humans (Enochs 1993: 86). In addition, the Ghost Dance of 1890 forced him to consider a means of gathering adult Sioux organizational force against such movements in the future. Moreover, he chose Independence Day in order to compete with the U.S. patriotic celebrations, which allowed certain traditional dances including war dances (Thiel 1989: 11). This first Congress made the Pine Ridge Lakotas aware that their North Dakota relatives were more progressive, wearing short hair and the like. The Oglalas wanted to catch up and start their own St. Joseph and St. Mary Societies. One of them said at the time that he felt "like a child breaking through the shell. . . . The Blackrobes by their teaching have hatched me" (in Digmann c. 1922: 28).

Sioux who received baptism had a difficult life ahead of them. They were required to attend mass; they were prohibited, at least publicly, from polygamy, the warpath, divination, superstitions, and consulting with medicine men. Their gentile relatives and friends ridiculed their Christian identity. The St. Joseph and St. Mary Societies provided a peer structure for mutual encouragement, under priestly guidance. Furthermore, these groups could lobby the reservation authorities against the old culture. As one priest noted, "an organized minority protected by law and a watchful police is a powerful factor in swaying public opinion" (Goll 1940: 38).

The congresses grew naturally from both Christian and Lakota institutions. The German Jesuits had promoted Catholic congresses in Germany, Austria, and Switzerland at midcentury, to foster devotion to God and Church, to encourage Catholic schools, and to lobby for Catholic rights during the *Kulturkampf*. When those Jesuits emigrated to the U.S., they initiated similar congresses among the Indians. American bishops organized devotional congresses for African Americans and for white lay Catholics in the 1880s, and Protestants, too, held summer congresses for their congregations in the late nineteenth century. For the Sioux, Catholic and Episcopal summer congresses served as traditional summer encampments; each *tiyospaye* traveled and camped as a unit, and pursued its goals of enhancing social solidarity, arranging marriages, and expressing religious values in common.

These sodalities and their annual congresses provided the Lakotas with the only viable means of leadership in their communities, since medical, military, and political authority had been wrested from them.

At the same time, the congresses served at first to diminish the role of Lakota women in public affairs. At the 1892 Congress on the Cheyenne River Reservation, Bishop Marty refused to allow the Sioux women to speak:

> In the Church it was held so from the beginning that the women had to keep silence in public affairs. Man has been appointed by God as head, to order and arrange. The women's honor and privilege it is to govern the house and to raise and . . . educate men. (In Digmann c. 1922: 32)

Marty's ban held for almost twenty years. By 1922, however, the women's speeches were found to be most edifying by a visiting priest (in *The Indian Sentinel,* October 1922: 542–545).

The congresses were also means by which Church officials could manipulate Sioux sentiment and organization in favor of the missions, and often against the U.S. government—which partially supported the mission educational enterprise but which was rarely friendly to Catholic endeavors. After 1905 the U.S. forbade the congresses from taking place on Independence Day.

Locally, sodalities met Sundays in conjunction with prayer services (or mass, when a priest might be available), and periodically for retreats. There was mutual encouragement and public confession, as well as entertainment. At these meetings the Indians expressed their spirituality and discussed their problems as Catholic Indians. A Jesuit reported about one of these gatherings:

> I do some preaching, but they do most of it themselves, and you would be surprised how excellent their sermons are. They do a lot of praying. They go to Mass every morning. All of them go to Confession and Communion at least once. Most of them go twice, and some every day. That may give you some idea of the sincere faith of some of these Indians. (In *The Indian Sentinel,* January 1952: 15)

Until 1896 a single Congress was held in the summer; however, from 1897 there were regional congresses. Concurrently the various Protestant bodies were also forming their own sodalities and congresses, and many Sioux attended all the congresses they could, as vehicles for social interaction, gambling, and politicking. Thousands of Indians attended these congresses, with perhaps only hundreds actually participating in all the religious activities.

Every year the members set up camp with horses and tipis in the early days, wagons, tents, and autos as the century progressed. Each congress constructed a bower where thousands of delegates gathered. Criers greeted dignitaries, including bishops and papal representatives. Everyone shook hands solemnly, then proceeded to the magnificent Eucharistic processions, devotions to the Blessed Sacrament, hymnody in Sioux, Latin, and English, and requiem services for those who had died during the year. Delegates gave speeches, passed resolutions (e.g., against peyote use and divorce, or for greater federal funding for Catholic boarding schools), put on plays about Catholicism's battle against paganism, and displayed the various sodality regalia.

At Holy Rosary Mission during one congress a Sioux Catholic said: "The new ways are better than the old. We have changed much and we owe all the improved conditions to the Black Gown. With my right hand I cling to the Cross, with my left I cling to the plow handle" (Catholic Sioux Congress 1920). At the 1933 meeting, Lizzie Whirlwind Soldier addressed the audience: "How shall a Catholic mother raise her children?" Ralph Eagle Feather expounded: "Why I became a member of the Catholic Church" (Catholic Sioux Congress 1933). At the fiftieth anniversary of Holy Rosary's founding, in 1938, one of the old-timers recalled at the congress how hard it had been to adjust to the mission school: the alien blackrobes, the regimentation of days of the week: "Strange were the teachings of the new religion; the sign of the Cross was a subject for laughter and regarded as superstition by the pagan Indians" (Catholic Sioux Congress 1938). Sister Lucy, a Native religious, addressed the congress in fluent Lakota and English. Everyone shook hands with her, and "It made everyone feel very happy" (Catholic Sioux Congress 1938). At the 1938 meeting there were 1,000 communions, 600 confessions, eighty-three confirmations, six first communions, and one baptism.

Although World War II scattered many of the sodality members, 1946 witnessed a Catholic Sioux Victory Congress, to celebrate the end of the war. By this time, however, the priests delivered almost every address, whereas in the earlier decades the Indians served as the speakers. The congresses of the 1950s attempted to meet the challenge of deteriorating social relations on Sioux reservations in the post-war era, and in the 1960s the congresses dealt with the growth of new Protestant sects on the reservations. By 1965 the majority in attendance were more comfortable in English than in Lakota, and so the rule was made: "ENGLISH OR BROKEN ENGLISH IS TO BE USED BY ALL" (Catholic Sioux Congress 1965). Old-timers who spoke no English would be provided translators, even though much praying and singing still took place in Sioux. By the 1960s very few priests spoke any Lakota, a change from the early days.

During the late 1960s and 1970s the congresses held panel discussions regarding the need for Catholic Sioux religious leadership and increased lay participation in Catholic organization. In 1962 a Jesuit observer opined that the Congress "is dying a natural death" (Tekakwitha Missionary Conference 1962); a decade later Lakota participants complained that the "Congress is not going any place. Same people, no new members" (Catholic Sioux Congress 1975). Older Lakotas of the 1970s appreciated the origin of the St. Joseph and St. Mary Societies and their annual Congress—one Sioux thanked Father Digmann for creating a Christian equivalent of the old Sioux societies whose function was to unify the people (Stolzman 1973–1978, February 13, 1973)—but their federating powers faltered in the modern day. The Congress marked its centenary in 1991 and the meetings continue, but they seem to be overshadowed by national, regional, and local Tekakwitha conferences. The Sioux have wondered whether they should subsume their congresses under the structure of the National Tekakwitha Conference and disband their own meetings. However, the Tekakwitha gatherings are not Sioux in origin and so don't seem "really Indian" to the Lakotas. They don't have the "old-timey feeling" that the older Sioux Catholics enjoy at their own congresses, speaking their own language and recalling their local days of yore. Maybe the Sioux Congress is "gathering dust" (Fargo, August 4, 1989); nevertheless, St. Joseph and St. Mary members are determined to maintain this particular form of Lakota spiritual organization.

CATHOLIC LAKOTA LEADERSHIP

In the early twentieth century Bishop John Stariha of South Dakota employed catechists as well as sodalities in order to solidify adult Sioux Catholic institutions. By 1909 he had thirteen paid and five volunteer Native helpers, some of whom were interested in spreading the Catholic faith and its forms to other Plains Indians (Thiel 1989: 31). Between 1888 and 1932 twenty-three catechists worked at Pine Ridge, all men, including both half-breeds and full-breeds. These catechists — Ivan Star-Comes-Out, Joe Horn Cloud, Albert Long Soldier, and the others — held lay services in their locales when priests were not able to visit. They helped the priests pray over the sick; they taught hymns, baptized in emergencies; their main task was to "try to bring in as many converts as they can" (Westropp n.d.: 8). The catechists also served as the eyes and ears of the priests, informing on their tribesmen who persisted in aboriginal spirituality or peyote rituals, and counting all the Indians who attended mass and received the sacraments.

Were any of the catechists prospective priests? Father Sialm, for one, doubted their ability to carry the administrative burdens of the priesthood, however useful they proved as helpers. In his "Retreat Notes" of 1930, the priest wrote rhetorically: "Are there any Lakota doctors or lawyers? Why should we expect priests?" He mentioned Nicholas Black Elk and other Lakota catechists, and asked if they were capable of running a farm, supporting a family: "What hope is there? Who is capable to manage his own household justly, reasonably — Christian like?" Drawing upon his forty-five years of experience at Red Cloud, he could not think of a single alumnus who, in his opinion, could serve well as a priest or brother: ". . . what individual is there to be called!" He was aware of a girl or two who had become a tertiary of the Sisters of Saint Francis, staying at Holy Rosary, living and dying a good life. But what of boys? He found "very little love for sanctification in *any big boy*!" Where could he find the spirit of self-denial, the love of God for God's sake, the devotion to the Blessed Sacrament, the constancy of humility? What Lakota even had a family that encouraged and displayed those virtues, thus forming the priestly character in their children? He concluded that the Lakotas were simply not ready to produce a priest: "I should ask the question: Did the Gypsies have any priests of their tribe!" And even if the Lakotas were to produce a priest, where would he serve? At home his relatives would tempt and undercut him. Even the half-breeds were incapable of serving a non-Indian parish: "An Indian priest for the whites!—Who will gladly accept!" So for the first half century, and indeed to this day, there have been no Oglala Lakota Catholic priests, even though there have been Episcopalian priests (e.g., Robert Two Bulls) and even a Russian Orthodox priest (Martin Brokenleg, now Episcopalian) from the Sioux. C. P. Jordan, a Rosebud Sioux fluent in Lakota, served as a priest at Holy Rosary and is currently at St. Francis. Several Oglalas have been seminarians, including Gerald Clifford, and most recently, Emil Her Many Horses, but none has received full ordination.

One of the most prominent catechists at Pine Ridge was Nicholas Black Elk of Manderson. Born in 1863, he began his career as a medicine man at the age of seventeen; however, in 1886 he joined Buffalo Bill Cody's Wild West show, the contract of which stipulated that he be a Christian. His letters from Europe were printed in *Iapi Oaye (Word Carrier),* the Sioux-language Protestant journal printed at the Santee agency in Nebraska. He was quoted in December 1889: "So thus all along, of the white man's many customs, only his faith, the white man's beliefs about God's will, and how they act according to it, I wanted to understand" (in DeMallie 1984: 9–10). He was probably a neophyte Episcopalian at the time, seeking as a Lakota holy man to understand all things spiritual.

When Black Elk returned to Pine Ridge from his European tour, his medical practices came into conflict with the newly established Holy Rosary Mission. Although his wife joined the Catholic Church, and three of his boys were baptized in the 1890s, Black Elk was not converted until 1904, when Father Joseph Lindebner, S.J., ejected him forcefully from a curing ritual. The legend has it that Black Elk was working with drum and rattle over a sick boy, when the priest arrived to provide last rites for the patient, already baptized. A struggle ensued between the two religious specialists, and Lindebner threw the Indian's sacred paraphernalia from the tent, then grabbed Black Elk by the throat, saying, "Satan, get out!" (in DeMallie 1984: 14). Black Elk was so overwhelmed by the priest's power and authority that he received baptism himself two weeks later, on the feast of St. Nicholas, from whom he took his Christian name. (Throwing doubt on this story is Steltenkamp 1987: 91–97.)

In the years that followed, Nicholas Black Elk became a catechist, earning $5 a month and proselytizing not only among the Sioux, but also the Arapahos and Shoshones. He and his second wife became pillars of Lakota Catholicism, with Black Elk appearing on the cover of the missionary journal, *The Indian Sentinel,* in 1926, an image of the pagan-turned-Christian, rosary beads in hand. One missionary estimated that

Black Elk brought at least four hundred conversions through catechetical duties. Father Westropp said of him:

> Ever since his conversion he has been a fervent apostle and he has gone around like a second St. Paul, trying to convert his tribesmen to Catholicity. He has made many converts. . . . Though half blind he has by some hook or crook learned how to read and he knows his religion thoroughly. (Westropp c. 1910: 12)

In the mission organs we read of his justifying veneration to Virgin Mary by biblical references; we learn of his spellbinding oratory, and his victory war whoops after completing a conversion. When Father Sialm organized a retreat for Oglala catechists in 1922, employing St. Ignatius Loyola's "Spiritual Exercises," Nicholas Black Elk initiated the vow: "We catechists resolve never to commit a mortal sin" (in *The Indian Sentinel,* April 1923: 78). Other Lakotas might refer to him derisively as a "cigar-store Indian" (in Holler 1983: 4–5); however, he persisted in his Catholic commitment, and it is said that he is buried with "The Road Picture" he used on his evangelical journeys (see Steltenkamp 1987: 108–133).

At the same time, Nicholas Black Elk never abandoned his traditional Lakota worldview, as everyone knows who has read *Black Elk Speaks,* written by the poet John G. Neihardt, and *The Sacred Pipe,* by the scholar Joseph Epes Brown. As a result of these books, Black Elk the traditionalist Lakota holy man has become world-renowned (Powers 1990). When Black Elk converted, he vowed to have nothing more to do with his guardian animal; he is purported to have said, "No more screech owl" (Steltenkamp 1987). Nevertheless, when John Neihardt arrived in 1930, seeking to interview an old-timer who remembered Custer's Last Stand and the Ghost Dance, Black Elk's traditionalism poured forth. On Decoration Day 1931, Nicholas Black Elk was noticeably missing from the Catholic Sioux Congress. He was with John Neihardt, relating his life story.

When *Black Elk Speaks* was published in 1932, "The Jesuit priests at Holy Rosary Mission were shocked and horrified at the suggestion that one of their most valued catechists still harbored beliefs in the old Indian religion" (DeMallie 1984: 58). In September of that year, a new American Commissioner of Indian Affairs, John Collier, visited Pine Ridge Agency, in order to promote his Indian New Deal. Collier was insistent that governmental rules against the practice of traditional

Indian religion be rescinded; indeed, he found much of value in aboriginal spiritual practice. At Pine Ridge he participated in a "Pipe of Peace" ceremony. There was a growing interest, even fascination, regarding traditional Indian spirituality—Neihardt's book was part of the trend—and the Holy Rosary missionaries were challenged by these developments. The following year the mission personnel produced a lengthy document, "Some Points on Catholic Indian Activities," accusing John Collier of undermining Catholicism, Catholic schools, and Christian influence on Indian reservations. The document accused Collier of spouting atheism, promoting communism on reservations, sponsoring paganism, and depriving Indians of their right to uplift themselves. In the view of the Jesuits, Collier wanted to keep Lakotas and other Indians as specimens in an American open air ethnological zoo, rather than helping them toward Christian culture (Red Cloud Indian School, Series 1/1, Box 1, Folder 5). A four-part series, "Some Facts about the New Deal for the Indians and the Wheeler-Howard Bill," in the *Catholic Daily Tribune,* April 5, 6, 14, and May 2, 1934, repeated these charges publicly. A historian says that the period 1932–1934 was filled with anxiety at the South Dakota Catholic missions, for the Indian New Deal threatened everything the missions stood for. "For the Government to countenance the restoration of pagan practices under the guise of allowing 'fullest constitutional liberty in all matters affecting religion, conscience, and culture' (quoting Circular No. 2970, January 3, 1934, which nullified U.S. prohibitions of Indian religion) . . . among a people for whom the missionaries had worked and died to Christianize seemed to betray a distorted sense of values on the part of officials" (Southall 1964: 66).

These events were not insignificant in regard to Black Elk's backsliding in print. In 1933 when the catechist was run over by a team of horses and a wagon, he asked for last rites and was granted them. Upon his recovery, he signed two documents now preserved in the Holy Rosary Mission archives (Red Cloud Indian School, Series 1/1, Box 1, Folder 5) in which he recanted and disavowed the contents of *Black Elk Speaks.* The first, typed in English and Lakota, and signed by Black Elk, his daughter Lucy C. Looks Twice, and Joseph A. Zimmerman, S.J., is entitled "BLACK ELK SPEAKS AGAIN—A LAST WORD," dated Holy Rosary Mission Pine Ridge, South Dakota, January 26, 1934. The second is a handwritten letter—but not Black Elk's hand—"Dear Friends," dated September 20, 1934, Oglala, South Dakota.

The first document claimed that the visionary and ritual content of *Black Elk Speaks* was "about people's ways of long ago, . . . not . . . about current ways." It would appear that when Black Elk was faced with possible death in the wagon accident, he promised to recant the book if the priest would give him last rites: "I called my priest to pray for me and so he gave me Extreme Unction and Holy Eucharist. Therefore I will tell you the truth." Just how much pressure was applied, we shall never know; however, it is clear that a *quid pro quo* took place. The recantation was apparently payment for Extreme Unction. Black Elk then stated that he was well aware of what St. Peter says of those men who forsake their faith (in 2 *Peter* 2). What *Peter* says is that those who accept Jesus and then reject Him are far worse than those who never accepted Him: the dog is returned to his vomit, the sow to her wallowing in the mire.

In the second document Black Elk claimed to have spoken to Neihardt of his Catholic faith, but that Neihardt left such material out of his book. In effect, the letter blamed Neihardt for dwelling on the past and accused the poet of inventing a paganized Black Elk. "Because I value my soul more than my Body I'm awful sorry for the mistake I've made," Black Elk concluded, and he reaffirmed the superiority of Catholicism over the Sun Dance, Ghost Dance, and Lakota medical practices. In both statements, Nicholas Black Elk was identified as a believing, normative, church-going Catholic.

And yet for the rest of Black Elk's life—he never served again as an active catechist after the *Black Elk Speaks* scandal, although he remained an observant Catholic—the Indian involved himself publicly with presentations of traditional Lakota ritual: e.g., appearing in Black Hills pageants, and instructing Joseph Epes Brown regarding the sacred rites of the Oglala Sioux. Two years before his death in 1950, Black Elk told one man that "he had made a mistake in rejecting" his Lakota practices for Christianity. "Perhaps, after all, the Lakota religion would have been better for his people" (DeMallie 1984: 72).

Nicholas Black Elk did work for thirty years as a devoted Catholic catechist. He knew his Bible and practiced his Catholic rituals religiously. Nevertheless, he interpreted some of his Catholicism through the Lakota worldview, thinking, e.g., of retreats as if they were vision quests. On the other hand, his interviews with Neihardt betrayed a Christian universalism, a peaceful moralism, that seemed to have reinterpreted Lakota traditions through Christian consciousness. He seems to have come to understand the Sun Dance, the sacred pipe, in terms of Christian values. Black Elk was a "creative theologian" (Holler 1983) who was able to understand two religious traditions in terms of the other. Thus, Father Sialm wrote in the 1930s that "in the last years he fell back into the old Indian dances without losing his faith." At the same time, "we seem to have two Black Elks: a catechetical Black Elk who never mentions the old ways and a traditionalist Black Elk who never mentions Christianity" (ibid.). It would appear that, while thinking of the two faiths in terms of each other, he kept them separate in practice. He compartmentalized them. He did not substitute one entirely for the other; he maintained "a kind of theological bi-culturalism" (Holler 1983). At Pine Ridge today some older people remember him as a catechist, whereas the younger Lakotas know him through *Black Elk Speaks.* At St. Agnes Church in Manderson, the parish priest complains (Pine Ridge, August 7, 1988) that everyone tries to turn Nicholas Black Elk into a "noble savage" when he was in fact a "man of the faith" in Manderson. Across the road in the Catholic cemetery, "Chief Black Elk 1858–1950" is buried with other members of his family, supposedly with the pictorial catechism he used on his missionary journeys. One Franciscan priest proposes that Black Elk be considered for sainthood, so holy and caring a man he was (Cavagnaro, August 3, 1988), and a Jesuit says, "On occasion I have prayed to Black Elk. He is really a holy man, he is a saint, I think" (in Archambault 1995: 163).

Recently a Lakota Franciscan sister, Marie Therese Archambault, has written a meditation (Archambault 1998) upon his career as a Catholic Lakota holy man, walking the two spiritual roads with integrity and grace. She states that "reflecting upon Black Elk's life enables us to understand how two disparate ways came together for him" (in *Bureau of Catholic Indian Missions Newsletter,* vol. 16, no. 4, May–June 1997). "Black Elk's Life," she says, "reflected his conviction that his people could live again spiritually in two ways: through the Catholic tradition he embraced and through the ancient Lakota traditions" (Archambault 1998: 7). In her view, Black Elk "lived two traditions integrally. He grasped the holiness of each, and lived it in a *wakan* way as the cultural boundaries of his time would permit" (87). He "brought unity to them in himself" (98), and in living such an existence of wholeness, he set an example for Indians, Christians, and others to follow. "I now consider myself his devotee and disciple," writes Sister Archambault; "he is also my brother in Jesus Christ" (59).

Yet Black Elk's great-granddaughter Charlotte (Gerald Clifford's wife) has his pipe and his amulets, the paraphernalia of his traditionalism, and she has a bag of tales about how Black Elk tricked various priests into thinking he was a thorough convert. Traditionalist Lakotas, traditionalist Catholics, and syncretists all draw upon Black Elk for justification and inspiration today. In the 1930s, however, his dual religiousness repelled the Holy Rosary authorities, and it helped end their experiment with Lakota catechists at Pine Ridge.

A letter from Father Sialm to Mr. Thomas Blind Man, dated March 28, 1934, indicated the need to assert authority over the catechists:

> Your word to me at the Mission should not go unchallenged, 'that the Missionaries don't care for the Indians?' . . . And you consider yourself a catechist. . . . Ungratefulness is very ugly and unjust. . . . Even God is displeased. (Red Cloud Indian School, Series 1/1, Box 1, Folder 5)

Sialm told Mr. Blind Man that Indians were tearing down the missionary work with their sins; however, the priest was ready to forgive the catechist's "insolent talk to me yesterday. But you ought to apologize."

By World War II, Holy Rosary personnel had decided that catechists were no longer necessary as part of the Catholicization process of the Lakotas. By then cars and paved roads made it easier for priests to get around by themselves, and the number of priestly vocations was large enough that catechists were superfluous. It was also felt that the catechists were not as trustworthy as had been hoped—Nicholas Black Elk being the most prominent disappointment—and in the weakening of authority caused by the New Deal there was need to impose priestly, hierarchical, non-Indian authority over the Indians. An experiment in Catholic Indian leadership came to a close, and clericalism became a controlling force at the mission in the 1940s and 1950s. The missionaries charged then that the Sioux Indians were too "unstable" (in White 1969: 14) for Catholic leadership.

After more than eighty years of Jesuit missions to the Lakotas at Pine Ridge, it was said two decades ago, "There has not been a single attempt on the part of the Sioux men to pursue office in the Church. . . . There is a deep inherited reticence on their part to put themselves forward as leaders" (Diocesan Permanent Diaconate Program, May 28, 1971) Hence, the Jesuits in the Diocese of Rapid City proposed to begin a permanent diaconate program for Lakota men. They recommended that the Lakota community nominate candidates to the priests at Holy Rosary Mission, who would then approach the nominees, telling them of the community support. Bolstered by that vote of confidence, perhaps some would begin training. Their plan of study would include not only priestly formation, knowledge of

Church and Christ, but also the "Church's sacramental system and possible parallels with Indian sacramentals" such as vision quests, sacred pipe ritualism, and the like. The diaconate training program was to "stress Indian truths and ways that are good and beautiful which will enhance western Church's Theology."

According to the 1971 plan, these deacons were to perform many of the tasks formerly managed by the catechists: reading scriptures at mass, leading prayer meetings, teaching religion classes, assisting priests with parish work. The deacons were trained to preside at wakes, assist at funerals, conduct devotions, give talks, provide instruction, take sacraments to the sick, assume some administrative functions, visit families, hospitals, and jails, and help with parish organizations. In 1975 this program went into effect, and a half dozen Oglala men have achieved the diaconate. The first American Indian deacon, Steven Levi Red Elk, was ordained in 1975 at Holy Rosary.

Despite the diaconate program of the past decade, Holy Rosary has not produced in a century of work the beginnings of a Lakota clergy. As one contemporary Jesuit writes, "Local Churches in many countries are able to boast of native clergy and lay leaders. The Indian communities of North America are a tragic exception" (Hatcher 1987: 91–92). The writer finds a paternalism in Holy Rosary's history that has never considered the locals ready to take over; there has never been enough trust in them. He recommends that there be more trust, and that there be more complete adult education programs, not only in priestly formation, but also for lay leadership. There is no reason to think, he states, that the Lakotas at Pine Ridge (or any other Indian group, for that matter) are incapable of producing their own spiritual leadership.

Among the females there have been more vocations. Clara Condelario was the daughter of a Mexican father and Sioux mother. When both died she came to live at the mission with the sisters, and was one of the first girls at Holy Rosary. She was the first Sioux girl to take a vow of chastity, and she belonged to the tertiary order of St. Francis, dying of tuberculosis in 1915 and being buried near the sisters in the Holy Rosary cemetery. Lucy Patton, another half-breed, took her tertiary vows in 1914, after fifteen years of schooling at Red Cloud (Sisters of St. Francis: 38).

Father Craft formed an ill-fated Sioux sisterhood in the nineteenth century, but not at Holy Rosary. In 1935 the Oblate Sisters of the

Blessed Sacrament was established at Marty, South Dakota, designed for Indian females of the Dakotas. From time to time letters came to Holy Rosary from Sioux girls seeking a vocation, e.g., one to Father Bryde in 1949: "I realize fully what I would be giving up as a religious—namely giving up men for God, that is being a virgin" (Bryde 1949). The provincials gave Holy Rosary priests the advice: "All should strive to foster vocations among those with whom they are working" (Provincial's Visitations, November 21, 1956). At Pine Ridge there have been perhaps a dozen sisters from the Native population in the first century.

Sister Genevieve Cuny, O.S.F., for several years a staff member of the National Tekakwitha Conference, has been a striking example of Lakota vocation in recent years. She attended Holy Rosary Mission for twelve years, coming from one of the prominent half-breed families on the reservation. Her Catholicism was already three generations deep at her birth, and she attests to receiving her faith not only from the sisters and priests, but more significantly from her parents. They were always praying, and she knew her prayers before ever entering Red Cloud School. Her parents were "like Jesus" (Cuny, July 11, 1987), always teaching to share, by example. She attended Sioux City College in Iowa and planned to marry, but after working for four years with the Franciscan tertiaries as a social worker, she decided to give her life to Christ. Only three or four Indian sisters were around when she made her decision; however, she has served as a model for other Sioux women as she has taught at Pine Ridge, Rosebud, and Standing Rock. Cuny views Lakota women as the active force of Catholicism at Pine Ridge. The women attend church services and take roles of leadership that reflect their economic status—women are more likely to have salaried jobs and are often the breadwinners these days. Lakota men suffer from acute unemployment (as high as 80 percent), alcoholism, and low self-esteem. Their "macho image," she suggests (Cuny, August 8, 1986), prevents them from seeking God's help or forgiveness, and they seldom participate actively in Catholic liturgical life. Tragically, she writes (in DCRAA 1979), Lakota men, suffering "serious social and psychological upheavals," perpetrate violence upon Lakota women. As a result she has sought Church and tribal protection for battered Lakota women, with the support of Sister Geraldine Clifford, O.S.F., also of Pine Ridge.

Marla Powers (1986: 183) claims that "Christianity has fostered the idea of male superiority much more than native religion has, particularly among the Catholics." She notes that there are many Oglala nuns but no Oglala priests, and she suggests that the Church "is reluctant to bring men into the priesthood, where they may be regarded as equal to white males." Native nuns are acceptable to the Church, she argues, because women are thought to be "subservient," and therefore are inoffensive to white male authority.

Although it may have seemed to some that Holy Rosary remained cloistered from the changes of the 1940s, such was not the case. The coming of paved roads, the use of automobiles, the installation of telephones, were all signs of modernity and put an end to the seclusion of the mission. Like so many other Christian experiments—the reductions of Paraguay, the Canadian reserves of the seventeenth century, the praying Indian towns in New England—there was an attempt on the part of the missionaries to keep the converts separate not only from their pagan tribesmen, but also from influences of the secular world. At Pine Ridge, World War II intruded. Hundreds of Lakota men took part in the fighting. The U.S. government usurped part of Pine Ridge—the area of Cuny Table (named for the family of Sister Genevieve)—for a bombing range. For these and other reasons, many Lakotas moved from the reservation to urban areas like Rapid City and beyond. The rural, isolated Sioux became enmeshed in modern American culture and the reservation was overrun by outside forces. The poor, undereducated Sioux became "the American lower-lower class, . . . the 'failure class'" (White 1965: 2).

The institution of Holy Rosary had enormous influence on the spiritual and cultural life of the Oglalas at Pine Ridge from the 1880s until World War II. All the outward signs—no matter what the Lakotas were thinking privately—indicated a strengthening of Catholic bonds and an outpouring of Catholic devotions. These did not end with World War II; indeed, the 1950s found a continuation and elaboration of devotionalism at Holy Rosary. Nevertheless, World War II seems a watershed, after which the mission held less prominent sway.

In the post-war years there was "racial prejudice" on the part of the Red Cloud mixed-bloods, who organized gangs to assert their dominance over the full-bloods (Red Cloud Indian School, Series 1/1, Box 3, Folder 3). Participants at the Catholic Sioux Congress found a slackening of spirit at their meetings. They noted that "The Second World War changed our men. They came back after seeing the world. . . . they couldn't live the same way" (Catholic Sioux Congress, February 15, 1983). Furthermore, there was a bridling under the increased clerical control over all aspects of Catholic Lakota life in the 1940s. "In old days the people were the church. Then when things changed they no longer felt in control" (ibid.). They experienced disaffection from the mission and from the Church.

Many of the new social outlets were unhealthful to the Lakotas. Adult and juvenile delinquency increased in the post-war years. Drunkenness became common and then epidemic. Innocents, especially women and girls, were "continually frightened and annoyed" by abuses. The police were not able to keep order and bribery became common. In 1950 the Catholic Sioux Congress drew attention to these trends and passed a resolution to call to the attention of the tribal council on each reservation the great increase in "disorderly and unlawful conduct among the people of the various reservations . . ." (Catholic Sioux Congress 1950).

Some Lakotas left the reservation to escape the disorder, and they traveled to Rapid City and elsewhere in search of jobs. Father Zimmerman went to Rapid City in 1949 in order to help Sioux from various reservations adjust to urban life. Bishop William T. McCarty built the Mother Butler Center as a chapel and social magnet for the Indians. McCarty hoped to merge the Sioux eventually with other Catholic parishes in Rapid City, "not keep aloof as Indians" (Scott 1963: 78); however, in the short run the Sioux needed a place of their own. In 1953 Father Zimmerman wrote from Mother Butler Center, saying that the newly urban Sioux were "bewildered" by city life, but since 60 percent of the Sioux were Catholic, they came right to Mother Butler to get oriented (see White 1960; cf. Feraca 1963: 7). Whatever the Sioux religious experience in Rapid City, urbanization was one factor that caused Father Bernard Fagan, S.J., to remark in the early 1960s that the number of Catholic Lakotas at Pine Ridge had been declining for a decade, even though the majority of Sioux continued to "die in the Church" (Southall 1964: 90).

World War II was one watershed; the Second Vatican Council of the early 1960s constituted a second. The first affected the Lakotas themselves directly; the second had its greatest immediate impact on the Catholic missionaries and other church personnel. Eventually, however, the effects were felt by the Lakotas themselves, and the ramifications persist to this day. In particular, Vatican II reconsidered the attitude of Catholicism to non-Christian religious traditions, lessening the tone of condemnation toward them and seeking reconciliation with members of other faiths. In the context of this pan-faith ecumenism, the goal of missions became problematic. If Catholics were to respect religious orientations other than their own, then the condemnation of those other religious traditions was out of place, and perhaps the whole missionary enterprise was outmoded, even wrongheaded. Vatican II brought about numerous outward manifestations of doubt. Catholic men and women doubted their vocations and left their orders in large numbers; many came to doubt the unique place of Catholic orientation in the world; at the least there was widespread doubt regarding Church authority. These conditions transcended any conditions at Holy Rosary; however, the provincial's visitation report in 1962 found, "There is a serious morale problem in this community" (Provincial's Visitations 1962), referring to the community of religious as well as the Pine Ridge population as a whole.

In the 1960s the Holy Rosary staff evaluated and reevaluated its mission and procedures, and asked in searching ways—ways very much at odds with the first seventy-five years of Holy Rosary methods—what the real needs of the Lakotas might be. Father Bryde, who worked at Pine Ridge from 1954 to 1967 and was school director during those years, wrote two tomes (1966; 1967) that attempted to understand Sioux values (e.g., bravery, individual freedom, generosity and sharing, adjustment to nature) in order to assess the Indian resistance to white values (e.g., material achievement, scientific conquest of nature, working every day, personal acquisitiveness, efficiency, practicality). Rather than condemning the Sioux values, Bryde's work was an attempt to praise those values, so that mission personnel might adjust their methods to the Indians. In the general correspondence of the Red Cloud Indian School archives there is an anonymous report dating from the same period, and perhaps even written by Bryde, that refers to the Lakotas as "the most naturally religious people in the world" (Series 1/1, Box 4, Folder 4). The priest complained that Catholic liturgy was forced upon them, which "inhibits the Indian's natural expression of prayer in his spontaneous response to God." The missionary activity of the church served to "harm him spiritually, confuse him, increase his guilt feelings."

When an Inter-Mission Board was established in the 1960s to monitor the mission enterprises at Holy Rosary and St. Francis, the members admitted that "there is much discouragement on Indian missions throughout the country today because the promising beginnings of fifty years ago have come to so little fruition today" (Inter-Mission Board 1969). The board recognized the "cultural disintegration that has been taking place especially with such rapidity since 1945. . . . In as much as organized Catholicism was once a part of the life of the Sioux, that much must Catholicism suffer as has the rest of the life of the Sioux suffered." What advice did the board have for its missionaries?

> The best studies indicate a minimum of 100 years or 4 generations for a culture to gradually disintegrate and then reintegrate around a differing set of cultural values. . . . The missionary must be prepared to bolster up the individuals caught in this cultural disintegration, rather than make life more difficult for them by imposing new demands and new sanctions that they are unable to bear.

The board stated that "the Sioux are still a very spiritual people, even if their lives often reflect patterns of social degeneration. They are much more spiritual in their orientation than is the typical non-Indian who may be teaching them the forms of Christianity." The board found in the Indians the virtues of faith, hope, and charity, predating their Christianity; therefore, the missionaries should seek and build upon those virtues, not only to help them become functioning members of the Church, but also to improve the functioning of Oglala society. Investigators reported that the old missionary condemnation of paganism, coercive acculturation, had created a

> dualism, a schizophrenic attitude in the converts to our Faith. According to their own confession, they humbly accepted what they were told and back home they practised (sic) what through centuries of religious behaviour and tradition they felt was their way God wanted them to live. No community can survive on such a dualism. (Leo van den Oetelaar, S.J., to Joseph Sheehan, S.J., 1970?, Inter-Mission Board)

There was now the realization that Lakota Catholics, particularly the full-bloods, had not given up all their aboriginal forms of religiousness; hence, the board suggested that a variety of liturgies might be necessary to meet the needs of a variety of Catholic persons: full-bloods, mixed-bloods, etc. What Holy Rosary resisted in the 1930s when it was recommended by John Collier and carried out by Black Elk, the missionaries attempted in the 1970s.

EFFORTS AT INCULTURATION

Holy Rosary Mission, like many other Catholic Indian missions, inaugurated a process of "inculturation" (Hilbert 1987: 144). The staff published traditional Sioux stories in Lakota language (*Ehanni Ohunkakan*) and in English ("Lakota Stories") as part of curriculum development. They produced *A Lakota and English Hymnal* in 1972 which was meant to reflect Sioux as well as Catholic ceremonial traditions. Although it was recognized that many Lakotas possessed deep devotion to the Blessed Virgin Mary and preferred the rosary to any Lakota religious form, and that these traditional Catholics would be scandalized by radical innovations (and many of them were indeed scandalized!), certain priests decided to cross the boundaries between Catholic and Lakota religious expression.

If the Holy Rosary personnel were to adjust liturgical and other forms of Catholic life to the local Lakotas, it was necessary to understand those persons' culture. Hence, a missionary anthropology was necessary. This process was nothing new at Holy Rosary. The first missionaries attempted to learn Sioux language, and priests such as Eugene Buechel left dictionaries, grammars, drawings, linguistic and ethnological notes, as well as collections of Lakota stories. Father Buechel was fluent in Lakota, and many of his writings were in Lakota language. No one could argue that he and a number of his coworkers lacked the linguistic and observational skills to understand the Sioux, and it may be that few non-Indian persons understood them better. Buechel's corpus was substantial and lacked condemnatory judgments regarding Lakota culture. Contemporary Jesuits such as Ray Bucko, S.J., are engaged in scholarly research among the Lakotas, studying, e.g., the relationship of sweat lodges to Sioux cultural order (Bucko, September 29, 1991; see Bucko 1992). The seriousness and sincerity of this work is beyond doubt, and Lakota religious practitioners are more apt to be candid with contemporary Jesuits than with secular anthropologists, recognizing in the priests a kindred spirituality.

In the late 1960s and 1970s, three Jesuits in particular set out to analyze not only Sioux religiousness, but also its similarities and relationships to Christian forms. Father Paul Steinmetz was the first. Steinmetz taught at Holy Rosary during three summers in the mid-1950s, and when he was ordained in 1961 he received charge of the Oglala parish. He furbished the church there with murals of tipis, buffalos, thunderbirds, sun, moon, horses, and other natural phenomena. Benjamin Black Elk and other Lakota Catholics designed the church under Steinmetz's supervision, "expressing the Christian Trinity in Lakota religious symbols" (Steinmetz 1980: 37), replacing the dove with an eagle, placing a pipe beneath the crucifix. Before long he bedecked Our Lady of the Sioux Catholic Church with an "Indian" Jesus hanging from the crucifix, a peace pipe, an eagle feather, and horse hair paraphernalia. The altar cloth read, "Wakan Wakan Wakan." An observer remarked that Father Steinmetz was "creating a revolution, returning to the Indians their own religious traditions. Surely, this was a Sioux, as well as a Catholic, place of worship" (Collins 1969: 16).

In 1965 Father Steinmetz began actively to use the pipe as a symbol of Christ, a gesture that some Lakotas rejected (why should *he* be entitled to employ a sacred pipe?) but others encouraged. Lakotas asked him to say mass at the Pine Ridge Sun Dance in the same year, partially to help validate the traditional ceremonial in the face of harassment by Lakota Christians who blared gospel music during the rituals. For two years Steinmetz said mass following the piercing rite, and in 1971 he prayed with the pipe at the Sun Dance, at the request of the Lakotas. He performed these syncretic acts because the Sundancers were Catholics; he saw no good cause to keep their dual religious identities separated.

In 1973 Steinmetz introduced a pipe ceremony at the Catholic Sioux Congress, and its use lasted until around 1980. Steinmetz wrote in 1969, "One starting point in the blending of traditional Sioux Religion and the Christian Religion would be to transform the Sacred Pipe into a Christian prayer instrument." For him the pipe was a "type of Christ," since Jesus mediates perfectly between humanity and God, as the pipe mediates "in an imperfect way. . . . The Pipe, then, is the great Sioux foreshadowing of Christ in His Priestly Office" (Steinmetz 1969: 20). If the pipe could be purified and exorcised, it could become, in Steinmetz's view, a means to Christ, not the hindering pipe the early missionaries condemned. Steinmetz asked:

When you have taken the Pipe into the Catholic Church, you have taken in the essential good of their religion. Does this mean that we need to take in all their religious values without careful examination? No, some of these must be purified or even rejected. (20–21)

The priest reported that some Lakotas objected to the use of the pipe because they had always learned from the missionaries that the pipe was impure; Steinmetz told them that he was "baptizing" the pipe so long condemned by priests to be now an instrument of Catholic prayer. One Catholic full-blood who at first was against the use of this pagan device, decided he "wanted to be the godfather" (21) of the pipe for Christian use. Steinmetz saw the use of the pipe as a means of reaching the many Sioux who were presently "leading double lives" (21), going through sweats or vision quests while maintaining Christian lives, but feeling guilty about their bi-religiousness. In classes he taught at Red Cloud he praised Indian heroes; in church he told the legend of the White Buffalo Calf Woman. He encouraged some young Lakota men to engage in vision quests and advised them about their spiritual experiences. He prodded Lakota Catholics to "'interpret Christianity through the symbols of their own heritage, rather than sacrifice their old beliefs and . . . their Indian identity'" (Collins 1969: 16). More than one Lakota expressed gratitude, as did Benjamin Black Elk, that Father Steinmetz had made it possible for Indians to practice traditional and Catholic rituals openly and in peaceful communion with one another, without fear of being unfaithful to Catholicism.

When asked if he was fostering paganism, Steinmetz replied that he was doing what Jesus did in substituting the mass for the Jewish paschal meal; he was fulfilling, not destroying, the Sioux religion. For Steinmetz, Jesus was the fulfillment not only of Judaism but also of Lakota religious tradition. He wrote that Lakota religion is "pre-Christian" (1980: 160 n. 2) in the sense that it prepares one for Christianity. Lakota religion can exist, he said, in a Lakota Catholic, continuously preparing the person for the "deeper understanding" of Christian faith. Such was the Jesuit's perception of inculturation. Quoting a Lakota Catholic, Edgar Red Cloud, Steinmetz wrote: "When the Indians knew Mother Earth, they knew the Blessed Virgin Mary but they did not know her by name" (161). More crucially, for Steinmetz, the Lakotas knew aboriginally of Jesus through their sacred pipe, without yet enunciating His name. By combining the pipe and

Christ, the priest hoped to fashion a profoundly fulfilling Lakota Catholicism at Pine Ridge.

Steinmetz had long-range hopes for the pipe: "Eventually, it may become an official sacrament" (Steinmetz 1969: 22) in Catholicism, but in the meantime it was a way of enriching Catholic prayer for the Sioux, and even for priests like himself. He found that the pipe's communitarian ethos—"For the sake of our relatives" (24)—was similar to that found in holy communion, and so he hoped to provide the Christian Sioux with the means to "Christianize his own tradition" (Steinmetz, May 1970: 84). In 1980 Father Steinmetz completed a doctoral dissertation in which he examined the functioning of the pipe among the Sioux in relation to Christian and peyote religious orientations. And in 1984, after leaving his Sioux mission post, he published a book about Lakota spiritual practice, meant as a guide to non-Indians. As a result of his experience with the Sioux, Steinmetz wrote in 1986 that Christianity is today overly legalistic and rational; "the Native American can help us rediscover symbol in creation so that the world can again become mysterious and meaningful. . . . Native American Spirituality gives us a sense of the sacramental nature of creation" (7). The attempt to understand Lakota religiousness led at least one priestly observer to praise Sioux spirituality over Christian forms, even while remaining an active religious, albeit not at Pine Ridge. He wrote: "I must confess that Lakota Religion has added a new depth to my priestly life" (Steinmetz 1980: 7).

Michael F. Steltenkamp, S.J., accompanied Father Steinmetz in his journey to understand the Lakotas, and since leaving Holy Rosary he has become an anthropologist. Like many of the priests, he has taken sweats with the Indians and participated with them in their religious services. In observing the Sacred Calf Pipe bundle, Steltenkamp enthused that being in its presence was like being in Bethlehem (1976). In 1982 he published a book portraying and praising Sioux ritual practice for a non-Indian readership. He has written a book about Black Elk (1987, 1993), documenting the Indian holy man's dual participation in Catholicism and Lakota spirituality.

William F. Stolzman came to Holy Rosary in 1966 and was ordained in 1971. He also served at St. Francis Mission. Between 1973 and 1979 at Rosebud Reservation he conducted regular meetings between Sioux medicine men and Christian clerics. They compared ceremonies and worldviews. They discussed daily and spiritual concerns, and they engaged in a sustained, profound dialogue rarely achieved between Indians and Christians (Stolzman 1973–1978; see below). There was a real interest on the part of Stolzman (1969, 1973–1975, 1975, 1982, 1986a, 1986b) to understand and validate Sioux religious practice.

Steinmetz, Stolzman, and other Jesuits may have wanted to syncretize the pipe and Christ, but many Sioux preferred to keep the two forms of religious practice separate. They didn't mind comparing them and understanding one in terms of the other, but in practice they wanted them segregated (Black Bear, August 4, 1988). It was one thing to compare the Christian rite of confession with the Lakota sweat lodge. Both have similar functions: to purify, to bring a person back into right relations with the holy and with humans. Nevertheless, one should not perform Catholic confession in a sweat lodge. Benjamin Black Bear, Jr., who participated in the dialogues conducted by Stolzman, found it ironic that some Sioux beliefs, e.g., those regarding ghosts and spirits, which were becoming decreasingly important to many contemporary Sioux, were being embraced by the priests like Father Stolzman. Also, it was the priests, rather than the medicine men, who promoted the comparisons between Catholic and Lakota ceremonies; the Lakotas found the comparisons often to be "stretching it a bit" (ibid.). Nevertheless, the medicine men came out of these meetings reassured that dual participation was acceptable in the modern era. They found a "verbalization" of what they had already been doing—practicing Catholic and Lakota rituals separately, each in its place and for its purpose. In turn, they were able to counsel young Lakotas to carry on this compartmentalized bi-religiousness. Still, for the Lakotas there remained the task of holding together their lives through their religious practices, both Lakota and Christian. Fathers Steinmetz, Steltenkamp, and Stolzman on the other hand, are no longer to be found at Pine Ridge—a comment upon the short-lived presence of Jesuit innovators.

There were many Sioux who resisted the liturgical innovations of the past decades, others who adopted them for a while, until Steinmetz and other Jesuits moved on. Some feared that syncretism and dialogue promoted by Jesuits would undermine their traditional Lakota religious identity. Some Jesuits accused Steinmetz and his cohorts of fostering paganism and watering down the uniqueness of Christianity. There were also many Jesuits at Pine Ridge who regarded liturgical reform as irrelevant to the Sioux crises of the 1970s. The AIM takeover at Wounded Knee in 1973 led some mission observers to focus not so much on religious as on political, social, and economic issues. Robert A. White, S.J., writing in the midst of Wounded Knee II, depicted intense Sioux poverty and alienation. He found among the Indians a culture of despair that constituted for the church and the government a "crisis" of policy. The Sioux insisted on remaining Indian; they rejected the melting pot. They wanted to make their own decisions and not be dependent on Whites. They were bitter and did not want to be anthropological museum pieces. There were tensions among the various classes of Sioux, but among them all there was yearning for autonomy, both from the U.S. and from the Catholic Church. He found over the years since World War II "the gradual de-Christianization of the Sioux . . . people," and he observed that

> The Sioux made a remarkable acceptance of Christianity, something most sincere, and they integrated this into their lives. Their Christianity was built into the rhythm of life of the reservation culture from 1900 to 1940 and when this collapsed the institutions of reservation Christianity collapsed with it. (White c. 1973)

The average age at Pine Ridge, White stated, was fifteen. These young Indians were poor and aimless. They were not guided by Christian norms, or any religious norms for that matter. They avoided religious leaders, both Catholic and Lakota, and constituted a "culture of excitement—seeking the thrill of the moment." He doubted that the Church and the American government knew how to treat these disaffected Sioux. Furthermore, the tragedy of the Sioux was not that the young failed to attend mass. It was that they did not have faith in the universe; they had no hope; they practiced little love. That is, they lacked the attitudes of religiousness that the missions tried and failed to instill. The aboriginal Sioux culture had religiousness galore, not only in form but in attitude. "But in the lower-class, alienated culture the Indian is de-religionized and de-humanized in the process." White argued that rather than trying to revive some old Sioux gestures in Catholic worship, the Church must try to answer the questions raised by contemporary Sioux culture.

White noted that in the early years of Holy Rosary, the St. Joseph and St. Mary Societies, the congresses, and the catechists were all institutions that worked with Sioux kinship communities, giving local neighborhoods a chance to organize and help themselves. They were community-builders at local, tribal, and even pan-tribal levels. But after the 1930s the Church neglected and even undermined local autonomy of Sioux communities in favor of regimentation and clericalism. Following the lead of some Latin American base communities, White encouraged Church-supported, lay Indian leadership programs. He argued that the Church should provide funding, training facilities, and support for Indian Catholics who wanted to serve and organize their people, who were willing to dedicate themselves but who did not necessarily want to be priests. He even argued in favor of ordaining as priests married Lakota men who were chosen for leadership by the Catholic Indian community. Such programs would have the effect of building community without emphasis on building church hierarchy. In effect, White argued for a Sioux liberation theology (see White, August 1969; White n.d.), and for several years he attempted to foster an effectively liberating Lakota base community, through the American Indian Leadership Council.

Middle portion of the Road Picture Catechism by Rev. Albert Lacombe, O.M.I., c. 1885, depicts the ways of good and evil.

Nicholas Black Elk (sixth from left, wearing moccasins) and other catechists convene at a Catholic Sioux Conference, Holy Rosary Mission, Pine Ridge, South Dakota, 1911. Used by permission of Special Collections, Marquette University Memorial Library.

Participants gather around the bower at a Catholic Sioux Congress,
Holy Rosary Mission, Pine Ridge, South Dakota, 1920.
Used by permission of Special Collections, Marquette University Memorial Library.

Corpus Christi celebrants perform a benediction at
Wounded Knee, South Dakota, 1930.
Used by permission of Special Collections, Marquette University Memorial Library.

Students dress as angels for a Christmas play,
Holy Rosary Mission, Pine Ridge, South Dakota, 1930.
Used by permission of Midwest Jesuit Archives; photograph by
Rev. Joseph A. Zimmerman, S.J.

Commissioner of Indian Affairs John Collier (center) confers
with Jesuits and other officials, Holy Rosary Mission,
Pine Ridge, South Dakota, 1934.

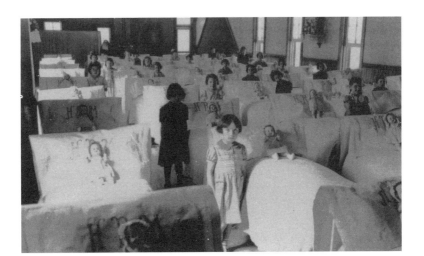

Students stand by their beds in the younger girls' dormitory,
Holy Rosary Mission, Pine Ridge, South Dakota, 1938.

Students enact the play, "Princess of the Mohawks,"
Holy Rosary Mission, Pine Ridge, South Dakota, 1938.
Used by permission of Special Collections, Marquette University Memorial Library.

Mourners perform a funeral for Albert Chief Eagle,
Holy Rosary Mission, Pine Ridge, South Dakota, 1943.
Used by permission of Midwest Jesuit Archives; photograph by Rev. Joseph A. Zimmerman, S.J.

Benjamin Black Elk prays with a pipe at the altar of the St. Agnes
Church, Manderson, South Dakota, c. 1971.
Used by permission of photographer Rev. Paul A. Steinmetz, S.J.

Holy Rosary Mission of the late 1960s and early 1970s was not of a single mind. If one looks during this period at *Red Cloud Country,* the fund-raising newsletter, one sees a mixture of old and new attitudes. Chief Red Cloud was still winning his fight for religious liberty by getting the government to allow Catholic missionaries among his people. Sioux children were at study and play. Yet Benjamin Black Elk was telling how he saw no clash between the pipe and the cross. In the newsletter, Indians' rights were upheld; their conquest was decried; their poverty bemoaned. Yet at Red Cloud Indian School, it was said, "they learn A NEW WAY OF LIFE." In volume 5, number 2, in 1968, Benjamin Black Elk was on the receiving end of a finger-wagging at the hand of Sister Serena, his first teacher at Red Cloud: "When I visit her," the old Indian was quoted, "she says, 'Now, Ben, you be a good boy.'" In private, however, the mission correspondence was far less condescending and far more critical of its own enterprise. As one internal memo stated in 1969, the mission was as "paternalistic" as the Bureau of Indian Affairs, possessing "colonialistic attitudes" (Inter-Mission Board). During the 1973 seige at Wounded Knee, Bishop Harold J. Dimmerling of Rapid City was still referring to the Pine Ridge Lakotas as "our Indian people." Acknowledging that the Indians wanted to wrest their lives from the external influences of the U.S. government and AIM militants, he failed to perceive the Church as a foreign presence among the Sioux. Rather than impeding Lakota self-determination, Catholicism was (in his view) a force aiding that goal. He concluded that "the Church has a great role to play at this time" (in *Our Negro and Indian Missions* 1974: 27). Robert J. Hilbert, S.J., remarked with more insight in 1978 that the history of Holy Rosary was the history of cultural destruction (Red Cloud Indian School 1978).

One hundred years after the foundation of the South Dakota missions, church personnel are vigorously engaged in asking themselves whether institutions such as Holy Rosary are meeting the ideals set forth, e.g., in Pope Paul VI's 1975 encyclical "Evangelization in the Modern World." The Jesuit John Hatcher—founder of the Sioux Spiritual Center in Plainview, South Dakota, mentor of the Lakota deacons, and director of a training program for Native American catechists—reminds us that today, just as a century ago, the Church is missionary by nature: compelled to preach the Good News, even to those who already have religious traditions of their own. These peoples have a right to hear the Christian word, to have their religious traditions completed, but not destroyed, by christianization. He notes that the role of mission is to establish a community of believers, a church. That is, the goal of mission is to move beyond mission, to create church life among the Lakotas, a church life that is true to local culture but in communion with the universal Church. The Church must be made incarnate in the local culture, but the gospel must be presented in full, without obfuscation or apology. The gospel will challenge cultures—all cultures; such is the nature of the gospel. The missionaries who engage in this mission activity are to preach the gospel and live it by example. They are to be zealous without being aggressive. They should represent the Church without attacking other Christian bodies. They should be concerned with the social needs of the local people; however, they are not revolutionaries or social workers. In the end, the missionaries are to melt away in favor of local leadership, including evangelized laity. The question is whether these ideals put forward by Pope Paul VI in 1975 have been an actuality in the history of Holy Rosary, or are active forces today.

Father Hatcher finds that the first seventy-five years of Holy Rosary displayed a plethora of zeal and preaching of the gospel; however, there was an excess of condemnation and an insensitivity to the Sioux themselves as cultural human beings. The Jesuits attacked the Sioux in order to force them into change.

Hatcher looks to Harold J. Dimmerling, who became bishop of Rapid City in 1969, preceding Bishop Chaput, as an example of contemporary mission ideals at Holy Rosary. He praises the bishop for initiating the diaconate program, for maintaining local Lakota parishes apart from Holy Rosary Mission itself, for supporting the Sioux Spiritual Center in 1977 to expedite deacon formation, and for speaking publicly in favor of Native clergy, lay Native leadership, social justice, and Indian cultural values, including Sioux liturgical forms. Dimmerling stated at the 1978 Tekakwitha Conference in Rapid City that the missionaries "must decrease so they can increase. . . . Missionaries should be willing to work themselves out of a job" (in Hatcher 1987: 66–67). Hatcher also quotes a Jesuit provincial in 1979, who wrote to the missionaries, "We are not to Americanize American Indians" (in ibid., 68). In 1985 the Wisconsin Province of Jesuits made it clear that their top priority should be a "self-sufficient Sioux Indian Church. . . . It is, ultimately, the Indian people themselves who must incarnate the fullness of the faith in their own culture" (in ibid., 73).

In the early days of Holy Rosary, Hatcher finds,

> the Indian people did not have a sense that the Church was their Church. All the decisions concerning life in the Church were made by the missionaries. The people were counseled to be obedient. They had to give up their old ways in order to be Catholic. Despite this admonition, they often practiced both the old religious ceremonies and Catholicism. . . . (83)

Even today, Hatcher claims, many missionaries distrust Indianness beyond a "veneer":

> Many missionaries still fear Indian religious practices are superstitious at best and devil worship at worst. It is acceptable for Indian people to decorate the Church with Indian art and to wear costumes at the liturgy. It is another thing for the missionaries to accept the Sweat Lodge, the Sacred Pipe Ceremony, or the Sundance Ceremony as valid and healthy ways of praying. (106)

Other missionaries tell the Sioux which practices they should incorporate into Christian worship, and when and how, without letting the Indians decide what there should be of symbol syncretism. He also reminds his fellow Jesuits that "there is no golden age of Sioux culture. God is found today in the culture as it is today. . . ," not "in a romanticized past nor . . . in some ideal future" (114).

Hatcher asserts that the contemporary Sioux "are starving for spiritual nourishment" (135), even those who already have received baptism and attend mass on Sundays. The mission of the contemporary Church at Holy Rosary and elsewhere is to provide that nourishment to people who feel unworthy and undereducated, who are anxious about failure and criticism, and who fear the missionaries themselves. Hatcher concludes that the missionaries must admit the injustices of the past and seek forgiveness from the Sioux, effecting a "reconciliation" (144) between Holy Rosary personnel and the Pine Ridge Catholic population, both of whom represent the Church. He is currently a consultant in the Lakota Inculturation Task Force, created by Bishop Chaput in 1994, working with Lakota Catholics to determine which Lakota rituals can be used in Catholic liturgy, and which of these can best prepare the way for the gospel. He hopes to overcome fears among churchmen and Lakotas alike regarding Native ritualism in order to effect inculturation. Rejecting the notion of non-Lakota Catholic personnel enacting Lakota ceremonies for which they hold no authority, he plans to develop indigenous leadership which will respect the varieties of Lakota religious affiliation and praxis (see Hatcher 1996/1997).

A RANGE OF RELIGIOUS ORIENTATIONS

Although virtually all of the Indians at Pine Ridge are nominally Christian, there is in reality a range of religious orientations on the reservation. First, there are the Catholic Lakotas who have felt encouraged to Indianize their liturgy, as well as participate in Sioux religio-cultural ceremonies. These are the Lakotas about whom William Powers speaks when he describes "dual religious participation" (August 2, 1988). Black Elk's great-granddaughter Charlotte says that her people were able to become Christians without leaving behind their Lakota traditions. They are good Christians, insofar as they have a relationship to Jesus, but not in the sense of identifying themselves exclusively as Catholics (August 2, 1988). This "bi-religious" (Holler, late 1980s) mode is perhaps the normative stance among the Lakotas. Among this group there are those who compartmentalize their religious practice, even though the religious ideas from each tradition may interpenetrate one another; and there are those who syncretize their religious practice. The former tend to be those who are more embedded in traditional worship; the latter feel comfortable with Catholic worship but like the old-time Sioux ambience in their Christian liturgy. (And, of course, there are Lakotas who do not want anything to do with Christianity.)

Gerald Clifford, coordinator of the Black Hills Steering Committee and an accountant with an engineering degree, is one Lakota Catholic who embraces both religious traditions without trying to combine them. He is a "Lakota Sioux Indian activist who is also a practicing Catholic" (Walsh n.d.). Between 1962 and 1968 he studied to be a priest in the Camaldolese Hermitage in California and the Benedictine Theologate in Rome, leaving short of final ordination when his mother died and his father needed his help. Gerald chose to honor his kinship responsibilities and aid his father in a time of crisis; he realized that it would be "irresponsible for me not to come home" (ibid.), and so he quit the seminary.

He did not reject his Catholic faith; however, after nearly six years of studying and practicing Christian spirituality, he returned to Pine Ridge and discovered *Black Elk Speaks,* in which he found his own Native spirituality. He joined Father Robert A. White's American Indian

Leadership Council, which met each weekend to create a plan for re-structuring Lakota society: to take over the schools, create Lakota colleges, run Native businesses and law enforcement, and to revitalize Lakota spirituality. The Council brought him together with Charlotte Black Elk; they married in 1969. For over two decades he has chosen to express his religiousness through Lakota forms: sweats, pipe ceremonies, the Sun Dance. At the same time, he continues to participate in Catholic liturgical life: lovingly, but not without ambivalence. He recalls whippings from the Jesuits at Red Cloud School. He claims that the priests discouraged Lakota men from pursuing religious vocations. He sensed Jesuit condescension toward Lakota adults. Nevertheless, he identifies himself as a Catholic, and several years ago he helped establish a Rapid City diocesan Office of Native American Concerns.

Second, there are non-Catholic Christians: primarily Episcopalians and Congregationalists; however, there are now over a dozen Christian denominations at Pine Ridge today, in addition to Half Moon and Cross Fire peyotists. The relations among these groups is relatively friendly, even ecumenical, although more so among the older denominations than the newer ones. Among the Lakotas themselves, there is less differentiation among the various Christian bodies than there is among non-Indians.

Third, there are those who have been baptized, but who want nothing to do with Christianity. These are born-again pagans who have attempted to return to Native religious practice, or to neo-traditional forms, and they oppose the Catholic use of their Sioux traditions. Indeed, they are anti-Christian in their tone.

There are strong Lakota feelings against Catholicism and Christianity in general. To many Indians at Pine Ridge, Christianity has been and continues to be the white man's religion, accepted, understood, and rejected as such. When there are resentments against the Whites—as there are to this day—the Whites' religion shares in the onus. For the Lakotas, all non-Lakota institutions, including all those of the Catholic Church, are peripheral to their existence and impinge on their autonomy and identity as Lakotas. Their major frame of reference is their Lakota relational community, and Holy Rosary Mission is perceived as a looming intrusion to that community (Brokenleg, August 3, 1988). Lakota children receive their education from Red Cloud; however, "they never set foot in a church again" (Clifford, October 16, 1991).

Resentment still exists against the decades in which Whites refused to permit traditional religious practices. This resentment is strong even among those who have forever eschewed those practices. Since traditional Lakota religious practice, with its emphasis on everyday behavior and its effect on relatives, was embedded in community life, the impingements were not only on liturgical form, but on the very way of life of the Lakotas, and Lakotas still resent White Christians for destroying that way of life. Many Lakotas perceive Christianity as the cause, not the cure, for contemporary Lakota social woes.

Many of these resentments have been expressed through militant organizations like AIM. Even those only tangentially touched by AIM have felt themselves radically disassociated from Christianity, although they were probably baptized in their infancy or youth. So Wallace Black Elk, Black Elk's putative grandson (Black Elk and Lyon 1990: xx), spent the middle 1980s preaching to the Indians and non-Indians alike, both on and off the reservation, about the salvific, New Age strength of Lakota religion. He and his wife, Grace Spotted Eagle, ran sweat lodges and self-help workshops based on semi-traditional Indian lore, teaching non-Indians how to make flesh offerings and conduct vision quests, in order to find a spiritual life superior to Christianity (Holler, late 1980s).

At the same time there are Lakotas who are attempting to follow a religious way of life which they refer to as the Good Red Road. It is based on Black Elk's teachings in *Black Elk Speaks,* and it entails a syncretism apart from Catholic authority. Leona Bull Bear is a middle-aged Lakota woman living in Kyle, married to a man who studied for the diaconate. She was studying the Bible, but a few years ago she and her husband decided that they needed to participate in Lakota religious life, practice the Lakota sacraments, get in touch with Lakota spirits. Her husband now speaks directly with the spirits. They have not turned their backs on Catholicism completely, but for now they pay attention to their Lakota ways (Bull Bear, August 4, 1988). For her the Good Red Road is roughly equivalent to the Way of Christ, only with specific Indian content. In her view the Lakota spirits can be dangerous, and one must be very careful not to be harmed along the Good Red path. On the other hand, she reports, Good Red Road adherents favor sweats to confession because they cannot trust priests to keep secret what they hear in the confessional. With the sweats one speaks silently and privately to the spirits and one is purified.

Some of the priests at Holy Rosary remark that the ethos of the neo-traditionalism at Pine Ridge is actually a restatement of Christianity. The very ideals of the neo-pagans are those of Catholic morality. "Let's face it," says Father David Shields, "most Lakotas today are Christian, and Christian ideas have suffused their religious thought, even if they don't recognize or admit it" (Shields, August 4, 1988). Father Pates, recently deceased, referred to the neo-traditional rituals—e.g., weddings officiated by Lakota medicine men—as "bobolink Christianity." He recognized that Catholicism fell on hard times among the Lakotas in the 1970s, a fact corroborated by many other interviews. AIM encouraged Lakota youths to disrespect the White teachers. Lakotas fell away in large numbers from the Church, but toward what? They experimented with sweats and other Indian rituals, but some found these unsubstantial and now that they are having children, they are returning to the Church. What is more worrisome than neo-traditionalism to the priests and to Lakota elders themselves is that so many of the youths at Pine Ridge have no religious orientation at all (e.g., Clifford, October 16, 1991).

Sensing the void, Holy Rosary staffers continue to preach the gospel. Says Shields, "I'm a Christian. I believe that Jesus Christ is the most complete revelation of God, and that His Church is the most complete means to reach God. But I try to say these things without arrogance toward other religions, including those of Indians" (Shields, August 4, 1988).

Finally, Lakotas, particularly older Lakotas, still engage in Catholic rituals. Indeed, there are traditional Sioux Catholics; many, but not all, of these are mixed-bloods. For several generations their families have engaged in Catholic institutional life and identification, and even today many of these prefer the Latin rite of their youth to an Indianized liturgy.

They attend Sunday masses at Sacred Heart Church in Pine Ridge. They place $20 bills in the offertory basket and greet each other and strangers with friendly "Peace" embraces. Their mass has no explicit Indian references, except to living and dead members of the immediate community. There are yellow-black-white-red cloths hanging, some Southwest bowls, a picture of an Indian hunter, and a painting of Kateri Tekakwitha, but the priest conducts the service according to standard non-Indian form. At St. Agnes in Manderson, with Father Joseph Sheehan, S.J., officiating, the scene is similar. A quiet crowd puts singles rather than twenties into the collection plates; these are poorer folks than the Lakotas at Pine Ridge. There are some "Indian" designs of the sun, moon, lightning, a tipi, behind the altar; however, the service itself is normative Catholic. After mass everyone retires to the Tekakwitha Hall behind church for donuts and coffee. There is real warmth between Father Sheehan and his parishioners, as they pray for the sick and the dead, as they chat about local matters. One does wonder, however, what the Lakotas are thinking in Manderson, the heart of Lakota traditionalism and Black Elk's scandal, when at mass Father Sheehan reads about Elijah competing with Jezebel's pagan priests. Elijah taunts them when their sacrificial offering is not received with any miraculous fire, despite their dancing about and gashing themselves. A fire burns Elijah's offering and he contrasts the pagan gods—of wood and stone and nothing else—to the God of Israel, the God of all. This is an old Christian message: the true religion conquering the false, and the parallel to a century of missionary preaching at Pine Ridge is not to be missed.

HOLY ROSARY, CIRCA 1988

Most contemporary staff at Holy Rosary avoid the triumphant consciousness of the first half century of the mission. They are no longer comfortable, as Father Westropp was decades ago, to depict the spiritual conquest of the Sioux: the great hunters of the old Sioux nation, now coming to schools, folding their hands in prayer. In the old narratives, there was Black Elk, the old medicine man, now a catechist. There were his people saying the rosary. There were pictures of hell that got the Indians to think about their afterlife. There were Sioux farmers. There was the misguided Ghost Dance; there was the "tragedy" at Wounded Knee. There came the good Samaritans: the priests and sisters. The Sioux converts were ever-faithful, in classroom, baseball field, carpentry shop, and dormitory. In the olden days the Indians dried meat, wore buckskin. Now they ate in the dining hall; worked the cream-separator, churned butter, washed, ironed, wore stockings and dresses; progressing from savagery to civilization under the guidance of Catholic institutions (Westropp n.d.).

Many Oglalas who have attended Red Cloud, like Tim Giago, see the history differently: "The system was wrong, and the system has changed, but too late for too many" (Giago 1978: viii). These Indian critics say that the teachers whipped them. They refused to let the Indians speak their own language. They erased individuality with militaristic discipline. They isolated the pupils from their families: "I still remember being strapped severely by Mr. John Bryde, who became a priest. In my time he was school principal at Holy Rosary Mission" (ibid., 2). The late Father Pates agreed with some of these criticisms, saying that when missions kept children from their parents for most of a school year, their parents never gained experience with parenting, and indeed whole generations of Lakotas have had little tradition of being parents, because of Holy Rosary Mission (Pates, August 5, 1988). The mission has exerted far too much control over Pine Ridge life for a century and the resentments are there: resentments for the "very severe" (Smith 1985: n.p.) discipline at Holy Rosary, that to the Lakotas seemed like torture, and resentment because childrearing was taken away from the Sioux parents. "In many cases the isolation from family life created not only the loss of culture through the loss of language, traditional stories and games, but the loss of self confidence, and per-haps, of self respect" (ibid., 20).

A Lakota deacon reports (Condon, August 5, 1992) that he has heard many expressions of pain from Sioux elders regarding their Catholic boarding school experiences. They felt "abused" and "mo-lested" at Red Cloud, and one elder said that she would want to "kill" one of the boarding school officials if the person walked in the door, to avenge her years of mistreatment. The intensity of these expressions call attention to whispered charges of sexual abuse in the boarding school. While mission authorities tried to douse youthful sexuality among the Lakota boys and girls—"Why was it wrong for us to love?" writes Tim Giago, "To want to be together, / Made to feel our love was evil" (Giago 1978: 22)—there are persistent rumors of seduction and scandal concerning the mission personnel (Berkemeier, August 6, 1988), several of whom garnered infamous reputations for sexual abuse (Thiel, July 28, 1989).

Agnes Picotte, an educator formerly at the University of South Dakota, and a full-blood Oglala who attended Red Cloud from the age of five, complained bitterly in 1978 that everyone who had author-ity at Holy Rosary was "not of my culture" (Red Cloud Indian School 1978). If her parents were allowed to visit, they had to deliver her back to the school by dinnertime, and then depart. As a child, she won-dered, "Could it be that they were not capable of taking care of me?" She wept by herself, away from the disapproving sight of the sisters. She cried from loneliness and from an acute sense of inferiority, realiz-ing herself and her parents to be "incapable" of authority or autonomy. She claimed that the mission programmed Indians to fail by usurping control over the upbringing of the generations.

Elizabeth Berkemeier, who was a special education volunteer teacher at Red Cloud, left the school, thinking that it was not a good thing for the Indians. It encouraged too much dependence, not only among the students, but throughout Pine Ridge Reservation. The mission has been and continues to be an overwhelming presence on the reservation: providing food, shelter, education, raising generations of Lakota children. Its permanence and stability prevent autonomy of the Lakotas (Berkemeier, August 6, 1988). The fact that there is an alien institution in their midst, teaching goals and ideals that do not come from the community, tends to create alienation from elders and community, producing personality disorders and anger toward the mission itself.

As a result one finds that the student response to Red Cloud has continued to be one of erratic attendance and early dropping out. The history of Red Cloud has been the history of runaways. No punishment would stop them from escaping the institution, out of loneliness, personal animosity, or downright hatred for the place. Father Sialm once wrote: "I have used the most severe [measures] . . . : whipping, locking up, fasting, mortifying their pride by wearing ridiculous clothes, etc. None of these made them quit" (Sialm 1912–1915). An observer once wondered why "so many Indian children persist upon running away inspite (sic) of so many being frozen to death or being crippled for life" (Red Cloud Indian School, Series 1/1, Box 1, Folder 4, 1922). Even the Cuny family boys ran away in the late 1930s. Today many Lakota children simply drop out as soon as they are permitted.

The primary critique of the mission—that it took over Sioux parental functions—is also a compliment to the place. Given the poverty and the dissolute character of Lakota society in the twentieth century, some Lakotas are grateful to Holy Rosary for the food, shelter, and other services (Powers, August 2, 1988). Even Charlotte Black Elk notes that in spite of the "mission bashing" that goes on among the Indians, there is a great deal of mutual respect between the present mission staff and the contemporary Lakota community. Despite Giago's critique of Holy Rosary, he has fond praise for modern-day Jesuits, including Father Pates (Giago 1984: 371–372), whose recent funeral was attended by hundreds of Lakota mourners. When Brother William Siehr, S.J., died in July 1991, his funeral was the largest anyone could remember at Pine Ridge. The decades he spent in the mission bakery had made him a legendary, beloved personage at Pine Ridge (Thiel, July 22, 1992).

Indeed, the graduates of Holy Rosary school who returned for the centennial—granted, they are the ones who are not permanently alienated from the place—spoke grateful praise for the school. Eileen Tibbits Jelovich graduated from Red Cloud in 1945, growing up as one of ten children to mixed-blood parents on the reservation. When she graduated, she left for the state of Washington, where she had a sister and other acquaintances who had attended the mission school. She had been "weaned" from her parents, nine months out of twelve all those years, and she wanted to "better myself" by leaving the reservation. There was "too much heartache" at Pine Ridge, and Red Cloud provided her with the means to escape. She married a non-Indian, worked in white society, had children, and returns only occasionally. She is what anyone would call acculturated, and that is what she wanted as a graduate in 1945. She is happy for her education and for her choice to leave. "I had to sacrifice something—being close to my parents," but she is glad she did. "It makes me madder than hell," she says, to hear Lakota children complain that the missions destroyed the Indians. "It was the best thing that ever happened to us." Throughout the centennial one frequently heard that the staffers were strict or "mean" and the punishments were plentiful: kneeling on hands, whipping, etc.; however, the results were good. One woman says that "it made me strong." They wish that Lakota children today had this kind of discipline but it hasn't existed on the reservation since the 1970s.

Mrs. Jelovich has "stayed with" her Catholicism. She raised her children in Catholic schools and she is glad to see that they are coming back to Catholic liturgical structures after a "hippie" phase, now that they are parents. A widow, she works as a cook for a parish rectory, and although she is a post-Vatican II Catholic, picking and choosing which elements of the modern Church to embrace or reject, she is little different from any other middle-aged middle-class Catholic woman in America today. She and others at the centennial reunion are Catholic Indians who have ceased participation in Indian religious forms. They converted and became mainline Catholics. Jelovich's mother went through six grades at Red Cloud; she completed all twelve grades. Her mother stayed on the reservation; she left. A study of Lakota Catholics today is not complete if her life story is omitted, even if it is a pattern only for a minority of Red Cloud alumni.

Indeed, an evaluation of Holy Rosary's first hundred years at Pine Ridge requires attention to a spectrum of viewpoints, including Father Steinmetz as well as Father Digmann, Sister Cuny as well as Mr. Giago, Ms. Black Elk as well as her famous forebear. There are old Lakota women today who say the rosary daily in their homes. There are mixed-bloods, proud of their White and Indian heritage and their Jesuit education. There are married couples, graduates of Red Cloud School, who argue with each other over whether to celebrate Christmas and other Christian holidays. Some feuding Catholic Lakotas won't attend mass if members of opposing families are present. Some Catholic medicine men hold sweats for visiting Catholic college students. There are many faces and many voices of Lakota Catholicism, a century after the founding of Holy Rosary Mission.

GERALDINE CLIFFORD, O.S.F.

One of the most profound of the Catholic Lakotas in the 1990s is Sister Geraldine Clifford, O.S.F. Sister Geraldine was born on the Pine Ridge Reservation, grew up at Holy Rosary, daughter of Robert Clifford (the athletic director and coach) and Geraldine Swallow Clifford, who taught in the grade school at Red Cloud. Presently Sister Geraldine teaches psychology at Oglala Lakota College on Pine Ridge and runs the St. Francis Home for Children, which she founded several years ago. For thirty years she served her order, the Franciscan Sisters of Charity, away from her home community. She trained novices and served as provincial superior at the motherhouse in Denver. Only recently was she "permitted" to return to her land and people, and she expresses regret at the decades of "deculturation" she underwent. She appreciates the "fine education" she received from the sisters at Holy Rosary and from Jesuits at advanced institutions such as Loyola in Chicago and Fordham in New York. Nevertheless, she wishes that her training had not meant assimilation to white life and alienation from her kinfolk—the very people she most wishes to serve. It is now her project to overcome the cultural loss and serve her fellow Oglalas (Clifford, October 16, 1991).

Prayer is a powerful force in Sister Geraldine's life, helping her to reach toward God's transcendence. She has absorbed the contemplative works of St. Teresa of Avila and St. John of the Cross, and she attempts to combine the "charism" of their prayer techniques with the ameliorative effects of apostolic social action, in order to live a helpful life of prayer. She and her brother Gerald, a former seminarian and more recently a Sun Dancer, attended an international convocation of Franciscan prayer in 1992, at which he prayed with a Lakota pipe, at his sister's urging. As a Catholic she has aspired to prayerful contemplation; however, the model she has followed most assiduously has been that of her Lakota grandmother, who raised herself to relation with the divine through traditional Lakota spirituality. Sister Geraldine tells people that the Lakotas knew God before the Christians came. Jesus is the fullest revelation of God, but the Lakotas were religious contemplatives who prayed to God before becoming Christians. Today Sister

Geraldine is attempting to achieve the levels of prayer once attained by her Lakota kin.

At Red Cloud Indian School the authorities kept her apart from Lakota culture. Her parents worked for Red Cloud, lived at Red Cloud, and yet they were treated like other Indian parents when it came to visiting their children. The priests and sisters regarded all Indian parents as intruders and dangerous influences. The goal of the boarding school was to break contact with the parents' culture, even if that culture was Catholic. The children belonged to the school, and Geraldine's parents were permitted only occasional personal contact with their children, sitting on benches in the hallways. In the summers, Red Cloud arranged for her to work off the reservation; hence, she rarely saw her parents, indeed hardly knew them after early childhood. As a result, she says, she became "completely acculturated" (Clifford, August 9, 1992).

She did not experience beatings or other overt violence at Red Cloud, but her brothers did, including beatings from Father John Bryde, who wrote so eloquently about Indian acculturative psychology. By the 1950s the Sisters of St. Francis were sending their problem sisters "to Siberia"—that is, to Indian missions. As a result, these sisters "acted out" upon the girls, including Geraldine's younger sister, who attempted to run away from the school and received a strap-lashing. Their mother was horrified, but in their father's view, "The Jesuits could do no wrong." Sister Geraldine comments that the Jesuits performed their tasks with "intensity and thoroughness." The result of their effective work was to "annihilate our culture" (ibid.).

When Geraldine was at Red Cloud, the Franciscan sisters did not allow Indians into their order. They told her as a youngster that she was "too close to paganism," because her grandparents had been gentile Lakotas; even though her parents were Catholics, she could not enter a novitiate when she first felt a religious vocation.

Her two aunts, Esther and Grace, were the saintly girls memorialized by the priests at Holy Rosary when they died in their youth. Both wanted to become Franciscan sisters but were refused admittance. Geraldine bore a striking resemblance to one of her aunts, and her vocation was understood by Lakotas and Holy Rosary personnel as a fulfillment of the deceased aunt's wish to take the veil. For a time, strictures interfered.

The rule changed; she joined the order, and in her years of training she almost never went home to Pine Ridge. The process of deracination from her family and culture, begun at boarding school, was completed. She found in the sisterhood a community that accepted her, and even elected her to positions of authority and responsibility. She has remained certain of her vocation, and she has continued to love her order. Despite her criticism of the alienating process by which she gained her training, she has never wavered in her prayerful love and service for God as a sister.

In the early 1980s Sister Geraldine attended a meeting of the Association of Native Religious and Clergy, a support group for Indian sisters, brothers, and priests. Other sisters were telling how much racism they faced in their orders; she testified gratefully that she had never experienced bigotry from her sister Franciscans. Upon consulting with members of her order and upon reflection, however, Sister Geraldine realized that the sisters treated her as if she were white because she acted exactly like a White. She was struck with the realization that through boarding school and novitiate she had "ceased to be an Indian" (ibid.), at least in the eyes of others.

She determined to move back to Pine Ridge and regain her relations with her sister, brothers, and extended family. She wanted to be with her people and to help them if she could, after thirty years of absence. The Franciscan sisterhood permitted her this goal; the question was: what would she do on the reservation? She did not want to live at Holy Rosary ("a ghetto," she calls it). She did not wish to serve the chancery office in Rapid City. She decided instead to teach at the Lakota-operated community college and to create a shelter for abused Lakota children. She and another sister built a nine-bedroom house where the children could live with her in a family setting. She did not cut ties with the Franciscans; indeed, she has served two recent years as provincial, and she is now spiritual director for Franciscan novices, who come to Pine Ridge to receive her guidance. Neither did she surrender contact with her alma mater; in fact, she is a member of the board of directors of the Red Cloud School. Her primary ministry, however—one might say, her prayer, her religiousness, her *wacekiye*— is to create a web of relations for needy Lakota children, serving as their foster-parent, their grandmother, and guardian. In the process she is reestablishing her own Lakota identity.

It has not been easy. In trying to learn Lakota language, for example, she experienced great frustration. Her teacher was Father Jim

Green, S.J., and she felt resentment that this Jesuit could speak with facility the language of her ancestors, while she stumbled through it. She rued that it was his mission predecessors who prevented her from speaking Lakota as a child, when she was a Red Cloud student. Now the Jesuits favor the teaching of Lakota language and culture at the school, while most Lakota board members think it impractical to teach the things of the past. They want their children to learn skills that will overcome contemporary poverty.

The Pine Ridge Reservation constitutes the poorest county in the United States, with 63.1 percent of the population living in poverty, according to Census Bureau standards. The annual per capita income is $3,417, and the tribal chairman refers to his constituency as a fifth-going-on-sixth-generation welfare state. This poverty causes Father Joseph Sheehan at Wounded Knee to comment: "I don't know what I would be if I were an Indian. I think I would be an alcoholic" (in Kilborn 1992: 1).

Sister Geraldine Clifford regrets that in the midst of this poverty Lakota youths have little or nothing to hope for; theirs is the culture of empty excitement, of cowboys and sports, of alcohol and abuse. In this context most Lakota youths want nothing to do with religion. They take their religion courses at Red Cloud; however, prayer means nothing to them. When they leave school, they abandon the Church.

These are the children Sister Geraldine is trying to reach. She says that it disturbs her, not because baptized Lakota youngsters refuse to embrace Catholic spirituality; would that they embraced traditional Lakota religion. Her sorrow is that they embrace nothing. They have no prayer, no spiritual relations, no human commitment.

So, in 1992 she took her foster-children to witness her brother Gerald, the former seminarian, enact a Sun Dance at the summer solstice. She and the children danced at the periphery of the Sun Dance grounds in support of his prayer, their *wacekiye* in kinship with his.

Similar patterns have prevailed among other Sioux peoples, at Rose-bud, Cheyenne River, Standing Rock, Devil's Lake, and other reserva-tions in the Dakotas, as well as among the Siouan Assiniboin at Fort Belknap and Fort Peck reservations and the Crows on their reservation in Montana. Jesuit and Benedictine fathers joined forces with several orders of sisters—the Grey Nuns (Sisters of Charity), the Sisters of St. Francis, etc.—in order to create an archipelago of religious and educa-tional institutions across the northern plains. These missions also reached the Siouans—the Crows and Assiniboins to the west and Win-nebagos to the east, and the Osages (see White 1997) to the south—as well as several Algonkian and the Shoshonean peoples.

Of all these tribes, "the missions among the Sioux of North and South Dakota have become the most important group of missions," wrote the editors of an evangelical Catholic journal in 1936. There were more than a hundred chapels, and as many as ten mission schools with over fifteen hundred Indian pupils. One half of the thirty-four thousand Sioux in the mid-1930s were baptized Catholics. "They lead simple, wholesome Christian lives, chastened by material privations. Their family life is sound and their attachment to the Church is strong" (*Our Negro and Indian Missions* 1936: 25; cf. Zens 1936: 13–56).

These Sioux Catholics engaged in the same agencies of Catholic cul-ture on their reservations. "I am hungry for It" (in *The Indian Sentinel*, 2, no. 3, July 1920: 142), said a Rosebud Sioux convert after walking thirty miles to receive the blessed sacrament. At Standing Rock the St. Joseph and St. Mary Societies members sought "forgiveness for any offense committed by a neighbor during the past year . . ." (ibid., 25, no. 1, January–February 1945: 8) by shaking hands all around at mid-night on New Year's Eve. "I have still to find my first real saint" (ibid., 25, no. 5, June 1945: 79), bemoaned a Jesuit priest at Rosebud; however, he and other Catholic authorities witnessed numerous acts of piety among the Indians: wearing crosses and rosary beads; walking the sta-tions of the cross; kneeling before shrines of the Blessed Virgin Mary; attending masses; participating in processions and novenas; reciting memorized prayers and catechetical lessons; attending Catholic congresses each summer; serving as catechists; receiving last rites, and so forth.

At St. Stephen's mission among the Arapahos in Wyoming, at St. Paul's among the Gros Ventres and Assiniboins in Montana, at St. Benedict Joseph Labre's mission among the Northern Cheyennes in Montana, at Sacred Heart Mission, Fort Berthold, among the Mandans in North Dakota, and at other missionary stations on the northern plains, the situations did not much vary. For many decades of the twentieth century the Church constituted the center of social and religious life, and the Indian children spent most of their hours in Catholic schools. At midcentury many of the Gros Ventres were said to be "as fervent in the practice of their religion as any Whites" (ibid., 24, no. 10, December 1944: 149), and it was claimed that "practically all of the 1,250 Arapahoes are Catholics, for the missionaries have been among them for several generations" (ibid., 28, no. 5, May 1948: 77).

A Jesuit among the Assiniboins wrote, "Usually the old men and women are baptized, confirmed, married in the Church, and are practicing Catholics, but the young ones coming up seem to be dropping away from the Faith" (ibid., 29, no. 9, November 1949: 138). In the post–World War II years the Indians of the northern plains were less tractable and the missionaries experienced impatience with the slow progress of the faith. The various Sioux persisted in traditional religious practices—Yuwipi, sweat lodges, and Sun Dances—and were reluctant to divide themselves according to strict denominational allegiance. Peyotism persisted as a religious force counterposed to Christianity. Indeed, it was reported of the Cheyennes, "The peyote cult has done more to counteract the work of the missioners than any other single factor." A Franciscan priest said that the "drug" had a "pernicious" effect on the Indians and "destroyed the faith as well as the love of spiritual things . . ." (ibid., 35, no. 3, March 1955: 38). A Jesuit among the Assiniboins had to remind himself that "they are only a few years out of savagery" (ibid., 29, no. 9, November 1949: 139) and continue with his christianizing work. The educators pressured the Indians to take "homecraft" courses in order to act out the roles of "*Christian* family life" (ibid., 40, no. 4, Winter 1962: 52), and to maintain monogamous marriage vows as "Mr. & Mrs. Joseph and Mary Christian" (ibid., 29, no. 5, May 1949: 72).

Over the past century the experiences of the Lakotas at St. Francis Mission on the Rosebud Reservation in South Dakota have been the closest to those of their relatives at Pine Ridge. Like Holy Rosary, St. Francis is said by the Jesuits to have derived from the will of a Lakota leader—in this case, the Brule Spotted Tail—to receive blackrobes as teachers and religious leaders. Recent commentators (Archambault 1995: 3–4; Markowitz 1994: 11–20) have shown that Lakotas of the late nineteenth century, like Spotted Tail, were at best disinterested in Catholicism when its institutions arrived at Rosebud. The century that followed at St. Francis resembled that at Holy Rosary, with "the suppression of the Lakota religious practice and imposition of Catholicism" (Archambault 1995: 12).

Recently Sister Marie Therese Archambault, O.S.F., a Hunkpapa Lakota from Standing Rock, has interviewed Rosebud Sioux associated with St. Francis Mission in order to learn what has happened to the Lakotas who grew up under "Catholic orthodoxy":

> Why did Lakota spirit and spiritual expressions survive even in the face of drastic measures to wipe it out? What form has Brule Catholicism taken? Do the Brule of the Rosebud identify themselves with Catholic spirituality, with Lakota spirituality, or with both—and if both, how do these two identities co-exist? (Ibid.)

Her study complements the findings of the previous pages. St. Francis authorities have tried to heal their relations with the Lakotas who have attended the boarding school over the years. They organized a gathering of St. Francis alumni in 1992 in order to reflect upon their Catholic-Lakota identity. They have changed their attitudes toward Lakota religion from condemnatory to laudatory. In 1995 the Rosebud Educational Society, Inc. (which is St. Francis Mission School in its contemporary guise) published a public expression of regret in a local newspaper, apologizing "to all who ever attended St. Francis Mission School" (ibid., 180).

Nonetheless, many Lakotas who were baptized in the Catholic faith and who underwent catechesis at St. Francis feel alienated from the Church. Teresa Archambault graduated from St. Francis in 1960 and spent two years in a novitiate. She says that she respects Jesus' humility and his solidarity with the poor, and that she feels close to Kateri Tekakwitha "because she is Indian and she is close to God. I do pray a lot through her" (in ibid., 47), she states, but she is disillusioned with the Catholic Church in general and with its manifestations on the Sioux reservations. In the midst of her people's poverty she finds an un-Christlike vanity among the priests. In her view, they never let her forget that

> It is "their" church. We think we have ownership to it, but when you go in, it is not our church, it is their church. They never say, "It is yours, what would you like to do?" It is theirs and we know it. . . . We do have a beautiful church. You know it is the most beautiful church that we have ever seen. But it does not belong to the people. If it did they should be able to put what they want in it and pray what they want in it. (In ibid., 44)

Albert White Hat's father was a catechist and Albert was baptized Catholic; however, he was so overcome by the fear of God and Satan and a sense of his own evil instilled in him as a youth, that he no longer considers himself a member of the Church. Instead he has become a Sun Dance leader every summer. "I believe in Christ," he avows (in ibid., 26), but not in the teachings or rules of Catholicism. Asked what it would take to make him feel welcome in the Church, he replies: "I think I would take the Catholic church on a Relative basis. It's a Relative and I respect the institution for what it stands for but it has to respect me also" (in ibid., 27).

Victor Douville carried his Catholic education into college, where he studied theology. He now teaches at Sinte Gleska University, one of the Sioux institutions of higher education. He recalls how the priests of his youth spoke of "the one true church," and yet when he thought of his grandmother, who still practiced the Indian religion and sang Sun Dance songs on her deathbed, he could not take seriously the notion that her soul was lost because she was not in "the one true church" (in ibid., 58–59). He decided that the Indian and Catholic religions were parallel roads to one another, each appropriate as means to right oneself with the divine. He engages freely in speculating about the polytheistic aspects of the Christian trinity, and he compares the Virgin Mary to the White Buffalo Calf Woman as mediators between humans and the sacred. His hope is that a Lakota Catholic Church will develop from the dialogue between the two religions, employing the spirituality of his people but also making use of Catholic institutions. In the present day, Lakota "social controls" are weakened, he states, and Catholicism might bring order to Lakota life, with its clearly articulated values and rules of behavior. He finds Lakota medicine men "unreliable" (in ibid., 66)—some are alcoholics, some seek personal gain from their practice—in contrast to members of the St. Mary and

St. Joseph Societies, who are selfless community leaders. Douville wishes that such local leaders could one day create a particularized Lakota Catholicism, in communion with the Roman Church but also serving special Lakota spiritual needs.

Deacon Benjamin Black Bear, Jr., suggests that the St. Mary and St. Joseph Societies once produced a viable Lakota Catholicism, of which he is an exponent. In his youth these organizations had already become part of the Lakota social order, "so there was almost like a tradition developed within that organization where a lot of traditional Lakota people joined when they became Catholic" (in ibid., 76). Lakota catechists, too, played an active role in defining and passing down Lakota Catholicism. They organized giveaways, gave speeches, and led prayer services, all under priestly auspices, but Lakota children thought of these services as integral parts of their lives, without dividing their activities into "Lakota" and "Catholic" domains. E.g., feasts and giveaways at Christmas and Easter were traditional Lakota behaviors, carried out according to the Catholic calendar, without disjunction between the two traditions. Unfortunately, he says, the St. Mary and St. Joseph Societies consist today of dwindling numbers of old women and men who failed to pass down their faith to the youths. The young are almost completely uninterested in Catholicism, and so the synthesis of Lakota and Catholic religiousness is a phenomenon of the past.

Today there are a hundred thousand Sioux in the United States; over forty thousand of them are counted by the Church as Catholics, including the almost ten thousand Lakotas at Pine Ridge and another five-to-ten thousand within the Diocese of Rapid City (Bartholomew 1992: 10–11). The Diocese of Sioux Falls reports over two thousand Catholics among its Sioux population. Two dioceses in North Dakota—Bismarck and Fargo—enumerate over twenty thousand Catholic Sioux. In addition there are several thousand Assiniboins and Cheyennes in the Diocese of Great Falls, Montana, and half of the seven thousand Arapahos in Wyoming's Diocese of Cheyenne are members of the Church (see Beaver 1979: 181–186; DCRAA 1976–1986).

Like the Lakotas at Pine Ridge, the other Catholic Indians of the northern plains have experienced disaffection from the Church during the past several decades, despite pastoral efforts to make Catholicism more relevant to the Native Americans' contemporary cultural realities. Special ministries to urban Indians, liturgical experiments, and

social programs have been initiated, for example, among the thousand
or so Catholic Winnebagos in the Diocese of Omaha, in an effort "to
bring back to the Church those who have abandoned it for one reason
or another" (DCRAA 1983). The bishop of Great Falls, Montana,
Eldon B. Schuster, observed "a deep spirituality" among the Assiniboin, Cheyenne, Crow, and other Indians of his diocese; he asserted
that "faith among the Indian people is still alive" (ibid., 1976). Another
prelate took a harder look at the dangers facing his flock on the northern plains: "The morality breakdown of the United States: abortion,
pornography, alcoholism, drugs, homosexuality, etc., etc., etc. is seep-
ing down to the reservations and if the trend continues I see no future
for our Indian children" (ibid., 1985).

Ironically, some committed Catholic Sioux have become angry
with the Church as it has turned over some of its assets to Indian authorities in order to achieve greater Native autonomy in social and educational matters. Witness the letter from a Crow Creek Reservation
Sioux to Monsignor Paul A. Lenz of the Bureau of Catholic Indian
Missions (ibid., July 26, 1985):

> I am 53 years old and a good Catholic being baptized by the good 'bene-
> dictines' and I'm self taught and try to understand the white man's ways
> and that seems impossible as, my culture, traditions and heritage disal-
> low me because I am not greedy and the almighty dollar is not my God.
>
> I was very fortunate and lucky to have been given my religious train-
> ing and education and to make my first Holy Communion, Solemn
> Communion, Confirmation and to go to Mass every day and to have
> religion as my fourth "R" in school on the Curriculum.
>
> Then the bottom fell out in 1976 when without input from the
> Catholic Indian people on the reservation, our Catholic school was
> given to the tribal government by the Benedictines of Blue Cloud
> Abbey. . . . Now the atheist dictatorship controls our school and the
> Catholic church at the school is empty and void every Sunday.

At a time when most other Sioux were retreating from Catholicism, at
least one man beckoned for greater Church attention to his people.

Sister Archambault comments (Archambault, June 14, 1997) that
wherever she goes in Sioux country she finds that almost no one attends Catholic services, and that the Indians have, by and large, left the
Church. She wonders, "If there was an historic, free and genuine acceptance of Catholicism by the Lakota, why has this acceptance not
made a greater difference in their spiritual life and human existence?"
(Archambault 1995: 180).

∗ II ∗

American Catholic Missiology

When the United States came into existence there were only a few clusters of Catholic Indians within the territories of the new nation, remnants of the French missions of an earlier era. Penobscots and Passamaquoddies in Maine, the St. Regis Mohawks in northern New York, Ottawas in Michigan, and Potawatomis in Indiana had maintained their Catholic identities and were glad for renewed association with the institutions of the Church. As Bishop John Carroll of Baltimore began to organize an American Catholic Church, he tried to meet their pastoral needs.

In 1805 the Holy See placed all of the Louisiana Purchase area under the care of Bishop Carroll. Ten years later the region became a separate diocese, and in 1827 it was divided into two dioceses: New Orleans and Saint Louis. Indians such as the Houmas in Louisiana received the attention of the former; the latter diocese took a role in the westward expansion of the Church. Jesuits established a home in Missouri in 1823 and took part in the evangelization efforts. In 1833 the Second Provincial Council in Baltimore petitioned Rome that the Jesuits be placed in charge of Indian missions in the west; this request was approved by the Vatican the following year.

American churchmen founded Indian missions and schools. Father Gabriel Richard opened the first American school for American Indians, the Spring Hill Academy near Detroit, in 1808. Jesuits followed with another "short-lived" educational enterprise in Missouri, St. Regis Indian Seminary, in 1824 (Tennelly 1967a: 400).

As we have seen in the second volume of *American Indian Catholics,* a revival of European interest in Native American missions boosted efforts among the Ojibways, Ottawas, Menominees, Potawatomis, Winnebagos, and Sioux in the American Midwest (then the furthest reaches of the Old Northwest), beginning in the 1830s. From Canada the Church reached south along the Red River to the Ojibways and their Métis kinsfolk before midcentury.

Even as the apostolic undertakings among the Potawatomis and others in the border states were "rendered futile by the apathy of excessive intemperance of the Indians" (Tennelly 1967b: 404)—only the mixed-heritage offspring of French traders took an interest in Catholic learning—Father Pierre Jean de Smet initiated his adventures in the Northwest beginning in 1840. As he and his fellow Jesuits tried to establish reductions among the Flatheads, Coeur d'Alenes, Kalispels, Crows, and Blackfoot in the Rocky Mountain region, Father Francis N. Blanchet entered Oregon country from Canada. Oblates joined the toil, making strides, e.g., among the Coast Salish along the Puget Sound in the 1850s and 1860s.

When the United States annexed New Mexico, Arizona, and California from Mexico in 1848, there were many thousands of Indians with lifetimes of experience with Catholicism. As we saw in the first volume of *American Indian Catholics,* Pimans and Puebloans were already acquainted with the Church, and in California many Native peoples had only recently been set adrift from the secularized Franciscan mission archipelago. In New Mexico Archbishop John B. Lamy tried to accomplish the Catholic development of baptized Pueblo Indians, "but few of them were willing to practice their religion. The Spanish Franciscan friars had been able to do but little during their long tenure, to break the tenacious hold of the native religion on these Indians" (ibid., 405–406), and Lamy was able to make only rudimentary progress. In southern California Father Anthony Ubach and a few other priests tried against all odds to care for the Mission Indians amidst the onslaught of the gold rush.

Through the 1860s Catholic missionizing efforts to the Indians were conducted primarily by European agencies. The American Church lacked its own clergy even to solidify the administration of parish life, much less to explore new fields. As Protestant ministers worked with the support of the U.S. Indian Bureau to christianize and americanize Native Americans (thereby aiding the march of westward expansion), Catholics remained aloof from the process. There were no Catholics, for instance, on the Board of Indian Commissioners, a blue-ribbon body which oversaw the conduct of the federal government's Indian policy.

Beginning in the 1850s the United States began to reduce drastically the land holdings of western Indian peoples and to establish reservations under the control of governmental agents. When a national program took shape in 1869 (Grant's Peace Policy, as it was called) to entrust the management of Indian reservations to Christian missionaries, the Catholics were left in the cold, having no members on the Board of Indian Commissioners. There was mutual distrust between the Church and Protestant America. Catholic clergy were perceived as foreign agents of Rome, subversive to American interests (see Prucha 1979: 57ff.). For their part, the Catholics were not interested in serving as tools of the federal strategy to make Americans out of Indians. At least in principle, Catholic missionaries wanted the Indians to be Christians, nothing more or less.

In 1870 the American bishops were attending the Vatican Council when the Indian Bureau was assigning Indian reservations to the Protestants. Many of these U.S. reservations were inhabited by Indian Catholics, who outnumbered the fifteen thousand Protestant Indians at the time. According to the Peace Policy, Catholic clergy were prohibited from entering the Protestant domains, in order to prevent sectarian squabbles. When the western prelates returned from Rome to discover an administration of Indian affairs stacked against their interests—only four of the forty-three agencies were delegated to Catholics, whereas the Church felt a right to as many as thirty-eight—they charged that thousands of baptized Indians had been denied their rights as Catholics and were placed under the missionizing control of Protestants. The Catholic prelates determined to organize a lobbying force in Washington, D.C. In 1874 the Catholic hierarchy under the leadership of James Roosevelt Bayley, the Archbishop of Baltimore, appointed Brigadier General Charles Ewing as an official emissary to Washington, D.C., someone who could lobby for Catholic concerns among the Indians. He was designated Catholic Indian Commissioner in the United States and Western Territories and was given a stipend by some New York Catholics.

General Ewing sensed the need for a clerical advisor, and Father John Baptist A. Brouillet came from the Pacific Northwest to serve in that capacity. Together in 1879 they established the Bureau of Catholic Indian Missions (BCIM, incorporated legally in 1881). The purpose of the BCIM was "to defend Catholic Indian missions" (in Fritz 1963: 93) against the all-Protestant Bureau of Indian Commissioners and the Grant plan that had doled out almost every Indian agency to Protestant control. Ewing and Brouillet's job (and that of their successors in turn, Monsignor William H. Ketcham, Monsignor William Hughes, Rev. J. Benjamin Tennelly, S.S., and at present, Monsignor Paul A. Lenz) was to gain as many reservations as they could for Catholic control, and to argue publicly for religious liberty (for Catholics) where Protestants were in charge.

The Catholics needed to raise funds. A lay agency founded in 1875, the Ladies' Catholic Indian Missionary Association, proved inadequate for the task. In 1884 the Third Plenary Council in Baltimore formed the Commission for the Catholic Missions among the Colored People and the Indians, in order to coordinate collections taken in every diocese of the country the first Sunday of Lent each year. The archbishops of Baltimore, New York, and Philadelphia played special roles in both the Commission and in the BCIM because only their realms were solvent enough at the time to render financial aid to the missions. In the 1890s Mother Katherine Drexel contributed her substantial holdings to found Indian schools (and the Sisters of the Blessed Sacrament to teach in them), at a time when the United States was retreating from the contractual support for sectarian Indian schooling, which had begun in 1873. Grant's Peace Policy had long since ended and the Bureau of Indian Affairs had opened its own boarding schools for Indian children. In 1896 Commissioner of Indian Affairs Daniel Browning ruled that only when government Indian schools were filled could Indians send their children to mission schools. This so-called Browning Rule stood until 1902, but by that time the United States was no longer willing to finance Christian missionary and educational enterprises among Native Americans. In order to pick up the monetary slack, the BCIM formed its arm of development, the Society for the Preservation of the Faith among Indian Children, heralded by *The Indian Sentinel* in 1902–1903. The Marquette League was founded in 1904, followed by the Catholic Church Extension Society in 1905. In 1917 the American Board of Catholic Missions supplemented these fund-raising efforts through the yearly Mission Sunday collections.

The last quarter of the nineteenth century witnessed a "surge in interest and activity" (Tennelly 1967b: 406) in Catholic Indian missions, overtaking Protestant efforts throughout the western part of the United States. A historian of mission history writes:

> Before 1870 the few Roman Catholic Indian missions were almost entirely a foreign mission of Europeans, and then the vigorous direction of the work by the new Bureau of Catholic Indian Missions made it the mission of the American Church. It began with reservations allotted under the Grant Peace Plan and quickly expanded, with special effort to revive or renew the long abandoned or dormant Spanish missions of the Southwest. (Beaver 1979: 32)

In 1875 twenty priests labored among the 25,000 baptized Native American Catholics, conducting fifty-five chapels and seven small schools. By 1900 there were 140 priests among 50,000 Indian Catholics, maintaining 175 missions and sixty schools (Tennelly 1967b: 406). Indeed, the last quarter of the nineteenth century was "the golden era of missions" (ibid.) in the West. Catholicism established it-self to varying degrees among the Flatheads, Blackfoot, and Coeur d'Alenes of the northern plateau, the Cheyennes, Crows, Sioux, Ara-pahos, and Mandans of the plains, the Ojibways, Winnebagos, and Potawatomis of the Midwest, the Pimas, Papagos, Navajos, Apaches, and Puebloans of the Southwest, the Colvilles, Yakimas, Spokanes, Umatillas, and Puget Sound Salishans—and many more.

Even as the mine of federal funds shut down after 1900, the Catholic missionary engines continued to fire. Schools consolidated their activities and increased the numbers of Indian pupils under their charge. As American vocations burgeoned, new orders of priests, such as the Capuchin, Marist, and Redemptorist fathers joined the efforts of the Jesuits, Franciscans, Benedictines, and Oblates. Religious com-munities of women, including the Ursulines, Dominicans, Sisters of Providence, several orders of Franciscans, Benedictines, Sisters of Loretto, Oblate Sisters of the Blessed Sacrament, and others, served as teachers throughout Indian country. Where Indian reservations lost further lands and were surrounded by county jurisdictions, a sort of secularization process took place and the Catholic Indians were "ab-sorbed into white parishes" (Tennelly 1967b: 407).

The Bureau of Catholic Indian Missions and the Commission for Catholic Missions among the Colored People and the Indians kept track of the progress of their evangelical campaign. Their respective or-gans, *The Indian Sentinel* (1902–1962) and *Our Negro and Indian Mis-sions* (1926–1976), published the records of the missionary labors: the names, locations, and personnel of the numerous missions and schools, the numbers of conversions and other statistical data, the stated goals and other attitudes of the missionaries in the field, as well as vignettes and photographs of Indian Catholics. To peruse these journals, which were succeeded by the *Bureau of Catholic Indian Mis-sions Newsletter* (1981–1998), is to gain an overview—the missionaries' perspective—of a century of American Indian Catholicism. What the *Jesuit Relations* were as expressions of the apostolic mission of New France in the seventeenth century (and as instruments of gaining rev-enue), these magazines have been for the twentieth.

At the beginning of the twentieth century the mission of the Church regarding the American Indian "race" seemed clear, if complex. The purpose of the BCIM and its granting agencies was "to bring from the darkness of pagandom to the light of Christianity the thousands that are still seated in the shadows of death, to preserve the faith of those who possess it, and reclaim those who have lost it" (*The Indian Sentinel* 1906: 5). To christianize the Indians was the prime goal, and it was serious business. So, too, was the felt responsibility to make over Native culture.

The Jesuits of seventeenth-century New France had experimented somewhat with models and methods of cultural relativism; the Rites Controversy put an end to such innovative liberality. For more than a century in China the Jesuits had coalesced Christian and Chinese theological terminology and permitted converts to engage in ceremonies in honor of Confucius and the ancestors. Upon protest from other missionaries (most notably the Franciscans) that the Jesuit regime was leading to syncretism and scandal, Pope Benedict XIV ruled in 1742 that the accommodations must stop. In his bull, *Ex Quo Singulari,* the pope condemned the Jesuits' ventures and prohibited Catholics from participating in rites of another religious tradition, no matter how bound they were in the social order. Missionaries were required to take oaths against allowing such rites among their neophytes, and all debate over the issue was to cease (see, e.g., Minamiki 1985: ix–xvi).

The Jesuits were quashed worldwide in the 1770s and reestablished in 1814. The new Society of Jesus possessed little of its previous accommodationism. Like the newly founded Oblates in Canada, the Jesuits in the United States took charge of Indian missions with zealous loyalty to papacy and dogma. There were exceptions—Father Pierre Jean de Smet was the most notable example among the Jesuits—but the missionaries of the nineteenth century were not eager to mix Native and Christian terminology or forms. Nor were those of the early twentieth century.

They could not prevent Native Americans from making of Christianity what they would. Indians may have thought of the sacraments as medicines and of the Church as a cult to be added to the panoply of tribal religious societies. They may have reworked biblical stories in light of their own oral narratives, combining Jesus the Redeemer and Coyote the Transformer into a single character or placing them at odds with one another (see Ramsey 1977: 443–451), or they may have imbued Christian hymns with indigenous meanings while singing them in their own languages (Rhodes 1960: 329). They may have received baptism for reasons that could better be called political, economic, sociological, or psychological, rather than religious.

The missionaries could not control the inner workings of Indian motivation and interpretation. On the surface, however, the Church had straight and narrow designs. As the author of a book on Catholic mission theory wrote (Schmidlin 1931), the duty of missionaries was to extend the one, holy, catholic, and apostolic Church to all peoples and incorporate them in its authoritative structure. Christianity was the incomparably true religion and Catholicism the only valid Christian body. The teachings of the Bible, the example of tradition, and the logic of faith all provided a rationale for the Church to send out its representatives to all lands and bring the sheep into the salvific fold.

As the missionaries tried to replicate the forms of the Church—its architecture, liturgy, ecclesiology, theology, and forms of piety— throughout Native North America, they also entered a strained alliance with U.S. policymakers. On the one hand, nineteenth-century Catholics felt themselves, and were perceived by Protestants, to be strangers to American culture. On the other, Catholics were becoming Americans, to the dismay of pontiffs and prelates when faced with Americanist heresies (secularism, libertarianism, pragmatism, materialism). By the twentieth century Catholics shared the values and prejudices of most Americans. In regard to Indians, Catholic clergy could be as denigrating to Native American custom and intent upon forcible acculturation as Protestant ministers or Bureau of Indian Affairs agents. Racism could exist in the heart of blackrobes as well as anywhere else.

A priest in Montana quoted a "kindly sarcasm" that "the Indian race was a race against time, and that at the moment . . . time was way ahead" (*The Indian Sentinel* 1909: 17). In his view, "the day of romance is past for the Indian, and the sooner he is taught to realize that the white man is no longer willing to carry his burden the better for him" (23). His advice, and the advice of other pastors of the early twentieth century, was for Indians to emulate white Americans, even though as Catholics the priests had much to criticize of American ways. Catholic clergy were intolerant of Protestant denominations, labor unions, secret societies, and any other organizations that threatened Catholic loyalties (Rosen 1895), but they found American Indian traditions singularly reprehensible. As a Jesuit missionary wrote of the Indians he knew, "Then sacredness of the marriage tie is entirely unknown to their pagan instincts, and their general morality is very low." Even their love for their children, he said, "cannot be very rational" and their religion was "only a mass of the most stupid superstitions. . . . Of course," he concluded, "the spiritual work among these degraded Indians has been anything but pleasant" (*The Indian Sentinel* 1909: 29, 30, 32).

The BCIM identified its cause primarily with that of the Church of New Spain and New France: "The Indian Missions of today are the continuation of the first glorious chapters in the history of the Church in the New World" (ibid., 17, no. 1, January 1937: back cover). "Imagine the fury of Lucifer and his infernal clans," penned the editors of *The Indian Sentinel,* "when Columbus planted the Sign of Redemption at San Salvadór, when Cortés cleared the idol-topped pyramid reeking with the blood of human sacrifices, and there raised the Cross in token of triumph over centuries old demoniacal sway!" (ibid., 1, no. 1, July 1916: 7–8). In their boarding school pageants the priests had Indian children reenact scenes of the Franciscans and Jesuits, brought by the Blessed Virgin Mary to America for the good of their Native forebears. Catholic martyrs, such as "Father Jogues . . . hanging in torture at the fiery stake while Iroquois danced beneath him in savage glee" (ibid., 35, no. 1, January 1955: 13), were the heroes of mission culture. But so, too, were American founders such as George Washington and Betsy Ross. In 1932, for instance, Catholic Indian boarding schools put on plays in honor of the American Revolution (ibid., 12, no. 3, Summer 1932: 114, 135, 143), and the Fourth of July was always observed with zest as part of the round of American civic holidays. Patriotism of a military stripe was a regular part of the mission regime in times of peace and war.

The tone of the Catholic mission journals was one of optimism, as the number of Catholic Indians accrued. In 1926 154 mission centers served close to a hundred thousand Catholic Indians on reservations. Two hundred priests, 450 sisters, and more than sixty brothers attended 340 churches and chapels (*Our Negro and Indian Missions* 1926:

27). For all the difficulties in convincing baptized Indians to give up divorce and remarriage—"about the only reason why some Indians who have become Catholics fall away" (ibid. 1927: 36)—and for all the competition from the pagans, peyotists, and the Protestants—"Unfortunately there are . . . well-financed ministers and Protestant catechists . . . whose chief object seems to be to undermine the influence of our missionaries among the Indians, most of whom are Catholics," wrote one bishop (ibid. 1928: 30)—the Catholic authorities perceived a furtherance of the faith. "Degenerate pagans became pious Christians," one author reported on the missionary toils of previous days. "Whole bands, and even whole tribes, threw away the 'medicine' and all the practices resulting from it and had been transformed into Catholic communities resembling closely in the practice of their religion the Christians of the Apostolic Age" (ibid. 1926: 29). In their own era the editors demonstrated palpable advances through the photographs they featured. Indian children were dressed up for first communion. A Native catechist instructed his fellows before a log cabin. Clerics and chiefs posed together, sharing their authority. Indian children made the sign of the cross. Many of the photographs—of Indian children at work in the mission fields, sitting in their chapel pews, playing their brass bands, lined up in front of their school bus—portrayed the priests and sisters in the positions of overseers, flanking their wards and watching over them. Christendom seemed in control throughout Indian country. One issue of *The Indian Sentinel* (1, no. 9, July 1918) was devoted to Catholic Indian efforts on behalf of the United States in the European War. Native girls were knitting clothes; young men were enlisting and already dying. Communities were purchasing liberty bonds and supporting the liberty loan. Even Papagos, receiving anti-American propaganda from Mexico across the border, were holding true to their country and thus demonstrating their marks of Catholic education, according to the reporters.

"The boarding school is our greatest hope," wrote the churchmen (*Our Negro and Indian Missions* 1928: 33), in overcoming the unchristian home environment of the Indians, and in those schools the Catholic youths of Indian country appeared to change their culture. A photograph of the "FIRST FULL-BLOOD INDIAN COMPANY OF THE CATHOLIC BOYS' BRIGADE OF THE UNITED STATES" (ibid. 1930: 27) at St. Labre's Northern Cheyenne Mission in Montana, decked in military attire, was evidence of their headway. "For years," a Jesuit wrote, "the adult Indians wanted only day schools, so that they could have their children with them as much as possible. This was simply canine affection" (ibid. 1929: 35). When the Great Depression began, however, Indian parents saved their children from starvation by sending them to boarding schools where the larders were well stocked. By 1930 the Catholic schools housed 8,500 Indian students—half of the Catholic Indians of school age, the other half attending government institutions (ibid. 1930: 28–29).

Although the Catholic Indian population was less than one-half of one percent of the total Catholic population of the United States at that time, the BCIM was committed to maintaining the Indian boarding schools, especially as the population of Indians began to increase from the nadir of 225,000 before the turn of the century. In the early 1930s the Church was in touch with Indians on two-thirds of the reservations, through thirty-two dioceses in twenty-one states (ibid. 1931: 26–27), and the Church authorities aimed to maintain that contact. At that time about one-third of the 340,000 Native Americans in the United States were said to be Catholics; another third were Protestants, and the last third were designated by the Church as "pagan" (*The Indian Sentinel*, 12, no. 3, Summer 1932: 99–101).

Catholic missionaries were concerned to foster the culture of Catholicism among the reservation Indians; both Protestants and pagans were obstacles to that progress. So was the "unchristian atmosphere of this country" (*Our Negro and Indian Missions* 1929: 34), including liberal secularists and moral relativists who would permit traditional Indian religions their full and public expression. Particularly during the Indian New Deal of the 1930s the Catholic mission personnel felt themselves in combat with the Bureau of Indian Affairs and its commissioner, John Collier.

When the BIA issued directives in the 1880s to suppress Indian dancing and other forms of religious expression, Catholic authorities raised no objection. Catholicism was as intolerant of other religions as the United States was of Native American traditions. Both Catholic and American forms of triumphalism conspired against the persistence of aboriginal faith. Some reservation agents allowed the Indians their dances at particular times during the year; when they did, the Catholic clergy complained. One Jesuit protested the practice in Browning, Montana, of Indians' celebrating their medicine dances in the week surrounding the Fourth of July. "Its celebration lasts about a week in

Browning, but in effect it lasts in the lives and doings of a great portion of the people, the whole year round" (*The Indian Sentinel* 1910: 28). In his opinion the festivities animated their dancing spirit, retarded their christianization, and gave them the impression that the U.S. government supported their "beaver dances, pipe dances, sun dances, grass dances" (29–30), and the like. In the Fourth of July's "far-reaching splendor Christmas and Easter are, so to speak, thrown into the shade" (28), the priest stated. "Can people, savage as they are, encouraged in such a folly from year's end to year's end, ever be truly civilized?" (31). The priest's answer was that the "Big Holy Day" (30) had to be stopped.

> But perhaps the Government may consider it out of place for it to bring violence to bear against the religions of the [Indians], since it must maintain liberty of conscience. Still, I think, the liberty of conscience tolerated by the Constitution concerns the worship of God, not such a worship as is clearly against the natural and divine law, as is the direct worship of the devil. . . . Now, the religion of the . . . Indians is devil-worship, clearly so; for although they will tell white people that they pray to God, yet we know that they pray to the sun, to the earth, to the rocks, and a host of other unintelligent creatures, to which they attribute divine power. God condemns such worship. . . . The religion of the Indians is openly and indisputably against the first Commandment of the Decalogue, for it is truly and clearly idolatry, like the worship of the Golden Calf by the Israelites, for which crime, by the command of God Himself, given through Moses, twenty-three thousand people were put to death in one day. (32–33)

The Jesuit did not recommend cutting down Indians for their faith; however, he thought their traditional religion deserving of extirpation.

In the early 1900s an appreciation was growing for the remnants of American Indian cultural heritage. The demise of Indians as obstacles to American expansion made them objects of commiseration to romantics and other sympathizers. The development of anthropology as a scholarly discipline lent validity to the notion that indigenous beliefs and practices were worth studying and even preserving. Some Catholic clergy in the United States and abroad played a part in the anthropological enterprise, interviewing Native informants and taking down accounts of Indian myths and rituals. Rev. Wilhelm Schmidt theorized about Native American theology (Schmidt 1933); Rev. Berard Haile used his post at St. Michael's mission in Arizona to master the Navajos' language and put together many volumes of their sacred texts. Sister M. Agnes Hilger, O.S.B., analyzed the social conditions and child life of the Ojibways. In 1926 Father John Cooper helped found the Catholic Anthropological Conference and edited the journal, *Primitive Man* (later called *Anthropological Quarterly*), in part to help missionaries understand the cultural foundations of Indian life.

By the late 1920s some Catholic missionaries sounded like social workers, as they spoke of Indian "maladjustment," the result of having been exploited and uprooted. "The problem before the Church," wrote one Catholic editorialist, "is not only to teach the Indian the truths of Christianity, but also as far as possible, to alleviate his distress and to teach him how to live a decent human life." Employing the anthropological insight that "Indian religions themselves are practical, woven as they are into the warp of Indian life," the writer exhorted missionaries to construct for the Indian convert "a practical religion . . . to replace the old faith in his daily life" (*Our Negro and Indian Missions* 1929: 26–27). Realizing with other reformers that the programs to de-indianize Indians during the previous decades had wrought debilitation along with cultural disintegration, churchmen began to question boarding schools and other means of deracinating Native Americans:

> The normal child is better off in his own home and the family is better off for having him there. The Indian child will now grow up in the place where he must afterwards make his own home, he will be better trained

in the responsibilities of family life, and he can form wholesome ac-
quaintanceships with his neighbors, Indian and white. (Ibid. 1934: 28)

John Collier imbibed the anthropological literature of his day, led a
crusade in the 1920s to protect Indians of the Southwest against a
land-grabbing U.S. Congress, wrote some tomes in praise of Native
spirituality, and was appointed Commissioner of Indian Affairs by
President Franklin Delano Roosevelt, where he formulated the Indian
New Deal. A keystone of his program was to grant Native Americans
the freedom of religion owed them under the Bill of Right's first
amendment. In 1934 he ordered all BIA employees to permit reservation Indians the liberty of their religious expression.

Catholic missionaries called Collier's principle a "disturbing element, conceived by anthropologists and others who have a flair for the
exotic," and now "injected into this plan by the present administration" (ibid. 1935: 26). Catholic editorial writers quoted the words of
the Secretary of the Interior: "We want the white neighbors of these
original Americans to learn to respect their religions and their ceremonies. We want the Indians to rebuild and develop their own cultural life" (in ibid.). They cited Collier, who wrote of "a great spiritual
stirring" among American Indians, an "awakening of the racial spirit"
(in ibid., 27), which must be encouraged, according to the commissioner. Against these goals the editorialists laid their objections: "But
to summon up the ancient tribal spirit and ideas, the animistic and
magical Indian religious systems, the primitive art and customs for the
purpose of effecting a wholesome social transformation, is to expect
from these influences something that they have never achieved" (28).
In the Catholic authorities' mind, only Christianity possessed the
power to help Indians adjust to their present circumstances.

Within a few years, however, the BCIM was paying at least lip service to Collier's ideals. Its director, Rev. J. Benjamin Tennelly, S.S.,
wrote in 1936 that "the Catholic Church also maintains that every person is responsible, not to the Government, but to God, for his religious beliefs, and has no desire that the Government should interfere
with the exercise of religion" (in Steinmetz 1980: 83). In 1939 Pope Pius
XII made use of anthropological language in writing the bull, *Summi
Pontificatus* (and his later encyclical of 1951, *Evangelii Praecones*), which
called for the preservation of indigenous cultures worldwide. Without
softening the call for missionary efforts, the pontiff countermanded the
directives of his predecessor two centuries previous. Whereas Pope

Benedict XIV had censured the Jesuits for their liberality regarding cultural expression in 1742, Pope Pius XII argued that peoples could become Catholics without denying them their rituals of civic and familial piety (see Enochs 1993: 151–152). The new ruling did not spell approval for all types of Indian ritualism—in the 1940s priests forbade Catholic Arapahos from taking part in sun dances and peyote services (*Our Negro and Indian Missions* 1946: 22)—but the stage was set for future flexibility.

In the early days of the Church in the Americas the missionaries had often attempted to isolate Indian converts from Euroamericans who might exploit and corrupt them. The reservations of the early twentieth century were modern analogues of the earlier reductions—controlled refuges for Indians on the road to acculturation—and the missionaries wished to be able to inculcate Catholic culture without the interference of other Whites. In 1887 the federal government had passed the General Allotment Act, which divided many reservations into individual land holdings and made it possible for non-Indians to purchase acreage within Indian country. The result was an invasion of the refuges. The editors of a missionary journal described the situation:

> Work among the Indians has been and still is most successful in places where there are relatively few white people. There they have their own churches and priests, particularly interested in their welfare. However, on many of the former reservations, where a large part of the present Indian population still lives, the whites predominate numerically, and the Indians are a merely tolerated, if not a despised class. Most white Catholics resent their presence at religious services, although they are often held in what were formerly chapels for Indians. It is not surprising that the latter are disheartened by this treatment and are inclined not to go where they are not wanted. In fact, where little . . . provision is made for their religious care, they drift into indifference. . . . An early Catholic education has proved to be no effective antidote against later neglect. . . . This is where—and why—leakage occurs. (Ibid. 1937: 28–29)

Even mixed-heritage Native Americans like the Ojibway-Métis of North Dakota with a long history of interaction with Whites felt overwhelmed by mainstream American Catholics. "They do not like to come to church with the whites," said one priest, "and were slowly falling away from the Church" until he said a special weekly mass for them (ibid. 1945: 27).

During the Second World War twenty-two thousand Indian men

and women joined the U.S. armed forces, and twice that number left their reservations to work in war industries. Mission organs paid tribute to these patriots (e.g, ibid., 22, no. 6, June 1942); nevertheless, Church authorities bemoaned the fact that "our Catholic missions have lost most of their able-bodied men" (ibid., 23, no. 2, February 1943: 20). At the end of the war many Indians left their reservations for urban life, partly by choice, partly under the prodding of the United States government, which instituted the Economic Assistance Act of 1952 to move reservation Indians to cities. In 1946 there were about four hundred congregations of Catholic Indians across the United States, numbering about 90,000. There were more than a hundred well-established mission centers with 64 mission schools (26 boarding schools with 3,518 pupils; 38 day schools enrolling 3,461 Indian students). One hundred fifty priests led these institutions, with the help of over seven hundred sisters, brothers, scholastics, lay teachers, and Native catechists. Another fifty Indian chapels were attended as out-missions from white parishes neighboring Indian country. Perhaps as many as 10,000 Indian Catholics had already moved to cities—making a total Catholic Indian population of 100,000 (*Our Negro and Indian Missions* 1946: 19).

Rev. Tennelly summarized the scene in the post-war period. Half of the Catholic Indians lived in the Southwest: Arizona, New Mexico, and California. A hundred years after the Treaty of Guadalupe-Hidalgo, there was still much to accomplish, in his view. "Despite the fact that that is a region in which the early Spanish missionaries worked, it is still preeminently a missionary field" (*The Indian Sentinel*, 28, no. 2, February 1948: 19), even among the Puebloans. Traditional peoples like the Navajos and Apaches were still "hostile" to Catholicism. The Pimas and Papagos were more "amenable" to the faith, and the Mission Indians of California were "docile, . . . earnest Catholics" (20). On the northern plains in the Dakotas more than half of the Sioux, approaching twenty thousand, were baptized Catholics, after a half century of missions. "Their family life is sound," Tennelly wrote, "and their attachment to the Church is strong" (20). In the Great Lakes area—Michigan, Wisconsin, and Minnesota—half of the Ojibways, Ottawas, and Menominees were members of the Church, perhaps ten thousand; some reservation communities were "almost entirely Catholic" (20). In the Northwest—Idaho, Montana, Oregon, and Washington—there were still pockets of Indian Catholicism (e.g., among the Coeur d'Alene, Flathead, Blackfoot, Crow, Umatilla, and Coast Salish); however, these once-flourishing missions had been undermined by the breakup of reservations, leaving many of the Indians dispersed and impoverished. There were small reservations with successful missions in Wyoming (Arapaho), Kansas (Potawatomi), Mississippi (Choctaw), Louisiana (Houma), Maine (Penobscot and Passamaquoddy), and New York (Iroquois), and smaller operations in Oklahoma (Osage); Alaska had over four thousand Catholics among its Indian and Eskimo populations.

After a half century of glowing vignettes of Indian Catholic piety, and a doubling of efforts and effects from 1900 to midcentury (see *The Indian Sentinel,* 30, no. 1, January–February 1950: 3–5), there were some sobering observations about the net result and future prospects. The editor of *Our Negro and Indian Missions* wrote in 1948: "Work among the Indians at the present time lacks the spectacular setting of the pioneer period, when the Gospel was everywhere a novel message and was often accepted with ready and apparently unfeigned enthusiasm." These conversions were often sincere, but other Indians were only curious rather than committed. "Then came the period of hard, prolonged work of fully instructing and training the converts and of laying a patient siege to the unconverted. Our Indian mission work is now in this stage" (20). Despite the pious acts of Indian Catholic individuals, wrote one priest, "the faith of the majority is still weak and the work of strengthening it involves many phases of Christian living" (24).

Through the 1950s, 1960s, and 1970s, the number of Indian Catholics continued to grow: 105,000 in 1953, with uncounted numbers in western states who were "assimilated into the parishes in the towns and cities where they are living" (*The Indian Sentinel,* 33, no. 2, February 1953: 19); 111,000 in 1957, counting 873 converts in the previous year (ibid., 37, no. 1, January–February 1957: 3), an increase of 7,500 converts between 1950 and 1960, bringing the total to 128,000 by 1962. In that year the greatest concentrations of Indian Catholics were in Arizona (22,000), New Mexico (17,620), South Dakota (16,500), Montana (12,160), North Dakota (9,566), California (8,950), Washington, (6,905), Alaska (5,730), Minnesota (5,646), and Wisconsin (5,498), with Native American Catholic populations in Oklahoma, Michigan, New York, Utah, Oregon, Wyoming, Idaho, Maine, Nevada, Mississippi, Kansas, Nebraska, and Colorado, in descending order (ibid., 40, no. 1, Spring 1962: 3–5, 12; the list neglected Louisiana). At the same time in Canada, over 110,000 Indians and Eskimos were counted as Catholics, served by five hundred missionary priests and sisters. The Church conducted forty-one boarding schools with 6,500 Indian pupils (Pouliot 1967: 401–402).

For all the statistical increase, the churchmen found cause for discouragement. Many Indians, they said, "cling to their old beliefs and practices. Bizarre as these [may] seem to us, they are meaningful to Indians and have practical values in their estimation. The making of converts and of real Catholics has been and is generally a difficult matter" (*Our Negro and Indian Missions* 1960: 24). Clergy assigned to Indian ministry found their tasks a hard grind, since "the prospects for success among the Indians are never great or dramatic. From a human point of view, it is not especially rewarding" (ibid. 1961: 31). Especially with Indians traveling between reservation and city, "one Indian requires five times the attention a white man should receive to be a basically good Catholic" (ibid. 1961: 30). As a result there were more priests and churches per Indian than for any other ethnic group in the United States in the early 1960s.

As a result, outreach slowed as the pastors tried merely to hold onto the Indians already in the fold and make them into parishioners rather than perpetual objects of missionization. One priest wrote that his goal was "to make the Indian people more aware of their responsibility to practice their religion faithfully, and to support their parish. Many of the older Indians," he said, "are somewhat lackadaisical in fulfilling their religious duties, and are slow to appreciate their personal obligation to support the church" (ibid. 1963: 32). "I realize," said another cleric, "that many of my Catholic Indians, both on the reservations and in established communities, are more or less lax in the fulfillment of their Catholic obligations . . ." (ibid. 1964: 28). Despite a 60 percent increase of Indian Catholics between 1940 and 1966 (ibid. 1966: 23), the future of their faith seemed less secure by the later date.

Even in the Catholic schools—by the mid-1960s there were thirty-nine day schools, eleven remaining boarding schools, and four combined institutions—the nine thousand Indian students were proving less tractable than they once appeared. "Although Indians are generally docile in school," asserted Rev. Tennelly of the BCIM, "most of them lack real interest in studies and ambition to learn, thereby reflecting the attitudes of their parents, who do not cooperate with the school or become involved in the education of their children" (Tennelly 1967a: 401).

Ten thousand Indians were added to the Catholic rolls during the 1960s. By 1970 the Church counted 141,573 Catholic Indians on reservations, with another 25,000 in cities of the western United States. Nonetheless, "nowhere have Indians been easily induced to enter the

Church. While many of their ancestral customs and ideas have been modified or forgotten, their religious beliefs and customs have often been little altered" (*Our Negro and Indian Missions* 1970: 24). "Sometimes one wonders if the results of all this missionary work is worth the effort," uttered one disgruntled priest (ibid. 1971: 32).

A hundred years after the founding of the BCIM there were 156,728 "practicing and nominal Catholics" (ibid. 1976: 24) among the reservation Indian population, and baptized Indians by the tens of thousands in non-mission parishes. Over 6,000 Indian children attended thirty-nine Catholic mission schools and 265 priests still worked in the Indian apostolate. And yet the numbers of schools and priests were diminishing in the post–Vatican II era. In some regions Indians were reverting to the "primitive Indian religions" (ibid. 1975: 28) of their tribes, and the progress of the previous century seemed in jeopardy.

In the 1940s and 1950s the public face of the BCIM often appeared both complacent and expansive. "MUSIC HATH POWER TO CHARM THE SAVAGE HEART" (*The Indian Sentinel,* 25, no. 6, September 1945: 96) read a caption for a photograph of a mission school orchestra. Despite some doubts about the progress of the Indians' faith, the Church continued to build chapels, convents, schools, and other missionary edifices. One story featured an "autobiography" of a mission dormitory (ibid., 33, no. 10, December 1953: 155–156). In private, however, the missionaries were having their doubts.

In 1939 a group of missionary priests, particularly from the northern plains, formed a support group named for Kateri Tekakwitha, the famous Mohawk convert of the seventeenth century. These priests felt isolated at their posts. Their ministry was "*to,* not *with* the Indian people" (Fargo, August 3, 1989), according to a Capuchin who was there at the beginning of the Tekakwitha Missionary Conference. The priests needed to talk to one another annually about the work they were trying to accomplish and the alienation they were experiencing.

Many of their discussions focused on practical questions: how to meet the economic and social needs of Catholic Indians moving to the cities in the federal relocation program of the 1950s; how to apply the insights of the liturgical movement of the 1950s to Indian reservations. Minutes from their meetings reveal the doubts these priests had about the approaches they were employing and the responses of Indians to missionary labors.

At the 1956 meeting a Benedictine priest suggested that "We should

use our ingenuity to adapt [the liturgical movement] to Indian customs, tendencies, practices, etc." (Tekakwitha Missionary Conference
1956: 3), perhaps even going so far as to use English language at mass.
Another Benedictine replied, "Perhaps, the Mass isn't as natural to
them as some of their group activities; not as natural as it is to us" (4).
Yet another acknowledged that "the Peyote Cult has the advantage
over us here. They have more participation since they have their own
bishops, priests, etc." (6). And a Jesuit among the Sioux admitted that
"Even Catholic Indians refer sometimes to Yuwipi as 'our religion' because they feel at home in it" (6). The priests recognized that, even
after many decades of effort on the reservations, "While we have generations of Catholicity behind us, they are still primitives, and somewhat frustrated primitives" (6). They were still drawn to their traditional religious practices and they were apt to quit the Church if it
conflicted with their yearnings. Parents were not passing down
Catholic practices to their children. Many of all ages were eschewing
the sacraments. A Benedictine noted that "Many pray at home, but
that's the end of it. Practically they are no longer Catholics." And he
added, "Even some of the older people are going 'tribal'" (7), attending powwows and peyote rites.

How to gain their attention? Should priests turn around at mass
before the consecration of the host and announce, as one priest did,
"O.K. boys, you are about to witness the greatest miracle of them all"
(in ibid., 6)? Might there be a "toleration of things otherwise undesir-
able" in order to show good will to the Indian culture? Had one priest
gone too far in taking a group of Catholic Indian children to a peyote
meeting to attend a burial of a baptized comrade? The priest admitted,
"Maybe I was wrong but I think we're going to win more back by love
than harshness" (6).

In 1962, the year in which the Second Vatican Council began under
the leadership of Pope John XXIII, the problems were the same. Indians rarely attended mass and seemed to regard the missionaries' presence as an imposition. One Catholic Indian explained to a Jesuit that
"the Indian thinks the Catholic Church is a White Man's religion" (in
Tekakwitha Missionary Conference 1962: n.p.). This was especially
true for Indian Catholics who made their homes in urban areas and
were faced with the prospect of joining a non-Indian parish. "I know a
couple," reported a Benedictine, "who went to church every Sunday
for 29 years. They left the reservation. They never went to church. The

reason was they did not feel at home." "Indians feel discomfort in presence of Non-Indians," explained a Jesuit, and the Benedictine admitted
that "Whites do not want to mix a minority into their own parish"
(ibid.).

Some priests suggested the most effective way to enforce Catholic
identity among Native Americans was to deemphasize their Indian
identity. "We should teach that he is an Indian not first. He is first a
Human being, then an American, the third an Indian," asserted one
cleric. Others disagreed, saying that Indians ought to be proud of their
own ethnic loyalties. A Jesuit reminded his fellow priests that for many
years both Church and State in America had prohibited Indian cultural
expression. Boarding schools, both parochial and federal, had produced untoward effects on Indian families and the sense of Native self-
worth. "It's penance to go to Church for an Indian. Russia has never
made their suppressed people speak Russian or think Russian. It's a
difference in frame of mind," he concluded, urging his fellows to respect Indian perspectives (ibid.).

THE SECOND VATICAN COUNCIL

We have seen at Pine Ridge that the Second Vatican Council (1962–1965) led to a reevaluation of missiology. It is the purpose of this chapter to examine the changes which have occurred in Church teaching and practice regarding Native American ministry over the past three decades since Vatican II. We shall see that in circles beyond the Church the old evangelism has fallen into disrepute, and that even within Catholicism new attitudes have arisen which have shaken the confidence of apostolic action. This has been a generation of alteration, apology, and experimentation.

The Catholic missionary journals of the twentieth century presented a picture of purposive progress, even though behind the scene the missionaries were having their doubts—not only about their rates of success, but also regarding their motives and methods. A few priests like the Flemish Oblate Roger Vandersteene, who served the Crees of northern Alberta from the post–World War II period, were already promoting an "interstitial," syncretic religious development among Native Americans, espousing inculturation before the term became current. When Vatican II offered an opportunity for discussion about all matters of theology and ecclesiology, these doubts and innovations found voices and received public hearing. Church leaders considered and even embraced the notions of ecumenism and interfaith understanding. No longer was the Roman Catholic Church to look with contempt upon other Christian denominations, and even Jews, Moslems, and members of other religious traditions were to be allowed the integrity of their faith. There was a newfound respect for individual conscience and cultural expression, accompanying the decentralization and declericalization of Church authority.

All of these factors filled the pages of major Vatican II documents (see Abbott 1966). In the "Pastoral Constitution of the Church in the Modern World" *(Gaudium et Spes)* the Church authorities stated that Christ's church is not coterminous with the visible Roman Catholic Church, allowing for God's law to exist beyond official Church boundaries. The "Declaration on the Relation of the Church to non-Christian Religions" *(Nostrae Aetate)* suggested that non-Christian religions can contain truth about God, and the "Constitution on the Sacred Liturgy" *(Sacrosanctum Concilium)* sought ways to harmonize Catholic liturgy with local cultural forms. The "Decree on the Church's Missionary Activity" *(Ad Gentes)* upheld the duty of Christians to share their salvific faith with other peoples; however, the "Decree on Ecumenism" *(Unitatis Redintegratio)* and the "Declaration on Religious Freedom" *(Dignitatis Humanae)* both emphasized the importance of individual free choice and warned against a triumphalist attitude toward peoples of other religions.

These documents were deeply and broadly felt throughout the American Church; those clergy and religious with Native American ministries attempted to implement the teachings of Vatican II, even if it meant refashioning their pastorates. Growing Indian traditionalism and the inroads of Protestant fundamentalism were competition enough to make the missionaries reconsider their approaches, but Vatican II actually changed their minds about their mission. They began to look at American Indians afresh in the light of the new good news of Pope John XXIII's revised apostolate, and in that light the Indians looked less like the deficient beings of old, in desperate need of the saving grace of Catholicism, and more like victims of genocide and oppression. Vatican II made churchmen take new, hard looks at their own Church, and in the new equation Catholicism appeared somewhat complicitous in the Indians' downfall.

CULTURAL CRITICISMS OF EVANGELISM

Non-Catholic Indians and other critics of the Christendom began to press the argument that missionization over five centuries had brought more harm than help to Native Americans. The Sioux scholar Vine Deloria, Jr., led this charge in his pathbreaking book, *Custer Died for Your Sins* (1970), which became required reading for thoughtful missionaries. "While the thrust of Christian missions," Deloria wrote, "was to save the individual Indian, its result was to shatter Indian societies and destroy the cohesiveness of the Indian communities" (106). Deloria put forward the proposition that aboriginal Indian religions were replete with spirituality before the coming of Christianity, a religiousness which fit and enhanced the cultures of the Americas. Missionaries served to destroy the traditional faith of Native Americans while debilitating their societies. Deloria wrote that "by 1930 the majority of the Indian people had a tradition of three generations of church life behind them" (113); however, denominational authorities refused to grant the Indian Christians congregational status, keeping them instead as missionary wards. Hence, the life of Christianity continued to be a foreign element in the Indians' lives. Since the 1930s and the Indian New Deal's relaxation of prohibitions against traditional religious practice, Christianity had lost its hold on its nominal Indian members. The development of the Native American Church and the resurgence of traditional religious expression seized Indian loyalties, even while many Indians kept membership in Christian bodies and participated in Christian ceremonialism.

A Cherokee scholar noted that Christian denominations, ruled by non-Indians, broke apart the solidarity of Indian communities. "Only the native people themselves," he asserted, "can integrate a new religion and then use it to make life consistent for themselves. An outsider cannot do this and usually only succeeds in doing the opposite." He concluded that "in many Indian communities the church is like a huge crowbar crammed into a delicate machine" (Thomas 1967: 24). In 1975 the militant American Indian Movement (AIM) named Christianity (along with educational institutions and the bureaucracy of the United States government) as one of the three major enemies of Native Americans ("Indian Unit Names Three Top Enemies," June 18, 1975), and as recently as 1993 an American Indian Lutheran minister blamed Christian missions for their historic role in creating a contemporary culture of "Indian dysfunctionality" (Tinker 1993: 118).

The more restrained voices of scholars found Christian missions among North American Indians to be wanting. One missiologist called them "among the least impressive in modern mission history. . . . in general Indians have accepted the white man's religion in its externals without understanding its internal meanings" (Turner 1973: 54). He noted that there was virtually no Indian leadership in Christianity, either in Catholic or Protestant circles (cf. Stuart 1981), and he observed that there was renewed opposition to Christianity among many contemporary Native Americans. An anthropologist theorized that the Christian missionary enterprise was, ironically, an "agent of secularization" (Miller 1970: 14) among Native Americans, undermining traditional religiousness and infusing rationalism and scientism as powerful elements in modern Indian life. "Nearly five hundred years of American history show that interaction between Indians and Christian spokesmen produced tragic results," according to a historian. "White clergymen who tried to convert natives may have been prompted by altruistic ideals, but their daily activities helped destroy the cultures of people they wanted to aid" (Bowden 1981: xv).

Social scientists were particularly hostile to missionary endeavors. Over the twentieth century they had developed the concept of cultural integrity, which stipulated that each people (culture) possesses its own patterns of behaviors, symbols, values, and meanings, all derived through a process of organic adaptation, all having useful societal functions, and all integrated with one another. In such a framework each individual gains identity and purpose by growing up, learning, and participating in an integral culture. In the viewpoint of social scientists, missionaries were intrusive agents of cultural transformation, making judgments on Native ways and destroying cultural integrity by coercing change.

In the eyes of many social scientists, each culture possesses its own set of religious codes, and no one set is inherently superior to another. The religious relativism of social science did not accept the Christian missionary idea that Christian codes are superior to all others or the conceit that gospel and Church are supracultural entities. Rather, Christianity constitutes a culture like any other, with no special claims on the good or the true. Its morals have their own genealogy, born of particular historical circumstances. For social scientists, then, Christian missionaries were doubly obnoxious, in that they falsely claimed the right to make judgments on other cultures, and in that their actions undermined the cultural integrity of people—like American Indians—who neither wanted nor needed missionary intrusions (see Stipe 1980).

Catholic missiologists had already accepted, at least in principle, the notion of cultural integrity by the 1960s. Instead of condemning a particular aspect of a culture, they said, we should understand what role it plays in that culture. Ideally, missionaries should look for linkages between the essence of Christianity and indigenous ways and values. Missionaries should try to make Christianity fit with local cultures, rather than destroying them (see Luzbetak 1961). Missiologists recalled that the early Church had encountered paganism in the spirit of accommodation and adaptation. Heathen religions of Europe had lent their liturgical and artistic forms to Christianity, as the Church expanded according to the principles of nativization and inculturation. It was in the Age of Discovery that the Church became less tolerant of new cultures, and the Rites Controversy sealed off indigenization for two centuries, until Pope Pius XII's liberalizing reversals, *Summi Pontificatus* (1939) and *Evangelii Praecones* (1951). "One of man's most basic rights," a missiologist wrote in the 1960s, "is his right to his own national distinctiveness and culture." In addition, "the supranational nature of the Church calls for missionary adaptation." Moreover, applied anthropology and the history of missions both demonstrate that the most "effective" missions are those that appeal to local cultures, becoming "immersed" in them" (Luzbetak 1967: 121). The Church of the 1960s wished to accommodate all cultures, but it needed to decide "what is essential for the unity of faith, and what might be termed as the accidentals of the Church" (122).

Thus, in the period immediately following Vatican II, the Church had adopted the language of social sciences in emphasizing the cultural grounding for varieties of human experience. "[You] are tearing to tatters the basic fabric of Indian life" (Lunstrom 1973: 5), wrote a faculty member at Campion Jesuit Residential High School to a Jesuit missionary among the Sioux, expressing the concept of cultural integrity in critiquing missionary aims and procedures.

In practice, some Catholic missionaries found cultural integrity to be a romantic and impractical notion. "Our doctrine on original sin and on the unity of the human race do not lead us to expect to find any race anywhere set apart by a noble life based on lofty ideals . . . , just doing what came naturally," said one churchman, who chided his fellows for carrying "idyllic notions about Indians" (Barry post-1965: 1–2). "I think missionaries should be freed from the assumption," he stated, "that they are dealing with a centuries-old, noble, or lofty culture, and so allowed to judge the Indian culture by its works. I think they will find that they are dealing with a cultural vacuum in which fragments of older cultures serve only to confuse people" (3). To speak of cultural integrity when dealing with people who underwent cataclysmic changes over many generations was, in one critic's view at least, a fiction. The present situation, he said, was that Indians' lives were in shambles, and they would do better to adapt to the American, Christian culture around them, rather than harkening back to remnants of the half-remembered past.

Even if missionaries were willing to acknowledge the integrity of cultures, they were not eager to espouse relativism when it came to the question of religions. The whole history of Christian missionization was bound up in the claim that Christianity as a religious system exists *sui generis*. According to the Church, the Indian should not be allowed to think that aboriginal religion was comparable to the true faith: "In Christianity he has the religion revealed by God, which is far superior to his old paganism" (ibid., 8).

In the 1960s it was still possible to express such an idea in so many words. The most recent generation has found such utterances distasteful, even though many within Catholicism have continued to hold similar sentiments. These judgments did not become wrong; they just became outdated, publicly unfashionable. Nobody argued these ideas out of existence; they merely got washed over by new, more romantic, more liberal, more anthropological thought (see Birmingham 1976). Icons of the Church like Thomas Merton (see Merton 1976) began to meditate upon the worth of Native American spirituality. The seminaries began to train clergy according to missiological principles appropriate to Vatican II theology (*Our Negro and Indian Missions* 1969: 28). At the Tekakwitha Missionary Conference in the late 1960s the priests were asking themselves how they might update their efforts in light of new concepts of Church (see McMullen 1969). In 1971 the

Oblates in Canada urged the Canadian Catholic Conference to foster a Native church, with local customs, social structures, and charisms (Grant 1985: 210).

Among the Lakotas in the 1970s a recently arrived Jesuit took stock of his order's place in history and suggested to his fellow priests that "the Church is an unjust structure," reflecting white mores, holding power to itself while trying to "civilize" Indians in a paternalistic manner (Hilbert 1975a). He said that missionaries like himself are carriers of an arrogant American culture, condemning Indian ways while pretending to be above criticism themselves. They must be more conscious of their cultural baggage, he argued, and more critical of American socio-politico-economic structures—and less critical of Indians (Hilbert 1975b). Other Jesuit mission staff felt the need "to work on problems relating to Indian culture and the ways in which this affects their practice of religion" (DCRAA 1976).

Capuchin Father Gilbert F. Hemauer, who was soon to be the head of a revamped Tekakwitha Conference, tried to lay down guidelines for a new kind of Catholic evangelization among Native Americans. "The urgent need exists," he wrote, "to recognize the 'Good News' Native American people and cultures already possess in their rich traditions and ways of living" (Hemauer 1976: 1). Through a process of pre-evangelization, clergy must learn who these people are culturally and what is sacred to them: "Missionaries need to understand and appreciate the manner in which God has made Himself known to Native American people throughout the centuries: in their beliefs, religious symbols, covenants, teachings, stories, myths, art and music" (4). Only then could catechesis take place, in which Church teachers could adapt the basic core of Christianity to local particularities. "Unconsciously," he said, by coercing and condemning Indians, "the Christian Churches have contributed to the cultural disorientation and dislocation of the people" (2). It was time, he exhorted, for a cross-cultural dialogue between the "basic core of Christianity and the basic core of Native American tribal religious traditions" (Hemauer 1977: 132).

APOLOGIES

In 1977 the United States Conference of Catholic Bishops issued a statement on American Indians in which they expressed the convictions of post–Vatican II Catholicism. They argued that the Church's authenticity as a community requires respect for "distinctive traditions, customs, institutions and ways of life of its peoples" (*Statement of U.S. Catholic Bishops on American Indians* 1977: 1). Drawing especially upon the "Pastoral Constitution of the Church in the Modern World," the bishops emphasized that in the work of evangelization, "the Gospel message must take root and grow within each culture and each community" (ibid., 3).

The bishops were not turning their back on missionization. Indeed, they praised the work, past and present, of the Bureau of Catholic Indian Missions and its funding arms. The bishops acknowledged the charges of some critics that Catholic missionaries have not always respected Indian cultures, and they underscored the responsibility of the Church to "appreciate American Indian history, cultures and spirituality" (9). Nonetheless, they stressed, the "center and foundation" of the Church's calling is to proclaim the good news: "God's saving love revealed by Jesus Christ in the Holy Spirit" (1). The duty of the missionary Church, they argued, is to preach the word of Jesus' incarnation, death, and resurrection, through which "salvation is offered to all people as a gift of God's grace and mercy" (2).

The bishops' statement iterated the need of the Church to promote social justice for American Indians within U.S. society. Given the American experience of damaging Indian cultures in the process of nation building, given the present state of Indian life with its poverty, uprootedness, cultural decay, and wardship to the United States, the Church must be active in seeking legislative and other means of redressing hurts. Social justice is "not foreign to evangelization" (3), the bishops said. Neither certainly is the aim for more Indian leadership—clerical, religious, and lay—within the structures of the Church.

Although the bishops voted overwhelmingly to issue the statement of 1977, there was sharp debate in which several, including Bishop Jerome J. Hastrich of Gallup, sought to eliminate references to past mistakes by Catholics and others in their treatment of Indians. "I would like to remind the Indians of the great benefit the Church has been to them," Bishop Hastrich said, and he asked, "Who are we to criticize the honest efforts of our government?" In his view the statement should have accentuated the "glorious history" of the Church among Indians, and they ought to be reminded that they "need Christianity badly." He objected to the apologetic tone of the pastoral statement and to the emphasis upon social activism. "A certain Sister was pushing" for the material needs of Indians, he wrote; others were more concerned about urban poverty than the more crucial duty to "evangelize" Indians. We bishops, he said, should "stick to faith and morals," instead of being swayed by "agitators. . . . Solving social problems is not the answer," he concluded. "It's a matter of converting the Indians to Christianity" (DCRAA 1977). The Second Vatican Council made it possible, even imperative, for those in Native American ministry to reconsider their aims and techniques; however, it did not establish a single-minded pastoral program. Rather, it engendered debate and set into motion a wide range of initiatives on the part of Church representatives. In general the Church attempted to move from the "imposition" or "translation" of Euroamerican Christian structures to a process of "adaptation" to local cultures and conditions. This adaptation of the Christian core has been called "indigenization," "contextualization," "localization," and "inculturation" (Angrosino 1994: 824–825; Peelman 1995: 84). Whatever name it has gone by, "the move from the exclusivist religious position in which conversion into a Eurocentric world view is a primary motivation, to an inclusivist position which acknowledges diversity of religious and cultural expression is a radical shift for Catholicism" (Grim 1991a: 18).

The shift has included a reconsideration of five centuries of evangelization in the Americas. How should the contemporary Church judge its historic role regarding Indians? We have seen in the first volume of *American Indian Catholics* that modern Church authorities have tended to defend the practices of the earlier missionaries, even when their activities were intertwined with the abuses of colonialism and when they employed coercion in treating Native American neophytes. Even those who have criticized particular missionaries, e.g., Padre Junipero Serra, have argued that in the main the Church has been good to Indians over a half millennium (McDonnell, July 1987: 22); some bishops have insisted that the Church has "nothing to apologize for" (in Starkloff, October 12, 1990) in its long history of Spanish American missions. In 1992 Pope John Paul II emphasized the salvific import of the Columbian encounter. In the same year the new bishop of Port-land, Maine—the Most Reverend Joseph John Gerry, O.S.B.—wel-comed Indian Catholics to an annual Tekakwitha Conference gather-ing by acknowledging a long history of disasters brought to the New World by Europeans. Despite the diseases and dislocations, however, he stated that we should not forget the "blessings" of the Columbian exchange, particularly the "spreading of the good news" to Indian peoples (Orono, August 5, 1992).

Other churchmen in the United States and Canada—most fa-mously, the bishops of Seattle in 1987 and the Oblates at Lac Ste. Anne in 1991—have issued apologies for the Church's treatment of Indians over time: for the destruction of Native spirituality in the overall of-fense against Indian cultures and for collusion in imperial expansion (see Grim 1991b: 3; Johnson, Midwinter 1988; Waugh 1996: 6 n. 5). These apologies have called for reconciliation between Indians and the Church, and such a reconciling has required that Catholic authorities listen as well as speak to Native Americans.

In 1989 the papal nuncio, Archbishop Pio Laghi, attended a "listen-ing session" (*Bureau of Catholic Indian Missions Newsletter,* 8, no. 7, October–November 1989: 2) with Native American Catholics in South Dakota. Missionaries in the field have testified that their best pastoral work took place when they stopped preaching ancient doctrines and instead began to converse with Indians about their experiential con-cerns. Listening to Indians has required a shift in clerical attitudes, not only toward Indians, but toward laity in general. Taking on the lan-guage of Vatican II, some priests have come to the conviction that they are "ministering *with* a people, as well as *to* them"; that the laity share the mission of the Church; and that the Church consists of the People of God, including the "Native People of God" (Fargo, August 3, 1989). This "ecclesiastical populism" has regarded the priest as a "'server' who helps implement the vision of the congregation" (Gualtieri 1980b: 50).

In order to comprehend the visions of Native American congre-gants, priests have begun to identify with them and their problems. Pastors such as Father Hemauer and others (JINNAM, January 28, 1985; Mittelstadt, January 18, 1987) have confessed their failings to their flock: admitting their own alcoholism and declaring themselves to be sinners among sinners, in need of mutual regeneration. Rather than standing above and beyond the Indians, clergy have entered into dialogues with them. In the following chapter we shall observe the rhythms of a theological dialogue among Jesuits and Lakotas in the 1970s. In many other locales dialogues have taken place in a general attitude of cultural, liturgical, and personal sharing over the past two decades.

Part of that sharing has focused upon issues of social justice for American Indians. Catholic ministries have taken an interest in strengthening Indians' family and community life, providing economic assistance or the counseling of social workers. At the same time, the Church has been wary of taking a paternalistic role in contemporary Indian society, preferring to let Indian authorities accomplish their own reforms according to their own standards. Father Ted Zuern, a Jesuit, has served as public conscience for the BCIM for more than a decade, writing a monthly column, "Bread and Freedom . . . Justice and Faith" (Zuern 1991), in which he has pressed home the sovereignty and special rights of Native Americans in the United States. Rebutting the likes of the Reagan administration in the 1980s, he has reminded those within and without the Church that Indians are culturally different from most Americans, and even where their culture is like ours, "they retain their tribal citizenship" (Zuern n.d.: 8). Based upon the expertise he has gained in ministries in Kansas, South Dakota, Minnesota, and Washington, D.C., he has taken the role of political activist, lobbyist, and coordinator of Jesuit mission political stances, and he has spoken publicly in favor of preserving and protecting American Indian religious freedoms, including those of traditional vision questing and partaking in peyote rituals.

Before the Second Vatican Council commenced, it was common to hear Catholic clerics speak of ending special Indian status within Church ministry. In an era of the melting pot ideal, when the U.S. government was intent upon moving Indians from their reservations to various urban locales and terminating the treaty rights of Indian tribes, the Church authorities wished to have Indian Catholics make "the transition from mission to parish." As Bishop Bernard J. Topel of Spokane said ("A Report on the Meeting of the Indian Missionaries of the Oregon Province," June 7–10, 1960), "I feel that we haven't asked our Indians to do things for the Church, to make sacrifices for it. What makes a good Catholic is the sacrifice the Catholic makes for the Church." The bishop wanted to see Indians carrying the financial burden of their white brethren in supporting Church services. From the nineteenth century Indian Catholics maintained their mission status, deriving funds from the BCIM or depending upon a parish in the vicinity to carry the expenses of the priests. In effect, the prelate and others called for a "secularization" of Indian missions which would make the Indian parishes self-supporting. "They'll be better Catholics for it," the bishop stated.

Since few Indian communities had enough money to pay for a parish church, the transition from mission to parish meant assimilating into non-Indian parishes, which meant that Native American identity within the local church would dissipate or disappear. Vatican II's emphasis on the cultural foundations of personhood—the realization that "individuals achieve their humanity through culture" and that "the Church embraces all cultures," as Bishop William S. Skylstad of Yakima said (Bozeman, August 7, 1986)—brought about a thoroughgoing shift in goals over the last several decades. Rather than downplaying Indians' specialness, missionaries have tried to accommodate Indian cultures in significant ways.

Not all churchmen have agreed on accommodation as a tactic or goal. We have seen in the first volume of *American Indian Catholics* that the Diocese of San Diego has decided in recent years to end special Indian ministry within its boundaries. Some clergy think that any form of adaptation of the Christian gospel to Indian culture produces a "weak-kneed Christianity," and that "attempts at indigenization now . . . would be artificial and forced—perhaps another instance of do-gooding white paternalism" (Gualtieri 1980b: 51, 54; cf. Gualtieri 1984). Among the orders of priests and sisters interested in Native American ministry, however—Jesuits, Oblates, Sisters of the Blessed Sacrament, and others—there is growing consensus that accommodation must be made to Native culture. The questions are: how much and of what kind? (Starkloff, August 7, 1986).

NEW /TRATEGIE/

When Archbishop Rembert G. Weakland of Milwaukee was asked by urban Indian Catholics "if he accepted and respected the Native American religions," the bishop replied that he "believes we all worship the same God—that many aspects of this worship are similar and form a basis for our mutual respect—that we can learn from each other" (Siggenauk Center 1985). For five centuries the Catholic Church in the Americas condemned Indian religions and sought as a matter of policy to convert Native Americans from their aboriginal spiritual traditions and to make them loyal Catholics. E.g., insofar as they held power, the Catholic authorities did not allow Indians under their control to venerate images of their traditional deities or to conjure spirits for the purpose of harming enemies or healing the sick. As short-term strategies, Catholic missionaries tolerated certain aspects of indigenous religions deemed harmless, or they tried to transform those aspects into Christian habits laden with Christian meanings. Directing prayers to God— even while smoking tobacco in a pipe—for a bountiful hunt, harvest, or cure from illness was acceptable; it was useful to employ Native terminology for a vision quest to designate a retreat. Some customs, like a sweat lodge, could be understood as cultural expressions with some religious import, but not strictly a matter of worshipping pagan gods; then they might be permitted. Some cultural patterns, such as polygamy or divorce, were preached against, not because they were matters of worship, but because they contradicted rules of the Church regarding proper social behavior. Some areas of Native culture, e.g., languages, were regarded neutrally in some instances, particularly in the earliest years of missions, but even these aspects came under attack in boarding schools in the twentieth century.

Indians made various adjustments to the range of demands made upon them. Insofar as they became Catholics, they may have eschewed all aspects of aboriginal worship, or they may have persisted in some practices, sometimes in secret from the priests. Whatever degree of cultural habit they may have retained, many Catholic Indians by the time of Vatican II still regarded themselves as Indians and held some aspects of their Native culture in high regard, although that regard could often be mixed with embarrassment or even shame.

It was now the task of the workers in Catholic Indian ministry to decide which aspects of Native cultures, and Native religiousness bound up in those cultures, were to be accommodated or even encouraged in Native American Catholic life. In Asia and Africa, as well as in the Americas, indigenous peoples since Vatican II have experimented with ways to "de-Westernize" Catholicism (Crossette, January 20, 1990: A4). As an indigenous Catholic priest from South India has stated, "My main purpose is to understand Christ within my culture" (in ibid.). How were churchmen to accept and respect Native American cultural elements and still guide Indians to the culture of Catholicism? Should pastors accept the Indians' music, dance, and other rituals within the context of liturgy, perhaps even considering them as sacramentals? In teaching Indian children, might a catechist draw upon Indian myths for moral lessons? Should missionaries consider Indian ceremonials as analogues to Catholic sacraments, and if so, what is their relation to one another? If Indian Catholics are not to be condemned for participating in a Sun Dance or thanksgiving for the corn, is it because these are cultural, rather than religious, ceremonies? Should the Church be encouraging syncretism or participation in more than one religious tradition? Over the past generation the Church has approached these and related questions in various ways, eliciting a range of responses from Indian Catholics.

When Rev. Jacques Johnson, O.M.I., first arrived at the Kisemanito Centre in Alberta, he found it necessary to overcome his prejudices against the curses, ghosts, and bad medicines of Indian religion, and to regard it as an analogue to the religion of the ancient Hebrews: monotheistic and moralistic. He concluded that in Catholic ministry to American Indians, "What we are better able to recognize today is that Indian people never were 'Pagans', rather they were Old Testament people. . . . God, in his own way had called them and groomed them over the years to become a holy people" (Johnson 1982: 131).

Other Canadian missionaries came to face the fact of "the co-existence of two religious systems, one aboriginal, the other Christian, in the same individuals" with a Native American Catholic population (Goulet, Fall 1982: 1). Rather than denying this reality, Rev. Jean-Guy Goulet, O.M.I., called upon the Church to guide Indians to rediscover their ancestral spirituality and re-envision it in a contemporary context. "A new era of missionary activity *is possible* today," he wrote,

> one in which missionaries and aboriginal people are called to become equal partners in experiences of personal and communal growth. The Church is called upon to help aboriginal people rediscover the God of their ancestors, and to reinterpret their traditional religion, so that they be better able to face the new situations they are in today. (Goulet 1984: 138, emphasis his)

Father Paul Hernou, who succeeded Roger Vandersteene among the Cree of northern Alberta, became less interested in manipulating Indian spirituality than in joining its ritualism. "I really believe that Christ is inculturating or incarnating himself in the Native cultures," he declared (Hernou 1987: 238). In his admiration for Native spirituality he deemed himself a pipe carrier and conflated pipe ceremonialism with the eucharistic rites of the Church.

If we listen to the audiotapes of weekly sermons given by Jesuits over the radio for almost two decades ("Sioux for Christ" 1963–1980) in South Dakota, we encounter the notion that "Christ is the fulfillment of the old-time Indian religion." According to this viewpoint, the old-time Sioux were "naturally religious," "always seeking God," and they prayed, "just as we do today in the 'Our Father.'" When they sought the divine in their vision quests, "the old-time Indians were really seeking for Christ," and thus "Christ and His word are the fulfillment of the old-time Sioux religion." When the Sioux prayed for life, they were reaching out for the Christian deity, although they did not realize it then. Now we see that "Christ is the food for that life" which the Sioux sought, and "the providence of God is seen in the sacred buffalo pipe." Moreover, the priests claim that "the holy woman of the sacred buffalo calf pipe and the mother of Jesus" are interconnected spiritually. Hence, "our pride comes from our double heritage of being Christians and Sioux Indians," according to the sermons.

"Sioux for Christ" expressed the idea held by many Catholic missionaries in North America, that Indian religions have "some divine value but requiring judgment, purification, or fulfillment by the Christian gospel." According to this framework, Indian spirituality is "valid but incomplete, needing to be crowned by Christ" (Gualtieri 1980b: 54, 55). The notion that Christianity is the fulfillment of traditional Native American religion has led many Catholic missionaries to consider the similarities between Indian and Catholic myths and rituals. One sister taught her Indian kindergarten children by pairing Lakota legends and New Testament parables, finding in them common messages and images (Palm 1985). As Lakota girls readied themselves for confirmation, they were reminded of their tribal ritual of former days, "Preparing for Womanhood" (Palm n.d.). In the Northwest, where Father Patrick Twohy found Indian Catholics abandoning the Church because of its irrelevance to their culture, he created a catechism with normative Christian instruction, but with frequent references to Indian customs and situations. His hope was that Catholicism could be "home" to Indians set adrift by a century of dislocation (Twohy 1984).

Another priest, Father Ron Zeilinger, produced a series of books for Lakotas which depict Jesus as "the great dancer suspended from the Tree of Cross. He was a warrior pierced on behalf of the people—that we might live!" (Zeilinger 1984: n.p.). The message of these books is that Catholicism promotes life as did the old religion epitomized by the Sun Dance, only more completely. The trappings of these books—the eagle-feather motifs, the Lakota terminology—are intended to appeal to the Indians' cultural heritage, and the central theme—a life of sacrifice—is meant to make sense to traditional Lakotas as well as traditional Catholics. What was Jesus' message, according to these books? That all beings are relatives and should be treated as such. What did Jesus do? He died for us, so that we could live, just as the buffalo once did for the Lakotas. Jesus is our food, a "true 'relative' making life possible for all" (ibid.). His sacrificial act—"the way of the cross" (Zeilinger 1985)—fulfills the ideals of Lakota spiritual existence and serves as a model for Lakota behavior in the contemporary world.

In the 1980s Catholic priests and religious, particularly Jesuits among the Sioux, began to take part in Native ceremonies like the sweat lodge, in part to show their solidarity with the Indians, but also to gain an appreciation for traditional spirituality (see "Spirit in the Wind," 1988). Some of the clergy extolled the beauty of Native American ritualism in print (e.g., Steltenkamp 1982, Steinmetz 1984), suggesting to New Age audiences the richness of Indian practices available to them. Others became anthropologists and wrote scholarly treatises about Indian ceremonialism (e.g., Bucko 1992). Indeed, the Jesuits have become the envy of anthropologists, because the priests have entrée into Indian rituals by virtue of their status as religious practitioners (Thiel, July 9, 1991). Taking sweats with Native Americans has become "the rage" (Steltenkamp, August 9, 1992) among Catholic personnel. Priests may feel uncomfortable in reconciling their role as Catholic leaders with their engagement in the liturgy of another religious tradition; however, their Indian hosts tell them to pray as Catholics, allowing each participant to worship God in his or her own manner. Priests have found themselves justifying the sweats, saying that they constitute an Indian means of worship, culturally suited to them (Hottinger, June 13, 1988). A Franciscan priest refers to sweats and pipe ceremonies as "sacramentals, means of touching the sacred," and he calls upon the Church to recognize them as such. The Church has always incorporated the rites of various ethnic groups in the sacramental practices of Catholicism, he asserts, regarding them as cultural gifts to the people of God. That is what makes the Church "catholic" (Cavagnaro, August 3, 1988). Some priests have become so enamored of sweats that they neglect other priestly roles. One Jesuit reports that when he visits an Ojibway community in Canada, the local chief asks him to say mass while the resident Jesuit is off at the sweats. "He likes the sweats, but we want mass" (in Steltenkamp, August 8, 1992), the chief explains.

Some Indian communities have rankled at priestly attempts to embrace their traditional culture at the expense of preaching the gospel and educating Indian youth. Canadian Crees often rejected the liturgical experimentation of Father Vandersteene. Having accepted the long-standing colonial program of deculturation, they did not wish to revive "traditional" religion in their Christian praxis. They preferred to be accepted as Canadian religionists, embraced by Whites, rather than ghettoized by the practice of drumming and smoking the pipe (see Waugh 1996: 292–306).

A Catholic Indian Congress in South Dakota in 1985 called upon the clerical orders to focus attention on schooling and catechesis: "The Catholic missionaries of the past have done what was expected of them by bringing the word of God . . . thru construction of schools, . . . discipline, and the teaching of the Catholic doctrine." The resolution concluded by chiding the pastors of the present day: "The follow up and continuation have been totally ignored and forgotten by this newer generation of Catholic missionaries" (DCRAA 1985). Indian traditionalists, on the other hand, have welcomed the liberalized attitude on the part of the Church, saying that if the changes of recent decades are "real and lasting, . . . never again will the priests tell Indians that the drum belongs to the Devil . . ." (Johnson, Midwinter 1988: 17). At the same time, however, traditionalists are wary that in the spirit of accommodation *they* will have to make the compromises. One Mohawk longhouse chief reminds the Church that the Iroquois have their own creation story, apart from the one found in Genesis. "We don't come from Adam and Eve, we come from the Skyworld Woman. To me, that part is not something to be reconciled" (in ibid., 17). Some Indians bridle at the notion that their traditional religious forms were no more than precursors and prefigurings of Catholic ceremonialism.

Within Catholic circles there are many who are at variance with Vatican II accommodationism. Some veteran missionaries see the program of inculturation as giving up on their evangelical vocation, and they say that it allows Indians to fall away from Catholicism. "They're going back to their native religion," one snorts. "Whatever that is" (Reilly, February 1979: 27). One Jesuit has commented that "TV does more to destroy story telling and their culture than any priest's condemnation of various practices" (JINNAM, February 23, 1984); another Jesuit blames the "new-aging" of Indian Catholics on Catholic sisters and other feminists who use Indian "odds and ends" for their own spirituality, out of disaffection with the "male, hierarchical, oppressive Church." In turn, they pass these practices to the Indians they instruct in schools.

Rev. Francis Paul Prucha, S.J., a scholar with considerable knowledge regarding Native American history, calls the adaptation of Christianity to Indian culture "hokum" (Prucha, July 21, 1986). The Jesuit historian argues that his fellow priests should be concerned with helping Indians survive in the modern world, rather than dragging them back to their ancestral past. He sees Indian Catholics with very little grounding in their tribal culture being encouraged by pastors, who should know better, to wear feathers and beads at mass, in a futile attempt to concoct an "Indianized Christianity." In his view, it is valid for peoples around the world to make Christianity culturally their own, but not to dredge up customs long abandoned, and in so doing to fabricate something self-consciously synthetic and ersatz. He asks his fellow Jesuits if they still believe that Christianity offers a uniquely important religious dimension to all peoples. Before Vatican II missionaries had no trouble with such a question; indeed, they answered it with an assurance that may have seemed cocksure to some observers. Today, however, missionaries have lost their sense of mission, their motive, their direction, and when Jesuits in Native American ministry gather to discuss their theology and strategy, their principles appear to be incoherent. Prucha acknowledges that today's Indian pastors surpass their predecessors in preparation, sensitivity, and stability of character. Indeed, he remarks that many priests assigned to Indian missions in the past were the "dregs of the order, those who couldn't make it elsewhere" (ibid., a charge echoed by Native Catholic clergy such as P. Michael Galvan, August 5, 1992), and the Indians knew and resented it. Such is no longer true, but he wishes that the Indian pastorate of the present had more starch in its Roman collar.

Father Prucha's disagreement with his liberal missionary colleagues is mild compared to sentiments expressed by some conservative elements within the Church. There are still Catholic personnel who refer to Native American ritualism as "devil-worship" (Cole, March 23, 1987) and are opposed to any sort of dialogue between Native American and Catholic forms of spirituality. Some conservative churchmen wonder why Indians today should be granted any spiritual autonomy when their cultures are in such disarray, with aimlessness and drunkenness abounding (in Gualtieri 1980b: 50). *The Wanderer*, a Catholic journal published in St. Paul, Minnesota, criticized the Native American liturgy which greeted Pope John Paul II in Phoenix in 1987:

> Featuring invocations to "Mother Earth," some sort of medicine man waving a feather in the Pontiff's face and the expressed exaltation of pre-Christian aboriginal culture, the meeting seems not to have been honestly evaluated anywhere in the Catholic press. (In *Bureau of Catholic Indian Missions Newsletter*, 7, no. 19, November–December 1987: 1)

Msgr. Paul A. Lenz of the BCIM calls this criticism "sad . . . sad . . . sad . . . perhaps even racist" (ibid.). He wants "to let Native Americans know that the Catholic Church cares about them" (Lenz, November 19, 1993), and so he travels to every corner of Catholic Indian America, encouraging Indian Catholics to share their cultural gifts within the setting of the Church. "Since Vatican Council II," he writes, "the Catholic missionary approach with Native American tribes has experienced both reevaluation and revitalization in light of renewed statement of church teaching and heightened Native American self-expression" (Lenz 1979a: 19); he approves of the liberalization which has occurred.

In the widely circulated BCIM *Newsletter*, Msgr. Lenz recounts some of his travels, e.g., a trip to the Yakima Indian Reservation in

1989 (ibid., 8, no. 4, May 1989: 1), where he heard Bishop Donald E. Pelotte deliver a "very meaningful homily" and a group of Lummi Indians sing "beautiful hymns during and after the Mass," and where he enjoyed a "superb dinner, really a feast." "I look forward to the fry bread on such visits," he writes, "and it was plentiful and delicious." The Indians gave him a gift of moccasins, which he wore to their pow-wow and thus "brought joy" to his hosts, whose Kateri League, he said, was active and "moving ahead for the Church." In his many contacts with Indian Catholics he witnesses what he calls normative, basic Catholic liturgy. There may be local variations—especially in the Southwest, a buffalo dance or an eagle dance—but more typical is the Catholic devotionalism of the St. Joseph and St. Mary Societies of the Sioux.

"There are so many fires I've had to put out" over Catholic Indian inculturation, the monsignor reports (Lenz, November 19, 1993). Some Indians complain that there is too much or too little Native content to Catholic liturgies, or that liturgies reflect one tribal group over another. For instance, at the 1976 Eucharistic Congress some Catholic Indians from the Southwest resented the attention paid to Iroquois, Ojibway, and Sioux cultural displays. He still receives angry letters from Catholics who think that the accommodation to Indian culture has gone too far, and even some members of the Catholic hierarchy think that too much attention is paid to one ethnic group, Native Americans, at the expense of other Catholic peoples in the United States. Lenz distributes funds (several million dollars annually, says Lenz, Potsdam, August 5, 1995) to dioceses with special Indian ministries and Catholic schools with Indian pupils, and he bankrolls the Tekakwitha Conference, which fosters Native American liturgies. "If it weren't for the director of the Bureau," he says, "the Tekakwitha Conference would never have developed" as it has in promoting Indian Catholic inculturation. For him, the BCIM is "the visible sign of a caring Church." For many Catholic Indians, the monsignor is the visible sign—the face—of the BCIM. His visage graces every issue of the BCIM *Newsletter,* and with a circulation of twenty thousand, he says, "wherever I go, people know me" (Lenz, November 19, 1993).

Each issue of the BCIM *Newsletter* carries Father Zuern's column, "Bread and Freedom . . . Justice and Faith," with its informed concern for Native American rights. In matters of social justice Father Lenz's Bureau tries to stand behind various Indian causes as much as it stands for an inculturated Indian Catholicism. A Carmelite brother with a doctorate in anthropology comments in this regard: "I think Native people should be very skeptical when the priest puts beads on his vestments. Window trappings like this do not serve the cause of liberation. But when the church supports initiatives of Native people, . . . then Native people should not turn away from a powerful ally" (in Johnson, Midwinter 1988: 16).

CARL F. STARKLOFF, S.J.

No emissary of the Church has thought more deeply and written more widely and intelligently about the future shape of American Indian Catholicism than the Jesuit priest, Carl F. Starkloff. Father Starkloff served for many years at St. Stephen's Mission in Wyoming among the Arapaho and Shoshone Indians, with a stint in the chaplaincy to Indian students at Haskell Indian Junior College in Lawrence, Kansas. Under the inspiration of the Second Vatican Council, and through the goading of Vine Deloria, Jr.'s "prophetic" (Starkloff, October 12, 1990) critique of "Missionaries in the Cultural Vacuum," he began in the early 1970s to reconsider the mission of the Church (and his own calling) to American Indians.

He came to the conclusion that there is a common ground of human experience in Indian and Catholic religions; he sought to proclaim that commonality, both to Catholics and Indians, and to overcome their suspicions about one another. Working from the principle that Jesus came to fulfill rather than destroy, Starkloff could see "no reason why such rites as the Sun Dance, Pipe Covering, and Sweat Lodge, as practiced by the Arapaho, should not be considered as possible 'para-liturgy,' and even as cultural settings for Christian worship for Indians who so choose" (Starkloff 1971: 338).

The Jesuit did not shrink from the idea that Christianity can improve tribal ethics through the paradigm of Jesus' selfless love; nevertheless, he sought to learn as well as teach. He saw a deep spirituality in Indians' notions of God, and in their "belief in man's creaturehood, the practice of prayer and sacrifice, ethical consciousness, a belief in life after death, and elaborate sacred ritual" (Starkloff 1974: 124). "If . . . we can develop a Christianity grounded in Indian culture or encourage a dialogue between the two," he wrote, "we may still be able to gain from the best of two ancient worlds" (20).

In ministering to Native Americans, Father Starkloff held back from insisting what "essentials" (Starkloff 1975: 8) Indians had to adopt in order to be called Christians. He encouraged missionaries to think carefully about their own cultural baggage before confusing it with the core of Christian faith: "What is essential is that the Christian truly preach Jesus Christ and not his own culture and his own biases" (13). Simultaneously, he exhorted evangelists to tread with a gentle humility when seeking to transform Indian cultures which entwine Indian religion, so as not to destroy the fabric of Indian existence. Starkloff warned against Christianity's continuing a "cultural invasion" among Native Americans, and he called his Church to the highest missiological ideals of modern times: "In Vatican Council II the Church for the first time since the first century began to realize its nature as a universal Church . . . open to *all* peoples and cultures and to cease being merely a *European* Church" (Starkloff 1982: n.p., emphases his).

Between 1978 and 1986 he was involved extensively with the reformulation of the Tekakwitha Conference, as it became a vehicle for Catholic Indian inculturation, and since 1981 he has taught missiology at Regis College in the Toronto School of Theology. One of his main tasks in Toronto has been to assist the Jesuits of Canada to establish Native Catholic leadership "for a renewed Church" (Starkloff 1989: 6). He has conducted much of this work at the Anishinabe Spiritual Centre, where he has led dialogues with Anishinabe Catholics for many years (see volume 2 of *American Indian Catholics*). For several years in the 1990s he has been helping fellow Jesuits in the state of Washington to develop innovative Indian ministries.

Father Starkloff describes himself as a theologian. When an Ojibway asks him what that means, he says that he is committed to interpreting the authoritative Christian tradition for his times. He characterizes himself as a "liberal" within the Church, his license to teach theology chronically endangered by Vatican oaths of fidelity and orthodoxy. He is sometimes "angry at the hierarchy of the Church" (Starkloff, October 12, 1990), but his vocation is firm to provide Indians a home within the Catholic tradition.

"The people among whom I live and work have suffered religious oppression," he writes, "and for them especially this means social oppression—in a country that prides itself on being a haven for the seeker of religious freedom" (Starkloff 1978: 802). He has asked himself how a Catholic ministry can help Indians today when historically the Church has hurt Indians while trying to convert them. Indians are beaten down, he says, partially by us churchmen (he includes himself in the depiction). The Natives do not trust us enough, he says, to enter dialogue with us; their young are alienated from their culture and community; alcoholism is a force in every home; spiritual apathy is rampant; there is virtually no reservation economic life. Is there anything missionaries can do for them? "What does the missionary in the field tell the bishops about 'inculturation' and structural reform when the tribal culture lies moribund in a growing majority of the young people, and the language promises to die on the tongues of the present generation of elders?" (ibid.). One Arapaho man spoke of his people to the priest: "They've been taught too well by now, Father, that Indian ways are finished" (in ibid., 803).

Instead of "brooding" about the disintegration of Native American cultures, Starkloff asks himself what "'solidarity with the oppressed'" can really mean, beyond a "mealymouthed phrase" (804). He suggests that one must experience powerlessness before gaining power, and he reflects upon the everpresence of death on the Wind River Reservation. The Arapahos continue to express their aboriginal culture in responding ritually to death. They give away gifts, paint their faces, and try to move forward together toward life's continuance. In observing their funeral rites, Starkloff finds that they possess, on their own without his help, the ability to heal themselves in the face of death. Rather than mourning for their supposedly dying culture, he aims to achieve solidarity with the healing power they still exhibit. "I believe that I function as a priest much better, in many cases, when I sit and listen to an elder encourage his people, than when I try to preach to them" (806). And rather than trying to reform their structure, he aims for solidarity with them as persons—wounded, for certain, but still vital.

Native Americans as a group may be poor, unemployed, sick in body and spirit. Too few possess educational and technical skills. Too many abuse themselves with alcohol and attempt suicide. These burdens, Starkloff declares (Starkloff, May 1979), do not constitute reasons to get Indians to be like us. They still possess the wherewithal to ameliorate their own suffering; a Catholic ministry ought to be in solidarity with them through their sufferings and their own solutions. Appreciation for their culture makes for better catechesis than providing a preestablished message for them to take in. He recommends to those in the Indian pastorate to hold off on delivering sermons until hearing what the Native Americans have to say about life. Listen to their myths; observe their rituals; meet them where their wisdom is, as well as their affliction. He finds much in common between Indian and Christian religious forms. Indians have their Native emphases on humility and pitifulness in the face of the divine. They believe that suffering is a path toward holiness, and so they fast and endure pains with patience and perseverance. They also express their spirituality through prayers of thanksgiving and adoration as well as petition. They have high expectations regarding the holiness of religious leaders, priests will have to improve, to meet their standards.

Starkloff's ideal Church ministry needs to pay attention to Native religiousness in order to help Indian peoples create their own local communities of faith, connected to the Catholic Church but possessed of cultural autonomy. The first step toward effective catechesis, then, is empathetic, open-minded dialogue—which is arduous labor. The Jesuit contends: "That one is doing catechetics and preaching in an environment of communication, common meaning, and community can never be simply assumed. In the dialogue with another culture," he states, "one must begin by assuming that such an environment of community can only be the product of hard work and educated sensitivity" (Starkloff 1979: 140). Dialogue will mean challenging as well as affirming one another, but challenges and affirmations must both rest upon comprehension. Starkloff's first goal is to understand Native Americans in order to communicate with them. He does not want the "good news" of Christianity to be construed as a prefabricated ideology of the Western Church (Starkloff 1981).

Father Starkloff began to participate in Arapaho sweats in the 1970s and he tried to understand the theological import of Arapahos' prayers in their Native tongue, in order to become a careful listener to their values and hopes. He wanted to join the Arapaho Sun Dance, but he "made the mistake" (Starkloff, October 14, 1990) of asking permission of the local bishop, who refused him. At the same time he entered into a long-standing missiological dialogue with Vine Deloria, Jr., who became a trusted colleague. Father Starkloff has become a confidant to many Anishinabe people during his recent years in Canada. He shares their sweats and their community concerns. They speak candidly with him about matters of ultimate concern—their myths, their visions, their medicines—seeing in him a religious man who responds genuinely to their concerns (Anishinabe Spiritual Centre, October 12–14, 1990). The Jesuit feels more at home with these Indians than with white priests who justify the policies by which the United States dispossessed Native Americans, or maybe worse, those who romanticize Native American spirituality in the context of New Age Creation theology. Having experienced the brutal heat and transporting intensity of prayer in the sweats—e.g., during a ritual of solidarity for the Indians during the standoff between Mohawks and Canadian military at Oka in 1990—he regards them as ordeals with complex Native meanings, not to be appropriated by Whites.

Starkloff acclaims the power of Indian spirituality to address the hurts of contemporary Indian life; however, his "theologico-pastoral" (Starkloff 1989: 3) role is to help Native American Catholics to shape an Indian Catholicism which is more potent for them than anything from the past. He does not call upon Indians to turn back to their aboriginal religion any more than he wishes to embrace the Catholicism of times past. He wishes them to create "religious renewal" (Starkloff 1985a) which will revitalize their existence in palpable ways. Looking at the history of revitalization movements in American Indian history—the Longhouse religion of the Iroquois, various prophet dances, the peyotism of the Native American Church—he sees no reason that American Indian Catholicism cannot serve uplifting and unifying purposes for some Native Americans, as long as Indian Catholics achieve "self-support, self-government, [and] self-propagation" (Starkloff 1985b: 71) in their local churches.

A Native Church will require Native leadership. It is time, Starkloff asserts, after five centuries of mission in North America, to turn the Church among American Indians into the *subject,* rather than the *object* of mission. Indian Catholics cannot become the people of God truly "until ministry becomes 'ministry-by' native people, rather than 'ministry-to-and-for,' in the top-heavy form imposed by the Church for so many centuries" (Starkloff 1989: 7). "My point is this," he writes:

> Jesus Christ invites the native peoples of this continent, even as he calls Christians everywhere, to be aware that they share in the gospel mission of the Church. He invites them, as he did those persons of his own time and culture, to assume their commission according to their incarnate historical reality. Accordingly, then, the 'sending Church,' at work among aboriginal people, has the duty to spare no effort to facilitate native ministry as a truly indigenous reality. (3)

He finds in Indian communities four types of extant traditional ministries: those which heal and sustain life; those which counsel and express values through words; those which conduct rites of passage; and those which seek to tap the power of nature for community use. Catholic missionaries have often claimed that such Native ministries were rendered obsolete by Christianity; Starkloff finds such claims incorrect. Hence, in Native communities there are leaders who are already serving their people.

Some of these leaders are Catholics who wish to combine their Indian and Christian traditions into a single, effective ministry which can gain Church recognition. Father Starkloff writes that the Church must move beyond its historical patterns in order to establish authentic local leadership. In the past the Church has relied upon Native catechists, female religious, and occasional priests; however, "in nearly every case, in order to function in Catholic ministry, the aboriginal person has had to be 'extracted' from his or her 'incarnational' situation and transformed into a minister according to European models" (37). For Starkloff, the inculturation of Christianity in Native American communities means locating the Church in the bodies of Catholic Indians.

Before Vatican II Catholic missionaries may have tolerated some aspects of Indian religious culture; however, they regarded that culture as superstitious or dangerous paganism. Inculturation was simply not a goal of the Church among American Indians, according to Father Starkloff. Even among theologians, only the rarest of Catholic exponents considered primitive religions to have anything of worth which might "enhance the Church" (41). And yet, Starkloff has found in his associations with Native Americans a spirituality which he thinks ought to be yoked to Catholic worship to create a revitalizing Native American Catholicism. He is even willing to promote "syncretisms" (Starkloff 1991: 7) between Native and Catholic spirituality, in order to help Indian Catholics fashion a Catholicism authentic to them.

At the Anishinabe Spiritual Centre Father Starkloff has heard Ojibways speak of the need to maintain their cultural and religious traditions with "a solid wall standing between" (ibid., 1) Euroamerican and Indian ways. An elder exhorted his people to permit no interference between Christian and traditional forms of religion. Let them stand, separated as it were, by a fence which would make the two traditions good neighbors to one another. Starkloff understands the motivation for such a stratagem, especially in light of the long history of Church condemnation of Indian religion.

In 1983 Starkloff was at the Northern Arapaho Sun Dance, when a ceremonial leader and practicing Roman Catholic said to him that he thought that the Whites' and Indians' religions would flow together one day like the Wind River and the Little Wind River, which become a single confluence in Wyoming. Following this metaphor through the writings of liberation theologian Leonardo Boff, Starkloff has come to the conclusion that "Christianity must be syncretic if it is to be an incarnate faith" (Starkloff 1989: 14). The Church's future depends, he states, upon its ability to accommodate, mix with, agree to, translate, adapt, and adopt indigenous religious traditions. Starkloff looks forward to a day in which Indians will no longer maintain "two religions"—a Native one for "earthly well-being" and a Christian one for entry into the afterlife, which is what Indians sometimes say they do. The Jesuit writes that "this distinction causes me shame and chagrin," and he adds, "Christianity must prove itself in the arena of human suffering and oppression; that alone is the solution" (Starkloff 1991: 12).

In order to become relevant to Indians' lives, Christianity must speak the language of Indian communities. Native speakers have said to Starkloff, "Our language *is* our theology" (Starkloff 1989: 51). He tells how Arapaho Catholics used to refer to God in their own language as "the White Man Above" (Starkloff, October 12, 1990). In effect, they were praying to someone else's deity, the "white invader who held the power" (Starkloff 1989: 50). Even in their prayers they felt alienated from the religious tradition to which they had been converted. Finally in the 1970s an Arapaho woman complained that the term for God was "too white" (Starkloff, October 12, 1990), and she got the medicine men to change the name to an older Arapaho usage for God, "Old Man Above," "the-one-over-all" (Starkloff 1989: 51). This was their way to inculturate Christianity.

In the same way, Indians need to name and perform their traditional rituals as Catholics. Starkloff has participated in Native rituals for years, and he has found in them the spirit and the ethics of Catholic Christianity. He sees no reason for Indian Catholic ministry to eschew sweetgrass and sage blessings, peyote services, sweat lodges, vision quests, rites of passage, child-namings, smudgings, green corn and sun dances, and the like. Even non-Indians can enrich their spirituality by participating in such practices, under the leadership of Native American Catholics. The Jesuit suggests that non-Indian Catholics might grow in their own religious faith by observing some of the values exhibited in Native communities, e.g., the attention paid to ancestors and the spirits of the dead in general. Starkloff recalls that the Wyoming Arapaho Catholics receive the Eucharist in their cemetery every Memorial Day, as they bless and clean their family plots, and he recommends similar acts of piety among other Catholic ethnicities.

Starkloff is not suggesting that every type of syncretism is proper. He does not wish to engage in "extravagant romantic encomiums to native tradition," in which "the critical dynamic is absent." For him, syncretism should not be a "yielding to an overblown and fulsome—often condescending—praise of the natural beauty of native practices, and of natives as instinctive altruists" (Starkloff 1991: 24). This may assuage liberal Catholic guilt but it is unrealistic. He says that churchmen need to practice "discernment of spirits" in evaluating Native American rituals for use by Catholics. He acknowledges that sorcery exists among American Indians, and the Church cannot incorporate the spirits of such behavior into its ministry. "No malevolent power can harm one who trusts in the sovereign Will and tries to live out the universal values" (Starkloff 1989: 59), he writes; nonetheless, the Church must move carefully in assimilating the religious expressions of American Indians, "reinterpreting and recasting them" (14) into the sacramentalism of Catholic life.

For the past twenty years and more, Starkloff has engaged in dialogue with American Indians, both Christians and traditionalists. Some Indians have declined his invitations to converse; others have addressed him bluntly to make up his mind (and the mind of the Church) whether Indian ways are acceptable or not. The Jesuit has shown a remarkable ability to elicit candor and deflect anger without sacrificing his principles (Starkloff 1993). His aim has been to achieve rapprochement between Indian and Catholic religious traditions, with the hope that "perhaps in due time a unified world view might emerge freely and spontaneously, following collaborative reflection" (Starkloff 1991: 12). He sees in Our Lady of Guadalupe a syncretism which has fulfilled the spiritual senses of many millions of Mexicans over several centuries—"whether she has in effect displaced an earlier spirit, or is simply a new embodiment, is largely a matter of terminology" (14)—and he would like to see similar flowerings in the United States and Canada.

When he reads through the Relations of the seventeenth-century Jesuits of New France, he is reminded that representatives of the Church once allowed and even encouraged certain forms of syncretism, for instance, sweat lodge ceremonies as prayers, and feasts of the dead as All-Souls' Day pilgrimages. Today he sees similar moves in the Church—drums and sweetgrass at mass, for example, —and he applauds them; however, they are merely steps toward a greater end. If they are but an accommodationist missionary ploy to get Indians back into the churches—and Indians are already suspicious of such techniques—they will serve no effective purpose. If, on the other hand, they lead toward an Indian Catholic initiative which addresses contemporary Native American needs, then the meeting of the two spiritual rivers will have the potential to fertilize the future.

OTHER EXPONENT/ OF INCULTURATION

In Canada the Oblate priest, Achiel Peelman, has sought aims similar to those of Father Starkloff. For more than two decades he has been involved in the Canadian Summer Institutes for the promotion of American Indian leadership in the Church, as well as the Tekakwitha Conference in the United States, and he has been associated with *Kerygma* (1967–1993, now called *Mission: Journal of Mission Studies*) at St. Paul University in Ontario, a magazine devoted thoughtfully to the question of inculturation in Native American Catholicism. In his book *Christ Is a Native American,* Peelman attempts to imagine "the Amerindian vision of Christ" as a way to help develop "local theology" (Peelman 1995: 16) among Indian Catholics.

Before a large audience of Native Americans in 1984 at the Shrine of the Canadian Martyrs in Ontario, Pope John Paul II declared:

> Thus the one faith is expressed in different ways. There can be no question of adulterating the word of God or of emptying the Cross of its power, but rather of Christ animating the very centre of all cultures. Thus, not only is Christianity relevant to the Indian peoples, but *Christ, in the members of his Body, is himself Indian.* (In ibid., 13, emphasis his)

In his book Father Peelman asks what we might mean to say that Christ is an American Indian: "There can be no Amerindian church without an Amerindian Christ. But who is this Indian Christ Pope John Paul II referred to . . . ?" (ibid.).

Like Father Starkloff, Peelman believes that "inculturation is the key concept for a truly theological interpretation of the encounter between Christ and the Amerindian cultures" (16), and he employs "interreligious dialogue" in order to flesh out Christ's incarnation among Catholic Indians. He notes, however, that this dialogue is not only a matter of persons from different religious traditions communicating with one another. For Indians such a dialogue is internal, a matter of "a personal experience of integration" (17). That is, Indians tend to syncretize Native and Christian forms of religiousness in their own lives. That is where the dialogue takes place for them; that is where the two rivers of faith blend.

In their encounter with Christianity, Peelman argues, Indians have continued to surprise missionaries by conducting ceremonies in which they combine Native and Catholic elements. "The religious situation of many Amerindians," Peelman states, "can best be described as religious dimorphism: the simultaneous or successive belonging to two religious systems" (158). Father Peelman asks, "How can one justify this simultaneous belonging to two religious systems which have practised mutual exclusion in the course of history?" (80). Native Americans have not given up their ancestral spirituality, and he looks to it to discover "the hidden face of the Amerindian Christ" (96). In discussing the similarities between Indian ceremonial pipes on the one hand and Christ's mediatory role on the other, Peelman gains insights into the meaning of the Eucharist. He suggests that the Church examine the pipe in order to learn more about "the spiritual powers which live in the Indians' sacred universe" (148), and he exhorts both Indians and churchmen to "abandon their traditional parochialism" (149) in order to share their religious profundities. We need to turn to the dialogue between those Indians who are trying to integrate Christian and Native religions, and to those Christian ministers who are "truly moved by Amerindian spirituality" (90), in order to uncover Christ's Indian identity. This enterprise of christological inculturation must reverse the missionizing process, in which the Christian God was presented to Indians as someone who demanded that they change their ways of life. God must have seemed like an oppressor to them, Peelman suggests, or at least the God of the oppressors, and he wonders "how can the 'God of the oppressors' become a liberating God for them" (86). Peelman thinks that missionaries have placed themselves too often as arbiters of the gospel message. They have insisted that Indians respond to the Good News of Christ in prepackaged ways, not allowing for Native cultural needs.

This is where inculturation becomes key for Peelman. "Its prefix, 'in,' reminds us of the demands of the incarnation of God in the person of Jesus," he writes. "Its root, 'culture,' asks us to take into account the richness and variety of human culture" (91). He continues:

> *Inculturation, in fact, is something that happens between the gospel itself (the seed) and the receiving culture (the soil).* The role of the sower, the missionary church, remains very important, but is secondary with respect to the people who receive the gospel. . . . Jesus, the Christ, is himself the main actor in the inculturation process, because he is the Word

proclaimed by the church and received by peoples. He is the way, the truth and the light. (92, emphases his)

Because Jesus made Himself a cultural being, a Jewish person, He can do the same in every other culture on earth. He proclaims Himself to people of all cultures, who must integrate themselves to Him. The missionary sows the seed (Jesus), but is not the seed himself. Peelman says that the Church must have *"the capacity and the courage to welcome responses to the gospel which, to the missionary who has sown its seed in a foreign soil, are creative, unique, original and properly unheard of"* (92, emphasis his). Christian ministers must accept the fact that there will be cultural "responses of faith which often exceed our expectations and predictions" (92). So, for example, if Indians find themselves akin to the dispossessed Canaanites of the Old Testament, rather than Israel's Chosen People, we must understand the insight in such a recognition, because it arises from the reality of Indians' historical situation.

Father Peelman has engaged in sweats, vision quests, and dialogues with Native Americans, and he describes himself as a *"participant observer"* (99, emphasis his) of Indian religious realities. In his conversations with Indian Catholics throughout Canada he has found the process of inculturation already taking place for them, internally. They have joined Christian and Native ritualism, and they have begun to think of Christ in Native terms. Montagnais Indians have said to him, "For us, Christ is Indian. He speaks and thinks in Montagnais when we address him in our own language" (100). Urban Indians in Winnipeg have identified Christ with their daily struggles, revealing Himself "in the brokenness and in the suffering of all the native people who are lost between two worlds" (107). A medicine man told Peelman that "Jesus would have been a good Indian! He prayed and fasted" (109).

"The Amerindians are a wounded people" (163), the Oblate states. Hence, Christ appears to them as a healer. Indians have always combined medicine and religion, and in Jesus' ministry they correctly perceive his own healing role. Medicine men in tribal communities today often call upon Christ as well as other medicines to help their compatriots with their ills, hurts, societal dislocations, and feelings of sinfulness. They see Christ as a powerful, but pained person, like themselves, a "wounded healer" (173). Thus, a Native artist depicts Jesus as a persecuted, suffering Indian, with braids, eagle feather, and sacred herbs. "Natives can identify with the sufferings of Jesus," Peelman declares, and the artist "wants to show that native spirituality and Christianity are not that far apart. His art is a form of reconciliation between the two religions" (177). It is that form of reconciliation that Peelman wishes to engender.

Is Christ a shaman? Does He have a place in the sweat lodges, the medicine wheels, and the spiritual therapies of Native Americans? Might Christ's healing powers complement the local medicines and also be acceptable to the institutional Church? Father Peelman does not have definitive answers to these questions, but he wants Indian Catholics to pursue them. It will take some doing, he says, to get Indians to think of Christ as someone who is beneficial for them on their own terms. A Native American woman has said to the Oblate: "The missionaries never told us that God was good for us. The only thing I remember from my religious education is fear and hell" (in ibid., 175). Only when she began attending Alcoholics Anonymous meetings did she come to understand that the Christian gospel reveals a God of reconciliation as well as judgment. Peelman wants Native Americans to begin thinking of Christ as a liberator as well as a healer—in political, as well as personal and social matters—and he wants that liberator to take the appearance of a Native American.

Missiological theorists in North America like the Jesuit Starkloff and the Oblate Peelman have urged for an active implementation of the inculturative process. Higher-ups in the Church hierarchy are more cautious in their public statements. Francis Cardinal Arinze, an Ibo from Nigeria who is president of the Vatican's Council for Interreligious Dialogue, addressed the Tekakwitha Conference annual gathering in Fargo, North Dakota, in 1989 on the topic of "an authentic response to the call of Christ in His Church" (Fargo, August 3, 1989; see *Tekakwitha Conference Newsletter,* 8, no. 5, November 1989: 1–8). Although his homily called for Catholic dialogue with traditional religions and he had kind words for tribal peoples' spirituality, he delivered stern warnings against "romanticizing" and "canonizing" Native American culture in all its elements. He mentioned "negative elements" which form a part of traditional religion and culture and he said that "inhumane and un-Christian" aspects pervade all cultures. "The point is," he argued, "that Christians cannot close their eyes to whatever is incompatible with the life and teachings of our Lord and Savior Jesus Christ." Indigenous cultures may contain in them much that is beneficial; however, the Church must scrutinize and judge all cultures, working to expunge those features that fall short of Catholic standards. Cardinal Arinze said in his homily that God made us many in our many cultures, but He made us one in His image and likeness. We should aim toward the oneness of our being.

Cardinal Arinze is reported to have said once that there are two kinds of traditional peoples: those who have converted to Christianity and those who will. At the Tekakwitha Conference he received the applause of an enthusiastic audience who heard him invoke the terminology of inculturation. With a smile he received the blessings of eagle feathers and sage from the Ojibway priest, John Hascall (Fargo, August 3, 1989). The following year in the Vatican at a conference on culture and worship, however, the Cardinal warned against those Catholics who are "immoderate in their desire to promote cultural awareness in the liturgy. They are angry. They rush. They are not sensitive enough to the need for unity in the Church. They oversimplify issues" (*Tekakwitha Conference Newsletter,* 9, no. 4, December 1990: 2), and thus produce polarization in the Church. "Some people overstress the importance of inculturation in the liturgy. They speak and act as if they no longer realize that revelation transcends the cultures in which it finds expression." And finally, "The cultural heritage of a people does not have an absolute character" (3).

Pope John Paul II has modulated his support for inculturation with an insistence on dogmatic and liturgical propriety. In various settings in the Americas, in Asia, and in Africa, the pontiff has enthused over the "rich ethnic panorama" (in Dionne, July 5, 1986) represented by tribal peoples in Christendom. He has spoken in favor of indigenous peoples' rights to their lands and he has praised the locals' traditional values, "which modern society is in danger of losing" (in Suro, November 23, 1986). In Canada in 1984 and 1987 his central message to Native Americans was that "Catholicism can be synthesized with native traditions" (Martin, September 16, 1984). In both the United States in 1987 as well as in Canada, he received the ceremonial burning of sweetgrass and accepted eagle feathers as gifts, gestures much appreciated by the Indians. The pope told North American Indians that their heritage constitutes a gift to the Church, and as we have already quoted above, his utterance regarding an Indian Christ has been "a Magna Charta" (in McDonnell, July 1987: 22) for Indian Catholics eager to make Catholicism fit their cultural patterns.

In effect, the pope has seemed to embrace inculturation as the new stance of the Church. Some Indians have asked, however, if the pope's statements constitute "a dramatic shift in a centuries-old policy," or "merely the selling of the same product in a different package" (Johnson, Midwinter 1988: 14). One scholar has called the pope's combining of inculturation and evangelization a "new evangelization" (Grim 1991a: 1) program, and there is a question where this agenda will lead:

> Will the new evangelization be accepting of revered Native religious beliefs and practices such as: the ancient healing ministries of the shamans, the world renewal rituals, the complex oral traditions, and the values of Native cosmologies? If the new evangelization within Catholicism does not adequately address complex cultural and religious contexts, such as cosmology, can it be said that Catholicism is returning to the earlier period of initial dominating encounter with Native American traditions? Will Catholicism retreat from contemporary efforts to engage in authentic interreligious dialogue? (Ibid., 2–3)

"These new Christians," the pope said of Indian converts to Catholicism, "knew by instinct that the Gospel, far from destroying their traditional values and customs, had the power to purify and uplift the cultural heritage which they had received" (in Martin, September 16, 1984). In so saying the pope has emphasized the spiritualizing effect of Christianity upon Native culture, an attitude in keeping with the evangelizing past. In his 1990 encyclical, *Redemptoris Missio,* the pope has asserted forcefully the need of all peoples to become familiar with Christ, and he has criticized the "religious relativism" (in Simons, January 23, 1991) which undermines the missionary spirit of the Church. The pontiff is not against interreligious dialogue, but he thinks that there has been too much sympathy expressed in the recent past for religious traditions beyond the realm of Christendom. He does not deny the possibility of non-Christians' attaining salvation; however, his encyclical declares that all salvation comes from Christ and most fully through the Church.

During the marking of the Columbian quincentennial with all the charges of colonization and genocide, the pope and his emissaries have reaffirmed a half millennium of missionizing in the New World. Even as the North American bishops have emphasized their commitment to reconciliation and inculturation, "by respecting the culture which the Gospel embraces and which in turn embraces the Gospel" (*Tekakwitha Conference Newsletter,* 11, no. 1, March–April 1992: 27), they have continued to emphasize the continuing christianization of Native peoples.

For all the liberalizing of Catholic evangelization since the Second Vatican Council, the missionary impulse has remained intact.

In Latin America the same countervailing impulses continue to intersect. In a recent book, *The Indian Face of God in Latin America* (Marzal et al. 1996), four Jesuits (three of them anthropologists) examine "the image or images that the Native Americans of today have of God," in order to bring about "a second evangelisation" which will be *"truly inculturated"* and *"truly liberating"* for American Indians (1). The authors depict the contemporary religious cultures of the Tseltal Mayans of Mexico, the Quechuas of Peru (descendants of the Incans), the Aymaras of Bolivia, Peru, and Chile, and the Guarani of Paraguay and Uruguay (the first inhabitants of the Jesuit reductions of the seventeenth century), meditating upon the ways in which these Indians have combined Christianity with their tribal cultures.

Observing a half millennium of contact with Christianity, Marzal and his associates wish to see "the coming together of the church and the cultures of Native American communities" (2). They recognize that the Church must first overcome its history of condemning indigenous religion and collaborating with the forces of colonialism. Churchmen need to do more, Marzal contends, than merely tolerate syncretistic expressions, waiting patiently for them to disappear over time. Rather, the Church should understand, evaluate, accept, and incorporate Indian religious expressions, if Indians are to have a place in the Church of the next millennium.

In Latin America as well as in the United States and Canada, contemporary Catholic evangelizers consider culture a crucial category in their mission: "The point of emphasizing the importance of culture in the evangelization process has been to recognize how much culture shapes our very being in the world. Without addressing those powerful forces that make thought and expression possible, evangelization remains incomplete and, frequently, superficial" (ix). At the same time the missionaries recall Pope Paul VI's words in his 1975 statement, *Evangelii Nuntiandi,* in which he emphasized the evangelical goal to transform, "through the power of the Gospel, mankind's criteria of judgment, determining values, points of interest, lines of thought, sources of inspiration and models of human life, which are in contrast with the Word of God and with the plan of salvation" (11). The priests reaffirm that Christian faith, "by its very definition" (ix), judges all cultures critically and seeks to christianize them, expunging evil and raising up good.

The authors understand that such judgments are not always easy to make, or accurate in their discernments, and that the process of transforming cultures in the New World has often demoralized Indian peoples. When a group of Latin American Indians urged Pope John Paul II in 1985 to "take back the Bible, for it had not been Good News to them in five hundred years of domination and subjugation" (ix), they may have been justified in their bitterness, one author suggests. For that reason, the authors present "the Indian face of God" in contemporary Latin America, so that the Church will help preserve acceptable aspects of Indians' religious culture and promote inculturation.

Father Manuel M. Marzal, S.J., explains that in many cases in Latin America there was an initial era of evangelization, followed by a period in which, due to the expulsion of Jesuits, revolutions, etc., Indians were given freedom, *de facto,* to reshape their Christian beliefs and practice. "This freedom, which they did not have during the first evangelisation, came when these indigenous peoples had already been fundamentally Christianised. Thus the result was not the radical restoration of the original indigenous religions, but rather the 'Indianisation' of Christianity," Marzal argues (18).

"The Indian Face of God in Latin America," Marzal states, is the result, not of pastoral inculturation, but of Native peoples' syncretism; it arises from

> their efforts to make the Christian message more comprehensible and to conserve certain enduring traces of the aboriginal religion. It is this syncretism which I have called the other face of inculturation. If inculturation is the evangelists' systematic and conscientious effort to translate the universal message of the gospel into the religious categories of the target society, then syncretism is the inverse process by which those who have been evangelised try to retain vestiges of their own religion, not so much in opposition to the Christians as in reclothing the accepted tokens of Christianity in the appropriate aboriginal religious forms. (18)

Marzal highlights certain aspects in Latin American Indian religious cultures: "the sacred dimension of ecology," "the unity of the whole person (body and soul)," "the role of the senses in religious experience" and thus "the logic of the physical and the sensual," the images of saints "as a pantheon of angelic beings," animistic elements, "which horrify us" monotheists, but which may symbolize the one God's "providence and transcendence," and the varied liturgical forms (dancing, fasting, etc.) by which a people approach the divine. Taking a stance similar to that of Fathers Starkloff and Peelman, he exhorts the Church in Latin America to understand and, ultimately, to embrace these forms of syncretism.

Beyond Catholic missiological circles, criticisms have persisted in recent years concerning the new Catholic evangelism. It has been said that the American bishops are "subtly patronizing and imperialistic" when they offer, however gently, the Church's so-called "universal message" (Fittipaldi, Spring 1978: 74) to American Indians. How can there be true dialogue between Catholicism and local culture, one asks, when the Church regards itself as transcendent to the Indians' local particularity? To ethnologists, it is apparent that Catholicism is a culture like any other, possessing its own flaws and limitations. Its claims to primacy in the salvific process remain unproven, unprovable, and indeed, improbable, considering the sorry history of Christianity among the indigenous peoples of the Americas. An anthropologist uses the phrase, "imperialist nostalgia" (Kozak 1991: 15; see Rosaldo 1989: 69), to describe the new evangelism of the contemporary Church. Having stripped Indians of their authentic culture, the author declares, churchmen now look back with romantic fondness at the Indians' moribund traditions. Those in Indian ministry even try to revive selected aspects of past Native ways—those customs deemed harmlessly quaint: the smoke, the feathers, the talk of Mother Earth—and to encourage "the use of pan-Indian concepts and objects for the invention of a new pan-Indian Catholicism" (Kozak 1991: 15). Another anthropologist remarks that "there is an underlying assumption that inculturation is something that the Vatican, out of a sense of *noblesse oblige,* is in a position to grant; it is calling people to the truth and only uses cultural forms to induce people to heed that calling" (Angrosino 1994: 830). In this perspective, Catholic inculturationists can afford to take the stand they do because contemporary Indian culture possesses little of its aboriginal force. Elements odious to the Church—polygamy, human sacrifice, vengeance warfare, etc.—were driven out of Indian cultural patterns long ago. Today Indians pose virtually no sovereign threat to anyone; if anything, their present condition elicits pity. Thus, liberals in the Church can pander to Indian sensibilities, even entertaining the "myth of the noble savage . . . spoiled by meddlesome missionaries" (Grant 1985: 205). Churchmen can tell Indian Catholics to embrace their traditional culture because there is so little left of it.

At the close of the Second World War, large numbers of American Indians left their reservations, seeking jobs and an escape from rural poverty. Having experienced the world beyond their home communities, either through military service or wartime factory jobs, these men and women sometimes decided to move to nearby towns and cities.

United States policy in the 1950s encouraged such migration, particularly through the Employment Assistance Program of 1952, which provided moving and limited living expenses for urbanizing Indians, supplemented in 1956 by vocational training directed by federal agencies. National policymakers regarded Indian reservations as economic wastelands, and the best thing for Native Americans would be to terminate their associations with land and tribe and relocate their identity to an urban setting.

The next several decades witnessed a monumental migration of Indian populations, an urbanization that has led to significant social shifts. Today close to two-thirds of all United States Indians live in cities. Some have joined the working and white-collar classes; others have experienced poverty, disorganization, dislocation, and alcoholism. Large numbers have returned to reservations; others travel back and forth between rural and urban locales.

Tens of thousands of these urban Indians are Roman Catholics. Over the last half century the Church has encountered the challenge of establishing a ministry to these Catholic Indians, as the Native Americans have felt a spiritual uprooting of substantial dimensions. Some Indians have attended Catholic parishes without reference to their ethnic identity. Others have separated themselves from the institutional Church. Still others have sought religious solace in the company of their tribesmen and fellow Indians from various nations, and the Church has responded by creating special ministries to them.

In Gallup, Tucson, Albuquerque, and Los Angeles, in Milwaukee, Chicago, and Minneapolis, in Rapid City, Sioux Falls, Salt Lake City, and Denver, in Spokane, Tacoma, and Seattle, in Sault Ste. Marie and Grand Rapids, in Syracuse, and elsewhere across the United States, the

Church has initiated urban Indian ministries, with varying degrees of commitment and success.

The Franciscans remarked as early as 1947 in Gallup that the hundred or more Catholic families who had moved there were "hesitant about attending the local parish churches because they feel that they are not wanted" (in *Our Negro and Indian Missions* 1947: 25). Having been accustomed to segregated life on reservations, and having felt the sting of overt and subtle racism, both in and out of the Church, many Indians felt uncomfortable in congregations dominated by non-Indians and preferred to keep their distance. In Gallup the diocese created St. Valerian's Indian Center in 1947, the first of the urban Indian centers conducted by the Church in the modern period.

Others were to follow in the 1950s, as diocesan personnel perceived the social dysfunctions of urban Indians and the need for caring guidance. "These maladjusted Indians," wrote a missionary editorialist, "create a religious as well as a social problem" (ibid. 1952: 24), and it behooved the Church to act. Baptized Indians were not finding their way to Catholic churches; without chapels and community centers for them, they and their offspring would be lost to the Church. "There is a *great loss* of Catholic Indians who are 'relocated' in large cities," according to a report to the Tekakwitha Conference. "A woman working with the Catholic Indians in *Los Angeles* reported that one per cent of Catholic off-reservation Indians made a Catholic adjustment to city life" (Tekakwitha Missionary Conference 1957: 5, emphasis theirs). Later surveys in the same agency suggested that of the 288 Catholic Potawatomi in Topeka, only forty-four practiced their religion with regularity. In Chicago, only two of twenty-five Indian families tried to practice their religion. In St. Louis, it was said, "there is very little attendance at church" among the Indian Catholics there. The children of these citified Indians would not be baptized and would "probably revert to paganism" (ibid. 1958: 11). In Minneapolis and Milwaukee, it was claimed, only five percent of the Catholic Ojibways practiced their religion. "Unless something is done, much of our work back here on the reservations during almost a century of effort will go to naught" (12). In the Northwest, Church personnel recognized that urban Indians needed to be integrated into the mainstream, and it was up to the Church to provide organized parish life that would draw Indians in (e.g., special Indian masses) and make them part of the whole (e.g., integrated parochial schools) ("A Report on the Meeting of the Indian

Missionaries of the Oregon Province" 1960). In South Dakota a bishop wrote as recently as the late 1970s that urban parish priests needed to be converted from "the attitude now so prevalent that these [Indians] are 'second-rate' people" (DCRAA 1979), in order to foster outreach at the parish level. Those with a history of evangelizing Indians called on the urban churches or the missionary orders to create Indian churches, similar to national parishes of ethnic immigrants from Europe.

In Rapid City the Catholic Sioux came to the diocese for spiritual and social help, and in the 1950s the Church responded with a Catholic Indian community house that became a center of Indian life in the city. With a church, basketball court, and a hall for suppers, dances and other gatherings, the Mother Butler Center received extensive Indian use, under the direction of the Jesuit fathers and Nardine sisters. Madonna Hall was a haven for Indian girls amidst the evils of urban life.

The Jesuits regarded it as their responsibility to establish an Indian ministry to the Sioux in Rapid City, not only because there were several thousand Indians in the city even by the mid-1950s, but also because the Society of Jesus had a commitment to the Sioux, having evangelized them for several generations. One Jesuit (White 1959) described a "typical" Sioux man's transition to Rapid City. On the reservation the Indian and his family knew the Church personally through the priests and sisters, the chapel and the school. In Rapid City, however, he could not bear to attend the parish church, where everyone else was white, wealthy, and strange. So, the Mother Butler Center provided a place where a Sioux could attend mass with his own people, and where his children would receive religious instruction. The Church personnel helped him locate health care, counseling, and a credit union. He could bathe, wash his clothes, and exercise in the Church facility, all in the company of other Indians. In this way, the Jesuits' long-standing missionary enterprise followed the Sioux from reservation to town.

Over time the Mother Butler Center grew into an Indian parish, named for the Jesuit martyr, Saint Isaac Jogues, embracing close to a thousand practicing Catholics among the five thousand Indians in Rapid City. It is one of three such "personal parishes" ("to be established based upon rite, language and nationality of the Christian faithful within some territory or even upon some other determining factor," according to canon law, in *Tekakwitha Conference Newsletter,* vol. 9, no. 1, March 1990: 16) among American Indian Catholics in the U.S. today. The other personal parishes are in Tucson and Milwaukee.

Indians have lived in Tucson throughout the twentieth century, most prominently the Yaqui refugees from Mexico and the nearby O'odham (Papagos). The Yaquis brought with them their own church organization and ritualism, and they kept largely to themselves. The Papagos came to town in sizable numbers in the 1950s and 1960s, and so the diocese opened St. Nicholas Indian Center in 1969, to keep the Native Americans from feeling lost in the urban neighborhoods.

A decade later the diocese recognized the swelling numbers of Indians, including many who were neither Yaqui nor O'odham, and the Church established six parishes to meet their spiritual and physical needs. Catholic personnel handed out Bibles and devotional literature, in explicit competition with fundamentalist Protestants who were "attacking these people away from the Church. . . ." Some of these evangelicals practiced the "'burning of the Saints' (pictures and statues)" (DCRAA 1980) in their conversion of Catholic Indians.

Catholic authorities wished to counteract the Protestant incursions; they also desired to win more loyalty from the Yaquis for the Roman Church by keeping a closer eye on them. In the late 1980s the diocese created of the six churches a single parish, Blessed Kateri Tekakwitha Parish, under the pastorship of Father Daniel McLaughlin of the Missionary Servants of the Most Holy Trinity. By the 1990s the "personal" parish had as many as five thousand Indian congregants, mostly Yaquis and Papagos, attending masses said in Spanish with occasional hymns in Yaqui language.

AN EXPERIMENT IN MILWAUKEE

An extended look at the third of these Indian parishes, the Church of the Great Spirit in Milwaukee, established officially in 1989, can offer insight to the workings of urban Indian Catholicism. Milwaukee has about ten thousand Native Americans, including Ojibways, Menominees, Winnebagos, and Oneidas from Wisconsin environs, but also people from other tribes. No one knows how many Catholic Indians there are in the city, but estimates suggest about three thousand.

In 1977 a delegation of Milwaukee Indians led by the Menominee/ Ojibway John Boatman sent a letter to Archbishop Rembert G. Weakland, requesting a Catholic ministry to Native Americans. Although the Indians attended several parish churches throughout the city, they felt the need to worship together, in order to express the pan-Indian culture that they were developing together. They complained that, despite some personal outreach by a few clergy, there was "no spokeman, no program, no agency" (Siggenauk Center, Box 1, Folder 1) in the urban area. Weakland responded by hiring Sister Margaret Troy, S.S.M., for a half-time Native American ministry in St. Michael's parish, where many Catholic Indians lived. She hoped that she could coordinate her ministry with an archdiocese-wide effort to reach Indians in order to make them feel a real rapport with the Catholic Church, with a Native spirituality to offer all.

Sister Troy perceived among the Milwaukee Indians a problem of poor morale, and she wanted to encourage expressions of Indian religiousness in order to bolster self-esteem. The Indians needed to hear, she thought, that their spiritual ways were not only acceptable—after many years of missionary condemnation—but even uplifting and inspirational. Having worked for a short time on a Menominee reservation, she was sympathetic to Native American feelings. At the same time, she was well read in the theory of liberation theology, and she was determined to allow the Indians to decide their own agenda in regards to the Church. Over a period of years she listened to their concerns, until she felt capable of elucidating "what *they* say is needed" (ibid., Proceedings, 1977–1978, emphasis hers). She tried to organize best by organizing least ("I came backwards into the organization. . ., backwards on purpose," Troy, August 3, 1989), allowing herself to become an agent of the Indian Catholic will rather than promoting her own.

She noted the Indians' manner of interacting: their reluctance to assert themselves or interfere with others; their tendency to say yes, even when feeling otherwise, so as to avoid disagreement; their avoidance of hierarchical structures; their humility. She hoped that the Catholic fellowship she was fostering in Milwaukee would respect their ways. She observed that they were "thirsty for spirituality," and she wished for the Church to succor them; however, she acknowledged that the "Church has been instrumental in bringing about loss of culture," and as a result the "Indians are lost to Church," even the Menominees, the great majority of whom were baptized Catholics. In a context of cultural demoralization and widespread alcoholism, she desired to "help them to realize their own dreams for the progress of their own people" (Siggenauk Center, Proceedings, c. 1977–1978).

Through the archdiocesan Commission of Human Concerns, a group of Indians, including Ojibways (e.g., Anita Hamly), Lakotas (e.g., John Clifford), Menominees (e.g., Mildred Kaquatosh), and people of mixed heritage (e.g., John Boatman), initiated the Siggenauk Project, named after a pan-tribal Indian leader from the era of the American Revolution. Years later it was observed that Siggenauk's name meant "red winged blackbird" ("Native American Parishes Promote Spiritual Heritage," February 1990), a bird whose colors encompassed the hues of humankind: red, white, yellow, and black. The Project organizers wanted their movement to be "a visible sign of the Church's interest in Indian people" (Siggenauk Center, Box 1, Folder 1). They determined to establish a center for Indians to gather under Catholic auspices, for the purposes of advocating social justice for Milwaukee Indians and for mutual support, coordination, and comfort, as well as for spiritual and liturgical development. The archdiocese funded the Siggenauk Project (with help from the Bureau of Catholic Indian Missions) and used Cursillo (a Catholic leadership retreat program) as a "leadership training vehicle" (ibid.) for the Indians. Later Milwaukee instituted a permanent diaconate program for Native Americans.

Despite a will to create a single center for Milwaukee Indians, the existence of several different tribal groups made for immediate and enduring factionalism beneath the surface of pan-Indian sentiment. In the first years there were charges of financial mismanagement among the various lineages, as some thought that money was being used "to buy the favor of those in the Indian community" (ibid., September 25, 1979). To this day, different families claim sole responsibility for creating the Siggenauk Project, without reference to the contributions of others (Troy, August 3, 1989).

There were some Indians who were put off by the emphasis on Native liturgical forms. Anita Hamly wrote:

> I have a concern about the undue amount of Native American religion that John Boatman wants to put into this Christian program. . . . I don't remember us wanting to hire drum chiefs before. I really have to take a stand on this point. I am a Christian! That means I have one God—Yahweh—and my brother is Jesus Christ who sends the Holy Spirit to comfort and guide men. . . . This is a Catholic group right now—I'd like to see the Christianity flowing throughout it with no distortions.

She recalled that at a Tekakwitha congress attended by the Milwaukee contingent, a majority of Indians did not want to see Native innovations in Catholic liturgy: "People were too afraid to have a return to the witchcraft that is in the Native American Religion that they didn't dare even incorporate things like symbols, etc." (Siggenauk Center, September 25, 1979).

It wasn't only John Boatman and other Indians who were angling for a resuscitation of Indian ritualism in a Catholic setting. Sister Margaret Troy regarded the expression of Native culture as her special mission, in the spirit of Vatican II reforms. She wanted the Siggenauk Project to revive Indian spirituality, even if the revival alienated some of the conservative Indian Catholics in the group. Anita Hamley left the project and eventually moved from Milwaukee. The Siggenauk group continued with its experimentation, for instance, using Indian fry bread for Eucharist and employing drums, feathers, sage, cedar, and other elements of Indian ritual in the Catholic services as sacramentals. At the same time the community included "very strict Catholics" like the Ojibway Connors family. "If my parents miss mass on Sunday," says Jolene Connors De Cora, "they think it's a mortal sin, and will go to confession before going to mass again" (Fargo, August 3, 1989).

The Siggenauk Project aimed to revive Indian spiritual forms; it also had the goal of drawing Indians, baptized but estranged from the Church, back to the sacraments. In 1981 Sister Troy told a reporter, "This is not an Indian parish, . . . nor is it trying to replace the parish.

We seek to reach the unchurched Indians . . ." (in Siggenauk Center, Newsclippings). The project leaders added that "many Indian people would like to receive the sacraments, but they feel strange and unfamiliar in their parishes. Often they are afraid of being turned away so do not even try to approach the Church." Native elements in the liturgy were designed to "ease their anxiety" (ibid., Box 1, Folder 1).

At Tekakwitha meetings the Siggenauk Indians learned ways of conjoining Native and Catholic religious forms, and they invited Tekakwitha clerical liturgists such as Fathers John Hascall, Ed Savilla, Georges Mathieu, and Sisters Kateri Mitchell and Genevieve Cuny to speak and lead services. Hence a "blending" (Box 1, Folder 3) of Indian and Catholic elements was brought about. In 1984 the Siggenauk community held a Native American Spiritual Day, "A Gathering of All Faiths." There was an attempt to balance Native and Catholic ritualism: a mass and a powwow, Catholic prayers like the Apostles' Creed during a "traditional meal" with a giveaway at the close.

Throughout the 1980s the Siggenauk Project served as a rallying agency for political causes deemed advantageous to Indians and other poor denizens of Milwaukee: Hunger Task Force, Youth Employment Programs, Women, Infants and Children, Alcoholism Rehabilitation, Nutrition Services, and the like. A Social Justice Committee wrote letters to congressmen against budget cuts brought about by the Reagan administration; complained about anti-Indian slurs in the local media; and offered help to incarcerated Native Americans in regional prisons. A newsletter alerted Indians in and around Milwaukee of events and programs, both Native and Catholic: powwows, feast days and schedules for Indian catechesis. Thus the Siggenauk Center became a touchstone for Native American culture in the city and beyond, to Indian communities throughout Wisconsin.

The Siggenauk Indians acquired a pastor, Father Ed Cook, in 1983, and with his support the community moved toward the "historic moment" (Newsletter) in 1989 when the Siggenauk Center attained the status of a "personal" Indian parish. Father Cook enunciated the goal of the parish: "We're working toward forming a new rite, . . . a Native American rite that is equal to other rites in the Catholic Church" (in Newsclippings, October 27, 1988). He, Sister Troy, and the Indians on the parish board called for all Indians, Catholic or not, to make use of the Siggenauk Center: "Blood quantum is unimportant—If you have one drop of Indian blood, and consider yourself Indian—you are" (Box 1, Folder 3).

The Siggenauk parish became known as the Congregation of the Great Spirit. In its "Statement of Purpose, Goals and Objectives" (ibid.) in 1989, the parish board delineated four types of ministry: spiritual (weekly meetings, support for Indian ministry, interfaith contact), human (volunteer programs, funding for funerals, a food kitchen), social (programs for youth, elderly, imprisoned) and cultural (workshops by elders, instruction in Indian languages). With financial and moral support from Archbishop Weakland and organizational energy from the likes of Sister Troy, the parish initiated many activities, leading one local observer to say, "There's more going on here than in any other city in the country in the way of Catholic Indian programs" (Thiel, August 1, 1989), even though Milwaukee ranked 25th in U.S. urban Indian population. When a delegation of Milwaukee Indian Catholics attended the 1989 Tekakwitha Conference, they realized how far they had advanced, as Indians from other cities complained of lukewarm support from their local hierarchies.

The creation of the Siggenauk parish in Milwaukee has not meant the fulfillment of American Indian Catholicism in that city; nor has it brought to a close the factional disputes among the Indian families of the area. Tribal allegiances still exist within the community, keeping it from unity; however, Father Cook serves as pastor to all, and Sister Troy, who left the city so that the Indians could develop their own leadership free of her influence, visits on weekends. The Siggenauk Interfaith Spiritual Center moved to the site of the former Concordia College campus, and the parish is playing a role in the formation of Native American consciousness in Wisconsin. For all its growing pains, the Congregation of the Great Spirit serves as an example to other Catholic Indians hoping to establish urban parishes, and in 1997 the parish helped host the annual meeting of the Tekakwitha Conference in Milwaukee, putting itself forward as an urban paradigm of Indian Catholicism.

For the most part, however, citified Catholic Indians still bemoan their isolation and decry the lack of initiative taken by the Catholic hierarchy to create Native American urban ministries. Hopeful reports surface from time to time about the integrating effects of urban parishes. "There seems to be a growing desire on the part of our Native Americans and our white people to worship together," a bishop wrote (DCRAA 1976); "practically every one of our congregations is composed of white people and Indian people and there is less hesitancy on the part of our people to go to church together." Nevertheless, many urban Indians have felt neglected and lost in parishes dominated by Whites. Some have become non-practicing Catholics; others have totally abandoned their Catholic identity (Thiel, July 21, 1986). Since 1989 the annual Tekakwitha convocations have gathered urban Indians interested in increased Church involvement in their spiritual lives, in order to address concerns and stem the tide of defections.

Mort Dreamer, a Northern Cheyenne, is a civil engineer for the Bureau of Indian Affairs in Washington, D.C. He has lived in the nation's capital since the 1970s, associating with other Indians on the job but worshipping on his own, almost anonymously, in a Catholic parish. For nine years, he says (Fargo, August 3, 1989), he put his envelope in the collection basket each week, received the Eucharist, but felt invisible in the church. Finally, "emptiness overcame me," he confides. He forced himself to overcome the feeling he had of not truly belonging to a white parish—all Indians feel this, he suggests. In an act of bravery he introduced himself as an Indian Catholic to the pastor. The priest responded by giving prominence to Dreamer's ethnic identity in the congregation.

As the only Indian in the parish, Dreamer took it upon himself to remind the community of Kateri Tekakwitha's place in the liturgical calendar. On one Thanksgiving day he addressed the parishioners in his Northern Cheyenne regalia, to remind them that Indians still exist in America. "It was the first time," he remarks, "that eagle feathers and warbonnets were walking around our altar." The congregation responded with enthusiastic support, and before he knew it, he had been elected president of the parish council.

On the other hand, he was unable to interest his fellow BIA employees in forming a Kateri Prayer Circle. He admits, "I failed miserably" to interest detribalized urban Indians in Catholic Indian spirituality. "They thought I was from some underground." For Dreamer, then, his Catholic community includes virtually no Indians.

From other Indian Catholics one hears similar plaints: of alienation from non-Indian parishes; of neglect from the archdioceses; of failure to organize, and of a need to express their Indianness in urban Catholic settings. Chet Eagleman of Grand Rapids, Michigan, claims (ibid.) that, although urban dioceses have the opportunity to request money from the BCIM for urban Indian ministries, more often than not the urban bishops seem to care little for special Native needs, and the Indians are unable to apply for funds themselves. "The Church completely ignores us," he asserts. "You can grow old and very grey, waiting for the archdioceses. . . . You have to do it yourself."

Eagleman and Sister Marie Therese Archambault, O.S.F., a Hunkpapa Sioux of Denver, have tried in the 1990s to raise Catholic hierarchical concern for urban Indians, but without demonstrable effect in either Indian's eyes. The BCIM has encouraged the urban archdioceses to apply for funds in order to create Indian ministries, but without sufficient response. Sister Archambault says that, despite some excellent urban Indian programs in Milwaukee, Chicago, and Seattle, very few churchmen listen in the archdioceses she visits as an advocate for urban Indian Catholics. She wonders who will help the "lonely Indian living in the city who wants to stay Catholic without being white" (Potsdam, August 5, 1995).

Still, there has been progress in several cities: in Spokane, where the St. Aloysius Catholic Indian Community has functioned since the late 1980s with the inspired multicultural energy of Joan Staples-Baum; in Syracuse, where the Iroquois Catholics of the city worship prominently at St. Lucy's Church; in Cleveland, where a Native American Ministry keeps in touch with hundreds of Indians from diverse backgrounds. Sister Joan Lang, C.S.J., the Cleveland ministry director, says (Lang, July 8, 1992) that these Indians—Navajos, Mohawks, Apaches, Pimas, and others from across America—have little in common beyond their "Indianness." The youngsters have little to do with their tribal culture, and even less with Catholicism. She tries to "help them relate to the Church," although they "do not comprehend really well" the theological aspects of Catholicism. At best she tries to help them when they are sick or when they need money. "I love them. I hang onto them," she states.

Despite Chet Eagleman's dissatisfaction with urban archdioceses across the United States, his local episcopate has been active for almost two decades in organizing a Native American ministry. The Diocese of Grand Rapids began a Native American Outreach Program in 1982, in order to reach "those who had felt alienated from the Church" (DCRAA 1983). Fred C. Chivis, Jr., a Huron/Potawatomi, identified the Indian Catholics in an eleven-county area, imported Father John Hascall to celebrate Indian masses, initiated a prison ministry to Native Americans, and established a regional awareness of Kateri Tekakwitha's cause.

In 1990 he was succeeded by Shirley Francis, who now conducts the Native American Apostolate with the help of her husband, Simon, a Michigan Ojibway. Both of them are converts to Catholicism. In Grand Rapids they found a multi-ethnic parish, St. Francis Xavier—made up of Blacks, Hispanics, Vietnamese, as well as Indians, including biracial couples—where they are both very happy. Mr. Francis says that they all get along wonderfully, sharing their "colors and cultures" in a "charismatic" setting.

With this satisfying parish as a base, Mrs. Francis has helped develop a handful of Kateri Circles through the Grand Rapids territory. She tries to keep in contact with many of the 2,400 Catholic Indians in the diocese—Potawatomis, Ottawas, and Ojibways, in rural as well as urban settings. She says that the Indian people she has encountered have a lot of anger toward the Church. They recall times past when they were segregated, even in Catholic burial grounds, from Whites; they fear hierarchical authoritarianism and are put off by monetary obligations. Nevertheless, they are "hungry to come back" to Catholic spirituality, if given the opportunity. She tries to make rapprochement possible by encouraging Indians to employ Native "sacramentals" in their Christian worship. She tells of "ghost suppers" that take place among Catholic Indians on November 2 each year, a "christianized" version of the ancient Anishinabe feast of the dead, placed after All Saints' Day in the liturgical calendar. The Indians visit from house to house, sharing food with the living and making burnt offerings to the deceased. She and her husband join these devotions as part of their ministry. Shirley Francis also urges Kateri Circle members to participate in National Tekakwitha Conference conclaves, in order to share their Native and Catholic traditions (Francis and Francis, August 6, 1992).

Since 1983 the Salt Lake City Diocese has had an Office of Native American Ministry, with Sister Lorraine Masters, O.L.V.M., as director, treating with the small population of Catholic Utes and other Indians in the vicinity. Father Paul Ojibway, S.A., directs outreach to the thousands of Native Americans from over a hundred different tribes in Los Angeles. The Archdiocese of St. Paul–Minneapolis conducts an active ministry among the thousands of Catholic Ojibways in the Twin Cities area. In Chicago the Anawim Center is in its second decade of operation—first as a Kateri Circle, then as a storefront, and since 1987 as an American Indian center and Ethnic Ministries Office. There are over a hundred different Indian national groups in Chicago, many of them intermarried with non-Indians. The Anawim Center attempts to help these urban Indians deal with "issues of violence, gangs, and the consumer culture of the city, while raising our children with a sense of their own cultural identity and spiritual heritage" (*Tekakwitha Conference Newsletter*, 12, no. 3, September–October 1993: 2).

A COLLEGE CHAPLAINCY

The Catholic Church has needed to provide special ministry to Indians not only in cities but also in other institutions where Catholic Indians have found themselves away from their reservation homes, such as prisons. Catholic ministry has attempted to follow Indian youths to governmental boarding schools over the last century. U.S. employees have not always welcomed the Church in these institutions—Protestants have usually dominated their bureaucracy, and to make official adjustments for a Catholic presence could be construed as a breach of church-state separation—and in many places there is a history of tension between school administration and Catholic priests.

Haskell Indian Junior College in Lawrence, Kansas, has housed close to a thousand Indians at any one time, from dozens of tribes across the United States. A fourth to a third of them have been Catholics, and throughout the century the Church has provided at least an unofficial chaplaincy. In the early part of the century, assertive priests like the Ojibway Father Philip Gordon attempted to insert their ministry into the daily life of the college, and when school officials resisted, the priests caused trouble with the Bureau of Indian Affairs in Washington, D.C.—Haskell being a BIA institution. In later decades Jesuits and other priests kept a visible presence, to make sure that future leaders of Indian America would remain firm in their Catholic faith.

Today Father John Cousins is the Catholic chaplain at Haskell, maintaining a Catholic Center in a Victorian-style house across the street from the campus. The Catholic Center was dedicated in 1986, but the BIA will not permit a Catholic property on the college premises. "Luckily," Cousins says (Fargo, August 3, 1989), because in his position he does not have to deal with government bureaucracy, and because Catholic Indian students can come to their Haskell College Catholic Campus Center as a kind of refuge, leaving the federal campus behind and gathering for sacraments and counseling. Cousins's main goal is to offer them a place where they can be themselves, as Catholic Indians, in a "home" environment. They watch television, study, play cards, and snack on popcorn and hotdogs. The priest makes himself available past midnight on most nights, without trying to schedule too many formal events.

Father Cousins sees close to two hundred students per year—almost all of the Indian Catholic students at Haskell—with eighty or more attending services regularly. Surprisingly to Cousins (Cousins, November 29, 1991), many of those who frequent the Center are those who do not practice their Catholicism at home on the reservations. Those who are Catholics at home often rebel and stay away from the Catholic Center while away at school. The students who come to the Center are primarily from the Southwest—O'odham, Apaches, and Puebloans—and from Alaska, mainly Yupik Eskimos. He notices more men than women at mass in the Catholic Center chapel.

The chapel has Pueblo designs painted (by students) along the walls. The altar has a chalice and cruets made in Southwestern design and an eagle feather sitting atop it. There are pictures of Indian leaders all around the Center. Cousins says that he tries to "adapt" (ibid.) Catholic services to the Indians, but it is hard because they come from so many tribal and regional groups. He cannot favor one over the others. In addition, he is not qualified from an Indian point of view to perform Native American rituals, and the students feel themselves to be too young to enact their tribal rituals themselves. At one service in 1991 he invited four Catholic Indian students to perform blessing rituals in the four directions. Three of the four students called home first to get permission from "medicine men" to perform the blessings. Cousins continues to be wary not to push the Catholic Haskell students toward liturgical innovations for which they and he are not qualified; still, he wants them to express Indianness in his Catholic Center.

Father Cousins's diary contains written comments from students regarding the importance of the Center to them. They find the place peaceful and joyful, a home away from home. They appreciate his good advice, and they attest to finding Christ within the Center walls. This is a place to get them through their problems of adjustment to Haskell life; it is a place, they say, to strengthen their Catholic faith. Recent graduates often call to maintain contact with the chaplaincy. Like the urban centers maintained by the Catholic Church, the Haskell Catholic Center is an attempt to keep Catholic faith alive among Indians who are away from their reservation communities.

JOBRIETY MINIJTRY

Catholics engaged in ministry to American Indians recognize that special attention must be paid to the overwhelming problem of substance abuse. Given a climate in which "almost 50 percent of all young Indians have serious alcohol or drug problems, according to the Indian Health Service" (Egan, March 19, 1988: 1), Indian communities and individuals are trying to ameliorate the conditions associated with Native intoxication: maladaptation to white cultural demands, economic depression, and spiritual uprootedness. Many Indians participate in the twelve-step program of Alcoholics Anonymous, which includes the belief in "a Power greater than ourselves," a "decision to turn our will and our lives over to the care of God *as we understand Him*," and an admission "to God, to ourselves, and to another human being" of the exact nature of our wrongs, asking God "humbly . . . to remove our shortcomings." This "spiritual awakening" (Alcoholics Anonymous 1976: 59–60) has had a significant impact on Native concepts of spirituality over the past generation and has helped frame the Catholic response to Indian drunkenness.

At the same time, Indians beset by alcoholism are trying to revive their own traditions, "old religious values, including various forms of Christian-influenced native rituals" (Egan, March 19, 1988: 54). Some Indians in the United States and Canada have turned to drums, songs, sweats, and shamanistic healing to treat the problem. One of the most successful sobriety programs among Native American Catholics has been "The Pilgrimage," begun in 1985 on the Blackfoot reservation in Montana and adapted for other Indian communities. Word of mouth has spread the news about this innovative program throughout Indian country.

Fathers Victor E. Langhans and Ed Kohler created the idea for the Pilgrimage by combining elements of Alcoholics Anonymous with the format of a Cursillo (Catholic leadership) retreat. The priests hoped that by ritualizing the A.A. message, turning it into an "event" with sacramental dimensions, they would effect a radical change, a "conversion," in the lives of Native alcoholics that might have a lasting impact on Blackfoot (and other Indians') existence. Thousands of Blackfoot had already gone through Cursillo training, so the priests could build upon a Catholic ceremonial familiar to the Indians without explicit reference to aboriginal Native ritualism (Langhans 1986: i–ii; cf. JIN-NAM, January 31, 1987).

The Pilgrimage employs several leaders: a rector, a spiritual director, a cook, etc. They constitute a continuously replenished organization that evolves from event to event, with a newcomer serving an apprenticeship, and then moving on to membership and eventual leadership. There is no central or clerical control, although Catholic authorities in local jurisdictions have tried to maintain a normative Catholic character to the proceedings. Present leaders are always recruiting new leaders for the next event. Furthermore, at an event there may be as many staff-leaders as there are pilgrims; therefore, there is a great opportunity for one-to-one contact and, over time, broad-based, "Indian-run" leadership. In this way the program resembles Cursillo. As in A.A., a person "takes a step" by helping others, thus creating a leadership of healed healers (Green, August 4, 1988).

The procedure of the three-day ritual is to make the Indian alcoholics do several things—to talk, feel, and trust—which substance abuse has erased from their lives. On the first night they meet people in a social setting. They introduce themselves informally, snack, joke, and learn a little about each other. Everyone stumbles through the insecurity of a new situation but feels solidarity with the others going through the same process. Several people who have already gone through the regimen relate dramatic stories and provide encouraging speeches. The next morning the participants are encouraged to face the fact that substance abuse has made their existence unmanageable. Then they are urged to turn their lives over to a "higher power"—God, the Church, the Pilgrimage leadership—as an act of trust. In this the Pilgrimage resembles the first few steps of Alcoholics Anonymous; however, there are also explicit references to Catholic belief. The Indians are asked, "Who is our God? Who is my Savior? What is the gift of Faith?" (ibid.), and other catechetical questions. They are asked to renew their baptismal vows. They listen to readings from the Bible. They engage in sacramental anointing with water and oil. Among some tribes, such as the Lakotas, these Christian elements are supplemented by sweats and the pipe rituals of medicine men; however, the Blackfoot do not mix in Native ceremonies.

The second full day is calculated for more introspection. The participants make an examination of conscience, go to confession, and relate their defects privately to others going through the Pilgrimage. At the end of the day small groups put on skits having to do with their problems and the potential healing to come. These dramas are preludes to the public self-opening that fills the evening, when individuals testify publicly about their alcoholism, emptying the burden of their solitariness with "charismatic fervor" (Grim 1991b: 6).

Throughout the several days the pilgrims receive encouraging messages from relatives and friends, delivered by the leaders. On the last morning there is a potluck feast, at which the pilgrims are reunited with the community. They receive congratulations for having "survived" the experience, having rid themselves of a "false sense of being this individual, alone." The pilgrims now relate the journey they have taken—their "death and resurrection"—and try to articulate "what will I do with my life" (Green, August 4, 1988).

The Pilgrimage does not end at the conclusion of the ritual. The healed become healers for others. There are monthly meetings with their class of pilgrims and quarterly meetings with larger groups. Graduates call each other regularly, offering help at times of temptation and self-doubt. In this way the short course becomes a longer step toward recovery and sobriety.

The Pilgrimage has helped give rise to Catholic sobriety ministries on many Indian reservations. The lay deacon Harold Condon and his wife Geraldine devote much of their parish ministry on the Cheyenne River Sioux Reservation to combating alcoholism. Myron Littlebird of the Northern Cheyenne reservation in Montana credits a parish anti-alcohol program for his recovery and pins his hope for his tribe's future on Catholic action. "If we don't do something about alcoholism," he declares, "we are just not going to survive as a people. . . . The Church is in our recovery" (in Walsh 1990b: 22).

✳ III ✳

Catholic Indian Leadership

HIJTORICAL INTRODUCTION

In his 1979 survey of North American Indian Christian communities, the renowned missiologist, R. Pierce Beaver, charged that "the Roman Catholic Church is the most colonial-minded of the churches and has done next to nothing to raise up Native American clergy and religious" (Beaver 1979: 42). At the time he could locate only eleven Indian priests, fifty-two sisters, and one brother in the United States and Canada, out of a Catholic Indian population of two hundred thousand. A decade later a Catholic agency suggested that over time there had been as many as thirty priests, ninety religious, and two bishops in North America of definable Indian descent (Fargo, August 3, 1989). A spokesman for the Bureau of Catholic Indian Missions estimated that about fifteen Indian priests, a dozen brothers, and fifty sisters were identifiable in the United States (Zuern, March 18, 1987) in the late 1980s, a figure that holds true in the present day, out of 350,000 Indian Catholics.

For the past century certain commentators have remarked upon the dearth of Indian priests (and of sisters and brothers, too, although we shall focus first upon the priesthood), and have sought to understand the sparsity. Catholicism is a religious tradition that makes explicit the theological, ecclesiastical, liturgical, and moral needs for a priesthood. Priests are necessary as mediaries between God and humans. They celebrate the mass. They serve the episcopal structure of the Church on earth. They teach, preach, and consecrate, and they absolve sins. Whatever influence laypersons have, the Church has historically relied on a priesthood for its continuance. In the implanting of Catholic tradition in the New World, the question of a Native clergy has been an issue from the start.

Scholars have noted that in New Spain the Church denied clerical vocation to Indians in the sixteenth and seventeenth centuries: "This was by no means due to the lack of interest and desire on the part of the natives, for many of them earnestly sought to be admitted; but by deliberate action of the authorities of the church they were excluded" (Braden 1930: 269). A Church synod in 1555 forbade the ordination of Indians, Blacks, and even mestizos throughout New Spain. "Lacking a . . . native clergy," one historian has written, "the Church of New Spain could never attain a sufficiently national character, and this fact, perhaps, explains in large part the history of Catholicism in Mexico and the hostility with which governments have persecuted it . . ." (Ricard 1966: 292).

Priestly orders such as the Franciscans passed internal legislation (e.g., in 1570) forbidding Indians from taking clerical vows. Even though Indians in Mexico could hold public office in the government of New Spain as early as 1530, they could not become priests. The Church provided Indian males with some theological training, permitted them to be porters, readers, exorcists, teachers, interpreters, acolytes, and even celibate lay brothers without vows, but they could receive no sacramental powers. The Church regarded Indians in New Spain as "neophytes," no matter how many generations their family had been Catholics; therefore, they were regarded as "incapable of reaching what was considered the summit of Christian perfection: total dedication to God within a convent" (Morales 1973: 39). Because they were descendants of infidels, they might return to the "vomit" of their forebears; because they were perpetual probationers, they were not capable of becoming "masters" over others, according to Mexican Church authorities (in Braden 1930: 272). Even progressives such as Bernardino de Sahagun came to the conclusion that Indian men were too unchaste, intellectually inept, and lawless to represent the Church as priests (see Ricard 1966: 218–231).

Only in the late seventeenth century did certain Mexican Indians take their vows, by virtue of having been declared nobility by the Spanish Crown. For example, there were several Moctezumas who became Franciscans; their nobility overcame their inferior status as Indians. At the same time, dozens of mestizos joined the orders and diocesan priesthood of Mexico "sporadically" (Ricard 1966: 235) in the late seventeenth century, but they were not actively recruited by the Church and when they did receive ordination, they generally were given rural parishes with very local authority. Over the more recent centuries there have been numerous Mexican priests of full and mixed Indian descent.

In New Mexico the Franciscans would not ordain Pueblo men as priests, considering the Indians "an inferior race of ill repute, easily given to heresy. They were 'weak and frail' children of low intelligence who would remain perpetually minors in need of a father's guidance" (Gutierrez 1991: 166).

North of New Spain the constraints upon Indian priests have been less legalistic, but far more compelling. In the seventeenth century the Propaganda Fide expressed the "desirability of preparing Indians for priesthood" (Pizzorusso 1990: 22), and there was even a proposal to establish a Vatican procurator for such a Native ministry. Nevertheless, "No Indian, not even those converted, were allowed into the corridors of the Catholic Church's organizational power. . . . During the colonial period, nowhere in North America was there an indigenous clergy sent to Rome to study, though this happened in missions elsewhere, and requests to ordain baptized natives were made from the early 18th century onward" (23). We encounter reports of an unnamed Iroquois ordained as an Augustinian in Europe around 1650. This man was captured by Europeans as a child, grew up in Spain, and lived his entire adult life in Europe. He was an Indian by blood but culturally he was a Westerner (McGloin 1950: 49). Otherwise, the ordination of Indians waited, perforce, for a later age.

In the early nineteenth century several Native Americans found their way to Rome to study for the priesthood. The Ottawa Indian William Maccatebiness (Blackbird) of Michigan died in Rome in 1833, supposedly on the day he was to be ordained (Blackbird 1887). From California the Luiseño Pablo Tac entered the Urban College in 1834, along with a fellow Indian youth who died in 1837. Tac progressed in his studies, with the hope of becoming a missionary among his own people; however, he died of smallpox in 1841, before taking his vows (see Tac 1958). It is unknown how many other Indian men died in Catholic seminaries, before becoming priests; however, only one priest in the U.S. before the twentieth century—James Chrysostom Bouchard, S. J., ordained in 1855 and of mixed heritage—possessed positive Indian identity.

In Canada the Métis Edward Cunningham received ordination in 1890, followed in 1901 by another Métis, Patrice Beaudry; the former was at home in Indian culture, the latter preferred to live among white parishioners (Zimmer 1973). The most famous of the Métis seminarians, Louis Riel, left the Montreal novitiate shortly before leading the Métis Red River revolt of 1869. His fanatic religiosity fed upon his Catholic training and led to his fomenting the revolution of 1885, for which he was hanged. He imagined himself a priest, indeed, the pontiff for all humanity; however, he received no official vows (see Flanagan 1979; Riel 1976). In Canada the first treaty Indian, a Blood from southern Alberta, was ordained only in the 1960s (Grant 1985: 207), and to the present day fewer than a dozen First Nation men have become Canadian Catholic priests, including Milton McWatch, who in 1990 was ordained in the Diocese of Sault Ste. Marie (several years after the annulment of his marriage), the first Canadian Ojibway Catholic cleric (*Tekakwitha Conference Newsletter*, March 1991: 6). Knowledgeable observers are struck by the Canadian Indians' "unresponsiveness to what is most specific to this Church of the Whites: its clerical character" (Goulet and Peelman 1983: 7).

Why so few? An observer at a Catholic Congress in Baltimore in November 1889 counted priests from around the world, including Africa, representing myriad nationalities, but no full-blood Indian priests. So, he (Reilly 1890) put the question to a hundred priests and bishops in Indian ministry: why are there no Indian priests? He recorded their responses.

A Jesuit priest said that American Indians were the "remotest" of all nations from "Christian civilization," and thus "it takes more time to civilize them" (268); their "nomadic life" (269) was an obstacle to seminary training and sedentary service. Other priests suggested that Indian communities had not been long enough in contact with Catholic culture; several generations were necessary before Indians could produce their own Catholicity without missionary guidance. Only then could they produce their own priests. Only when their culture was autonomous and self-reliant, free from the governmental reservation system which had "broken down their spirit" (270), could Indian men express their leadership qualities in various manifestations, including the priesthood.

In the perspectives of many priests interviewed by Reilly, "The greatest bar, however, to the uplifting of the aborigines, has been the Indian himself. He is a child. His character is unstable. His moral fibre is not sturdy enough to endure prolonged sacrifices. His ideas are gross and his sentiments are not refined. He is too near nature to live a supernatural life" (271), and so he fails to produce priests. One missionary said that Indians lack spirituality. Another spoke of Indians' "materialistic heaviness of intelligence, crookedness of judgment, and especially inconstancy of will and purpose" (272). Indians might perform acts of self-sacrifice, e.g., in the Sun Dance, but they lack perseverance in spiritual matters. The white missionaries had mixed opinions about Indian intelligence and its potential; however, they agreed that priestly celibacy constituted a major obstacle to a Native priesthood. As one priest with almost three decades of experience among Wyoming Indians asserted, "there is only one reason why Indians do not become priests, and that is—they must marry" (274).

Rev. Francis M. Craft, a controversial missionary among the Sioux and himself of some Mohawk descent, criticized the Church in the 1890s for not encouraging more Indian vocations. Without denying the difficulties facing religious leadership among Native men and women, Craft condemned "the vile and unCatholic *race prejudice* that has hitherto been the cause of nearly all (and perhaps all) our mission troubles and failure" (Ewens 1988: 13). He objected to the notion that Indians were "too near nature to live a supernatural life" ("Native Indian Vocations" 1897: 345), citing the sophistication and wisdom of their religious and philosophical ideas, and he accused his fellow missionaries of attempting to dominate Indian populations. He asked how Indian communities could identify themselves fully as Catholics until they were empowered to produce their own priests.

Even though several American Indians achieved the priesthood in the first half of the twentieth century—the Potawatomi Albert Negahnquet in 1903, the Ojibway Philip B. Gordon in 1913, the Mohawk Michael Jacobs in 1934, the Potawatomi Georges Mathieu in 1937, the Mohawk George White in 1945, and the Blackfoot John J. Brown in 1948—many Church leaders mistrusted Indian vocations in principle and in practice. As we have seen above, Father Placidus F. Sialm, S.J., who organized Lakota catechists on the Pine Ridge Reservation in South Dakota, doubted the ability of Indian men to carry the administrative burdens of the priesthood, however useful they proved as helpers.

In 1939 the national Catholic organization for raising funds for Indian missions noted in its journal, *Our Negro and Indian Missions,* that Indians had a "deficient background" in religion before the coming of missionaries, because they had no priesthoods and no regular religious worship, beyond the occasional dance. As a result, the missionaries had to "inculcate habits of regular religious practices and a Christian community spirit upon this deficient background." It was necessary, therefore, for Indian communities to depend upon white priests for all religious leadership, "for Indian men and women often lack the initiative, or at least the experience and Catholic background, that would make them effective leaders" (27).

Only in the years following the Second Vatican Council can one find a concerted effort to create a Native American priesthood in the United States. Beginning in 1939 missionaries among American Indians had been meeting in an annual Tekakwitha Conference. In 1965 the 26th conference met at Blue Cloud Abbey, South Dakota, to define the goal of Indian missions in the post–Vatican II context: ". . . to so firmly establish the roots of the Church that the community of the Indian Faithful may progress toward less outside dependence for economic support, for direction of local institutions, and for religious and priestly vocations" (Hettich 1966: 1). The missionaries attempted to understand the factors working against Indian vocations in order to remove the obstacles.

Historically, they found, Indians have clashed with non-Indians, not only militarily, but also culturally; the result has been a hybrid reservation culture that degrades Indian initiative amidst governmental paternalism. Indians have low socioeconomic status; they have difficulty defending their rights and dignity. They lack educational opportunities and must be content with tribal and national governments hostile to religious expression, either traditional or Christian. Many Indians, the missionaries said, are rooted only partially in Christianity, and paganism persists. In short, Indians are in a state of transition that does not promote Catholic vocations.

Psychologically, Indians are perforce preoccupied with material concerns. Given their poverty, religious and spiritual values appear irrelevant or dysfunctional, and the idea of a religious vocation is meaningless to Native communities. There is no home support for vocations; indeed, strong family ties prevent vocations that will, by necessity, pull the priest away from his relatives. Indians suffering from crises of inferiority and transitional identity, apathy, and dependence on paternalistic systems, are not the best candidates for the priesthood. In addition, Indians fear further restrictions upon their freedom, and in particular they have a strong aversion to celibacy, regarded as a white cultural value. The missionaries commented that much peer pressure works against Indian vocations: if an Indian man or woman leaves his or her family, it is an act of desertion. One priest wrote, "Many an

Indian who takes on the ways of the white man is bitterly talked about and criticized by other Indians . . . and this dread . . . of being different than their fellow Indians keeps them back" (ibid., 21).

The missionaries admitted that their ministry tended to discourage Indian vocations. They lacked vocation programs. They failed to adapt Christianity to Indian cultural forms. They fell short in creating schools that fostered Indian leadership or established a good image of Christianity itself. For some priests and sisters, "the Indian missions are regarded as a kind of 'Siberia' for rebels and recalcitrant members" (ibid., 26); no wonder Indian youths do not wish to emulate priests they refer to as "mean, crabby, unhappy, frustrated, phony, and a nag" (29). The priests "feel superior to the Indian, believe he is scum, that he has no morals nor intelligence nor responsibility" (28); as a result, the Indians form unpleasant notions of priests and the priesthood itself. The Tekakwitha Conference missionaries hoped to turn these conditions around, in order to develop more Indian priests.

Over a dozen men of immediate Indian descent became priests in the United States from the 1960s to the 1990s; throughout this period the Church articulated the goals of Indian vocations and Indian Catholic leadership in general, including lay readers, catechists, and permanent deacons, as well as the religious roles of sisters, brothers, and priests. During this time, many persons, Indian and non-Indian, Catholic and non-Catholic, have suggested various models by which Indian Catholic vocations and leadership might function.

Some have assumed that Indian communities desire hierarchical roles in the Church: "We realize that having an Indian Bishop would be everything that Indian people could hope for" (Tekakwitha Missionary Conference, August 1970), said one group of non-Indian clerics. Assuming a central place for normative male priesthood within the Church, and projecting shortages of white priests in the future of post–Vatican II America, some have urged Indians to take their rightful place in a hierarchical Church (JINNAM, February 9, 1984). When Pope John Paul II addressed thousands of Indians in Phoenix in 1987, he called young Indians to the sacerdotal life. He exhorted them to listen to Jesus' call: "He will not let you down" (Phoenix, September 14, 1987). As the Tekakwitha Conference became a gathering for Indian Catholics, homilies addressed the issue of Indian vocations. "More than ever before," said one white priest, "we need Native priests." He called Indian parents to "challenge" their children to "serve our Church as priests and religious," and to "pray for this gift among your own children" (Fargo, August 3, 1989).

At the same time, questions have been raised about the appropriateness of the priesthood for Indian peoples. Some have argued that traditional Indian leadership is more "circular" than "authoritarian," "emerging naturally" from the gifts of individuals in particular situations. According to this view, Indian individuals perform "situational leadership" within their communities, which recognize natural talents that can serve as gifts to their people, within a short-range context. The notion of a person serving as a priest for life, with fatherly authority over a community, is foreign to Indian ways of thinking, some have said (Mitchell, August 7, 1986). Missionaries who have hoped that their Indian parishioners will one day put Anglo clerics out of a job, taking over their own Catholic Church locally, have not necessarily encouraged the Indians to become priests. Indeed, they suggest that non-hierarchical, lay leadership according to Indian models is more useful for Indians within the Church, and perhaps for the Church as a whole (Mittelstadt, January 18, 1987).

Others have asked, if Indians are to become priests, whom will they serve? This question asks not only *where* they will serve—in their home community? in other Indian ministries? in non-Indian parishes?—but where their loyalties will be placed. Will their authority derive from their personal standing among their own people, or from the status vested in them by the local bishop representing Rome? Will they have a goal of building a local religious culture that adheres closely to local values, responsibilities, and symbolic expressions, or will they reproduce, more or less, normative Catholic forms and meanings? Will their training in the spiritual life include instruction in tribal sacred ceremonies, and hence will their liturgical outpouring incorporate Native calendars, regalia, mythological references, and ritual gestures? Or, will they serve, more or less, like white priests, theologically and liturgically? An Episcopalian priest and ethnologist, Peter Powell, praised Catholic proposals for Native American clergy, but warned against their being too "white-centered. . . . Only when Indians see the Church producing Clergy who will preserve Indian tribal cultures, and who will be holier than the Holy Men of old; only then can the Church expect to win Indian people to Christ" (Powell, September 24, 1970). A statement of Jesuits working in Indian ministry (JINNAM,

August 14, 1985) called for the Church to free itself of attitudes that impede Indian leadership; to listen to Native peoples about their models of Christian leadership; and to encourage the development of indigenous theologies and liturgies in connection with Native vocational training.

For the past thirty years, the questions of Indian Catholic vocations have necessarily been tied to the questions of inculturation. "[T]he Church needs to take root in each Native culture," writes (Hatcher 1996–1997: 12) a Jesuit with long and effective service in the American Indian ministry, and this happens most palpably through ordained leadership. The sum of these questions is directed at Indian Catholic priests themselves (and sisters, brothers, and deacons, too): how shall they embody Catholic faith in their Indian personhood? It is the purpose of the following section to examine the lives of several American Indian priests and religious, not to recommend how they ought to live, or how they should have lived, but to observe the complex contours of their Indian Catholic leadership and service.

JAMEſ BOUCHARD, ſ.J., AND ALBERT NEGAHNQUET

If one looks at the lives of the first American Indian priests, one can see either the submergence of their Indianness in their public ministry, or the tensions created by their desire to assert their Indian identity in the face of Church policy to mute it.

James Chrysostom Bouchard, S.J. (*Watomika*, "Swift Foot"), a Delaware Indian, a convert to Catholicism in 1847, ordained a Jesuit in 1855, and a missionary in California from 1861 to his death in 1889, was the first American Indian ordained to the Roman Catholic priesthood in the United States. Born in 1823 in Indian Territory (now Kansas), Watomika was French on his maternal side—his mother having been captured by Comanches as a child, and having lived her adult life as a thoroughgoing Comanche, married to a Delaware. Watomika grew up culturally as a Delaware-Comanche: hunting buffalo, participating in war parties, paying close attention to his dreams and visions. When his Delaware father was killed in a battle with the Sioux, and his mother returned to her Comanche relatives, the youth was approached by a Protestant missionary who sent him to school at Marietta College in Ohio. He became a Presbyterian; then he converted to Catholicism, in St. Louis.

In becoming a Christian, Watomika overcame the admonitions of both his parents. He said of his father, that he "was not only ignorant of the Christian Religion, but also a bitter enemy of it & all who made profession of it" (in Miller 1989: 172). His mother, "much more Indian than white, taught him to regard the religion of the white man as an invention for deceiving and destroying the Indian and despoiling him of his land" (McGloin 1950: 43). At the same time, when he embraced Catholicism, he seems to have reached for the faith of his mother's family, and he took her French name—Bouchard, or Boucher—as his own.

His biographer writes: "Watomika, while later living his life as James Bouchard, Jesuit, and while engaged in his significant apostolate in the Far West, chose not to emphasize his Indian origin or pre-Christian tribal years. While not denying the truth concerning his origin, he chose . . . to be habitually silent on the matter" (ibid., 42).

Nevertheless, his Native heritage "was common knowledge among other American Jesuits" (Miller 1989: 167). Bouchard wrote a brief memoir of his Indian youth at the request of the famous Belgian Jesuit, Pierre Jean de Smet, penning it in the third person. He distanced himself from his Indian identity, at least in public (his private papers burned in the San Francisco fire of 1906); however, in his adult years he was fond of speaking Delaware, quoting tribal lore, and he kept in regular contact with his Indian relatives. Indeed, the night before he died, he received a letter from his brother, back home in Kansas, addressed not to "Father Bouchard" but to "Watomika," at his San Francisco address.

Bouchard's early Christian spirituality reflected his Delaware patterns. He fasted devoutly and regularly while at Marietta College. He referred to Christianity as "the Great Medicine of the White Man" (in McGloin 1950: 53). While in seminary he recorded one of his dreams, in which,

> a celestial guide conducted me into Heaven, and there showed me, far in the upper Heaven, five circles of glowing stars, in the center of which there was one star more significant than the rest. Asking my guide the meaning of this, he responded: "The outer circle represents those members of the Society of Jesus who die out of office; the fourth represents all who die as rectors; the third represents the missionaries of the Society; the second represents those who have died as provincials; the first represents the Generals—and the central luminary represents St. Ignatius, the holy founder of the Society of Jesus. . . ." (In McGloin 1950: 64)

The pattern of this dream corresponded to the paradigm of visions experienced by Delaware (and other Algonkian Indian) youths in their quests for guardian spirits, in which a spiritual guide leads the Indian to the sky to gain cosmic knowledge. Obviously the content of the dream bore the stamp of his Jesuit training and concerns.

Father Bouchard was openly critical of government policy toward the Delawares and other Indian peoples. As an Indian, but also as a Catholic, he criticized the materialist liberalism of American culture, "whose only God is the almighty dollar" (in ibid., 75). It was his desire, as a Jesuit and as an Indian, to serve as missionary to his own people—if not the Delawares, then at least the Indians of the West, and he hoped to accompany Father de Smet on his missionary journeys; nevertheless, his superiors forbade such a vocation. Because of the conflict between his wishes and the order's commands, he came close to quitting the

Jesuits, but by 1861 he made a decision to remain. Even though an instructor of his reported that he wished "to devote himself to the salvation of the Indians" (61), he went as he was told to California, where he had an illustrious, although controversial, career as preacher and Catholic organizer from Salt Lake City to Hawaii, from Vancouver to San Francisco. When he arrived in the West, he said he felt in "exile. . . . I fear my going to California is too much like Jonas' fleeing from Nineveh. . . . How gladly would I go back to Kansas!" (87). Nevertheless, he submerged his Indian longings and came to identify publicly with his non-Indian Catholic flock. He even went so far as to adopt and express the bigotry of Irish Catholics against the Chinese in California, speaking of himself as one of the "white race" (100). It is doubtful that he ever engaged actively as a priest in the theological or liturgical admixture of Catholicism and American Indian religiousness.

A half century after Bouchard's ordination, and more than a decade after his death, the second Native American became a priest; indeed, he is often referred to as the first full-blood Indian priest in the United States: Albert Negahnquet (Leading Cloud). Born in Topeka, Kansas, in 1874, he moved with his Potawatomi family to Indian Territory as an infant. After a Catholic schooling he attended the College of the Propaganda in Rome and was ordained in 1903. Immediately he received a commission to serve as priest to Creek, Cherokee, and other Indian peoples, as well as white Catholics, within Indian Territory and beyond. He took the assignment eagerly, writing of his vocation to the priesthood as one "which I could do nothing else but obey. With such convictions I have never wavered" (Negahnquet, March 18, 1903).

Little is known today of Father Negahnquet's clerical career; however, he retired in the 1930s and in 1941, three years before his death, he was laicized. Why did he leave his ministry, and then his priesthood? Until someone performs firsthand research regarding his life, one can only note that "there is evidence that it might have been related to problems of cultural conflict and racism within the Church" (*Bureau of Catholic Indian Missions Newsletter*, April 1991: 2).

PHILIP B. GORDON

If there are only suggestions of cultural conflict in Father Negahn-quet's career, the Ojibway Philip B. Gordon's vocation bore the cross of constant turmoil with the Church. If Father Bouchard allowed his Indian persona to lapse in public, Gordon proved less docile in sub-merging his Indian identity. As a result, his whole life as a cleric proved a bitter struggle against Church authorities.

Philip B. Gordon was born in Wisconsin in 1885 of mixed French and Ojibway ancestry; his Indian name was *Ti-bish-ko-gi-jik* ("Looking into the Sky," or "Gift of Heaven"). His half-blood grandfather had served as choir master and interpreter for the famed Slovene mission-ary bishop, Frederic Baraga, and had wanted to become a priest in his youth. As an adult, he took an interest in Western schooling, and passed to his descendants a proficiency in various languages (English, French, Ojibway, Latin) and a love for learning of all kinds. Philip's fa-ther was a chief of the Indian Police and an interpreter at the Indian Agency at Odanah, Wisconsin.

Gordon attended St. Mary's Mission School, under the tutelage of Franciscan sisters and priests. His success as a student led him to fur-ther schooling apart from his Indian associates. Three of his brothers became doctor, lawyer, and dentist, and like them, Philip emphasized adaption to the ways of Whites. He used to say, "The Indian traditions must be preserved, but in books" (in Delfeld 1977: 41). As a youth he and his closest friend, Mesabi, attempted vision quests, but whereas Mesabi received a powerful vision and returned from it confident in his future as a traditional religious specialist, Philip's dreams were said to have been confused and insignificant to himself. He returned from his quest "unresolved. . . . He had found no spirit to guide him through life. The Christian faith of his grandfather was in conflict with the old Indian traditions" (26).

In 1903 Gordon applied for entry into the Provincial Seminary of St. Francis in Wisconsin, but received the reply that "doubts have been expressed concerning your vocation to the holy priesthood" (43). The doubts concerned his Indian identity; at the time the Franciscans still questioned the ability of Indians to become priests. He attended a

Catholic college instead, graduating in 1908, at which time he was admitted to St. Paul Seminary in Minnesota, where he began his priestly studies.

While in seminary Gordon took an interest in Indian missions in the United States, and felt that he was preparing himself for a ministerial life among Native Americans. He wrote to the Bureau of Catholic Indian Missions in 1909, requesting information about Indian missions, and during his several years in theological training in Rome and Austria—where he learned to speak fluent French, Italian, and German—he maintained his dream of becoming a missionary to his Indian people and kept up a correspondence with the BCIM.

When he returned to the United States in 1913 to receive ordination, he visited Ojibway missions in Minnesota and yearned for an assignment there or at his "home" at Odanah, Wisconsin. He observed several hundred Ojibway "pagans" at Red Lake, Minnesota, twenty miles from a priest; at White Earth in the same state, the local priest never visited the Indian reservation, he claimed. Most of these Indians spoke no English and were "very ignorant (which goes without saying)" (Gordon, September 21, 1913), he reported; "truly, if I have a duty, it is to these neglected people."

At the time of his ordination, his relation to his Ojibway people was complex. On the one hand, he was foursquare in maintaining his Indian identity and locality, saying, "I want to live and die among my people" (in Delfeld 1977: 8). When he was ordained he asked that a war drum and peace pipe be constructed so that he could present them to his childhood friend, Mesabi, who was by then the hereditary medicine chief at Lac Court Oreilles Reservation. At the same time, he identified himself with the goals of the BCIM, asking its director, William H. Ketcham, to deliver a sermon at Gordon's first mass (he declined; Odoric Derenthal, O.F.M., who had baptized Philip, gave the sermon instead). Gordon was a Catholic priest intent upon spreading the faith and institutions of the Church among "pagan" Indians.

Unhappily for Father Gordon, his Ojibway ministry was cut short. After several months of serving the Wisconsin Franciscan priests—Fathers Derenthal, Aloysius Hermanutz, Chrysostom Verwyst, and others—he received a transfer to a non-Indian parish, and from there he went to Catholic University in Washington, D.C. Gordon felt beloved among the Ojibways: "The Indians received me very well and come for miles around when I officiate here or there" (Gordon,

March 6, 1914), and he was a forceful defender of the "grand old Church" of the Catholic faith (April 22, 1914) against the forces of Protestantism. He was just coming into contact with the newly formed Society of American Indians, a national agency of Indians with political and social concern for Indian welfare, but he was initially suspicious of its Protestant bias.

At the same time, he fell immediately into rancor with the Franciscans, who dismissed him from their service. Father Derenthal disparaged Gordon to the BCIM, complaining that the Indian priest would not preach in Ojibway language, claiming not to know the verb endings and refusing to study them. Instead, he charged, Gordon spent his time "bumming around as he pleased," tending to his "extensive useless correspondence." The Ojibway alienated the white priests with his concern for his salary, and he spoke to the bishop in a "very saucy, impolite way before a crowd of people" at a Corpus Christi liturgy (ibid., September 21, 1914).

Father Gordon felt deprived, having been removed from his vocation of "working among my own" (ibid., April 22, 1914), and it took Father Ketcham of the BCIM to remind him that "a priest is ordained for priestly work first of all" (April 24, 1914), among Whites as well as Indians. His parishioners were now Irish, German, French, and Polish families, at least until he was transferred to the national capital.

In Washington, D.C., he collected money for Indian missions, and he also came into contact with politically active Indians from around the nation, including, e.g., Charles Alexander Eastman and Carlos Montezuma, the Sioux and Apache physicians. Before long he joined Montezuma's Society of American Indians.

In 1915 the BCIM sent Gordon to Lawrence, Kansas, where he served for a year as chaplain to the Catholic Indian students at Haskell Institute, the federally funded college for Native Americans. At Haskell Father Gordon combined his Indian and Catholic loyalties in a personal crusade against religious discrimination at the Institute. In Gordon's view—and evidence shows him to have been correct—the authorities at Haskell functioned as Protestants, discouraging Catholic Indian organization and spirituality among the student body. Gordon felt the Protestant bias as an affront to his Indian and Catholic sensibilities, and he carried out a campaign in which he tried to uphold the rights of Indians and Catholics alike.

BCIM Director Ketcham recommended Gordon to the Haskell

ministry as a smart, well-educated Indian priest, liked by Whites as well as Indians. Ketcham noted that although Gordon was almost a full-blood, "he has the aggressive ways and manners of a white" (ibid., February 16, 1915). Indeed, Gordon entered the fray at once, defending Indians as potential Catholics against the prejudices of his fellow priests, and insisting upon his full access to Indian Catholic students at Haskell. Gordon expressed his Catholicism fiercely in demanding time and space to meet with Catholic Indians students at Haskell, avowing that "this injun is on the war path" (September 27, 1915) against Protestant administrators. Before long the Commissioner of Indian Affairs became incensed at Gordon's "stirring up things at Haskell," as Father Ketcham put it (October 13, 1915), and he threatened to remove Gordon from his post. The BCIM and the cardinals it represented were embarrassed by Gordon's violation of "ordinary proprieties" (November 19, 1915) in his rude correspondence with government officials, his sermons against Haskell Institute and the Indian Bureau, and his letters to the parents of Catholic Indian students, protesting YMCA and YWCA activities at the Institute. Gordon claimed that "several Catholics have lapsed into Protestantism from the effects" of these activities, and he called for the parents to "help us to keep your children Catholic" (November 1915). Although Ketcham approved of Gordon's struggle against Protestant biases and told him to stick to his principles, he also feared for the political fallout from the Ojibway's vociferous zeal.

Gordon regarded it a right of Catholic Indian students to receive the sacraments and he decried administrative decisions that kept the Indians from their priest. "One of my Catholic boys died last night," he wrote, and Gordon did not hear of it for ten hours: "The boy died without the Sacraments, without a Catholic at hand! What a commentary on Catholics in Government Schools!" (ibid., December 27, 1915). Gordon wanted to see "compulsory attendance of Catholic students at mass, and he invited non-Catholic Indians to attend Catholic services, so they could learn more of his faith. In 1916 Gordon won his battle for compulsory mass attendance, and his victory made the Protestants wary that Catholicism was taking over at Haskell. Before the next academic year began, Gordon was removed by the BCIM from his chaplaincy.

For the next year Father Gordon served the BCIM as an itinerant preacher and fund-raiser. He investigated conditions at other boarding schools; he preached against peyotism among the Potawatomis; he visited Indian communities in Oklahoma, Nebraska, South Dakota, and Montana, demonstrating the living reality of an Indian priest. He competed with Protestant missionaries and took an interest in the conditions of Indian peoples wherever he went. By August 1916 he was serving on the editorial staff of *American Indian Magazine,* the organ of the Society of American Indians, and in October of the same year he attended a Lake Mohonk Conference, where gathered national reformers of Indian policies.

Throughout this stint, however, Gordon resented the fact that he was not given an Indian parish. He complained, "I certainly realize that a visitation of a mission does very little good except in showing the Indians that an Indian can become a real live priest" (ibid., December 8, 1916). He made his desires clear: "If I was my own 'boss' you may be sure that I would have appointed myself to some Indian place a long time ago" (in Delfeld 1977: 62). He lobbied for an Indian mission post, leading to thoughts of resigning and friction between himself and his superiors within the Church. He wrote in 1917, "The Indians need me, dear Bishop, and you are not the one to allow the call of the Redman to go unheeded" (in ibid., 64).

In 1918 Father Gordon achieved his wish and took over an Ojibway parish at Reserve, Wisconsin. Neither Father Derenthal nor Father Ketcham had high expectations of Gordon's success; the BCIM director hoped that God would grant Rev. Gordon "prudence and make him a useful man" (Gordon, February 27, 1918). Before long, however, Gordon's dual loyalties to tribe and Church fell into conflict with one another and he faced a crisis of his own making, of his own being, as a Catholic Indian priest.

At Reserve, Father Gordon found a log church built by the Indians for the Franciscans. He wanted to create a church that would combine Indian and Catholic religious symbols. He felt that the missionaries had tried to bring the Ojibways too quickly and thoroughly away from their aboriginal worldview and symbolic meanings; therefore, he wished to build a church that would be a "connecting link," as he put it, "which would sagely bring Indians from paganism to Catholicism." He aimed to construct a church and a ministry that would "reach the Indian's heart" (in Delfeld 1977: 71). He and the Ojibway Catholics built an edifice with stained glass windows picturing the rising sun, arrows, crossed peace pipes, tobacco, with the Christian cross above them all. Deerskins hung from the confessionals and at the altar. Ojibway women fashioned altar cloths with Indian designs, and Gordon's house was made in the shape of a tipi. A power project partially flooded the reservation and the church was never completed; however, its plan revealed Gordon's desire to include at least the outward representations of Ojibway imagery in Catholic worship.

At the same time, Father Gordon took an active role in Ojibway politics, serving in the government of the Lac Court Oreilles Band and becoming a vocal agitator against the Bureau of Indian Affairs and its local bureaucrats. He took up the cause of Indian land claims, and even attempted to run for Congress, until the local bishop stopped him. In the turmoil of World War I, Gordon began to publish an Ojibway language newspaper, *Anishinabe Enamiad,* in which he accused the Franciscans—Fathers Derenthal, Hermanutz, and others—as well as his bishop, J. M. Koudelka, of "Teutonic origin" (Gordon, August 1918) and pro-German sentiment in the war. He charged that both Church and State were falling short in their commitment to social welfare, and urged his fellow Ojibways toward more strident demands for amelioration of their conditions. An Indian Service employee complained to the BCIM concerning Gordon's activities: "These Indians are very material. Father Gordon could well afford to concern himself with their spiritual and moral needs alone, but he has chosen to make this part secondary to their material side" (ibid., September 5, 1918). The Catholic Bureau brought these complaints to the Apostolic Delegate with the message that "we are much worried over Fr. Gordon's conduct. . . . It would perhaps be better if the Bishop took him away from the Indians entirely . . ." (ibid. 1918). Father Ketcham suggested that Gordon be appointed an army chaplain: "the Bishop should send him now; once in the army he will have to submit to discipline & this may save him" (ibid.).

Gordon's particular ire was directed toward the boarding school where local Ojibway children were sent, and where, he said, they "became almost strangers to their folks . . ." (ibid., December 1, 1918). He wanted to establish a type of public school for the Lac Court Oreilles Ojibways, staffed by lay teachers, and he ordered the Sisters of St. Joseph from their teaching posts on the reservation, calling them incompetent and chiding them for their refusal to sing with the Indians in church choir. His complaint against the boarding school was one thing, but his attack on the sisters aroused strong opposition, both from Indians and Whites. The sisters made it clear that they had no confidence in Father Gordon, appealing to federal authorities, who found it ironic that Gordon was publicly criticizing his own Church operations, "of which he is supposed to be the priest in charge" (ibid., March 1, 1920). Gordon arrived at his Ojibway post in 1918; within two years he was the subject of governmental, as well as ecclesiastical, investigations, and he was being termed a troublemaker, "placed in the Bolshevik class," Gordon said (April 23, 1920). Church officials were embarrassed by his outspoken criticism of the Indian Bureau and by the fracas with the sisters. His bishop feared the scandal of Gordon's public disobedience and wondered if he should not remove him.

Gordon succeeded in removing the sisters from the day school at Reserve, after first refusing them the sacraments. He solidified his authority among the local Ojibways and became president of the Society of American Indians, using his position as a secular pulpit from which he delivered tirades against the Bureau of Indian Affairs. Church officials rankled over his politicization of the ministry, and local Ojibways chafed under his regime. In 1923 some of them brought charges of sexual improprieties against Gordon to the Indian Bureau, which commissioned the prominent Sioux author and physician, Charles Alexander Eastman, to conduct an investigation. Eastman's report inferred truth in the charges and Gordon was forced by Church superiors to resign his Indian post in 1924, although the BCIM thought that Eastman's conclusions outpaced the evidence. In resigning, Gordon asserted that the campaign against him constituted a successful attack to prevent his continued critique of the Indian Bureau. He was reassigned to a non-Indian parish, and he petitioned the diocese to get his Indian post back, to no avail. He reminded the Church that the pope had called for an indigenous clergy for tribal peoples; still, he was kept from an Indian ministry. From his new parish, "a typical farming district," he decried his treatment: "Isn't it strange that all my activity in behalf of the Indians has not as yet drawn a single word of either thanks or appreciation from my superiors, that is, the Bishop and [the Bureau of Catholic Indian Missions]. . . . or is Indian work ever the most ungrateful task?" (ibid., May 16, 1924).

For two more decades until his death in 1948 Father Gordon maintained his public Indian identity: protesting against the governmental ban on Indian dances in the late 1920s; encouraging the passage of Indian New Deal legislation created by his friend and Commissioner of Indian Affairs John Collier in the early 1930s; blessing the president and members of Congress in an invocation in the House of Representatives in 1943. "Bless, O Great Spirit, the Kitche Manito of our forefathers . . ." (in Delfeld 1977: 135), he intoned. Nevertheless, Church officials denied him a return to Indian ministry. He remained alienated from what he considered his true calling as a priest.

It is worth noting that the son of Philip Gordon's cousin was ordained a priest in 1983. Kevin Gordon has taken great interest in his uncle's clerical career, and like his uncle he has served within his home state of Wisconsin, although not in Indian ministry, thus far.

MICHAEL JACOBS, S.J.

Born on the Caughnawaga Mohawk Reserve near Montreal in 1902, ordained a Jesuit priest in 1934, Michael Karhaienton Jacobs spent almost the entirety of his ministry among Mohawk peoples. From 1936, almost until his death in 1988, Father Jacobs lived at or near the St. Regis Mohawk Reservation straddling the St. Lawrence River between New York State and the Provinces of Quebec and Ontario. Jacobs's family were Catholics and steel workers; his family worked in Canada near his home, and his brothers built skyscrapers in New York City. Michael joined them but was frightened by the dangerous heights; he opted for the priesthood. He attended Jesuit novitiates from 1922, and after ordination served briefly at Caughnawaga and Auriesville, New York.

He began as a temporary mission helper for the Diocese of Ogdensburg (St. Regis also is part of a Canadian Diocese of Valleyfield) in 1936, eager—he wrote to his bishop—to "start off for this 'great missionary adventure.'" He looked forward to teaching the Mohawk children, visiting their families, and strengthening the Church presence in a community that had begun almost two centuries earlier as a Catholic enclave. He referred to himself as a "devoted Indian-Jesuit Missionary" (Ogdensburg, April 28, 1936) in accepting his assignment. He was grateful to the bishop, Joseph H. Conroy, for "the great privilege . . . to work among his children of the Mohawk Tribe," and he asked "God, through the powerful intercession of Our Lady" (ibid., May 7, 1936), for success. He took great pleasure in teaching the Indian boys and girls to recite the Hail Mary in Mohawk, and to validate the use of Mohawk in St. Regis liturgies. In a census he compiled when he first arrived, he located 392 Catholic families and 96 Protestant families making up the population of 1,552 persons on the reserve. Although the Indians were suspicious of his census-taking, they received him cordially, including the Protestants, whom he hoped, some day, would "return to the True Fold" (June 25, 1936). Father Jacobs spent the summer at St. Regis before taking another position.

In 1938 he returned as assistant pastor of the mission, as the diocese turned St. Regis over to the Jesuit ministry. Bishop Conroy did not regard the Mohawk highly—"Frankly I have no great regard for the ability of Father Jacobs; he seems to me to be a visitor—not a leader or worker" (ibid., July 7, 1937)—but he needed the priest's fluency in Mohawk language to lead liturgies and to communicate to the people the Church's regard for them. The St. Regis Indians were concerned that their community would be split into a Canadian and American parish; the bishop expressed his desire to "preserve your unity as a Nation insofar as possible and consonant with your precious heritage of the Catholic Faith" (December 23, 1936). For their own part the St. Regis governing council affirmed their desire for Christian moral training within the educational curriculum, and reminded the bishop that they had been "traditionally christian [sic] for several hundred years, and 92% belong to one Christian Church" (October 24, 1937).

Father Jacobs entered a Mohawk community that held dearly to its Catholic faith, its Mohawk rites—a privilege granted by the papacy—and its sovereign integrity. Initially these conditions made his ministry a welcomed addition in the community, and he commented upon an "Increase of Faith" (ibid., July 13, 1939) among his parishioners in the first year of his service. More Indians attended mass, received sacraments, and joined Catholic sodalities. He initiated devotion to the Blessed Virgin and to the Sacred Heart of Jesus, and he found hospitality in the Mohawk homes. The Indians were "happy to see their priest," he wrote. "They try to show their appreciation in giving him what they have. I come home every night loaded with vegetables: corn, carrots, cabbage, potatoes, preserves, oats barley buckwheat, they give what they can and they give generously" (October 24, 1939).

Father Jacobs was a conservative Catholic priest in regards to theology and parish ecclesiology. Church teachings were authoritative; dogma was sacred; and the power of the priest over his parishioners was paternal. He did not shrink from scolding them for their sins, and he let them know what a privilege they possessed in having a Mohawk priest among them. When he returned from his first vacation in the summer of 1941, he reported that the Indians "begged me not to leave them any more." They thought that he had left permanently, because he had "scolded" them before leaving for a month, suggesting to them that he was through with them. "I was wrong," he said, "and I think, kindness is still the best policy with them" (ibid., June 8, 1941).

The St. Regis Mohawks were jealous of their control over community matters and institutions, and they were suspicious that Jesuits planned to usurp control over their community center, formed in 1939. Still, they trusted Jacobs. Their parish council attested (ibid., April 8, 1946) that, "although he is a Jesuit, they still like him, because he is an Indian." Jacobs himself fell out with the Canadian Jesuits, who, he said, refused to learn Mohawk and who regarded him with disdain. He considered an attempt to sever St. Regis from the Canadian province and made it known to his fellow priests how popular he was among his Mohawk flock. When he returned to the parish after a lengthy recuperation from an illness, the Indians greeted him by lamenting his absence ("We missed you so much. . . . It was lonesome while you were gone"), and by packing the church and giving hundreds of dollars for his support. He crowed, "No other priest before ever had one-fourth of the material support that they have been giving me since I am their pastor" (June 17, 1946). To celebrate his return the parish held a Corpus Christi procession, with a brass band and a lacrosse game at the community center. With his funds Father Jacobs provided some of the lacrosse equipment, and he noted the Indians' gratitude: "They feel that Fr. Jacobs is for them; he is with them; and what I love most, is that they are so happy when I am with them and they have confidence in me" (July 10, 1946). They accompanied him on pilgrimages to Montreal and to Caughnawaga, where they performed devotions in honor of "Our Indian Saint, the Lily of the Mohawks" (ibid.), Kateri Tekakwitha. Jacobs found their faith strong; all they needed was an Indian priest to serve as their shepherd.

In the early 1950s Father Jacobs noted that in disputes between the "elective" and "traditional" chiefs at St. Regis—the former were created by the Indian New Deal of the 1930s; the latter derived authority from the aboriginal League of the Iroquois—he took sides with the more "progressive" elected officials. By the end of the decade the traditionalists had gained power and influence, not only in matters of political jurisdiction, but also in the religious loyalties of the Mohawk community. The 1950s saw a resurgence of the Longhouse Religion, the traditional Iroquois spirituality reformed by the Seneca visionary Handsome Lake and his followers in the early nineteenth century. The proponents of this "traditional" religion won adherents with spiritually grounded appeals for Mohawk national sovereignty, and Father Jacobs found himself in "stiff competition" with them for the hearts and minds of his parishioners. There was no Longhouse at Caughnawaga when Jacobs grew up, and he found their "traditionalism"

new-fangled and wrong-headed. He wrote that the members of the
"'Long-House' with their extreme nationalism," i.e., their claim to
constitute a "'Sovereign, . . . Independent Nation,' are making head-
lines and are very belligerent." He continued:

> They have made some gains for a while; but with the help of God and
> the Intercession of Our Blessed Mother—The Month of May Devo-
> tions, every night—The Month of the Sacred Heart and still more
> prayers and sacrifices—with much patience and humility, I hope we will
> be able to hold the *Fort* and reclaim the souls that are being fooled by
> Satan. (Ibid., April 29, 1959)

At a moment when Jacobs was celebrating his twenty-fifth anniversary
of ordination, and when he was—at long last—made superior at St.
Regis, he and his Church were falling out of favor with his fellow
Mohawks.

In the 1960s Father Jacobs came to struggle against his fellow Mohawks at St. Regis, which was now coming to be known by its
Mohawk name, "Akwesasne," under Longhouse influence. He had to
admit that the Mohawks were not "Church-goers" (ibid., February 10,
1961); that they were "*financially irresponsible. . . .* If we insist that they
give and give *regularly,* they will stop going to church, because it costs
too much—and the priest wants only money" (February 14, 1961).
When a group of Mohawks on the American side of the reservation attempted to create a Catholic church of their own—they were justifi-
ably protesting a regulation that required them to show their identity
upon crossing the U.S.-Canadian border—Jacobs asked, "What kind
of men are they?"

> Are they stubborn? Protestant mentality? I answer *yes,* and *crooked-
> minds* and a tendency to *Nationalism,* Neo-paganism-Long-house lean-
> ings, protestant notions of running a church. The *fascination* of *Church
> trustees;* they will finance the church—in their minds it means it is their
> Church, their own like the protestants; they will get the money; they
> will handle the business; and they will assume the direction—*they will
> run the priest,* as in Protestant Churches. (Ibid., *sic*)

The Mohawks, even some of the Catholics, were coming to identify
themselves more thoroughly with their traditionalist rhetoric and values, and Jacobs was finding himself on the outs with his own people.
He blamed their disaffection from Catholic authority—his authority—
upon the "poison" of a "pagan public-school system" (ibid.), but at the
basis was their self-conscious uprising as a people:

> This is the hardest *problem: the nationalism* of *these Indians* . . . 'the
> threat of the Long-house-Indians', which means Neo-paganism; their
> irresponsibility . . . their quick-change of mind . . . im-maturity . . . in-
> constancy . . . their fickleness, their laziness . . . they are prone to super-
> stition . . . and above all their vain-pride: 'The Country is theirs' . . .
> 'White-man = intruders' . . . 'White-man—no good, cheat Indians'
> 'Priest destroy 'Our ancient faith' . . . It is *paganism* and *diabolical*. . . .
> (Ibid., *sic*)

So critical was Jacobs of the Mohawks, that he was forced to add, in
writing to his bishop, "I am not running down the Indians—Many are
good Indians, believe me" (ibid.). He was compelled to explain to his
Church superiors why the St. Regis Indians were not attending mass
regularly, and in so doing, he distanced himself from them:

> I am not looking for excuses, but we must try to understand, their men-
> tality, their character, their way of thinking, as *Indians,* and relatively re-
> cent converts to Christianity.
>   The sound principles of Christianity, belief in the Articles of Faith,
> seven Sacraments—all these truths, they believe and they accept and
> practice, I hope, enough to be saved. . . .
>   Concerning Mass, frequent reception of the Sacraments, supporting
> the Church, Catholic education, Church societies, working for the
> Church, they haven't got it. (Ibid., March 9, 1961)

Why? Because they have been "wards" of the state and Church for two
centuries; they have received everything without working for it. They
haven't paid taxes; nor have they supported the Church, yet when they
die, they expect to go to heaven. Jacobs acknowledged that St. Regis
had existed as a Catholic enclave since 1752, and that fact meant "transforming the mentality of our Catholic North American Indians." At the
same time, however, "we still have to work hard . . . before we can say
that our Indians of Saint Regis Mission are equal in Faith, religious
Convictions and Fervor, like the Irish and the French-Canadians, who
have embraced the Faith many, many centuries before the Indians of
North America did" (ibid.).

Jacobs recommended that St. Regis Indians on the American side
of the reservation attend the Catholic church in Hogansburg, at the
border of the reservation. He knew that racial animosity made the Indians unwelcome in the white community, but he also criticized the
Mohawks for their own desire for segregation within the Church. He
wanted them to feel part of the Roman Catholic Church, rather than
to identify themselves merely as Mohawk Catholics. Given the mood

of Mohawk nationalism of the 1960s, Jacobs's integrationist model found little favor among the Indians, even as the Diocese of Ogdensburg insisted that priests from nearby towns accept Indians in their parishes.

Under investigatory pressure from the diocese to demonstrate the Mohawks' Catholic faith, Jacobs became more stridently zealous in the pulpit. He told his people in his Mohawk sermons that missing mass on Sunday "constitutes a mortal sin, and deserves punishment in hell" (ibid., May 6, 1961). He blamed their absence at mass on patterns of weekend drunkenness and condemned them for it. As he preached hellfire and damnation, his parishioners turned against him, treating him as an intruder representing an invasive Church, and worse. Complaints came to the diocese, accusing Father Jacobs of financial irregularities in favor of his relatives on the reservation. Jacobs responded, "I suppose some people are critical and jealous of my affection for my family"; however, his family activities were his "hobby," his "recreation, . . . priestly hours well spent" (May 3, 1961). Factional jealousies undermined the remainder of his pastorate at St. Regis, but underneath them lay Jacobs's unceasing opposition to the "paganism" of the Longhouse, which drew more and more Catholic Mohawks to its fold.

In 1965 the diocese replaced Jacobs as pastor; however, he continued to live at St. Regis for another two decades. During this period, the priest became more sympathetic to the political aims of the traditionalists, and although he continued to condemn the Longhouse religion, he identified himself with Indian causes. In 1969 he said of himself, "I am still a staunch defender of the Faith and a fighter for the Rights of Indians . . ." (ibid., January 23, 1969), and he attempted to form a Catholic organization to promote Iroquois treaty rights. He began to use his Indian name, *Karhaienton,* which he had let lapse in correspondence for several decades. As his priestly duties subsided, his Indian identity came once again to the fore. Jacobs's presence in St. Regis parish was an obstacle to the authority of several non-Indian pastors, including his successor, Rev. Francis Arsenault, S.J. They were constantly reminded that he spoke Mohawk, they didn't; he was one of the ethnic community, they weren't; he was regarded with some affection; supposedly they were not. Jacobs's familial allies undercut the Jesuits who replaced the Mohawk priest, whose old age was spent in physical and mental decline, but who continued to oppose the Longhouse. He called its members pagans and communists; in turn, they attacked him publicly for his rigid authoritarianism. Katsi Cook, a distant niece of Father Jacobs, bridled under his "unyielding" and "unrelenting" Mohawk sermons, in which he told his compatriots, "'You'll go to hell if you go to the Longhouse! . . . They are witches who worship Satan and do bad things there.'" As a result of his clerical tirades, "Father Jacobs was not someone I considered an uncle," she recalls (Cook, Midwinter 1988: 12–13).

"Jacobs was not a tolerant or kind man," writes Doug George-Kanentiio (March 4, 1998), whose childhood home was but a few dozen yards west of the rectory in the village of St. Regis, and who was baptized by Jacobs and served him as an altar boy, but who has long been an eloquent spokesman for the Longhouse. "He was, according to my experience, overly fond of alcohol, a habit which caused him problems at Akwesasne and alienated many Mohawks." Most important, however, was his opposition to the traditionalists, which served to alienate the Mohawks from Catholicism. Writes George-Kanentiio, "Much of the Church's difficulty in retaining the support of the parish was due to Jacobs himself." Ironically, his non-Indian successor, Father Arsenault (whom Jacobs undermined), played a key role in mediating between Catholics and traditionalists. "He was the first priest," George-Kanentiio says, "to enter the Longhouse" and treat its members with respect and he took a firm stand on aboriginal rights, which won him considerable admiration among the Longhouse people. Jacobs, the Native priest, never gained that trust among his own people.

Father Jacobs maintained his foursquare Catholic faith in his retirement, proclaiming, "The Catholic Church—is our Mother—our guide—our protection—our Hope." He never ceased to regard the Catholic Church as the one, holy, catholic and apostolic faith, and he urged it upon his fellow Native Americans: "The Religion of the Indians of all North America—must be the Religion of Christ—Our Master and Our Redeemer" (Jacobs and Egan 1973, 1989). As a priest he had little sympathy for the ecumenism and inculturation pronounced by the Second Vatican Council; he was not about to make spiritual or liturgical compromises with the Longhouse. "Tribal jealousies" (JINNAM, June 29, 1984) and familial factionalism limited his effectiveness, at least from the 1960s, leading some observers to doubt the wisdom of placing an Indian priest or religious among his own people (Egan, July 9, 1989), even though today some of the older, conservative Mohawk Catholics recall him with fondness (Cook, August 7, 1993).

The difficulties Father Jacobs had in serving his fellow Mohawks—
difficulties also experienced in later years by the Mohawk sister Kateri
Mitchell—led Rev. George White, O.M.I., the first St. Regis Mohawk
priest, ordained in 1945, to seek assignments outside his home community. Orphaned as a boy, White was raised in Ogdensburg by Grey
Nuns before entering the Oblate juniorate and novitiate. He did not
know who the Oblates were when he joined. All he knew was that he
wanted to become a missionary priest, perhaps a Maryknoll. He
thought of going to China. When he was ordained he volunteered for
Indian ministry in the Yukon; however, his order sent him instead to
Brazil, where he spent his first seventeen years as a priest, serving as a
missionary to Indians there. Then he served in various parishes in the
United States (presently in Connecticut), but never at St. Regis. On
the fiftieth anniversary of his ordination he comments that St. Regis
has always been Jesuit territory, and after all, he is an Oblate. He maintains contacts with relatives, coming back for brief summer visits, but
he has built his priestly life away from home and regards himself, basically, as a "stranger" in St. Regis (White, August 5, 1995) and does not
plan to become involved in its agitations. Father White is enthused
about the cause of Kateri Tekakwitha's sainthood, but he has attended
only one Tekakwitha conference (at St. Regis), despite attempts by
Msgr. Lenz of the Bureau of Catholic Indian Missions to get him involved. Lenz calls him "a hard man to track down" (ibid.) for Indian
ministry, and White acknowledges that he has developed other interests in his priestly career.

GEORGES P. MATHIEU AND JOHN J. BROWN, S.J.

In 1937 Father Georges P. Mathieu received his ordination in La Crosse, Wisconsin, and until 1972 he took parish assignments, hospital pastorates, and CYO administrative posts in various sites in the Midwest. A 1962 newspaper article described him as "a descendant of one of Chicago's oldest families, tracing his ancestry back through Mark Beaubien . . ." (Mathieu, June 15, 1962), one of Chicago's first non-Indian inhabitants. Ten years later, however, Mathieu received appointment as Director of Indian Apostolate for La Crosse and revealed himself publicly to be an American Indian.

Father Mathieu did not discover his Indian heritage in 1972; indeed, he grew up in the western extremity of Chicago near the remaining grounds of his Potawatomi ancestors. The Treaty of Chicago had taken most of the Potawatomi territory, leaving only an Indian cemetery (still in existence), around which the remnants of the Potawatomis congregated, Mathieu's family—part French, part Indian—among them. His family members were practicing Catholics; they spoke no Potawatomi language and performed no Indian rituals. Nevertheless, they knew of their Indianness, including their relation to an ancestor who first encouraged the Potawatomis toward Catholicism in the early nineteenth century.

In his youth, Mathieu's parents received visits from Father Philip Gordon, who encouraged the boy toward the priesthood, but who warned him against public disclosure of his Indian identity: "Don't let them know who you are, Indian" (ibid., February 8, 1982). Gordon and Mathieu felt that the Church was hostile to Indians and other men of color becoming priests, and so Mathieu hid his Potawatomi roots, even though he was "always conscious of Indianness: Became more conscious in seminary" (ibid.).

As a priest, Mathieu paid no especial attention to Indian ministry or to Indian social causes until the late 1960s, when he began to visit Winnebago Indians within the Diocese of La Crosse. They felt alienated from the Whites of his own parish, whom they regarded as bigots, and they associated Mathieu with his congregation. The Winnebagos did not accept him until he learned some of their language and was able to joke with them. From that time Mathieu prodded his diocese to recognize its Indian clientele and pressed for an Indian ministry, with himself in charge.

Even then, he did not identify himself publicly as an Indian, for he feared that a Church that had denied Father Gordon an Indian vicarship for most of his adult life would deny him an Indian post if his ethnic identity were well known. Following his appointment to the Indian Apostolate in 1972, Father Gordon made his heritage public, e.g., wearing the feathers of the Prairie Band of Potawatomi in marking the tricentennial of Père Marquette's exploration of the Mississippi, in 1973. In the same year he delivered supplies to Indian activists under siege at Wounded Knee, on the Pine Ridge Reservation in South Dakota, and he lectured Mayor Richard Daley of Chicago on the needs of the large Indian community in that city. His bishop in La Crosse resented his public posturing; however, for the next two decades Father Mathieu expressed an Indian Catholic identity and espoused a special Catholic ministry to Indians. In 1980 he was one of five Indian priests who distributed communion during the beatification ceremonies for Kateri Tekakwitha in Rome, and although he retired from active diocesan ministry in 1977, he continued to serve Catholic Indians until his death in 1996. Wisconsin Indians sought him out, and he attended Tekakwitha congresses to share in Indian Catholic liturgies. A newspaper reporter observed him at ease with himself in 1980: "Father Mathieu is obviously satisfied that he has found a role now in helping Indian people the best way he can—and found himself, too, at last" (in ibid., July 6, 1980).

Father Mathieu found a welcome at the Tekakwitha assemblies and in the Association of Native Religious and Clergy (ANRC). When he went to Rome in 1980, he said, only four other priests in the U.S. regarded themselves openly as American Indians: John J. Brown, Roch Naquin, John Hascall, and Charles Leute. Over the past decade he enjoyed observing the growing numbers of Indian priests ordained, and priests declaring their Indianness. He also enjoyed engaging in pan-Indian ritualism within Catholic circles: smoking the pipe, greeting the sunrise, purifying in the sweat, and he was thankful to Pope John Paul II for his support for liturgical changes that permitted Indian ritualism.

At the same time, he perceived a continuation of racism within the hierarchy of the Catholic Church in the United States, a bias that makes it difficult for Indian priests to fulfill their vocations. He claimed (Mathieu, September 14, 1987) that bigotry has stood in the way of hierarchical advancement by Indian clerics, and in general he found the hierarchical Church to be "a mess: the fact that the Church didn't fall apart centuries ago is a sign of the Church's divinity." But was he ready to give up his Catholic ministry to Indians? He retorted that his "retirement" was a "dirty, unfounded rumor." He planned to be active among Indian peoples until he died, and he fulfilled this promise.

During the 1980s Father Mathieu's closest Indian associate at the annual Tekakwitha conferences was John J. Brown, S.J. Brown was a Blackfoot Indian who grew up in the eastern United States, attending Catholic schools in Philadelphia and obtaining his theological degree from Loyola University in Chicago. He joined the Jesuit order in 1935 and received his priestly ordination in 1948. Unlike Father Mathieu, Brown spent much of his priesthood in Indian ministry and was active in the conversations among Jesuits in Native American ministry. He was never reticent in declaring his tribal heritage, although he did not grow up in a Blackfoot community.

Just as he was completing his ordination, Brown was actively supporting the goals of the newly founded National Congress of American Indians: to secure Indian rights as citizens, to enlighten the misperceiving public about Indian legal status and reservations, and to "preserve Indian cultural values." In frank correspondence with Archbishop Edwin V. Byrne of Santa Fe he defended the role of the NCAI, formed by "a group of us Indians," and he compared the Bureau of Indian Affairs to the past colonial administrations of Spain, France, and England. Although he applauded the preservation of "Indian cultural values," he had contempt for the Indian New Deal and various organizations concerned with "preserving us as anthropological guinea pigs, or 'atmosphere and scenery' for railroads, hotels, and Chambers of [Commerce] that had no other tourist bait to offer" (Brown, December 15, 1947). He rehearsed how Commissioner of Indian Affairs John Collier "began dictating how the Indians could be made more Indian. This alienated both the Indians and the Indian service people."

> Thus there arose charges of fostering Communism instead of tribal ownership, of favoring paganism instead of Christianity, making ceremonies religious instead of social, of re-introducing so-called Indian marriages and divorces, of permitting wholesale gambling on the score that it was Indian culture, and fostering the peyote cult on the plea that

it was a native religion, and hence protected by the U.S. Constitution, and finally, of substituting a very inferior type of education by labeling it "Progressive," etc. The result was trouble. (Ibid., January 5, 1948)

Father Brown never ceased to speak out regarding Indian issues, according to his own standards.

ROCH NAQUIN

Roch Naquin was born into an Indian community in 1932 and has lived most of his life among his people, the Houma Indians of southernmost Louisiana. Naquin grew up in Isle de Jean Charles, at the edge of the Gulf of Mexico. His family is Houma, although they possess Cajun forebears, and his grandfather used to tell him that they were intermarried with Choctaws from Mississippi. His father was a trapper, working the watery land for muskrats, minks, nutria, raccoons, and the occasional otter; his mother was an herbalist with great pharmacological expertise. Like the Houmas in general, they spoke French, the Houma language having been lost over the centuries, along with most religious and cultural traits. His father served as a "traiteur," treating headaches, swellings, bleeding, sore throats, fever, and kidney and gall bladder ailments by massaging the ailing part with his hands and making the sign of the cross. He would also pray for nine days straight, "like a novena," and he would prescribe herbs recommended by his wife. He was a "person of prayer" (Naquin, November 20, 1990), like other Houma traiteurs of his generation. Roch Naquin can recall no instances of Native spirituality during his youth in the 1930s; Catholicism was the spiritual currency of his people.

As a boy Roch wanted to become a priest. However, the local priest did not encourage him and the schooling did not prepare him for the clerical life. Racism was an overwhelming fact of Houma existence; Houmas were not permitted to attend school with Whites, nor were they welcome in white church services. The Church maintained a separate ministry to the Houmas, and when the Indians shared liturgy with Whites, they were segregated in the rear of the building. In such an environment, the Catholic clergy did not seek Houma vocations, nor did Catholic or public schools provide a substantial education. The school in Isle de Jean Charles had no books for the eighth grade, so when Roch began the school year, he learned that he was to repeat the seventh grade assignments. He and his peers took the hint and dropped out of school.

He soon landed a job on an oyster boat. After a time in the Gulf— the crew would spend twenty-seven days out, three days on shore—

a new priest was at his parents' house: "'You want to become a priest? Yes? You can't become a priest working on an oyster boat.'" The pastor offered to find Roch a place to finish grammar school, so that he could begin seminary. Bypassing the "strict segregation" of the immediate area, the Sacred Heart Brothers further north admitted him. In 1950 he completed grammar school and entered St. Joseph's Seminary, north of New Orleans. He was still learning English, and so he "dragged behind" the other novices, yet the rector would not expel him from the program. After his first year, Roch conferred with his parents about his vocation; he doubted his ability to continue. "Momma had a lot of devotion," he recalls, and her encouragements led him to return to seminary. Only after becoming ordained in 1962 did he learn from her that when she was twelve, she promised God that if she ever was to marry, she would pray that her son would become a priest. This she had done all the years of his youth, without telling him. Today Father Naquin is brought to tears, recollecting his mother's faith.

For twenty years Father Naquin served non-Indian parishes in Louisiana; however, in 1982 he agreed to take a post at St. Eloi in Theriot. In the 1960s Catholic parishes in the Houma area moved toward integration, and St. Eloi was a mixed ethnic congregation. Only after a thirty-day retreat did Naquin agree to face the tensions of racial mixing. He had learned that his status as a priest did not earn him entrée to all-white establishments, and there were times when he was "shown the door." Like other Houmas, he was prepared to mingle with Whites, but with a sense of propriety: "I can move about but I know where I'm not wanted." Naquin worried that he would not be accepted as an Indian priest in an Indian and White community.

His fears did not materialize, and then in 1988 he was asked to take over as pastor at Holy Family Church in Grand Caillou, the scene of integrationist struggles in the past, but now a large mixed ethnic congregation. He had heard "so many negative things" about Holy Family: that the parishioners, especially the Indians, were "not responsive"; that they did not attend mass. He was told that the residue of racism created "jealousy" between the races and the people of the parish were "against one another." Father Naquin prayed for eight days, before acceding to the wishes of his bishop and to an inner voice that told him to "stop giving excuses for not coming to the banquet." He thought, "'Banquet? This parish is a banquet?' But I promised obedience and I obeyed the bishop. I came and here I am."

In his decade at Holy Family, he says, he has not encountered a hostile or indifferent congregation. Rather, "I've been accepted, embraced. . . . It has been a real blessing," bringing him "growth as a man" among "good, dedicated people," Indian and White. He has had the support of white deacons working under his egalitarian style of leadership. Parishioners come to him for advice. He has been involved in Cursillo and Catholic Family movements, Young Christian Students, and Young Christian Workers. He has blessed the fishing fleets and spent his days in the homes of the faithful in a "ministry of presence." He has served his flock, roughly half Indian, half White—there are some Blacks, too—and with intermarriage occurring more and more frequently, he looks forward to the day when "99 percent of the parish will be able to say, 'I'm part Indian.'"

Attending mass at Holy Family Church (Houma, November 18, 1990), one is impressed by the buoyant esprit throughout the congregation, composed primarily of Houmas and Whites. Many receive communion; all appear lovingly attentive to his homily and the liturgy, which bears the marks of Father Naquin's charismatic faith. He embraces his parishioners. He leads a chorus of "Happy Birthday" at the end of mass. He tries to make the young and aged feel beloved by their congregation and their Church. "Father Roch is a good priest" says one elderly Houma man, who brings the pastor venison. "He hugs me and calls me 'papa.' He knows I am good" (Francis, November 21, 1990).

In Grand Caillou Catholicism is a faith shared by Indians and Whites (as well as Blacks), despite a history of virulent racism. Father Naquin realizes that his is an integrated parish, and although he is secure in his Houma identity, he never says "I'm Indian and I'm proud of it." He will not risk alienating his white parishioners by emphasizing his Indianness. But, in the words of a Cajun priest who was instrumental in the integrating of Grand Caillou in the 1960s (Boudreaux, November 18, 1990), it is a "sign of God's providence" that Roch Naquin has become a priest and now means so much to his Houma people, as a symbol of their Catholicism and their identity. In the white priest's view, the fact that the Houmas are thriving is a proof that a people cannot be kept forever from their freedom; God's activity in the world will not permit a people to be pushed into the corners and never get out. The Houmas are coming out, and Father Naquin is their leader.

Because of the Civil Rights movement of the 1950s and 1960s, bigotry is not "the thing to do" anymore in the Houma parishes, although individuals may feel animosity toward members of other races. Societal norms are against active bigotry—even though one can hear whispered comments about the "Coonies" in Holy Family Church (Houma, November 18, 1990). The presence of Father Roch Naquin, however, has provided an enormous impetus toward overcoming racial prejudice in his parish. The prayers of his mother, the encouragement by his parish priest, the second chances offered by his teachers, have paid off concretely in the respect won for his Houma people in their congregation.

Moreover, his presence has had an impact on Houma Catholic faith and self-esteem. Since Father Naquin has become the Holy Family priest, the Houma attendance has increased considerably at the sacraments. He serves as a palpable symbol of Houma social progress. As one Houma woman says,

> That time, they didn't have an Indian priest. Now we have Father Roch. . . . That time they wouldn't even look at you. They would have killed an Indian priest that time. . . . I used to pray for a colored priest, for them to be under a colored priest. But God took care of us giving us Father Roch. . . . They never thought they would see an Indian priest on the bayou. Now they hug and kiss him. (Boudreaux and Beaudreaux, November 21, 1990)

Father Naquin's symbolic importance affects Protestant as well as Catholic Houmas. He started an Association of Ministers in his area in 1989, in order to join in programs of common interest to the ten churches around Grand Caillou. They hold ecumenical services and discuss issues of local concern. Over half of these clergymen are Houmas, all of whom have familial relations with the Catholic Church. One of these, who calls himself a "Catholic Methodist" (Verret, November 18, 1990), speaks of the inspiration Father Naquin has provided to himself and other Houmas, in a community that had been marked by intense prejudice. In the 1960s, the Houma Methodist says, he would find Naquin's picture on the walls of Houma homes, so proud of him were his people that he had completed a B.A. and become a priest. To this day, Father Naquin is held in great esteem, as well as affection, by his people, even though—so far, at least—none has followed him to the priesthood.

CHARLES J. LEUTE, O.P.

A great difficulty for Indian youths interested in the priesthood has been the adjustment to seminary life. Training for priesthood has necessarily meant a separation from family and neighborhood, and all the loneliness that such a separation entails. For Indians the alienation has been doubly felt, because they have found themselves objects of curiosity and sometimes scorn within the novitiates. James Bouchard felt slighted by his fellow Jesuits, although he sensed that it was his American, rather than Indian, identity which aroused the condescension of the European Jesuits. Pueblo youths in the 1920s who entered the novitiate of the Franciscan Fathers in Ohio were faced with crowds wanting to gawk at the Indians. Juan Estevan Chavez, a Cochiti youth, remarked, "I felt ashamed when I faced the big crowd. They did not know what to make of me. I believe I would want to spend the rest of the afternoon in the woods if I have to do that again" (in *The Indian Sentinel*, 5, no. 1, January 1925: 35). From time to time there have been reports of Indian seminarians, particularly in the Southwest; however, the rigors and trials of seminary life have kept their vocations from reaching fruition.

Charles Leute is a Dominican priest, descended on his father's side from the Sauk-Fox people, although he, his father, and his grandparents before them did not live in any Indian community. Leute was brought up with a knowledge of his Indian patrimony, and both his parents instilled in him a sense of special responsibility to Indians. Nevertheless, he grew up in white society. He was not "Indian" in language or culture, he says, but in sentiment he was and has continued to be. Even though the Dominicans had no Indian missions in the United States, Father Leute insisted upon Indian ministry for himself.

Leute states that he "experienced more discrimination in the seminary" (Leute, August 7, 1986) than at any other time in his life. Instructors and novices made comments to him about "firewater," and other slurs were common, even chronic. He also encountered resistance from his order regarding Indian work, and he had to struggle to achieve his goal of ministering to Native Americans. As a Dominican, Leute wanted to follow in the tradition of the sixteenth-century priest

Bartolomé de las Casas and his predecessors who had lectured the Spanish authorities from the pulpit against the "mortal sin" of enslaving Indians. Leute had to convince his Dominican superiors that Indian ministry was a worthy Dominican tradition.

Ordained in 1969, Father Leute served under the Jesuits on the Oglala Lakota reservation at Pine Ridge for fifteen years, and he has continued to labor in Indian ministry in Minnesota and now in North Dakota. When he first worked among the Lakotas, he did not announce his Indian heritage and he was treated by them as a white man. In organizing sweat lodges, the Lakotas wondered if they should admit him. Permitting him entrance tentatively, they came to accept him fully, when "the spirit revealed" his Indianness to those within the lodge. He was gratified to be acknowledged as an Indian. Yet, in general, he has felt alienation both from Indians and Whites. "One is suspect, one is laughed at, one is questioned from both sides" (ibid.), he remarks. Nonetheless he has tried to live his life as a priest within both Indian and white worlds, serving the Church, but also serving Indian peoples.

In his ministry he has encouraged and trained local Indian leadership, e.g., permanent deacons. In 1975 he wrote of three Lakota deacons, hoping that "the priestly work might soon be placed into their capable hands . . . to ensure the solid, indigenous growth of the Church among our Lakota Sioux people" (Leute, June 28, 1975). He has also favored mixed Indian-Catholic liturgies, in order to bring about Native cultural expression within Catholicism, even though at first the mixture resembled "scrambled eggs" and made the Indians "uncomfortable" (Leute, August 7, 1986). He has shared ecumenical services with the Native American Church (peyote religion) and he has favored Indian religious expression, even though many in his order think that Indian liturgies are foolish and misdirected. He has been active in ANRC, seeking ways to accomplish the task of inculturation, even though he himself grew up apart from Indian ritual life.

Father Leute does not criticize Native religious forms; however, he serves as a Catholic priest because he believes that Christianity offers aspects of religion that are supremely valuable to Native Americans. Christianity offers a focus upon God as a person who treats all humans as persons; the Christian tradition, as he sees it, does not allow one to treat another person or oneself as a thing. He believes that Christianity is unique, in that it is the "direct creation of the Spirit." At the same time, he avows that Christianity "completes," but does not "negate" (ibid.) traditional Indian faith. For poor Indians, Christianity offers "hope." It helps them see that they are better than their conditions seem to make them. It helps them understand that their problems are not ultimate. It offers them perspective, not by promising them pie in the sky, but by providing them a means of identifying with, orienting themselves toward, a personal, transcendent God who cares personally about them. It is this Christian message that Father Leute brings to his Indian ministry.

JOHN HAICALL, O.F.M. CAP.

For the earliest Catholic Indian priests, the question of Indian identity was issue enough—should they declare themselves openly as Indians in a culture and a Church that looked askance upon such Natives?— without asking to what degree their priesthood should express their Indianness, ecclesiastically, theologically, or liturgically. It was important for Father Gordon to serve his Ojibway people and to adorn their church with signs of their Indian culture. Neither he nor any of the priests before the Second Vatican Council attempted to syncretize Indian and Catholic forms of spirituality, or to inculturate their Catholic worship, beyond the most superficial decorative designs. The Capuchin priest John Hascall, ordained in 1967, has proclaimed his Indian identity not only among his fellow Ojibways but also to diverse Indian peoples, and celebrated his Indian religious culture in synthetic combination with his Catholicism.

Hascall was born in Sault Ste. Marie in 1941, the son of an Ojibway woman and a Cherokee-Irish father. His mother's roots were in the Garden River Reserve in Ontario, but he grew up in the Sault city in Michigan. His parents were poor and Catholic; he was one of ten children in "a loving family" (Hascall 1984). He recalls his street-kid fear of the big Union Carbide hills where "every so often, someone would be burnt to death when he slipped into the acid water holes around the hills" (Hascall 1988: 13). His father allowed his mother to lead the family as an Ojibway woman, teaching them her language; however, in the streets of Sault Ste. Marie it was not good to be an Indian, so she referred to her children as Spanish. It was only in the mid-1970s, shortly before her death, that she would speak Ojibway on the telephone with him and "recognized her language again" (Hascall 1980).

In the third grade he expressed an interest in becoming a priest, in reverent imitation of his local pastor. Although he had made his vision quest by this time, his parents encouraged him to form his Catholic vocation in the same manner as one prepares for a vision: doing without things, acting in a manner that encouraged mindfulness. They would tell him, "If you want to be a priest, you can't do this or that!" (Hascall 1988: 14). They sent him to a Catholic school, and even when his family moved to another town, his father drove him daily to the Catholic school. With the financial help of the bishop and the seminary, he attended St. Lawrence Seminary, and in 1959 he entered Capuchin Way of Life in Indiana.

In the seminary, he says, "I had left all that I learned in the forests of the North to the back burner" (ibid.). For a boy whose earliest religious experiences came in his vision quest—"I really didn't know Jesus Christ that well," he remarks, "but I knew the Father who created all things" (Hascall 1980) from the time of his puberty vision—putting aside Ojibway spirituality was an act of willful repression. A fellow seminarian advised him to be himself, an Indian, in his religiousness, and in his third year of theological studies his Capuchin advisor permitted him to "pray in the way of my people" (Hascall 1988: 14). Still, he was torn between his Indianness and priestly vocation. Only after his ordination did he permit himself to pray in ways particular to his Ojibway people, and only then "the dam broke loose and I began to grow again, after eleven years of suffering" (ibid.).

He was stationed for a few months in Milwaukee, but then took a post at the all-Indian parish in Baraga, Michigan, not far from his birthplace, among his tribesfolk. He was determined to perform his priestly duties—instructing, counseling, providing the sacraments— with explicit reference to Indian beliefs and practices, and with the support of the Capuchin Order. In those days, he found, the Church as a whole had no cultural understanding of Indian worship or theology. His diocese made no mention of his Indian identity, and his own people greeted his attempts at syncretism and inculturation with "silence and fear." He remembers:

> I was back on the reservation, but I faced a people who had given up our Indian ways and, in fact, feared me and the medicine of our peoples. It was as if I were a "pagan" priest. . . . The non-Indian peoples accused me of everything to get me out of Baraga. (Ibid.)

These were years of suffering for Father Hascall. He asked himself repeatedly what he was doing as a priest. He joined the militant American Indian Movement (AIM), only to break with the organization over its condoning of violence as a political tactic in 1972. He continued to question his own right to pray as an Indian, even while working with the Indian Ecumenical Conference of North America to find where Jesus fit into his Native ways. He tried to participate in the Tekakwitha

Conference but could not gain solace or insight from the non-Indian clergy who then filled its ranks. From 1974 to 1977 he wavered in his determinations, first to quit the priesthood, then to reject his Indian identity, then back and forth again. He recalls, "I felt worthless" (ibid.) through this period. He served at Baraga for nineteen years, but for the first decade he did not know how to express his Indian and Catholic identities with integrity and fulfillment. He perpetuated his suffering through alcoholism, despite the prayers of his mother and his own efforts to cure that disease acquired from his father.

As Father Hascall tells it, God and Our Mother answered his prayers and those of his mother. God revealed to him that the God Jesus was older than two thousand years and had revealed Himself to non-Christian peoples as well as to the Visible Church of Rome. God was present in Native people and in their spiritual ways. Hascall perceived that it was possible for him to be "one person, totally Native, totally Christian as Medicine Priest" (ibid.). While at mass, "I was given the privilege to rise from the altar to the cross to see our medicine people around the Cross of Christ" (ibid.). Hascall came to the realization that God, Jesus, was incarnate in Ojibway culture, and that he, the medicine priest, was correct in teaching and praying as an Indian Catholic.

For Hascall, the difficulty was not only in being Indian and Catholic, but in engaging in the spiritual medicines of the Ojibways while serving as a priest. As a youth he had learned healing practices of the Midewiwin Society, an Ojibway religious organization with roots in traditional Ojibway religion which developed as an institution among Great Lakes Indians several hundred years ago. As a member of the Crane clan he was born to medicinal practice and Midewiwin participation; indeed, his clan helped revive Midewiwin in the 1960s and 1970s when it was moribund. He was in a sweat lodge in Alberta when a crane flew overhead and around the lodge, calling upon him to express his Crane identity and perform his Crane duties as a member of Midewiwin. To this day Hascall feels this vocation as strongly as he does his Catholic priesthood.

In the late 1970s Hascall became a charismatic Catholic as a means of receiving God's revelation freely as it came. He overcame his destructive alcoholism. He rejoined the Tekakwitha Conference, as it became a medium for Indian Catholic self-expression, serving in the late 1980s as president. He joined, and then became coordinator of, the

Association of Native Religious and Clergy. Above all, he affirmed himself as "a medicine man priest, the only one in the world" (Hascall 1984). As early as 1972 he was proclaiming the mutual healing properties of Indian and Catholic traditions. At the annual Indian Ecumenical Conference on the Assiniboin reserve in Alberta he said, "The Eucharist is medicine. . . . We get our strength from Christ's body" (in Fiske 1972: 43). In the 1980s his mission was to heal his fellow Indians through his Ojibway medicines as well as the Catholic sacramental channels of grace.

He traveled widely in the latter half of the 1980s on behalf of the Tekakwitha Conference, visiting many Indian communities all across the United States and Canada, conducting sweat lodges, performing "healing masses" and retreats, blessing Native rituals, and preaching a message of Indian self-worth. The superiors in his order supported his peripatetic Indian ministry, and the Church hierarchy did not forbid him his syncretistic inculturation throughout the decade. He was very much in demand among Native and non-Indian Catholics (and some non-Catholics, too), so much so that he became worn out and quit the Tekakwitha presidency. After a stint among the Crows in Montana, he has returned to an Ojibway ministry in Michigan. Throughout this period he proclaimed his dual, yet single, role as medicine man and priest, and when asked, "How can you be a medicine man and priest at the same time?" he replied, "That's your problem, not mine" (in Hascall, Fall 1986: 7). After his struggles with anger, self-doubt, and alcoholism, he declared himself "as comfortable in the church as he is in the sweat lodge" (Johnson, Midwinter 1988: 15). As a result of his own experience, and as a result of his affirming revelation from God, Father Hascall has preached and practiced a message of combined Indian and Catholic spirituality. He has tried to do more than allow Indians to feel comfortable in their Indian ways; his goal has been for his fellow Native Americans to recognize and celebrate their religious culture as an effective and appropriate means of receiving grace and attaining communion with God and His creatures. "There is still a reluctance and terrible fear in our people of our 'traditional' way of life," he writes. "I'm experiencing so much of this as I travel from place to place." He observes, "We still have a difficult time to see how Jesus speaks through the 'way of our people.' We tend to see the dogmas and doctrines as Church. Yet, that is not what Christ intended" (Hascall 1988: 15).

In his public expressions, Father Hascall has addressed the lack of self-esteem among Native peoples. His opening words are often, "I am the most beautiful person in the world" (Hascall, July 19, 1986); or, he asks his audience, "Who is the most beautiful person in the world?"—prodding the Indians before him to respond exuberantly, "I am!" (Phoenix, September 13, 1987). With this attention-getting device he establishes the leitmotif of his homilies, that we all are worthy parts of God's beautiful creation. He wants Indians to feel good about themselves, as members of Christ's Catholic Church, and as members of their tribal communities. He wants them to embrace their Indianness and their Catholicism in a simultaneous prayerful action. He says:

> Since the early 1970's and the rise of our Native Indian identity and awareness, we have seen a grand exit of external Christianity among our peoples. Our Churches, in most places, are almost empty. Some of our people have left to follow the 'Traditional Way' of prayer. Many have left to follow the Fundamental Way of Scripture. . . . Many more, thoroughly confused, have left and a lot of these have thrown off prayer altogether. Why throw off prayer? I hear from the people, "I am not forgivable", "I am not worthy"! Sin and guilt, which were taught so stringently to our peoples, have gripped us to such an extent that when we drink and commit other major sins of lust and excess, we feel there is no hope for us. Our concept of God taught to us, or perceived by us, is that of a strict and merciless Judge rather than the all-surrounding Creator, Mystery, who takes care of the people and provides for all. (Hascall 1988: 15)

If the Church has always stressed sinfulness, doctrines, commandments, and fear of God, Hascall encourages them with a Creation theology that emphasizes their connections to God and their inborn ability to overcome their weakness. He attempts to heal Indians' sickness of heart.

In so doing, he places himself in their midst, as one of them. He refers to himself as an "alcoholic" (Phoenix, September 13, 1987) who might backslide at any moment. He tells his audience, "Don't put me on a pillar, I might be married tomorrow. Don't put me on a pillar, because I'll knock it down" (ibid.). He emphasizes his illnesses—he is a diabetic, like many Indian people—and reminds his listeners of his mortality and frailty. He says, "I'll probably die of cancer, which I pray for every day. . . . I pray every day to die, to go home" (Hascall 1984). As for healing, he downplays his own charismatic gifts, saying, "We Indians are gift-people," engaged in "healing ourselves. . . . Where I go, there are lots of miracles, not because of me. . . . I have no more power than you do" (Phoenix, September 13, 1987). He tells his fellow Native Americans, "I used to hate myself," until learning that Indian ways are the ways of God. Now he is beautiful, and so are the Indians around him.

Father Hascall speaks to urban Indians, to Indians from broken homes, and to Indians who are victims of chronic alcoholism, sexual abuse, and incest. He uses the self-healing language of Alcoholics Anonymous and other modern movements to help Indians struggle toward self-love and love of God. A central part of this struggle, he says, is the step of forgiveness. He does not deny human sinfulness, but he exhorts Native people to forgive themselves and each other. He also has called for forgiveness of the Church for its heritage of racism and colonialism. He recalls that at the Tekakwitha Conference of 1978 Catholic Indians accused the Church of mistreating Indians, and in the years that followed, Church representatives, including bishops, papal delegates, even the pope himself, asked for Indians' forgiveness: "Now I say, 'hanta yo, let's move on.' . . . The eagle falls if it stops moving forward. Let us move beyond our bitterness" (Hascall, August 9, 1986). In a temper of hope, he has said, "The Church is now making sense to us. The Church that once persecuted us is now listening to us" (Hascall 1984). He prays for rapprochement between traditionalists and Catholics, and encourages a spirituality that helps to heal political divisions, as well as the hurts within individual souls.

Liturgically, Father Hascall has joined his roles as medicine man and priest to enhance a holistic spirituality. Arriving at a retreat, he opens his medicine bag, zippered within vinyl attaché cases, and with sacramental care he lays out bowls from the Pueblos, baskets from the eastern woodlands, Navajo rugs, embroidered Ojibway cloths, tobacco, sage, cedar, braided sweetgrass, an eagle feather fan, a mink fur bag, a Sioux beaded prayer ball, and other paraphernalia, which he calls his "spirit helpers" and "protectors" (Hascall, July 19, 1986). He wears black vestments, black being his "sacred color" as an Ojibway and as a priest. He speaks Ojibway, then switches to English, translating terminology back and forth. He draws upon his Ojibway religious forms, but also upon the modes of more generic or cross-tribal "Indian" religiousness. He does not shy away from employing rites from other Indian peoples, for example, in tossing the Sioux ball to his audience, saying, "Whoever holds this, pray for the people, pray for all the people" (ibid.). A banner behind the altar proclaims, "Our prayers come on the beat of the drum" (ibid.), and indeed, a Native American sister keeps rhythms on a drum during hymns as Father Hascall says mass.

Hascall carries with him tapes from his native Michigan: of loon calls, rushing streams, thunderstorms, and other natural phenomena. During meditation he plays these Ojibway-based, but New Age–enhanced, sounds. When an intense thunderstorm sweeps through the area during the retreat, the Ojibway priest thanks the thunderbirds for visiting and giving their blessing. He explicitly compares the crucifix with the fourth degree of his Midewiwin Society; for him the four directions of the cross correspond to the four grandfathers of the heavens. A thunderbird graces his chasuble; smoke blesses the chalice. Tobacco offerings abound in his services.

At the same time, his liturgy has the shape of normative Catholicism. The mass is at its center. There is the authority of the priest, leading his fellow Christians in prayer. He says that his spirituality consists of the "crucifix before me, the loons in the background" (ibid.), and although his sermon at mass uses the symbolism of the four directions, the sage, cedar, sweetgrass, and smoke, he reaffirms the "One God, . . . the Creator of All," also known as "Kitche Manito," the Ojibway term for the Great Spirit. There may be a theology of nature in Hascall's liturgy, but there is also a transcendent, monotheistic, Catholic theology. The fact is, his liturgy is appropriate as an Indian as well as Catholic ritual.

"Get rid of the idols we make of God," he intones (ibid.), to remind the Indians that the old gods are not ultimately real in and of themselves, but also to remind Christians not to criticize Indian "idols," since all concepts of God are only approximations of the divine. He is reminding his audience that "God" and "Kitche Manito" refer to the same "creator, love-source," and thus either term is relatively appropriate, but not complete by itself. Finally, he reminds us explicitly that our concepts of God arise from "our needs" (ibid.). This fact is not bad in itself, but must be kept in mind to prevent confusion between our needs and the ultimate divine.

In the midst of this theological discourse, Father Hascall attempts to establish a prayerful simplicity, which he identifies as an Indian and Catholic mode of meditation: "Listen to God. Talk to God. That's all" (ibid.). He wants those in his retreat to listen to God, and then talk to

God. He says of Jesus, "He is my friend. I can joke with Him." He suggests that we treat God intimately; we can "tease" God in conversation. Thus he tries to bring to a common level what he considers the essence of religion: communication between God and humans. He says that we relate to God in multivalent ways, as father, mother, friend, lover. All the aspects of love relations, he says, are the aspects of religious relation, and he encourages them all. He compares our prayers to the numerous calls of loons, singing across the Michigan lakes at night. He says that God speaks to us through the Bible, but also through leaves and grass and other aspects of His creation, as well as in the special revelations of vision quests.

Father Hascall brings to his retreat what he considers the "gifts" of Indian spirituality: the trans-verbal silence of dance, the unspoken prayers of smoke, both of which "empty us of our selfishness" (ibid.). He refers to God as "He, or She," reminding his listeners that in Ojibway language pronouns referring to the divine do not indicate male or female gender. He gives notice to the mothers and grandmothers and especially to "Mother Earth, who nourishes and heals us with her foods and medicines, upon whose body we build our homes" (ibid.). Of the creator, he states, "God is a mother to father us, a father to mother us" (ibid.). He claims that Indian religiousness has the quality of communal relationship, grounded in kinship bonds, from which non-Native Christians can learn. He does not deny similar spirituality in Catholicism, but for Indians there is an "emphasis on relationship" (Hascall, August 9, 1986) which he draws upon when serving as a medicine priest. Just as he brings the healing mass to Indian communities across North America, he brings what he considers his Indian spirituality to Catholicism. Hascall is emphatic in asserting the religiousness of Indian life: "We're not out there on the reservation doing nothing. We're struggling with our spirituality. We're struggling to see Christ" (Hascall 1984).

The medicine priest makes an impact upon the Indians and non-Indians who attend his services. In all his humility he possesses a charisma that turns others' eyes to him. They take his picture, touch him, and seek his attention. A Pueblo man says that Father Hascall is "a prophet, like Moses." Everywhere he travels in Indian America he is beloved (Savilla, August 6, 1993). At Tekakwitha conferences he receives accolades from the Indian participants, for his spirituality and for his social concern. One can overhear conversations among

Catholic Indians: "We have to get our money together and bring Father John out" (Fargo, August 6, 1989). A Mohawk woman—a convert to Catholicism and a doctoral student in religion—who attended Hascall's retreat in Milwaukee in 1986 reports that she was trying at the time to assimilate to white culture, to avoid her Indianness. When she saw his combining of Indian and Christian spirituality, her Indian Catholic faith was invigorated. She takes umbrage at the caviling she hears about his liturgies, e.g., that he calls upon spirits beyond the realm of normative Christian theology. She says that it has always been the way for Catholicism to incorporate the spirits of non-Christian peoples, at least until Christians reached the Americas. For her, Indian and Catholic traditions need not be separate, and Father Hascall is doing the right thing by "incorporating other spirits, good spirits," into Catholic devotions (Shillinger, August 5, 1993). An Ojibway woman living in Tacoma describes the effect of Hascall's visit to her urban community: "His presence has . . . been a healing process for Native and non-Native communities, as people witness the beauty of Native American spirituality that they do not always have access to" (Urban Catholic Indian Ministries 1989: 2). A Swinomish elder from the Seattle area attests to her "belief in Jesus, Blessed Kateri and Father John Hascall" (Seattle, August 7, 1993). Non-Indians are impressed by his liturgies, which they call "simple," "beautiful," and "down to earth." "Nobody could fault it," said one elderly Catholic sister of his retreat (Hascall, July 19, 1986), for its "proper mixture of Christian and Indian elements." A prominent Jesuit historian of United States Indian policy (Prucha, July 21, 1986), compliments Hascall for his sincerity in combining two living faiths as an Indian Catholic priest.

There are some, however, who are put off by his charismatic effusiveness. An Indian woman from the Northwest complains of his "Baptist" style homiletics, calling him, "Father Amen" (Fargo, August 4, 1989). A northeastern Indian woman says of Father Hascall, "I can't stand to listen to him. Just when he's getting into something, he has to say, 'Amen, Amen, Amen!'" (Jacko, October 12, 1990). In general, Hascall receives his greatest acclaim from urban Indians, or from those Indian communities that have lost consistent touch with their own tribal traditions. They see in him an authentic Indian religious practitioner, whose liturgical forms can provide a model for themselves. In general Ojibways respond enthusiastically to his rituals, because they recognize their own aboriginal faith in his religiousness. Non-Indian Catholics, especially sisters who are seeking alternatives to normative Catholic liturgy, are drawn to Hascall's Indian gestures and his references to nature and a gender-inclusive deity. On some reservations, however, Hascall receives a cool reception (Chaput, August 3, 1989). It is said that his appropriation of elements from various Indian religions offends the sensibilities of locals, jealous of their distinctive prerogatives. What right does he have, they ask, to wave this feather, burn this herb? Pueblo Indians in particular are put off by his pan-Indian ritualism at Catholic services (Pelotte, August 6, 1993). At San Juan Pueblo, for example, Hascall's "charismatic presence" at Sunday mass overshadowed the regular pastor and the local Pueblo leaders. The San Juan Tewas regarded him with "bewilderment, bemusement, and toleration," that he should try to join together two religious traditions—Catholic and Indian—that the Pueblo people have always "kept separate, because of the intolerance of one toward the other" (Ortiz, January 23, 1987). Hascall's trademark question—who is the most beautiful?—and his emotionalism in urging the congregation to tell each other they love each other rub across the grain of Pueblo reserve in social relations. Tribal jealousies have also contributed to resentment toward Hascall, as Indian communities, e.g., those of the Sioux, have rankled under the public attention paid to this Ojibway priest.

Over the past several years, at least since 1989, Father Hascall has come under increased criticism, not from Pueblo Indian Catholics determined to keep Indian and Catholic religious forms separate, nor from Sioux Catholics envious of Hascall's repute, but rather from members of the Church hierarchy, including two Indian bishops, Donald E. Pelotte, S.S.S., and Charles Chaput, O.F.M. Cap., and some non-Indian priests. In 1989 Hascall ended his executive association with the National Tekakwitha Conference, perhaps under pressure from the board of directors, much to the dismay of many aggrieved Indian Catholics who asserted that he "should be retained as our spiritual leader" (Fargo, August 4, 1989). For the next three years at the annual Tekakwitha meetings, Hascall's liturgical syncretism sparked "charge and counter-charge" (Thiel, December 3, 1991) in public disputes. Hascall insisted upon a joining of Indian and Catholic symbolic expressions during the mass, including the Eucharistic core. The Indian bishops would have nothing of it. Bishop Pelotte charged Hascall with disrespect for the propriety of Catholic sacred ways. A priest should dress properly and should celebrate the Eucharist according to official sanctions (Pelotte, August 6, 1993). Bishop Chaput said that Hascall's lengthy mass for elders in Tucson in 1990 was outside Church liturgical norms; in effect, Hascall's liturgical experimentation was "parallel to the church" rather than "in the heart of the church" (in Walsh, October 31, 1992: 330). In 1991 at Oklahoma City Father Hascall refused to perform the liturgy according to strictures he was faced with, setting off an "explosive time" (Thiel, December 3, 1991) among Indian Catholics. Non-Indian priests referred to Hascall as an "icon" and a "parody" (Orono, August 7, 1992), and an official for the National Conference of Catholic Bishops spoke sarcastically of Hascall as "just a humble little medicine man" (ibid., August 5, 1992). One Jesuit questions Hascall's status as medicine man among the Ojibways—is the Crane clan really responsible for healing within the tribe? is Hascall really a member of Midewiwin?—and notes that back in seminary nobody knew that Hascall was even an Indian; he refers to the priest as a "born-again Indian" (ibid., August 6, 1992). Another Jesuit finds him "manipulative, always having to be in control" (ibid., August 7, 1992), and yet another speaks of Hascall's "delusions of grandeur: 'sent by the elders, sent by the spirit, sent for the people.' I think he needs treatment" (ibid., August 8, 1992). A Native sister speaks ominously of "Jim Jones possibilities" (ibid., August 7, 1992).

Father Hascall has been hurt by the criticism, and in turn he charges that the Church is turning away from a decade and more in which the many flowers of Indian Catholicism were encouraged to bloom. He feels that now the Church is telling him that he cannot be an Indian in his Catholicism. "The church has raped us of our whole Indian way" (in Walsh, October 31, 1992: 330), he asserts. He has become "the most vocal critic" of the Tekakwitha Conference, charging that the Conference has "become part of a church 'that holds us down as Indian people, that doesn't allow us to be ourselves as promised by the doctrines of the church and the Second Vatican Council. . . . Unless it begins to treat us as equals, there is no hope for us'" (Walsh, August 17, 1992) At the Tekakwitha convocation in 1992 in Orono, Maine, Hascall spoke of the "burden of the priesthood" given to him by God. He said that to be an Indian, and particularly an Indian priest, today is to experience much "persecution" (Orono, August 7, 1992).

In this context Father Hascall conducts sweat lodge ceremonies for the Catholics attending the annual Tekakwitha conference. Even the two Indian bishops so critical of him partake of one service. Each sweat takes four hours, and as Hascall pours the sage-scented water over the steaming stones, his Indian spirituality unfolds. He leads each portion of the service in honor of a direction of the universe. He dedicates his prayers to the earth, to his human and non-human relatives, to women, to the elders, to animals. His fellow Indians—Apaches, Ojibways, Penobscots, Lakotas, and others—enunciate heartfelt concern for the hurts of their people: their alcoholism, their diabetes, their poverty. There are speeches against the irreverent secularism of white culture.

When Hascall speaks, he lays out a theology that draws far more from Indian religiousness than from Catholicism. The sweat lodge, he says, is our mother earth's womb. He elicits the spirits of bear, mink, the grandfathers, earth, and God. He states repeatedly that all religions are equal and the same. He says, "God equals Great Spirit equals Kitche Manito equals Wakan Tanka equals all other names of the divine" (Orono, August 7–8, 1992), and no religion has preeminence as a spiritual expression over the others. Hascall tells the men in his midst that he has tried to resign his duty as Crane clan medicine man, but his elders will not let him. Thus he chooses to call himself "medicine priest," with variations in his identity as he travels from location to location around Indian America. Throughout his service Hascall emphasizes the healing that comes from forgiveness and purification; the sweat is like a confessional rite in which the participants seek catharsis from their hurts and sins. Hascall himself gets on his knees, head on the ground, and begs passionately to the earth for pity and forgiveness. It is an emotional prayer, expressing the beseeching spirituality of charismatic Catholicism and Ojibway spirit questing, combined. At the close of the service Father Hascall "absolves" the men of all their "sins" (ibid.), and the cycle of prayers is complete.

If Hascall has severed his relationship with the Tekakwitha Conference for the present—and it seems that he has; witness his absence from the annual meetings since 1993—he has not given up his goal to celebrate an Indian Catholic religiousness. In July 1993 he conducted a three-day mission in Baraga, Michigan, where he is now stationed at the Most Holy Name of Jesus–Blessed Kateri Tekakwitha parish, and there have been rumors (Pelotte, August 6, 1993) that he is forming an organization to fulfill the task of spiritual syncretism. There is some anxiety, but no indication, that he will go the way of the Black American priest, George A. Stallings, Jr., who created his own church in 1989 out of alienation from the American Catholic institutions. It has been Hascall's hope as a priest to establish modes of spirituality that are healing and comforting for Indian Catholics. He has believed in the possibility of syncretistic rapprochement between Indian and Catholic forms of religiousness. At this time it appears that his goal will not be easily met, at least not on his own terms, and not within the Tekak-witha Conference. Perhaps he will accomplish his goal within other channels, but at present he is suffering seriously from diabetes and his eyesight is failing. A friend describes him as "a spent priest, a bent priest, who sees better now with his heart than with his eyes" (Cloud-Morgan, October 16, 1995). Despite his ailments he remains active in local Indian causes and his faith is strong.

DONALD E. PELOTTE, S.S.S.

Whereas Father Hascall has been the most visible Indian priest in the United States over the past decade, the highest ranking and most famous Indian clerics in the Church are now bishops Donald Pelotte and Charles Chaput. Although neither grew up in Indian communities, with viable Indian culture, their episcopal elevations, in 1986 and 1988 respectively, have been heralded as breakthroughs for Native American leadership within the Roman Catholic Church.

Donald Pelotte was the first American Indian to become a bishop in the United States, at the young age of forty-one. In 1945 Pelotte was born of an Abenaki father and a French Canadian mother, who raised her family in pious poverty in Waterville, Maine. At age fourteen he entered Blessed Sacrament Fathers and Brothers' Eymard Preparatory Seminary in Hyde Park, New York. He later attended Fordham University, receiving a Ph.D. and writing his dissertation on the American priest, John Courtney Murray. One of the strongest influences on his priestly training was the Catholic Worker Movement of Dorothy Day.

Throughout his formation he did not identify himself actively as an Indian, nor did he have any contact with his Indian heritage. When he was elected provincial superior of his order in 1978, he was a "backwoods boy" (Pelotte, August 6, 1993) whose cultural experience was parochial, consisting of his Catholic family life and his priestly education. As provincial he traveled to far-flung locales, including Vietnam, India, parts of Europe, and east Africa. He was "agog" at the range of cultural gestures he found among Catholics in these various areas. In some places the people treated Catholic priests with reverential devotion; in other places the communities went naked. He found the variations of food symbols, the roles of women and the aged, the nomadic movements of these different Catholic peoples to be dizzying. He had to ask himself the question, "What is essential to be a follower of Jesus?" (ibid.). When he asked this question of his fellow Catholics, even his fellow priests, the answers were as various as the cultural practices he witnessed. It was this experience of cultural multiplicity of Catholic peoples that led Pelotte to a consideration of Indian cultures in relation to the Church. In 1980 he went to Rome to help celebrate the beatification of Kateri Tekakwitha. There he met several other Indian priests and had his first contacts with the Tekakwitha Conference staff. Later that year he joined the Tekakwitha board of directors, a step toward his emerging Indian identity and a sign of his concern for Catholic Indian inculturation and social welfare. Bishop Pelotte has said that as a priest of the Blessed Sacrament, "the Eucharist has been my whole life," as a symbol of "unity," but also of "brokenness," as Christ's body was broken for us (Orono, August 8, 1992). In approaching Indian ministry, Pelotte came to consider the ways in which Christ shares in Native Americans' brokenness, as well as in their unity with humankind.

In 1986 Pelotte was appointed Coadjutor Bishop of the Diocese of Gallup; only in 1990, when Bishop Jerome J. Hastrich retired, did Pelotte become the Ordinary—the youngest Ordinary of a U.S. diocese. His consecration was a celebration of Indian symbolism. Zuni and Apache dancers donned their costumes. Pelotte himself read the House Made of Dawn chant of the Navajos. Rev. Robert F. Sanchez, then Archbishop of Santa Fe, exhorted him, "Never forget your roots or your cultural origins. . . . They will serve you well" (in Peterson, May 7, 1986). Other Indian religious, including Father John Hascall, spoke of Pelotte's consecration as a great step forward for Indians, a chance "to build our own church" (in ibid.). The new bishop recognized the historic import of his elevation, only in different terms: "This really makes Indians feel part of the Church" (Pelotte, August 7, 1986).

Bishop Pelotte immediately set about the task of learning his new territory, the 55,000 square miles of New Mexico and Arizona comprising the Diocese of Gallup. Over half of the area's population, 200,000 of 335,000 in 1986, were Indians. Of the 45,000 Catholics under his jurisdiction, 20,000 were Indians: Zunis, Lagunas, Acomas, Navajos, and Apaches, primarily, with as many as thirty different Catholic Indian centers. (Today the figure is closer to 30,000.) Learning Spanish, studying Navajo, Pelotte attempted to know his flock. At the same time, Indians from around the country requested that he visit their reservations and their parishes, and they sought to embrace him, not as the bishop of Gallup, but as the Indian bishop. In attending Tekakwitha conferences, Pelotte has found an affectionate greeting, a friendly banter, that he has returned with touches, hugs, and smiling repartee.

Some have questioned his cultural roots, regarding him as a profound Catholic but only a nominal Indian. In 1986 a young Native man commented that Bishop Pelotte would have to "run the door" (Ballew, August 9, 1986), meaning that when someone becomes a sweat lodge leader, he must first perform the subsidiary tasks as a helper: opening and closing the door to the lodge. Pelotte had no real experience as a leader of Indians—his administrative track record as provincial superior meant little to them, and they resented the notion that he might speak for them—and although he was welcomed by many Natives with loving arms, he was required to "start at the beginning" (ibid.) as an Indian bishop.

Bishop Pelotte came to his job in Gallup with an acute awareness of the sorry physical conditions engulfing Indian people. He grew up in poverty, in a family broken by alcoholism. He had been moved profoundly by Dorothy Day's Catholic Worker Movement, and he possessed a vocation to ameliorate social dysfunctions insofar as it is possible. In his early sermons as a bishop, he told of his encounter with a young Navajo man, drunk and stumbling amidst the interstate traffic that courses through Gallup. He asked, "Why? . . . no direction . . . lost in a world of drugs and alcohol . . . ," and he responded that such an existence is "common to many of us Indians" (Bozeman, August 9, 1986).

After many years as bishop of Gallup, Pelotte says that he still has great enthusiasm for his labor. In his homilies he has replaced the drunken Indian, the symbol of how difficult his job would be, with a march on Santa Fe that he participated in and helped plan. Something had to be done about the domination of alcohol in the lives of Gallup Indians—alcohol provided by "those good Italian Catholic distributors," he remarks (Pelotte, August 6, 1992); so, he and other Church personnel, as well as non-Catholics, brought the issue to the New Mexico state capital. The state responded by closing down drive-in liquor stores and by providing $1.5 million for alcohol treatment. What so pleased Pelotte was that various constituencies—Indians and non-Indians, Catholics and non-Catholics—worked together for a common cause.

This type of social activism has characterized Bishop Pelotte's tenure. He has supported the late Mother Teresa's Missionaries of Charity who conduct a soup kitchen and provide other services in Gallup for Navajos and other local Indians. He already has plans for an

AIDS treatment facility within the diocese, even though the disease has yet to devastate the Indians of the Southwest. He cares about social justice issues throughout the hemisphere. In the year of the Columbian quincentennial, he spoke publicly of the slaughter of Indians in Guatemala, where he traveled in 1991, and he has praised Leonardo Boff, a cleric of liberation theology who has condemned the Vatican's slowness in addressing issues of injustice in Latin America. Referring to the ongoing conquest of Indians in the Americas and the callous disregard for their social welfare, he states with fervor, "It can't go on" (ibid.). Compared to the atrocities visited upon the Indians of Latin America in the present day, the spiritual dislocation of United States Indians, the call of Indian Catholics for Indian liturgies, seems relatively unimportant to him. "How trivial our issues are," he comments (ibid.).

At the same time, he is Bishop of Gallup. He focuses upon the Navajos, who are the major Indian presence in town. He has established a deacon-training program for them. He praises their Catholic spirituality as well as their traditional values. He travels by airplane to the remote northern and southern reaches of the diocese to visit the Apaches. He interacts with the Catholic Pueblo peoples at Zuni, Laguna, and Acoma. He tries to avoid requests for lectures outside his diocese, so that he can be with his people, the Catholic people, the Indian people.

He has experienced loneliness as a bishop and some rejection within the Church and within Gallup for his Indian heritage; not all his episcopal days have been happy or fruitful. There are some who whisper of his having a drinking problem. He has asserted his authority over the priests and sisters in his diocese in ways that they have sometimes found heavy-handed. His greatest difficulty, however, has arisen in his relations with Indian Catholics who have persisted in calling him a "come-lately" Indian with no sustained commitment to Indian liturgies within the Church. Pelotte has chafed under these "very painful charges" (in Walsh, October 31, 1992). He has attempted to participate in Indian sweats, for example at the Tekakwitha Conference in Orono, Maine (August 6–7, 1992), but without great enthusiasm, finding the experience "touching, but exhausting." He has proven his dedication to improving Indian social welfare; he has shown tireless energy in bringing the Church he loves so dearly to Indian peoples within and without his diocese; he says that he desires to achieve the most profound kind of Catholic inculturation among Indian peoples. These goals are more important to his ministry than expressions of traditional Indian religiousness, per se. For that he has received the animus of many Indian Catholics, most pointedly at the 1992 Tekakwitha Conference in Orono, where he almost quit the board of directors, and had to be soothed by his fellow bishops into celebrating mass after he erupted in anger at his critics.

When Bishop Pelotte was consecrated in 1986, he and Father John Hascall saw the historic importance of the event in different ways; the difference is significant here. Hascall wished for Indian Catholics "to build our own Church." Pelotte wished Indians to "feel part of the Church." To this day the visions of these two ordained Indian men constitute countervailing goals within the Indian Catholic circles. They may be complementary aspects of the same vision; they may not be ultimately in opposition to one another. But at this time they appear as conflicting forces.

CHARLEſ J. CHAPUT, O.F.M. CAP.

In the context of these countervailing tendencies, Bishop Charles Cha-put has been a "very conservative" (Dixon, August 7, 1992) influence on the Tekakwitha board of directors. Born in Kansas in 1944, Chaput is an enrolled member of the Prairie Band Potawatomi, of Native American descent on his mother's side of the family. His grandmother was born on the same reservation as Albert Negahnquet, the first Pota-watomi priest. Chaput's immediate family, however, lived apart from their Potawatomi relatives. When he became bishop of the Diocese of Rapid City in 1988, amidst elaborate ceremonialism orchestrated par-tially by the Sioux peoples of South Dakota, he stated, "Although I was not born on the reservation and was not raised in a native cultural environment, I have a great love and respect for my native roots" (*Tekakwitha Conference Newsletter,* 8, no. 1, 1988: 2). When he speaks of "my people" (Chaput, August 3, 1989), he means the Potawatomis who converted to Catholicism in the South Bend area, and who were removed to Kansas. In 1986 these Potawatomis bestowed upon him an Indian name. They gave him a pipe, sashes, moccasins, and other signs of his Indianness. They provided him with a feast, so that he could feel more "Indian," more at one with the reservation Potawatomis (Puckee, November 24, 1991). They have kept in contact with him; several of them correspond regularly with him (Degand, November 24, 1991), and they look forward to his visits to their reservation. He is greatly comforted by their hospitality.

In 1997 Chaput was named archbishop of Denver. As bishop of Rapid City, Chaput openly embraced the Indians who make up almost half of the Catholics in the diocese. He supported the training of Na-tive American deacons and encouraged the development of Native clergy. He put his Indian identity up front, much to the dismay of non-Indian Catholics in South Dakota who still complain of Indian paganism. At Tekakwitha conferences he has received the joyful greet-ings of many Indians, and he has returned the compliment with enthu-siasm. Nevertheless, he has received the same sobriquet as Bishop Pelotte as a "come-lately" Indian, partially because of his theological conservatism.

Bishop Chaput remarks (Chaput 1988: 6–7) that the older generation of Indian Catholics "sometimes wondered if we can be ourselves,
be Indian people and be Catholics." In recent years Indians have received encouragement, he says, through Church-sponsored inculturation, "the process by which we can become fully Indian and fully
Catholic in this Church of ours." He supports inculturation, as an
archbishop and as a Potawatomi. He states that true inculturation will
make the gospel richer, giving Jesus an Indian face. But, he writes,
"each of our cultures is purified and then strengthened" by the gospel.
"Sometimes we tend to talk about our native ways as being all good,
and they haven't always been good. Each of our cultures needs to be
changed when it meets the face of Jesus. This is not only true about native cultures, this is true about our contemporary American cultures;
it's true about all cultures throughout the world" (ibid.).

For Chaput the Gospels are sacred; so is the liturgical core of
Catholicism, the Eucharist. He is not willing to see the central ritual of
the mass sullied by foreign acts, even if those acts are crucially important to Native religious traditions. In particular he has objected to the
conflating of pipe ceremonialism and the consecration of bread and
wine, the syncretism attempted most prominently by Father Hascall.
From "above" he has received the order: "Don't touch the Eucharistic
Prayer" (Chaput, August 3, 1989). Holding a pipe ceremony during
the transubstantiation at mass is, for him, a "multiplication of symbols, . . . just not good liturgy" (ibid.). Both communion and the pipe
stand for unity among the individual, the human community, the universe, and God. Hence, why do we need them both? Why should we
"tag on" the pipe, when it duplicates what the communion expresses?
He does not mind if feather-waving, eagle dancing, smudging, and
other Indian forms take place during the mass, as long as they are kept
away from the sacred heart of Christian sacramentalism. He does not
mind the pipe, but it should not compete with Christ's sacrifice celebrated in the mass.

In the same way, he complains that the Tekakwitha congresses have
emphasized Indian culture instead of celebrating Christ. The one
draws the focus of the Catholic Indians away from the other, and we
are at our best when we are facing Christ, he says. At the conferences,
he adds, "we are playing Indian" (ibid.), pretending that there is a single Indian religiousness to celebrate. We pick up bits of this or that ceremonial; we take them out of context; we combine rites that perhaps

should be kept apart. In so doing, we claim that we can "compartmentalize" our religious forms; however, we ultimately join the various aspects into confused patterns without integrity, perhaps without Christ at the center. He does not wish to encourage such a process.

In Rapid City, Denver, and at Tekakwitha conferences, Archbishop Chaput encourages Indian Catholics to increase their Catholicism. He supports Indian cultural expression but he is devoted to his Catholic faith, and as an archbishop he is committed to upholding Church authority. He questions why Native clergy, religious, and laypersons defer to Indian traditions and their practitioners, but not to Catholic traditions and their authoritative holy men in the hierarchy. He finds it ironic that fellow Indians will alter their behavior at the urging of a Native holy man, but they will pay little heed to the pope. Like Bishop Pelotte, he wishes that Indian clergy and religious would do more when they gather than "share their pain"—telling each other how out of place they feel in their religious communities and in the Church at large—in a "mutual support group" (ibid.). Like Pelotte, he has ordered certain Indian religious to subdue their criticism of the Church. Like Pelotte, he has encouraged his fellow Indian Catholics to address issues of social justice beyond their Native concerns.

In a speech at the 1986 Tekakwitha Conference (Bozeman, August 8, 1986), he said that Indians will become more Christlike when they care more about other people's problems than their own. Without denying the oppressive conditions of Indian communities—the racism, the poverty, the alcoholism—he called Native American Catholics to concern about world hunger, war, other types of violence, illiteracy, disease, the treatment of women as objects, the debts of Third World nations, mental illness, drugs, nuclear threats, and the lack of respect for the unborn and the aged. He exhorted Indian Catholics to be attentive to Church teachings on the economy, nuclear weapons, etc., and to learn more about what is happening in the world, as members of a universal (catholic) Church. "We are responsible for the whole world," he said, and although we should love those immediately around us, we need also to love "all God's people, not just our own." Rather than dwelling romantically on our own Indianness, he stated, we need to "evangelize our culture," instilling Jesus Christ's holiness into the daily life of our communities. Bishop Chaput has not denied the ability of Indian cultures to spiritualize the Church and the world, but his emphasis has been on the Christian sanctification of Indian lives.

CONTEMPORARY INDIAN PRIESTS

Since the late 1970s the numbers of priests of Indian descent and identity have increased: Edmund Savilla, an Isleta Pueblo Indian from New Mexico; P. Michael Galvan, an Ohlone from California; Paul Ojibway, S.A., an Ojibway who grew up in California; Diego Mazon, O.F.M., of mixed Apache-Zuni descent, from New Mexico; Peter Navarra, a Yaqui descendant, born and reared in California; C. P. Jordan, a Sioux from Rosebud, South Dakota, who as a youth referred to himself as "Irish Indian" (*The Indian Sentinel,* 6, no. 2, Spring 1926: 86), and who got his vocation at his aged mother's deathbed and so was ordained in 1985 at the advanced age of 68; Julian R. Nix, O.S.B., a member of the Assiniboin-Sioux Tribe from Fort Peck, Montana, raised in North Dakota; Raphael Partida, of O'odham (Papago) descent, bred in California; Anthony M. Garduño, of Chicago, descended from the Otomi Indians of Mexico; John L. Cavanaugh, a Sioux from Devil's Lake Reservation in North Dakota; and Thom Howell, of Cherokee and Iroquois descent. Some of these priests grew up on reservations; most did not. Several speak an Indian language; most do not. A few of them were raised with knowledge of distinct Indian spiritual forms; most were not. Most of them, however, are engaged in ministries to Indian peoples; all of them identify themselves as Indians as well as Catholic priests. Within their ranks there is uniformity in regard to expressing some aspect of their Indianness in their vocation; however, the degree and emphasis varies from priest to priest.

When Ed Savilla was in seminary, his superiors told him that he had to cut his long hair or risk dismissal. Here was the first Pueblo priest-to-be — his father is from Isleta, his mother is an Oneida Indian — and he was being expunged for having long hair. The Pueblo people expressed their dismay, and he was allowed to return to seminary, unshorn. He was ordained with long hair and has kept it long, in "physical solidarity" with his people. He regards himself as a "Native priest," rather than a "Roman priest" (Savilla, August 6, 1993); hence, he will not wear a Roman collar. Like Father Hascall, he prefers to say mass sitting on the floor, getting close to the earth. He interweaves gospel and Pueblo stories in the spirit of religious syncretism. Like Hascall, Father Savilla has received criticism from the Catholic hierarchy for his liturgical and theological experimentation. For example, a bishop wrote in 1983:

> I find Fr. Savilla's ecclesiology at best weak. He does not have an historical sensitivity to the developing Church nor an appreciation of how God's Spirit continues to touch the Church in growth and development. I just don't like negative aspersions cast at the Church which at times strike me as arrogant and ill informed. (DCRAA 1983)

The bishop also suspected that Savilla was heterodox in his notions of original sin, espousing a Creation theology rather than one of Fall and Redemption.

Father Savilla's loyalties have never favored the institutional aspects of the Church, including the Tekakwitha Conference, where grass-roots and hierarchical interests have sometimes come to clash. At times he has tired of "the politics of being a priest," having to be loyal "on both sides of the fence" (Savilla and Savilla, August 5, 1992). Nevertheless, he has no intention of leaving the priesthood, nor of abandoning his Pueblo identity.

Michael Galvan's grandmother always thought that when she went to church, she ceased being an Indian; then she would come home and regain her Ohlone Indian identity again. When he left for the seminary, she asked him, "Are you going to stop being who you are? . . . Will you be uncomfortable at home?" (Bozeman, August 8, 1986). He was uncomfortable at first in the seminary, the only Indian amongst strangers, not a single relative among them. Through the Second Vatican Council, however, the Church learned that Indian Catholics like Galvan could best be Catholics when they were expressing their Native culture; indeed, "if we stop being who we are, we cannot be Catholic" (ibid.), in Galvan's words. Encouraged by the Vatican II reformulations, Father Galvan has employed catechetical methods that combine Native and Catholic features in ways that are appropriate both to Catholic and Indian senses of propriety. In the process of inculturation, however, Galvan's focus is upon Jesus and His Church. He asks, "How does one be Native and Catholic at the same time?" but he follows this with another question: "How does one become transformed into Christ?" (Galvan, May 1987: 2). Like Father Savilla, he uses parallel gospel and tribal stories that enrich one another. But like Bishop Chaput, he seeks to "challenge Native peoples to examine our own Traditions and Cultures. As Jesus did thousands of years ago, the Gospel will challenge Native peoples in the areas of justice, forgiveness, and healing" (ibid., 3). He believes that liturgical change must come carefully, slowly, and that Eucharistic change must be approached with great caution, observing the "rules by which the Roman system works" (Galvan, August 5, 1992).

He and Father Paul Ojibway minister to California Indians. Ojibway constitutes the Los Angeles Archdiocese Indian Commission; Galvan serves in the Bay area, so that he can be close to his Indian relatives. Both of them recognize the hurt that christianization has visited upon Indians, in spite of the transcendent healing power of the Gospels and the sacraments. Both realize that Indians need to express their cultures religiously through Catholicism. Both recommend particular inculturative symbols—the use of drums, medicine wheels, nature symbols, native dances, etc.—as part of their catechesis and liturgy. Father Ojibway challenges the Church "to invite the Native American into a full maturity and dignity within the church, with our unique and treasured traditions, spirituality and languages intact and honored" (in Hall 1992: 68), and he chafes under the slow pace of liturgical change permitted by the present pope. At a recent liturgical conference in Rome he received an implicit message: "Talk about inculturation, but don't do it, at least not under this pope" (Ojibway, November 23, 1992). He looks forward to the day when meaningful inculturation will take place; in the meantime, he proceeds as he can, focusing on Catholic spirituality in an urban Indian context, and also seeking to serve the political needs of Los Angeles Indians.

In San Bernardino Diocese two priests of Indian descent, Raphael Partida and Anthony Garduño, try to meet the spiritual needs of local California Indians. Partida is the vicar for American Indians in the diocese. Like Paul Ojibway, neither priest grew up engaged in Indian ritual activity, but both have always regarded themselves as Indians, with a strong "family culture" (Partida, August 8, 1992). Like other contemporary Indian priests, Partida attempts to imbed Catholicism in Native ritual forms. He speaks of spirituality as an art form, a manifestation of a person's soul or spirit. All forms of spirituality, he says, are good, and therefore, Indians should express their Indian religiousness as part of their Catholic worship. Catholic and Native spirituality are two ways we have to express our soul. They are not in competition with each other, thus Indians should use them both (Partida, August 7, 1992).

Under the guidance of Father Hascall, Partida has developed sweat lodge rituals for California Indians, and in turn he has trained Father Garduño, helping him rediscover his Native spirituality first taught him by his grandmother. Both priests could be described as born-again Indians, in that they expressed little of their Indianness until they became priests; indeed, Father Garduño states that clerical visits to California reservations "triggered his interest in re-establishing contact with the Native American side of himself" (*Tekakwitha Conference Newsletter*, 9, no. 3, 1990: 4). In turn, the presence of these two priests, committed to Native religiousness, has caused an upsurging of Indian identity among Catholics in San Bernardino Diocese, causing some to complain to Partida, "There weren't any Indians here until you showed up" (Partida, August 8, 1992). Both of them have taken criticism for their Indian liturgies, e.g., Garduño's co-celebrating mass in Aztec regalia, offering sage to the four directions at San Juan Capistrano in 1991. If Fathers Galvan and Ojibway emphasize Catholic spirituality in Indian contexts, Fathers Partida and Garduño emphasize Indian spirituality in Catholic contexts. For all of them, the liturgical interplay between Indian and Catholic spirituality is crucial to their ministry among Native Americans. They may disagree with each other regarding the strategies of inculturation, the degree of Indian ritualism permissible at mass; however, they share a common mission to bring about an interpenetration between Indian and Catholic religiousness. As C. P. Jordan says, the days are gone when people in and out of the Church are "forcing Caucasianism on us," and he feels free to express "the best of both cultures" (in Doll 1994: 83), Catholic and Indian.

FACTORS INHIBITING VOCATIONS

There have not been many Native American priests in the past; nor are there many today. Considering the shrinking number of vocations in the American Church in general, one might conjecture that the difficulties in attracting and maintaining Indian vocations are comparable to those in the Church as a whole; however, the difficulties are far more formidable for Native Americans. There are well over fifty thousand priests (and a hundred thousand sisters) in the United States, in a population of 60 million Catholics. The figures of fifteen Indian priests and fifty Indian sisters, out of a population of 350,000 Native Catholics, are meager, both as raw figures and as ratios.

If we included all the Indian priests who claim any Indian descent, the figures might be higher. One might note, then, estimable personages such as Most Reverend Rembert G. Weakland, O.S.B., Archbishop of Milwaukee, who claims "some Indian blood," probably of the Susquehanna tribe, gained by ancestors in the seventeenth or eighteenth century. "When I was a boy," he writes, "we were hardly permitted to talk about this, as my great-aunts and -uncles thought it a disgrace. Now we are extremely proud of that heritage" (Siggenauk Center, December 8, 1977). There may be many other clergy with hidden Indian ancestry; however, among identifiable Indian Americans there are very few vocations today.

Why is this? At a session of the 1989 Tekakwitha Conference in Fargo, Catholic Indian clergy and religious suggested some causes. Rev. Diego Mazon, O.F.M., spoke of his own life when he said that he had always felt from white priests that he was not capable of achieving the priesthood: "You're not really worthy," the clergy told him, "You don't have the smarts" (Fargo, August 3, 1989). When he informed a Franciscan that he had a vocation, the priest "went into total shock. Of course, this was mainly because I was a mess," Rev. Mazon added. Other Native clergy agree that the Church continues to send at least subtle hints to Indians that they are not fully capable of sacramental powers and Church leadership, despite the presence of two Native American bishops.

Diego Mazon and other priests testify to their loneliness in the seminary, the wrenching from their Indian familial and cultural ties, the isolation from their communities. They have not found the company of their fellow seminarians a suitable replacement; indeed, some of them continue to experience what they perceive to be racist slights. When they see the difficulties that Indian priests have had with the Church in gaining assignments among Indian people and in expressing their Indianness as clergy, young Indians shy away from the challenges. They do not wish to give up forms of Native spirituality to become leaders in the Church.

The very process of book learning associated with priestly formation, involving over a decade of study in most orders, has put off some potential Indian priests. Diego Mazon comments that for Indians, "spirituality is learned by living." It is not an "intellectual" pursuit. He claims that the seminary learning was antithetical to the Indian way, because "I was never taught Franciscan spirituality and I never saw it lived." There was no "social intercourse" among the seminarians, as each one pursued his studies. He notes that today, "all the summa cum laudes, the magna cum laudes are gone from the order. All that are left are the dummies" (ibid.). Father Mazon suggests that the best way for Indians to learn to become priests is to live among Indian clergy and see them daily, to learn from their practice of spirituality. At the present, however, there are not enough Indian priests, and they live in ways isolated from their communities, so that no one can experience their spirituality firsthand.

Bishop Chaput adds that Indians still think of the Church as an institution foreign to themselves; the Church is not their own. They are content to act passively, allowing the Church to come to them as an outside force, rather than challenging themselves to embody the Church as leaders within its structure. Vocations symbolize a people's commitment to the Church, and he encourages Indian families to inspire their children to answer their calling from Christ. At the same time, he recognizes that as long as there are missions, Indians feel themselves to be "second-class citizens of the state, country, the Church." In order to make Indians fully part of the Church, he proposes to "do away with missions" in the immediate future: "A hundred years is too long to have missions among a people. . . . Dismantle them" (ibid.).

Two Canadian Oblates query the relationship between the inbred paternalism of the missionaries and the passivity of Indian Catholics:

What is their point as *missionaries*? Are they to devote themselves to ad-
ministering the sacraments or to evangelization and liberation? Are
they to be functionaries or prophets? Administrators or apostles? Theirs
is the most pressing of all missionary questions, one that is being asked
by persons like them all over the world: what are we still doing here?
Are missionaries to become merely stop-gaps in places where local
churches fail to produce enough priests and other ministers to do normal pastoral work? (Goulet and Peelman 1983: 15–16, emphasis theirs)

They point out that paternalism has been the pattern of the Catholic
missionary enterprise throughout North America and throughout the
centuries; it has inhibited Indians from taking responsibility for their
own religious lives.

Rev. John E. Hatcher, a Jesuit who directs the Ministry Formation
Program for the Diocese of Rapid City, suggests that Catholic clerics
have built a "dependent church" among Native Americans through a
system of "paternalism" (Hatcher 1996/1997: 12). Even today, he says,
Church personnel are slow to recognize the potential of Native Americans or trust them to be leaders within the faith; or worse, the churchmen ask, "If he or she does ministry what . . . am I going to do?" (in
ibid., 12). Hatcher asserts, "We must be convinced that anytime a non-
Native person does something a Native person can be formed to do,
the non-Native person has done a serious injustice to the Native
Catholic Church" (12–13), and he exhorts his fellow priests to relax
their authority in order to encourage Native leadership: "We must
drop our need to be in control and to be in charge. We must not step
in and solve Native people's problems for them" (13). For him the inculturation of Catholicism among Indian peoples depends upon the
promotion of indigenous leadership. When the Church commits itself
to the diversity found in Indian Catholic leaders, Indian Catholic leadership will emerge, committed to the Church. Another Jesuit, James
M. Dixon, adds that it is all-important for Indian men to step forward
into positions of clerical leadership because the non-Indian priests are
losing their commitment to Native ministry. Even among the orders
like Jesuits and Franciscans with a historic association with Indian
people, the priests are too peripatetic to make deep and lasting contributions to particular Native communities (Dixon, August 7, 1992).

Bishop Pelotte does not interpret the lack of Indian vocations as a
sign of incomplete commitment to the Church. On the contrary, he
says of the Indians in his diocese that "when they become Catholic,

they become Catholic. They are the best you'll ever see, . . . solid citizens in the Church" (Pelotte, August 6, 1993). In his view, Indians do not become priests primarily because of the strictures of priestly celibacy. There are many Indian Catholics who agree with this analysis. They say that Indians value their families, both those they are born into and those they wish to create, too highly to give up the foundations of kinship for the priesthood. It is bad enough to go off to a novitiate and experience cultural estrangement, but it is worse to live a whole life as a priest without the conjugal and parental intimacy that makes one, in the Indian worldview, a full human being. It isn't just that Indian youths are sexually active from an early age—like many of their white and black American counterparts, raised in the culture of Hollywood (Egan, July 9, 1989)—but that Indian cultures value sexuality as part of the life process. It isn't hedonism that makes Indians put aside notions of the priesthood—although hedonism certainly exists in contemporary Indian societies—but a philosophy of existence that includes sexual and parental activity as a necessary part of life. "Their morals are good," according to one Church authority (Lenz, November 19, 1993), but marriage, family, and sexuality prevent Indian men from joining a celibate clergy.

Canadian bishops visiting the Vatican in 1993 asked Pope John Paul II to consider allowing Indians of the northern provinces to become priests without taking a vow of celibacy. The diminishing number of priests in the far north is halting the growth of local Catholics' faith, they argued, and there are Indian vocations that could be brought to fruition if the rule of clerical celibacy were lifted. Without making a case for ending priestly celibacy in general, several bishops argued that particular aspects of northern Indian culture—that unmarried persons hold no authority, and that Native holy men function in coordination with their wives—would make married priests more effective among these Indians. The curial response was apprehensive. The head of the Congregation for the Evangelization of Peoples was said to fear that granting Indians a celibate clergy might "open up a floodgate of similar requests" (*Tekakwitha Conference Newsletter*, 12, no. 4, December–January 1993–1994: 11) from the tribal peoples of other continents. The pope listened to the request without agreeing to it.

Bishop Chaput rejects celibacy as the prime deterrent from Indian vocations. He tells how his order, the Capuchins, went to New Guinea less than two generations ago, and already there are forty indigenous

New Guinea Capuchins. These people, he says, are as family-centered and sexuality-affirming as Native Americans, but they also affirm their Catholicism through vocations. For him, the major factor is Indian alienation from white institutions—America, the Church—that have oppressed Indians. It is difficult for Indians to become leaders within those institutions.

Bishop Pelotte is "not very hopeful" that Indian vocations will increase in the near future, at least not until the codes of priestly celibacy are relaxed and Indians feel less estranged from the Church. Some Indian clergy note that Pope John Paul II recently suggested that celibacy is not essential to the priesthood, and there is hope that the next pope, or the one following him, will loosen the celibacy requirement, opening the opportunities for more Indian men to receive ordination. Others look to a future when Indians will regard themselves as integral members of Catholicism. For the present, however, celibacy exists, alienation exists, and Indian vocations are few. The Bureau of Catholic Indian Missions has "a lot of money" (Lenz, November 19, 1993) to support Indian priestly vocations but the funds go unspent, because the vocations aren't there. "Sure, it's upsetting," says Pelotte, "but it's the reality" (Pelotte, August 6, 1993).

OTHER MODE/ OF LEADER/HIP

In the present day, when there are not enough Native American priests, and when shortage of clergy and religious among American Catholics in general is perceived as a crisis, the Church is considering other forms of leadership among American Indian Catholics. Since the Second Vatican Council's Decree on the Church's Missionary Activity *(Ad Gentes)* and Pope Paul VI's encyclical "On Evangelization in the Modern World" *(Evangelii Nuntiandi),* Church leaders have experimented with alternative modes of indigenizing Catholicism, including:

> 1) the recognition of diverse ministries, especially among the laity;
> 2) the deeper rooting of ministry in the culture and society of particular locales; 3) the potential of indigenous spiritual realities, containing "seeds of the word," to become contexts for ministry by Christians in local native cultures. (Starkloff 1989: 73)

In short, here is an opportunity to deepen and embody the faith among Native Catholics beyond clerical vocations.

There is a long history in the Americas of training Native men (and women) for positions of local religious leadership. The Franciscans turned to "trustworthy natives" (Ricard 1966: 97) in Mexico to serve as *fiscals,* who assembled their people at mass and instruction; encouraged and enforced Christian morals and marriages; denounced idolatry; and even performed baptisms, visited the sick, comforted the dying, and buried the dead. The tradition of catechists and censors in Mexican parishes derives from this practice of the seventeenth century. As early as the 1640s in New France the Jesuits mentioned the existence of male and female *dogiques*—indigenous catechists who performed the duties of the priests, including the offering of public prayers, the holding of divine services, preaching, and baptizing. These captains of prayers served in the absence of the fathers, and also at their sides; they reported to the Jesuits regarding the spiritual progress and moral lapses of the nascent congregations of Algonkians and Iroquoians (Thwaites 1896–1901, 15:77; 17:25–57). The Jesuits were amazed among the Hurons, and not a little concerned, that converts conducted their imitations of confessions and masses in the absence of the fathers. The Indians wished to take over the forms they were learning, and the Jesuits insisted that the Indians learn that a priest had to preside over such sacramental events (ibid., 29:129). In encouraging local leadership, the Jesuits insisted upon their own authority. In a hierarchical and sacramental Church, indigenous initiatives could only go so far and then had to be suppressed.

In the absence of priests, out on the hunt, for instance, it was necessary for Natives to serve as prayer leaders. Some of the priests of New France trained these *dogiques* and in the case of the Micmacs, at least, taught them hieroglyphics beginning in 1677, in order to recall the words of the Christian prayers. When Catholic priests became unavailable after the British defeat of France in 1763, Micmac prayer leaders passed down Catholic modes of worship for several generations. When Father Christian Kauder restored a mission among the Micmacs in 1845, he found the hieroglyphic prayer texts firmly in use, and to some extent the depth of Micmac commitment to Catholicism was due to the autonomy of the local prayer leaders and village chiefs (see Schmidt and Marshall 1995: 1–15). Father Kauder praised especially the work of the Micmac village chief, Sak Plospel:

> Every day in the morning and in the evening Plospel calls all the Indians to communal prayer. In addition all pray the rosary. Before and after Mass there are prayers; even when they take a drink of water, they make the sign of the cross. On Sunday and feast-days they assemble under the leadership of Plospel for a Mass. Mass and Vesper are sung, also in absence of a priest, which is very often. (In Krieger 1993: 97)

The chief gave sermons, visited the sick, buried the dead, and even baptized small children in emergencies, as did his wife. Kauder reaffirmed the role of the local Micmac Catholic leadership and it has persisted to the present day.

In the northern realms of New Spain, explicitly among the Yaqui Indians, the Jesuits in the seventeenth century created local leadership that was supposed to remain subordinate to Church hierarchy; however, when the priests were banned by the Spanish Crown in the late eighteenth century, the Indians were left to their own devices. For the past two centuries the Yaquis have developed their own Catholic leadership without reference to Rome or episcopal authority. Their *maestros* became the authorities over local rituals, serving their communities rather than the Catholic Church, while maintaining the fundamentals of Catholic theology (combined with indigenous religious expression). To this day the *maestros* follow Roman Catholic ritual, using a missal and breviary. They employ standard Catholic prayers—the Our Father, Hail Mary, Apostles' Creed, Act of Contrition—and they continue to use the *alabanzas* (songs of praise) their ancestors learned from the Jesuits centuries ago. They pass down their knowledge to apprentices, using handwritten books to preserve their traditions. Women cantors lead the singing at ceremonies; sacristans maintain the candles, crucifixes, statues, and other accoutrements of the churches. Altar women arrange cloths and flowers and see after images of the Virgin Mary. Men and boys make up the Matachine Society, performing ceremonially during the Easter season, having made vows to Mary, dancing at vespers, fiestas, and other ritual events. Lenten ceremonial officials look out for the propriety of ritual events. The Yaquis have thus created their own local Catholic Church; they have indigenized Catholicism and established their own leadership, which for the most part is unrecognized by Church officials. The Yaqui communities in southern Arizona welcome the ministrations of ordained Roman Catholic priests; however, they reserve all religious authority to themselves, under God (see Painter 1986: 108–192; Spicer 1940: 117–194). Other Indian communities in the Southwest—Papagos and Puebloans—developed their own local Catholic leadership in the clerical neglect of the nineteenth century, and only reluctantly submitted to Church rule in the twentieth.

Church authorities in Rome and in the dioceses have wanted Indians to make Catholicism their own faith, but only under the doctrinal and ritual guidance of the hierarchy. Yaqui Church leadership is too indigenous for most Catholic officials. The other extreme—total hierarchical control over local Indian leadership—took place in British Columbia in the late nineteenth century. Based upon the Jesuit reductions in Paraguay of the colonial era, the Oblate priests established a system named after Bishop Pierre Paul Durieu, in which Indians were kept apart from the contaminating influences of non-Christians and non-Indians, and Indian policemen, catechists, bell-ringers, watchmen, etc., enforced the rules made by the priests. In these "missionary-controlled Indian communities" (Whitehead 1988: 13) of the Durieu System, the priests made all the rules—against medicine men, gambling, intoxicants, Indian ritualism, polygamy; they enforced daily prayer and catechism, Sunday observance, and separation of the sexes. The Indian chiefs, sub-chiefs, sextons, and the like served as instruments of the priests' authority and penal code, employing "a long series of punishments varying from the lash, a fine or black fast up to a

short prayer . . ." (Bunoz 1942: 194). Bishop Durieu appointed and de-
posed these Indian officials as he wished, and his courts made public
display of his rule. Although he encouraged Indian youths to consider
vocations, no Native in British Columbia ever became a priest. A
twentieth-century Oblate found this "providential, as there is no necessity to take chances with Indian priests (I mean pure blooded) as
long as we have enough white priests and white nuns who are willing
and anxious to dedicate their lives to the care of Indians both spiritually and materially" (ibid., 202).

In the early part of the twentieth century Catholic missions on the northern plains, the Southwest, and in Alaska, made use of Indian catechists among the rural Native populations. A Sioux, Fred White Coat, served St. Aloysius mission in South Dakota as early as 1905, followed by many other men and women in various Indian communities: Papagos and Pimas in Arizona, Lagunas and Acomas in New Mexico, Eskimos in Alaska, and others. The BCIM paid these workers $5 or $10 a month to deliver sacraments, lead prayers, and care for churches and the sickly in the absence of priests. Ivan and Margaret Sipary, an Eskimo husband and wife, served as catechists in Alaska beginning in the 1930s, when a priest came to visit their region but once a year. Sisters of the Blessed Sacrament trained as many as a dozen Pueblo women at Acoma and Laguna in the 1930s to serve as catechists and interpreters among their people, to great effect, according to a resident Franciscan priest:

> It is rare to see an Indian knit his brow in straining to catch the meaning of the Mass as it is given by one of these young catechists. . . . These same Indian catechists translated the stations of the cross at Acoma and Acomita during the past Lenten season. Both chapels were always crowded. It was evident that the Indians caught the significance of the devotion, their faces showing grief as they heard of Our Lord's sufferings and death. (In *The Indian Sentinel*, 15, no. 1, Winter 1934–1935: 5)

Mission agencies noted that Indian catechists were an important means of providing Native leadership in the local church, as well as Catholic leadership in the Indian community. Hence, one Catholic organ exhorted

> that the mission schools make it their main objective to train Catholic Indian leaders. Indians are being given a place in the Indian Service, and outside of this, there is need of outstanding Catholics in every Indian group to give Catholic tone to it and to be the backbone of the local congregation. (*Our Negro and Indian Missions* 1934: 29)

Hence, *The Indian Sentinel* (15, no. 3, Summer 1935: n.p.) beseeched its readers: "Will you support a catechist?"

It was the Church's hope that these catechists would become leaders of their Indian communities as well as servants of the Church. Thus, Conrad Lesarlley was not only an "exemplary . . . and zealous lay-catechist" (*The Indian Sentinel,* 16, no. 5, May 1936: 73) among the Zunis, but also an athletic coach at the local mission school. Frank Arrowside, a Rosebud Lakota catechist, was said to be "regarded by his people as a living saint" (ibid., 16, no. 8, October 1936: 122), in the model of Sioux holy men. Arthur Mandan became a Catholic and tribal personage on the Fort Berthold Reservation in North Dakota and Baptist Mathias among the Kutenai on the Flathead Reservation in Montana, the latter serving as elected sub-chief and peacemaker among his people. For a generation in the 1940s and 1950s the Papago catechist Laura Kirman developed the deserved reputation of a "holy woman" (ibid., 21, no. 8, October 1941: 123), as she taught at various schools, blessed marriages, recited prayers in Papago, and trained other Papago catechists to follow her path. Having "first heard the word of God," she said, at the Phoenix Indian School when Catholic nuns visited there, she wrote, "I am glad that I can work for Jesus, helping to bring His Church to my own people" (ibid., 22, no. 5, May 1942: 74). Two other Papago women were so eager in the late 1950s to become catechists that they flew weekly for over three months to Phoenix to complete their training and receive certificates to teach Catholic doctrine.

The names and deeds of these Indian catechists—Joachim Hairy Chin and Louis Crowskin of Standing Rock Sioux Reservation, Filomeno Lopez and John Francisco of the Papago Reservation, Marcelino Abeita, an Isleta Native serving at his wife's pueblo at Laguna—have become part of the Catholic heritage in several Indian communities, and one Indian catechist, Harry Blue Thunder of the Rosebud Sioux Reservation, received the annual Lumen Christi award of the Catholic Extension Society in 1992 at the age of eighty-six. He is the last of the old-time Lakota catechists, of whom as many as a hundred served what is now the Rapid City Diocese. Blue Thunder became a catechist in 1934, at the entreaty of a priest. His initial response was, "No, Father, I can't. I'm the roughest one!" (in Bartholomew 1992: 12); however, he had a vision of Christ praying among his people, and he realized that he was being called to the position—so, he relented.

The most famous of the Sioux catechists (as we discussed above) was Nicholas Black Elk of Pine Ridge, South Dakota, although his fame derives not from his Catholicism, but rather from the portrayal of his traditional religiousness in John Neihardt's *Black Elk Speaks,* published in 1932. After several decades of successful and well-advertised missionary work—he was said to have converted at least four hundred Indians to Catholicism by the early 1930s—he recounted his visionary Lakota spirituality as his living faith, and thus fomented a scandal among his Jesuit employers at Holy Rosary Mission, who directed him to retract in print his interest in his pagan past and identify himself publicly as a normative Catholic. Despite his retraction, and despite his continued observances at Catholic liturgy, the Black Elk brouhaha cooled Church officials to the continuing experiment with Indian catechists, and in the 1940s the numbers of these Native lay leaders ceased to grow.

The years following World War II did not put an end to Indian catechists; indeed, in 1962 there were still 118 of these lay Native Catholic leaders on the payroll of the Bureau of Catholic Indian Missions. Nevertheless, in the 1940s and 1950s clerical control over Indian communities tightened and local input diminished. Rev. John E. Hatcher, S.J., writes:

> The death of this breed of catechist was not simply the result of technology. A new generation of missionaries brought with them a model of mission which was very clerical and authoritarian. This model emphasized the importance of the priest in the christian *[sic]* community. The priest became the "Father" of the local community. . . . The net result was to create a Church that was completely dependent on outside help for its survival. (JINNAM, February 9, 1984)

A decade after the close of the Second Vatican Council, with its call for lay leadership in the Church, the American hierarchy began to train new catechists and permanent deacons, non-Indians and Indians alike, to fill in for the thousands of priests who left their orders and dioceses in the 1960s and 1970s. Today there are about ten thousand deacons in the United States, including more than a hundred Native Americans. The first Indian deacon was Steven Levi Red Elk, ordained in 1975 at Holy Rosary Mission at Pine Ridge, South Dakota. Harold J. Dimmerling, the Bishop of Rapid City, called Red Elk's ordination "the beginning of the fulfillment of a dream for native vocations" (*Our Negro and Indian Missions* 1976: 28). The Native priest, Charles J. Leute, O.P., said at the time of the earliest Lakota deacons that he hoped "the priestly work might soon be placed into their capable hands. . . . This marks a long milestone in our pastoral efforts to ensure the solid, indigenous growth of the Church among our Lakota Sioux people" (Leute 1975).

Over the last two decades the American Church has established close to a dozen Native American Ministry offices, spiritual centers that have trained Indians for Catholic leadership, including the model of the permanent diaconate. The most successful of these has been the Sioux Spiritual Center, *Manpita Na Maka Okoigna,* dedicated in 1980 in Plainview, South Dakota, in the Diocese of Rapid City. Its founder, Rev. John E. Hatcher, S.J., described it as "a Holy Place where [Sioux] can be lifted up to share in the tradition of the Sacred Pipe and the powerful reality it foreshadowed—the Risen Lord Jesus" (DCRAA 1980). In his training guidebook, *Builders of the New Earth* (Hatcher and McCorkell 1975–1976: xvi), Father Hatcher writes that "Jesus Christ did not destroy the way God has worked with the Indian peoples throughout the centuries. Rather he fulfills and completes the history of God searching for the Indian peoples." He hopes through the training program to educate Indians as lay-leaders (reading scripture at mass, leading prayer meetings, teaching religion), lectors (presiding at wakes, assisting at funerals, conducting Lenten services, serving the parish council), and catechists (taking communion to the sick, distributing communion at mass, preaching with supervision, and baptizing when no priest is available). Only after three years of training can a candidate ask to become a permanent deacon, and only then can he preach on his own, lead a parish, and be ordained with a bishop's approval. Hatcher states that the deacon represents Christ in serving his home community; his task is an everyday duty that includes selfless devotion from the deacon's wife. Hatcher warns that Indian deacons will arouse the opposition of Satan—"This is a difficult and frightening work" (Hatcher and McCorkell 1986: 3)—that will place the deacons in the protecting hands of God. Although the Sioux Spiritual Center is designed for Lakotas, the theology of the guidebook is normatively Catholic: emphasizing a catechism of sin, salvation, sacraments, Church, Jesus' victory on the Cross, and the crucial importance of human relations with Him. In recent years the Center has held a training institute, "Basic Directions in Native Ministry," which has instructed potential deacons and catechists from across Indian America in the principles of inculturation.

Other dioceses have developed their own Native ministry programs. The Jesuit Charles Peterson began an extensive system in the 1970s among Alaskan Eskimos, supplemented now by a Jesuit program of continuing religious education. There are already several dozen Eskimo deacons. The Anishinabe Spiritual Centre in Espanola, Ontario, has been training Ojibway and Ottawa deacons since 1977, under the leadership of Michael Murray, S.J. Since 1986 fellow Jesuit Carl F. Starkloff has instructed advanced candidates, including ordained deacons, toward a Bachelor of Theology degree at the Anishinabe Spiritual Centre. Oblate priests, led by Jacques Johnson, O.M.I., established the Kisemanito Centre in Alberta for the training of Native religious leadership in 1979. Since there were no men forthcoming for the priesthood, the Centre accepted women, deacons-in-training, even couples, for a two-year program of catechetical study. The students received training in theology; learned to lead Cursillo, youth groups, and Marriage Encounters; and they made home visitations among the surrounding Métis and nearby Crees, in order to become catechists. By 1990, however, the Kisemanito Centre had closed, at least temporarily.

In the meantime other programs have begun. In 1989 two Jesuits in Spokane, Dick Marcy and Tom Colgan, initiated the Kateri Northwest Ministry Institute in order to address the shortage of priests in the

Oregon Province. With several locations—at Great Falls, Montana, and LaConner, Washington, as well as Spokane—its purpose is to train American Indian Catholics for lay ministry, including permanent diaconate. Other dioceses, including Gallup, New Mexico, and San Bernardino, California, have called for Native ministry training programs, and throughout the United States Indian men have entered diaconate programs not especially designed for Native Americans. The Sioux Spiritual Center and the Alaskan program have been most fruitful in producing Indian deacons—several dozen at each—without watering down the theology or the leadership training, while at the same time meeting Indians where they are culturally, making them comfortable where they have not been, in seminaries. In the continental U.S., Father Hatcher's program is considered (e.g., by Pelotte, August 6, 1993, and Lenz, November 19, 1993) a model of inculturation, producing the embodiment of Indian Church leadership.

In order to foster solidarity among Indian deacons throughout the U.S. and Canada, Merlin Williams, himself a permanent deacon of Ojibway descent in the Archdiocese of St. Paul–Minneapolis, founded the Native American Deacons Association (NADA) in 1988. Deacon Williams serves as liaison between the more than one hundred members of his organization and the Tekakwitha Conference, of which he has been a member of the board of directors. The bulk of his membership in NADA comes from Alaska, Ontario, South Dakota, Arizona, Minnesota, and Mississippi, but another dozen states and provinces are also represented.

Like American Indian priests, the Native deacons take various paths in accommodating their Catholic identity of leadership to their Indian culture. On the one hand, Deacon Daniel Nez Martin (a Navajo who was a member of the Franciscan Friars for eighteen years, and who has taught Navajo language at Window Rock High School, Navajo Community College, and Prescott College) addresses what he perceives as the deep indigenous religiousness of his own people in preaching and instructing for sacramental preparation: "We are a prayerful people, following the 'beauty way path' or the 'Pollen way' as we call it" (in *Tekakwitha Conference Newsletter,* July–August 1992: 6). In his instruction and liturgy Catholic faith meets Native faith.

On the other hand, Don Goodwin, an Ojibway deacon from White Earth, Minnesota, states, "I don't think there will be a day when my religious belief will ever fit totally into the Catholic religion. . . . I do not believe that all our traditions can be put into the Church. We have our Sacred Drum, which cannot be brought into Church, yet. The Medicine Men say it cannot be brought in" (in Hemauer 1982: 1, 4). His fellow Ojibway, Deacon John Spears, who died in 1990 after serving the Twin Cities Indian community for over a decade, took a different stand. In his Red Lake community he was a pipe carrier and a holy man, as well as a deacon; he preferred to be known as a Catholic: "'I love being Catholic,' he says. 'I love being a Catholic deacon'" in a Church whose spirituality coincides with his Native religiousness: "the Indian spirituality is just another side. Part of the generosity of God" (*Tekakwitha Conference Newsletter,* 8, no. 1, 1988: 23). At his funeral in Minneapolis in Holy Rosary Parish, over forty Catholic deacons were present, including Merlin Williams and Don Goodwin (who performed a pipe ceremony). Larry Cloud-Morgan, the Ojibway peace activist and artist, offered a homily and a sacred drum. Members of AIM sang honor songs to the Catholic deacon, "the Apostle of the Street and of the Poor" (St. Paul and Minneapolis 1990).

Some of the Indian deacons are of mixed ancestry—Edwin D. Poulin is Apache, Tarahumara, and Iroquois—and in their ministry in urban areas they must accommodate a variety of Native ethnic communities. Working for the Native American Ministry Office in Milwaukee in the early 1990s, Poulin drew upon spiritual training from a Lakota teacher in order to heal urban Indian prisoners and drug users from a variety of tribes. He was "especially concerned with the practice and living of the traditional Native American rites" and he taught "how they are compatible with the Catholic Faith" (*Bureau of Catholic Indian Missions Newsletter,* June 1990: 2); however, he used a variety of Indian religious features for a variety of Indian people. Roger Cadotte, of French and Ojibway descent, grew up with Catholic spirituality, and only in the midst of studying for the diaconate did he begin to attend Indian liturgies. Ronald Boyer, ordained a permanent deacon in 1987 after studying at Regis College in Toronto and the Anishinabe Spiritual Centre, is an Ojibway living among his wife's Mohawk community at Caughnawaga, Quebec, and he is never unaware in his ministry that he is a foreigner, both ethnically and spiritually, among in-laws and others who may not be completely receptive to an Indian outsider (Boyer, August 11, 1986; Starkloff, October 12, 1990). Sometimes Native deacons make use of traditional ritual when their communities least expect it. The Ojibway Dominic Eshkakogan was ordained a deacon in 1984, right before the visit of Pope John Paul II to Midland, Ontario. Eshkakogan had always spoken against Native spirituality, and so his fellow Ojibways were surprised to find him greeting the pope with a traditional Ojibway rite.

The Lakota deacon, Benjamin Black Bear, Jr., emphasizes the continuity between Catholic and Indian values. This fourth-generation Catholic says that over the years the Lakotas have expressed their traditional concepts in Catholic contexts, often using the terminology of their traditional culture. His catechist father, for instance, would console Lakota mourners at Catholic wakes, funerals, and burials, but he drew upon his experience as a medicine man to create an effective language of comfort within his community. When Black Bear serves as a deacon, he uses the lessons and the language imparted by his father, and he finds that they harmonize with Catholic teachings. Deacon Black Bear located his vocation as early as high school; even then he knew that he was being called not to a generalized priesthood but to particularized service in his own community. "At that time the most valuable thing that I would pass on to them," he attests, "was the Catholic faith" (in Archambault 1995: 78), a Catholic faith expressed in Lakota terms.

Today he finds little of conflict between Sioux and Catholic ways, e.g., in the practice of family life—at least now that his ancestors have given up their polygamy. Both traditions speak of the permanence of marriage, the purpose of the "marriage act" to produce loving, supportive families. Parental and spousal love are highly valued in both Catholic and Lakota cultures. For Black Bear, the problems facing the contemporary Lakota family are not those deriving from Indian-Catholic tensions of identity, but rather alcohol abuse, early pregnancies, and single parent families—problems that exist in white as well as Indian homes throughout America. As a deacon he hopes to heal Lakota families by exhorting his fellow Indians to carry through values that are both Native and Catholic (Bozeman, August 8, 1986).

His fellow Lakota, Deacon Victor Bull Bear (who died in 1996), experienced dysfunctions in his own family—some of his children use drugs and alcohol, he said (Fargo, August 4, 1989)—and he, too, tried to heal physical and spiritual wounds with a combination of Catholic and Native spirituality. Deacon Bull Bear performed a Catholic sweat ceremony at Pine Ridge, not only for his own people, but also for visiting Catholic college students (Thiel, July 9, 1991).

Most Indian deacons, however, such as Alexander Roy of the Salt River Pimas in Arizona and Moise Bacon, a Montagnais from Betsiamites, Quebec, elect to live among their own people, and indeed, they are trained to do so. Deacon Harold E. Condon, a Cheyenne River Sioux from South Dakota, has served as a pastoral minister and counselor, dealing with personal and family issues, counseling against alcohol use, healing, and educating in his own community, since he was ordained in 1985, after training at the Sioux Spiritual Center. As a deacon, he says (Condon, August 5, 1992), he is in a perfect position to mediate between two groups whom he regards as his own people: the Cheyenne River Sioux and the Catholic Diocese of Rapid City. He is the Church representative on the reservation, and the reservation representative in the chancery office.

Deacon Condon symbolizes a breed of Catholic Indian leaders who have experienced the painful fracture of twentieth-century Native life, have undergone healing, and are able to express a thoroughgoing faith in God's salvific power on earth. His parents divorced, and then his father died. Harold and his eight siblings went to foster homes and blamed their mother for the family's disintegration. The children drank heavily and became "dysfunctional." After counseling, all but one have stopped drinking alcohol. Condon himself has been married for nineteen years, has three children, and would like to devote his ministry to caring for the many Sioux children of broken homes. Both he and his wife, Geraldine (Fargo, August 4, 1989), state that their marriage is invested in his deaconship. Indeed, they took all the training courses together, and in fact they say they share the diaconate as a "deacon couple" (in Walsh 1990b: 13). She organizes women in prayer and other activities that match her husband's ministry step by step.

In 1984 their eldest son got cancer. He was cured by massive radiation on his arm, the use of which he regained through physical therapy. Two years later he developed what looked like a cancerous spot on his knee. His father put holy water on the knee and prayed over it. The spot disappeared, and Condon is not shy to term the event a "miracle," only one of several such incidents he has been involved with during his diaconate. He does not expect the miraculous all the time, but he trusts God to heal all wounds in His own way. When Condon's uncle died, Condon asked God why; God answered, "He is with me now. I healed him spiritually" (Condon, August 5, 1992). The deacon avows that there are different kinds of healing; he does not expect physical healing all the time, but he does expect God to hear his prayers, and those of his fellow Sioux. When he speaks at Tekakwitha gatherings, as well as in his local Sioux community, he encourages Indians to pray for God's healing.

There are many who say that the healing of Indian communities can best take place when the Native Americans take leadership in the healing process, through the Church as well as other institutions. The priesthood is one such role of leadership; the diaconate is another. Some Church officials regret that the only reason many Indian deacons are denied the priesthood is that their marriages disqualify them from a celibate clergy, and at the present the Diocese of Sault Ste. Marie is attempting to have its Native deacons ordained as priests (Starkloff 1993). Others are satisfied with the goal of an Indian diaconate as a means to establish Catholic Indian leadership, but they decry the small number of Native deacons so far. "We want more," declares a Bishops' Conference delegate on the Permanent Diaconate to an Indian audience (Fargo, August 3, 1989).

OTHER LAY LEADERS

Some suggest that the Church must recognize different modes of spiritual leadership, beyond the ordination of priests and deacons. Among the O'odham, as well as among other Indians, particularly in the Southwest, Cursillo—the "small course in Christianity" which trains persons for an "intense, emotional" expression of faith in action in the light of Vatican II reforms—is currently a means of developing Catholic leaders. Cursillo-trained Pimas and Papagos in the Diocese of Phoenix are "sober" leaders, involved in "apostolic action" on behalf of their communities, intent upon being good Catholics by sharing publicly, holding communal meals, singing, and teaching scripture (Dixon, August 7, 1992). In the Northwest, it is said, Cursillo "is helping our people to have an authentic experience of *being* the Church" (JINNAM, November 4, 1986), a claim attested to by the Flathead Johny Arlee (Bozeman, August 8, 1986).

Among the Mississippi Choctaws there are elected "church chiefs" —mostly men, but women, too—who lead prayers, translate sermons, and conduct parish business on behalf of the community as well as the Church. Several Choctaw men are now training for the permanent diaconate; however, the church chiefs continue to function (Placilla and Culhane, August 5, 1992). In many Indian communities there is a new generation of catechists, women and men, who wish to teach Catholicism to their children. The Diocese of Rapid City, among others, has been eager to train them (Bartholomew 1992: 17).

Part of the difficulty in conceptualizing and achieving Indian Catholic leadership is that leadership in a Catholic context and in a traditional Indian context are two very different things. The pattern among most Indians was for a non-hierarchical, *ad hoc* leadership, in which individuals took positions of power as their skills warranted On the other hand, the concept of a priest (or deacon), especially where the training and ordaining bodies lie outside the Indian communities, is hierarchical. A leader is imposed on a community from outside and above. The community might not accept that person as a leader, even though he is a priest or deacon, although in many cases the mantle of white authority grants that individual enough status to claim community leadership. But to some Indians, the notion of a labeled leader, a priest, whose chain of command lies in his order, in his diocese, and in his Catholicism, smacks of political imperialism. It has been a pattern in U.S.-Indian relations that the Whites have tried to establish "chiefs" with whom they can treat on their own terms. Often they have set up supposed chiefs—men who were pliable to the white powers—who have not represented their community's interests or will. The same potential exists for Indian priests (and deacons); they can be Catholic agents for social and religious control in their communities, and their leadership is sometimes suspect.

As a result, Indians have called upon the Church to recognize not only the Indian priests and deacons (and women religious) as spiritual leaders in the Native communities, but also to "affirm Indian leadership" (Cuny, August 8, 1986) by recognizing traditional modes of spiritual authority: local holy men, Native American Church roadmen, the medicine men whom the Church attempted so strenuously to supplant for several hundred years. Is it realistic to expect the Church to work with these Native leaders, some of whom may be Catholics, but others of whom the term "pagan" might fit? At least one Indian sister answers emphatically, "Oh, Yes!" (ibid.). A non-Indian priest adds that the Indian Catholic leadership he encounters is most frequently lay. He suggests (Mittelstadt, January 18, 1987) that the Church is probably too "priest-ridden" anyway, and the future of Catholicism, not only Indian Catholicism, might lie in following the non-hierarchical Indian model.

In numerous Indian communities there are lay Catholic leaders who are truly the souls of their parishes. Elaine Cook, the Akwesasne Mohawk who has served for years as secretary of the St. Regis rectory and has chaired most of the lay committees in the parish, organizes a pastoral outreach committee to visit the sick and other persons in trouble. The committee performs corporal works of mercy for the Mohawk community under her leadership. She also organizes the parish's annual expedition to the Tekakwitha conference, and she helps establish local Northeast Tekakwitha conferences periodically. She takes some teasing from her fellow Mohawks about being "Sister Elaine" (Fonda, July 14–16, 1989) on the reserve, but she is clearly admired as a model by her people. Her devout Catholic leadership does not set her apart from her fellow Mohawks, although her children sometimes strain under the yoke of her ideals; one says, "I wish you didn't work

at the church, so I could be bad" (ibid.). As one priest dies and another
replaces him, Elaine Cook provides continuity in the Mohawk
Catholic tradition, explaining local customs to the new cleric and beseeching her fellow Mohawks to have patience with the ways of the
new pastor. There have been times when she has wanted to withdraw
from her active service to the Church, especially when her role as mediator between priest and parish tires her out (St. Lucy's Church, November 6, 1993). On the other hand, she is willing to stand (successfully) for election to the national board of the Tekakwitha Conference
(*Bureau of Catholic Indian Missions Newsletter*, 15, no. 9, November–
December 1996).

The same model of lay Christian leadership can be found in the persons of George Stevens or Joan Dana among the Passamaquoddies of
Maine, Lorena Dixon or George Arviso among the Luiseños in California, and many other local saints, unsung beyond their communities. Wilma Henry, "an exceptionally dedicated Catholic and an outstanding Native American woman" (DCRAA, June 21, 1985), has
received recognition regionally as the first lay person from the Diocese
of Gaylord, Michigan, to be elected to the board of directors of the
Michigan Catholic Conference. She is also a member of the national
board of directors for Church Women United. Her leadership has
transcended her Indian boundaries.

LARRY CLOUD-MORGAN

One of the most prominent figures in contemporary American Indian Catholicism is an Ojibway layman, Larry Cloud-Morgan (*Wabash Ti-Mi-Gwan,* or "Whitefeather"), baptized at his birthplace at Red Lake, Minnesota, but now in his mid-fifties without institutional Catholic identity. Activist, artist, playwright, liturgist, and translator, Mr. Cloud-Morgan has lived on several Ojibway reservations and reserves in the United States and Canada, as well as in Chicago, Milwaukee, New York City, Minneapolis, Mexico City, and in prisons in three states.

His father, of the Loon clan, was a devout Catholic who attended mass daily and prayed the rosary. He brought Larry to Ste. Anne-de-Beaupré in Quebec on pilgrimage, bearing a bundle of tobacco, which he left, with money, at the shrine in the basilica. The family name was "Cloud," but a doctor named Morgan helped deliver his father in a difficult birth, so they "honored" the doctor by taking his name.

His mother was a Bear. She had Episcopalian affiliations but as a girl she attended St. Benedict's School on the White Earth Reservation, where the Catholic sisters taped her mouth shut in public for speaking her language. For this humiliation she avoided the Church. She wanted Larry to become a warrior, like many of his famed Pillager Ojibway relatives. For a while he attended military school for boys in Illinois.

He grew up in Minneapolis and Leech Lake among Ojibway Catholics, Episcopalians, and traditionalists. His grandmother said her rosary while braiding her hair each day, counting the prayers by the knots. A woman friend of his mother crossed herself whenever her car came upon dead animals on the road. Larry perfected his reading of English at church schools, but at home the Ojibway language persisted along with the familiarity of Indian values and rituals. He was proficient in both Ojibway and English languages, and as a youth he served as a translator who traveled among the Ojibway villages of the Canadian border region.

His grandfather gave him his first book, *Joan of Arc,* and Larry read it aloud to his dog. He told the dog that one day the two of them would march like the saint, but with banners, not with weapons. Larry continued to treasure the book, but he rejected the heroine's soldiery and the warrior traditions of his family. Rather, he followed the sensibilities of his grandfather, who told traditional stories about hunting animals, but who was himself a vegetarian. The old man loved the earth so dearly that he ate soil and grass. He taught his grandson to love animals and to question the nobility of warfare. Larry's mother altered her dream for her son: he would be a reader, a communer with nature, an understander of systems, governments, and Church.

Larry wanted to become a priest. In the early 1960s he attended Marquette University, and he also studied at St. John's Abbey in Minnesota, where he was a roommate of Matthew Fox, now the New Age priest, whose Creation theology embraces Native American spirituality, learned at least in part from Larry Cloud-Morgan. Tiring of theology, Cloud-Morgan moved to Chicago to enroll in the Art Institute. While honing his skills as a painter, he worked as a luggage buyer for Marshall Field & Co. in the 1960s and 1970s.

Church officials saw him as a potential priest and offered to pay for his seminary training, but he decided against the priesthood. He feared that the process of priestly training would take him away from his people, placing him in a non-Indian setting where he would be asked to function as an "expert" Indian, speaking for Indians but detached from his community. He would become like a cousin of his, a lawyer who became a judge and in short time was making rulings against his fellow Indians. John Spears, the Ojibway deacon, was Cloud-Morgan's mentor; he encouraged the young man to accept either the priesthood or the diaconate, but Cloud-Morgan refused, to Spears's disappointment.

Cloud-Morgan loved the silences of the Benedictines and the meditational writings of Thomas Merton; he loved the activism of Daniel and Philip Berrigan. But he could not bear the confines of the priesthood. Indeed, he came to find the Church itself as a stifling presence. As an Ojibway man he found a universal Church among a community of tribal people to be a paradoxical, imperial, overbearing, conforming institution, one in which rules come from the top, from afar, not from his community. The Ojibways' tradition was to create all values and religious practices locally. He came to wonder if a reconciliation between the universal and the tribal was possible.

Cloud-Morgan remarks that the Ojibways intermarried with their beloved French associates in the fur trade and lumber camps, honoring them by taking their names and incorporating them into their clans. They liked the Frenchmen's deity and took Him as their own. In Cloud-Morgan's terms, the Ojibways "became Catholics first and Christians later" (Cloud-Morgan, January 26, 1992). They participated in the liturgical mysteries of the French and later of the Irish, whom the Ojibways liked as fellow people of the soil. Nevertheless, engagement in the Catholic liturgy was a "ceremonial commitment to life, having nothing to do with salvation" (ibid.) or a universal Church. They were merely adopting the ritual forms of their French and Irish neighbors and their religious specialists, the priests. Only over the generations did the notion occur to the Ojibways that Christianity was an all-encompassing religion that demanded exclusive loyalty and possessed a theology that called for a Christian way of life. The Germans arrived in Minnesota, and the Benedictine sisters taped your mouth shut for speaking your language. Their God seemed different from the one introduced by the French. The Ojibways had no aboriginal concept of a "religion" as an institution that established prayer, ritual, doctrinal truth, definitions of sacrality, and a way of life. The phenomena of what we call the religious life were all present in Ojibway traditions and had Ojibway terminology to describe them, but only with Christianity was there a "religion" to put them all together in a single, authoritative, sanctioning complex.

Cloud-Morgan turned away from ordination, but he has continued to be associated, however ambivalently, with Catholicism. "I love the Church," he says (Cloud-Morgan, October 18, 1990), but it is the ritual, the architecture, the sacramental mysteries that he loves. He says that he likes to go into churches when the priests aren't around, and he suggests that Catholicism is most lovable when the church is empty and a person can meditate there alone. He carries on a friendship with Archbishop John Roach of St. Paul–Minneapolis and is engaged in translating the mass into Ojibway, but he denounces the institution for its treatment of women and for what he views as its hegemonic proclivities. He gains inspiration from a variety of sources, and his spiritual eclecticism, as well as his Ojibway traditionalism, cannot be confined by the universal singularity of Catholicism. "I have a relationship with Catholicism," he comments, "which borders on anarchy and resistance" (Cloud-Morgan, October 16, 1995).

When he attends mass, he thinks the liturgy through in Ojibway, evoking the Native cultural connotations that have persisted through Catholic forms. He states that there is a deep Ojibway particularity of Catholic concept and worship. Ojibways sing hymns, he says, that express traditional concepts through Christian words in Latin and English. They have a special response to the blood of Jesus, the offspring of the Great Spirit *(Kitche Manito),* killed on a crossed tree—a response that is explicitly and peculiarly Ojibway and embedded in their mythology. They regard themselves as deriving from the blood—"we came from that redness" (Cloud-Morgan, January 28, 1992)—that spilled from Jesus to the sand, which the winds stirred up to darken the sky after His death. He would like the mass in Ojibway to elicit these linguistic, emotionally-laden associations.

In translating the mass into Ojibway, Cloud-Morgan is as much a dramatist as a liturgist. Several of his plays—"Ishi," "Dream Catcher," and others—have been performed by a troupe of Twin Cities Indians and non-Indians; he is writing a drama about Bishop Frederic Baraga, whose Ojibway-English translations in the nineteenth century helped preserve and transform Ojibway language and culture (see Baraga 1973: 209). The Ojibway mass, for him, is yet another dramatic form, albeit the one dearest to his spiritual life. His goal is not to lure disaffected Catholic Ojibways back to the Church by having an Ojibway mass, but rather to express Catholic-Ojibway spirituality through the liturgical translation.

Cloud-Morgan actively combines Catholic and Ojibway elements in his own plays, for instance, in "Dream Catcher" (referring to a little spider web placed over an Ojibway baby's cradle to protect against unwanted dreams), in which Gregorian Chant accompanies Native dance. On the stage a statue of St. Teresa of Avila stands beside the skeleton of a sweat lodge—both symbols of self-abnegation and purification—and a deer dancer approaches them both for inspiration. His eclecticism embraces MacLaine as well as Merton ("The Gospel According to Shirl," he calls one of her New Age books, July 20, 1991); at his sister's funeral he arranged for Buddhist and Jewish religious practitioners to officiate. At the 1994 Tekakwitha congress in Minnesota he performed a pipe ceremony and left the pipe on the altar; however, the local bishop insisted that it be removed before mass began. The episcopal authority was anxious about the pipe's potential overlap with the central rite of Catholicism; for Cloud-Morgan the Indian and the Catholic rites make splendid sense together. He contrasts himself to an Ojibway

Catholic relative of his who will not attend traditional Ojibway funerals at Leech Lake because she abhors the paganism. He sings Christian hymns at wakes, but he also embraces Ojibway traditionalism. Cloud-Morgan revels in rituals of all kind, and he fulfills his vocation by performing all manner of Ojibway and Catholic prayer acts whenever he is asked—at namings, weddings, funerals, and other dedications.

Cloud-Morgan's Ojibway conservatism is as deep as his Catholicism and as wide as his eclecticism. He will not tell or listen to traditional stories in the summer months, following the strictures of his ancestors. He feeds a family of bears who visit his cabin at Ball Club Reservation. He prefers his Ojibway name, *Wabash Ti-Mi-Gwan,* to his "Christian" moniker, and he frequents powwows and sweat lodges throughout northern Minnesota. One of these rites led to his almost losing a limb in the winter of 1991; his diabetes made his extremities so numb that he did not feel the hot stone burning his foot. Oxygen therapy cleansed the infection, but he was too lame to dance in the Ball Club powwow the following summer, much to his dismay.

Some of his sweat lodge companions include Catholic priests such as Carl Starkloff, S.J. In one such ecumenical sweat at which Cloud-Morgan was the doorkeeper, a Presbyterian minister squeezed in last and was given the task of ladling water onto the stones. The minister was a novice, and like a sorcerer's apprentice he poured on too much water, creating an intensely hot "warrior's sweat." Cloud-Morgan became so addled that he couldn't remember the phrase ("all my relations") necessary to break the circle and open the flap. All he could think of was "All My Children"—a television show. One priest kept beating his chest and asking God for forgiveness for his sins; another had to be carried out when Cloud-Morgan finally remembered the correct formula to end the rite. He has taken many sweats with Father John Hascall and "loves him dearly" (Cloud-Morgan, July 20, 1991), embracing him in his troubles with the hierarchical Church.

At the same time, he expresses his love for Bishop Baraga and other early missionaries who took genuine interest in Native Americans. No one else in Cloud-Morgan's family has anything to do with Catholicism; they have moved on "to evangelism, to nativism, to nothingism," he remarks (October 18, 1990). They regard the old mission schools, like the one at White Earth, as haunted places where one can hear the cries of Indian children at night. They have decided that in the old days it must have been angels who sang songs at the schools at

night—"it couldn't be the nuns who abused us" (January 28, 1992)—
and their resentments keep them alienated from the Church. Cloud-
Morgan visits the school where his mother's mouth was taped shut.
Sumac trees grow from the walls. A cornstalk stands on the roof. He
says, "I have forgiven the missionaries. . . . I wanted to love that place
but I couldn't" (ibid.).

Larry Cloud-Morgan is a man committed to love and concord. Despite advanced diabetes which requires dialysis every other day, his
prayers are those of thanksgiving: "I am grateful to the creator and the
co-creators," he says, "for the permission to live another day" (Cloud-
Morgan, October 16, 1995). In conversation he is seemingly incapable
of contradicting whomever he is with. He craves agreement. He fin-
ishes your sentences for you, out of personal solidarity. This agreeable,
even lovingly servile man, this Ojibway Catholic dramatist, is a man
who placed himself so thoroughly against the United States government in the 1980s, that he spent four years imprisoned for his actions.
After several years in the peace movement, quitting his job at Marshall
Field in 1980 to focus on activism, he and three other members of the
Plowshares movement—the Oblate priests, Carl and Paul Kabat, and
the mother of eleven, Helen Dery Woodson—broke into a Minute-
man II missile silo near Whiteman Airforce Base in Missouri on
November 12, 1984. They pounded on the cement structure with a
jackhammer, distributed photographs of children and anti-war mis-
sives from parents, and poured blood on the site, in a cornfield one-
half mile from an elementary school. Then they waited a while, until
the military realized what was happening and arrived to arrest them.
They were convicted of willful destruction of government property,
conspiracy, trespassing, and impeding national defense.

The four activists conducted their own defense before the U.S. federal district judge in Missouri, who allowed them to express their motives, but told jurors to make their decision based strictly upon the letter of civil law. At the trial Cloud-Morgan—the only first offender at
this, the eleventh Plowshares action—identified himself not only as a
"Catholic Indian . . . carrying two spirits with him" (Bancroft, Autumn 1985), but as "a simple man who calls out to humanity" (in Fox,
March 1, 1985) to cease nuclear proliferation. During the trial he wore
a blanket, a symbol of his Indianness, and when he was sentenced to
an eight-year term (the Kabats received sentences of ten and eighteen
years; Ms. Woodson got eighteen years, and her children had to grow

up without her), he attempted to give the blanket to the judge for safe-keeping. The judge refused the gift, because to take it would be considered a bribe. Nevertheless, he remarked that he had never seen anybody as morally impressive as Larry Cloud-Morgan. Reporters and other witnesses at the trial concurred.

Before beginning his sentence, which lasted four years, Cloud-Morgan became active in the appeals process for the Ojibway radical, Leonard Peltier, imprisoned for allegedly killing government agents in a political South Dakota shootout. While in prison, Cloud-Morgan served as spiritual advisor to Indian inmates and continued to organize Peltier's defense. After release (he got time off for good behavior, but then returned to his anti-war activism and was jailed again) he has persisted in Peltier's behalf, while also remaining active in Clergy and Laity Concerned (CALC) in Minnesota.

His activism has won him accolades, occasionally from left-wing Christian organizations, but more prominently from the Libyan leader, Muammar Qadhafi. In 1991 Cloud-Morgan was one of several Native American activists who together received the Qadhafi Prize for Human Rights: an award of $250,000 which Qadhafi hopes the Indians will use in their struggle against the United States. Previous prizes went to Nelson Mandela and Palestinian children of the Intifada. Cloud-Morgan represented the Leonard Peltier Defense Committee in receiving his portion of the award. He and ten other Indian delegates became the board of trustees for the Qadhafi fund, and will decide how the money will be allocated to Indian causes.

Indian rights concern Cloud-Morgan, and he uses CALC as a forum for addressing these issues. He favors Indian sovereignty, fishing rights, land claims, and religious freedoms, but he is also very much aware of the nepotism and corruption of tribal governments, which he opposes at home on behalf of the traditionalist Ojibway chiefs. He states that "the tribal governments in Minnesota function like corrupt, dynastic, political machines. And they are set up constitutionally to function as such" (Cloud-Morgan, July 20, 1991). His stand against Ojibway tribal governments, like his earlier stand against the U.S. nuclear policy, has made his life difficult among his Indian relatives. At a time when he is approaching the status of elder in his clan, he is at odds with some kin who work for gambling casinos and tribal bureaucracies, both which he protests against. There is suspicion of him that carries over from his Plowshares action. A niece asks him,

"What is a Communist?" He asks, "Why do you want to know?" "Be-cause," she replies, "they say at school that you're a Communist. I told them you *were not*. You're *an Indian!*" (Cloud-Morgan, July 21, 1991).

In such a milieu, the issues of Indian Catholicism are only a part of Cloud-Morgan's life. He says that he used to get a lump in his throat at the consecration of the Eucharist—the miraculous mystery taking place before his senses. Today he gets that lump when Ojibway elders protest the corruption of their tribal government, he among them (Cloud-Morgan, January 28, 1992). He continues to be a Catholic In-dian leader but that leadership takes place apart from the Visible Church.

THE TEKAKWITHA CONFERENCE

On the national level, the Tekakwitha Conference has provided the means for several Indian lay Catholics to achieve positions of leadership. A former Miss Indian America, Vivian Juan, was the president of the Conference, having served in various capacities for the organization since 1985. The O'odham (Papago) graduate of Arizona State University (B.A.) and the University of Arizona (M.A.) has been active in a variety of Indian groups, including United National Indian Tribal Youth, Inc., and the American Indian Volunteer Project, as well as Catholic agencies, such as the United States Catholic Conference Campaign for Human Development Advisory Council. She receives high praise from the director of the Bureau of Catholic Indian Missions, Monsignor Paul A. Lenz (November 19, 1993), for her intelligence and "vision" as Tekakwitha Conference executive; at the same time, her success has caused complaint among certain Indian Catholics (Savilla, August 6, 1993) that her institutional loyalties pull her away from her own people at the grass-roots level.

Other lay women are now members of the Tekakwitha board of directors, including Beverly Bullshoe, a Blackfoot from the Diocese of Helena in Montana. She is a pastoral assistant in her parish and leads the Pilgrimage—the intensive alcohol-treatment program—on the Blackfoot reservation. Ms. Bullshoe has been successful in encouraging her people to attend church, fostering their Indian culture, and, as religious education coordinator, providing their children with Catholic family-oriented education on the reservation. She was recently appointed to the Bishop's Council of Laity of the Diocese of Helena, and she has completed a three-year program in lay ministry offered by Jesuits from Gonzaga University in Spokane, Washington.

Joan Staples-Baum was the primary organizer of the annual Tekakwitha conference in the state of Washington in 1993. She lives in Tacoma, although she hails from the White Earth Ojibway Reservation in Minnesota. She identifies herself as a multi-ethnic person, having African, Swedish, and Finnish, as well as Ojibway, blood. As a Catholic she tries to understand "all sides of me" (Seattle, August 7, 1993).

Phyllis DeCory, Lakota Director of Native American Ministry, Diocese of Rapid City, was delegate to the Interreligious Colloquium at the Vatican in 1994. She is presently a member of the board of directors of the National Tekakwitha Conference.

One of the most visible Indian laymen at the Tekakwitha convocations in the late 1980s and early 1990s was the Crow, Burton Pretty-on-Top. He has been involved in Cursillo; he is a member of the Franciscan Secular Order. Baptized as a child, he did not come to Catholic practice until his adult life, partially as a means of controlling his anger about white racism. He comes from a traditional family; his uncle, John Pretty-on-Top, is a shaman uninterested in participating in Christian ways. As a result, Burton regards his Catholicism as "adopted" rather than indigenous to him (Pretty-on-Top 1991: 4). That has not prevented him from public displays of Christian piety, at Tekakwitha conferences and most prominently on a pilgrimage to Assisi in 1986. At St. Peter's in Rome he collected rosaries for the many people back home who had asked him to receive for them a special papal blessing, and later in Assisi he asked Mother Teresa to pray over the sacramentals.

To the many Jews, Hindus, Buddhists, Sikhs, Shintoists, and other representatives of world religious traditions he met at the World Day of Prayer in Assisi, Mr. Pretty-on-Top was a colorful example of Indian Catholicism. Everyone wanted to touch his buckskin clothing and watch him (and his Uncle John) pray with their pipe. An Italian told him that the Crow men were like St. Francis of Assisi himself, close to mother earth.

It is Pretty-on-Top's combining of Indian and Catholic features that has made him so charismatic to those who have witnessed him. He makes authentic expression of Crow spirituality, even when engaged in Catholic ritual. For instance, he fasted for four days before attending the Assisi conference, treating it as a Crow man would: purifying himself, sacrificing bodily comfort in preparation for contact with the sacred. He says that Catholic and Crow religiousness are the same for him, both emphasizing self-sacrifice as expressions of concern for one's people. He notes that the major Crow ceremonials—the vision quest, the peyote way, the tobacco society, the sweat lodge, World Renewal, or Sun Dance—all require sacrifice; watching his wife's participation in the Sun Dance reminds him of his own gathering with the ecumenical prayer leaders in Assisi (ibid., 1–2, 5–6).

He recounts for a Catholic Indian audience a fast he made in the summer of 1987: four days and nights in the mountains of Montana without food or drink. He was approached by an evil spirit whom he kept at bay with a circle of cedar around him. Tearfully, Pretty-on-Top recalls falling on his face in thanksgiving at the close of his fast: "If you have faith, this is where you need it" (Phoenix, September 13, 1987). He remarks that "Indian spirituality, combined with the Christian ways, is producing something greater than the sum of its parts" (ibid.). Although his recent years have not been free of public controversy and personal mortification, he seems successfully to be combining Native and Catholic spiritual forms, to the edification of other Indian Catholics.

The Tekakwitha Conference has been a forge upon which national lay leadership has been formed, but also one that has battered some careers. It is difficult enough for an Indian priest to establish himself authoritatively among various Indian peoples *and* the institutional hierarchy; so much the harder for a layman. Frederick A. Buckles, Jr., was the first Indian American Executive Director of the Tekakwitha Conference. The Assiniboin-Sioux was born and raised on the Fort Peck Reservation in eastern Montana. A lifelong Catholic who received catechetical and parochial education, he graduated from the University of Nebraska and after military service he administered various Indian programs for twenty years before being appointed Tekakwitha executive in 1989.

Mr. Buckles wore his combined Indian-Catholic identity with seeming ease. He spoke of his father's medicine bundle and war bonnet as his "most sacred possessions," and described his son as "my little grass dancer" (Fargo, August 6, 1989). "I did not seek this job," he said, but when the board of the Tekakwitha Conference came to him because of his administrative experience, he prayed in the mountains, received "beautiful songs" from a meadow lark, consulted with the elders, and attended sweats, before agreeing to take the position. He promised his fellow Indian Catholics to heed their traditions as executive director, so that they, like him, could be proud of both Indianness and Catholicism. He said that Indians must be free to express their Native spirituality in Catholic services, and that there can be "no more lip service in these troubled times" on this emotional issue. The American nation, and Catholicism itself, he declared, need Indian spirituality, and he aimed to foster it. The outgoing director, Father Gilbert Hemauer, referred to him as a "fully Indian, fully Catholic man" (ibid.). Buckles himself affirmed his own syncretistic principle: "When we call the Spirit in our native tongue, we are calling to Jesus."

Buckles won the admiration of many Indian Catholics, but he lasted only three years in his job with Tekakwitha. In his acceptance speech, he vowed to learn how to "walk the minefields of the hierarchy" as he had maneuvered through the "minefields of bureaucracy" (ibid.) in his secular career. Nevertheless, in 1992 the board of directors fired him "for business reasons" (*Tekakwitha Conference Newsletter,* July–August 1992: 1), setting off a vitriolic dispute at the annual Tekakwitha meeting in Orono, Maine. Buckles's supporters, and he himself, publicly defended his policy of encouraging Native expression in Catholic worship. Board members claimed that his dismissal had little or nothing to do with liturgical issues; Bishop Pelotte, Burton Pretty-on-Top, and others insisted in private that the man was an "incompetent" (in Walsh, August 5, 1992) administrator. Lawyers for the board insisted that no public statement be made, since Buckles initiated a lawsuit against Tekakwitha. Signs at the Orono conference read: "Fred Buckles Gag Order on Board? What can we do? What is the Board hiding? Let's get it out" (Orono, August 7, 1992). Many Indian Catholics saw in Buckles's firing a matrix of issues symbolizing for them the problems facing Indian Catholic leadership. How much Indian ritual is acceptable in combination with Catholic liturgy? How much control should Indian Catholics have over their participation in the Church, and specifically in the Tekakwitha Conference, which has become the major vehicle for national Catholic Indian networking? How much distinction should be made between clergy and laity? A poster in Orono stated: "All Board members be Native & Laity." In the fracas that almost destroyed the Tekakwitha Conference in 1992, many Indian Catholics came to doubt the sincerity or effectiveness of the board in promoting Catholic Indian leadership. These disaffected people noted that the chain of authority in Tekakwitha comes from the hierarchy, is funded by the non-Indian Church, and has an agenda to support Indian Catholic leadership only if the initiatives of that leadership coincide with the will of those in charge. In effect, the critics of the Conference, including Frederick Buckles himself, charged the Church with co-opting Indian Catholic leaders: raising up Indian individuals to serve institutional ends, and knocking them down when conflicts of interest arise.

BCIM Director, Msgr. Lenz, says that Buckles's failure as an administrator—his inability to arrange for food for thousands of participants at the annual conferences; his inattention to details; his complaints about salary—led to his firing. At the same time, he acknowledges that Buckles's loyalties rankled the board. The Indian layman executive told the board, "I have to listen only to the people" (Lenz, November 19, 1993), and not to the board that elected him. Of course he had to go, states Msgr. Lenz, and "he's the loser," pursuing his lawsuit with diminishing funds. The board sought another Catholic Indian to head the Tekakwitha Conference—one Indian executive lasted only a week before personal problems forced him out—and Lenz comments, "If we put a white person in there, the Indians are going to be upset" (ibid.). An Indian priest, Paul Ojibway (August 6, 1993), wonders what lay Indian has the administrative and diplomatic acumen to direct the future of the Conference and negotiate with the bishops and priests who control the board of directors. He himself was wary of accepting such a position when it was offered him. In 1994 Richard L. King (Assiniboin and Ojibway-Cree) was named executive director of the Tekakwitha Conference, although he lasted only two years before resigning.

Two of Tekakwitha's most persistent critics have been Joseph and Peggy Savilla, he of Isleta and Quechan heritage, she an Oneida. He grew up in California, where his father served in the U.S. Navy. When his father died, his family moved to New Mexico, where he became increasingly connected to the Pueblo-Catholic faith of his mother's kinfolk. He met his Protestant wife-to-be in the Southwest, where she held a BIA post. When they married in 1947, she converted to Catholicism. They have four children, including Ed, the Catholic priest. The other children attended Catholic high schools and received a good education in the faith; however, they "went their own ways" (Savilla and Savilla, August 5, 1992) and no longer attend Catholic services. The parents pray for them and hope that they will return to the fold; their brother the priest jokes with them about having "fallen away" from Catholicism but he places no pressure on them to come back.

In 1981 the Savillas became involved in local aspects of the Tekakwitha Conference in Santa Fe. Archbishop Sanchez recognized their leadership potential—they both were trained in Cursillo and Christian Living programs—and asked them to be archdiocesan liaisons to the Native American community. From then until 1993 they served as codirectors of Native Ministries in Santa Fe, working closely with urban and reservation populations on a nearly full-time basis for very little pay. Joseph Savilla also held an appointment on the Tekakwitha Conference board of directors for six years in the 1980s.

Both Savillas have the highest praise for Archbishop Sanchez, even in light of the sexual scandal that cut him from the chancery. On the other hand, they are disapproving of the Church in general, particularly in its clerical hegemony. "You get so damned discouraged," Joseph says, by the hierarchical attitude that "they are the Church. We know," he adds, "that the Church is not that priest sitting there; it is the community of faith." Peggy would like Catholics to change the long-held habit of "treating the priest as if he were a god" (ibid.). "We are loyal to the Church and dedicated to the faith," they avow. "God has been good to us. . . . We've been blessed our whole married life." At the same time, they assert that the Church has "neglected the Native people," never training them for a Christian life beyond the recitation of catechism and the following of rules. In their Santa Fe ministry and in the Tekakwitha Conference they have tried to encourage Indians to take a stronger role in the Church, to get involved in decision-making, and to regard themselves as autonomous embodiments of Catholicism. It is this encouragement of lay Native leadership, they aver, that has gained them the onus of Conference clerics. Joseph "got kicked off" the Tekakwitha board for being too vocal. He would report on board meetings to other Indians, earning the enmity of his colleagues. Bishop Chaput told Savilla that he was "too self-righteous" (ibid.). For his part, Savilla felt that the Conference was conducted "like a gestapo operation. The attitude on the board was, 'Be loyal to us, or get off'" (ibid.). The Savillas compare their own struggles with the experiences of their son, and they conclude that the path to Catholic leadership for Indian laymen has been no less problematic than the path for ordained Indians.

The path of official Catholic leadership has been taken more often by women than by men, but the comparatively larger number of Indian women taking the veil (at least figuratively, these days)—there are approximately fifty Indian sisters in the United States today—does not mean that the path has been easy. Even though the Native women have often constituted the foundation of Catholic participation and leadership in their own communities, at least in institutional terms "the religious role of American Indian women within the Catholic Church has not been extensive . . ." (Mathes, Fall 1980: 25).

The failure of short-term experiments to recruit Native women to religious orders, for example in sixteenth-century New Spain and seventeenth-century New France, meant that it was not until the nineteenth century that American Indian women began to enter the sisterhood. In colonial Mexico the Church authorities decided that Indian females, as well as males, were incapable of lifelong devotion, even though aboriginal Aztec virgins had served their temples religiously.

Several Huron and Algonkian girls in New France wished to become nuns, but the priests in Quebec did not think them capable. French sisters acknowledged that the "little savage girls have intelligence, many of them had good dispositions and were easily won by gentleness." Nevertheless, they noted, the girls had "a strong aversion to constraint" (Thwaites 1896–1901, 44: 259). One Huron girl, Geneviève-Agnes Skanudharoura, took her final vows among the Augustine Sisters of the Mercy of Jesus in Quebec, happy in the haven of the nunnery against the beatings her parents gave her, just before her death of a lung disease in 1657. This, the first Indian American sister, was followed a generation later by a pair of Iroquoian women religious at the Hôtel-Dieu in Montreal: Barbe Atontinon (Onondaga) and Marie Therese Gannensagouas (Huron-Seneca), both of whom took the veil in the 1680s.

In the meantime, however, female religious leadership, including the taking of vows of virginity, had been evidenced powerfully in the Catholic Indian community of Caughnawaga, outside of Montreal. As we saw in the second volume of *American Indian Catholics,* Kateri

Tekakwitha, the Mohawk-Algonkian convert, baptized in 1676, became a model of self-mortification at Caughnawaga. She looked after the old and sick, prayed the rosary, and emulated Christ's sufferings in rigorous self-abnegation. With several other Iroquois women she engaged in acts of heroic penance, following the model of French nuns in Montreal, but also carrying out the traditional Iroquois customs of sacred virgins. In 1679 she took a perpetual vow of virginity, scourged herself with branches, and walked barefoot in the snow, intensifying her mortifications until her death in 1680. Her life and death became inspirations for Native and non-Indian peoples, and in the twentieth century the Church has come to consider her canonization. She wielded powerful religious leadership for the short time she lived at Caughnawaga without becoming a member of a religious order. Her influence in Catholic circles over the centuries has been phenomenal, to say the least, but she never became a "nun"—an important point to Msgr. Paul A. Lenz of the BCIM, who scolded an archivist for describing her with that title in a poster at a Tekakwitha meeting (Seattle, August 7, 1993).

The numbers of Native sisters remained negligible in the United States and Canada until the latter half of the nineteenth century. In 1850 Father George Antoine Belcourt founded the Sisters of the Propagation of the Faith, the first religious order for women of Indian descent. Of the several women who joined the sisterhood, most were Métis from Manitoba; their duties were to Indians and other half-bloods on the Canadian and North Dakotan prairies. When Father Belcourt left North Dakota in 1859, however, the order disintegrated. The latter part of the century witnessed only a few vocations. An Ojibway from White Earth, Jane Horn, became Sister Marciana in the 1880s. The first Sioux nun, Sister Maria Josephine Nebraska of the Sisters of Charity (the Grey Nuns), took her perpetual vows in 1887 and taught English to French children in St. Boniface, Manitoba, until her death in 1894.

Most Catholic clergy did not seek vocations among Indian women, and they were sometimes nonplussed when Indians asked to join a novitiate. Bishop Frederic Baraga told of an Ottawa girl who begged him to accept her into an Ursuline convent. She led a pious life, receiving communion regularly, and her parents attested to her desire for virginity. Nonetheless, he wrote, "I was surprised by such a request from an Indian girl, because this nation, as well as the Hebrew and

other ancient nations, esteem and desire only the married state"
(Baraga, June 23, 1859). When Indian women sought entry to convents, they were sometimes rebuffed, for example, Mary of the Kaskas-
kias, who was prevented from joining a religious order because local
Whites protested on racial grounds. The Church officials feared racist
reprisals, and she was refused.

Father Francis M. Craft, descended from the Mohawks and sent as
a missionary to the Sioux in the 1880s, put into motion an idea set forward by Bishop Martin Marty to establish orders for Indian women,
as St. Benedict had done among the Goths and St. Boniface among
the Germans in the Middle Ages. Possibly because of his Mohawk heritage, Father Craft wanted Indian women to emulate the intense spirituality of Kateri Tekakwitha. When Ellen Clark, a half-blood, became
the first Sioux to enter the Benedictine order in 1885 and was ordained
Sister Gregory the next year, Craft began to think seriously about
Sioux vocations. In the late 1880s he encouraged several Sioux to join
the Benedictine sisterhood, including the daughter of the Hunkpapa
chief. Josephine Crowfeather was known from her youth as an incarnation of the female ideal, the White Buffalo Calf Woman. Her father
had carried her as an infant into battle, and they had emerged un-
scathed; she was regarded by her people as a sacred virgin. Hence,
when she became Sister Mary Josephine, her vows were consistent
with her tribal image. Sister Josephine became Craft's "obsession"
(Foley 1997: 264). He referred to her as "my pet sister,—the only one
who really loved her brother, & merited his love & respect" (in ibid.,
265), and when she took her vows in 1889 he wrote, "I have an idea
that God may intend that I or some one should found a congregation
of Indian Sisters. I will do my part, if I find it is His holy will" (in
ibid., 277). The following year Father Craft was at the Shrine of the
North American Martyrs in Auriesville, New York, near Kateri Tekakwitha's childhood home, proclaiming the "Lily of the Dakotas,"
Catharine Crowfeather (as he called her), whom he was publicizing in
Kateri's archetype (Ewens 1988: 12). He sought to raise funds to establish an Indian sisterhood because, he claimed, his Sister Catharine was
being "persecuted" (ibid.), presumably by racists within the Benedictine order. The novitiate superior accused the six Sioux novices of having "no religious spirit at all" (in ibid., 13). Craft blamed these charges
on institutional racism, and took his girls off in 1891 to his own training ground, the Congregation of American Sisters (or, the League of

the Sacred Heart, as it was also termed), on the Fort Berthold Reservation. One of the Sioux novices, Sister Bridget Pleets, however, asked to remain with the Benedictines: "All have left me, but I will try to remain faithful to my heavenly bridegroom. . . . I am more happy when I'm alone among the white sisters than . . . with any of my companions near me, especially Sister Catharine Crowfeather, who caused more trouble than any one else" (in ibid., 14).

Catharine became the Prioress-General of the new order, but in 1893 she died of tuberculosis, shortly after taking her perpetual vows. Father Craft trumpeted her holiness, claiming that "Mother Catharine had made the blood-stained and bullet-torn cassock I wore at Wounded Knee into a habit, and wore it at her death" (in ibid., 17). (Craft was wounded at the famous Ghost Dance massacre, but he was apparently not wearing a cassock; indeed, that is why he was shot. No one recognized him as a priest at the battle site. See Jutz 1918a: 318–327.) By 1897 he was attempting, unsuccessfully, to have her declared venerable by the Church.

What did Father Craft's sisters do? They acted as teachers for a while; then he trained them as nurses. They were always poor, and they begged for food at Fort Berthold, although they also trapped rabbits, ate cats, and fished for their food. Father Craft controlled their lives, sometimes refusing to allow them to eat meat, and threatening those who wished to leave with violence. In 1897 there were some charges of immorality made against several of the sisters and some government employees. (Charges were also insinuated against Father Craft.) Although none of the accusations was proven, Craft decided that it was time for his nuns and himself to leave "the Indian service" (in Ewens 1988: 19) of their own community. He wrote in 1897, "I am traveling with all the Sisters to visit the Sioux Agencies. We are the guests of the Indians, who are delighted to see their Sisters, and receive us with all sorts of honor . . ." (in ibid., 20). The truth was that several of the sisters had already defected from the order; others were starving under his direction. Members of the St. Joseph Society—the male Sioux Catholic leadership—berated him for his mistreatment of the sisters, and by 1898 Craft was prohibited from entering any Sioux reservation by the Commissioner of Indian Affairs. One Indian agent went so far as to accuse Craft of "living in open adultery with these girls" (in Foley 1997: 396) and suggested a warrant for his arrest.

Father Craft found little support from the institutional Church. The local bishop and the head of the Bureau of Catholic Indian Missions feared that the charges of immorality leveled against the Indian sisters might have some truth. As for Craft, the bishop believed him innocent: "The lonely life at that mission is enough to drive anyone crazy," he wrote, "he is a freak, but—I believe he is moral" (in ibid., 361). There were some suggestions that the Sioux women were "no Sisters in the true meaning of that word" (in ibid., 379), because they had made their vows to Craft rather than to a bishop. One bishop offered to make them real sisters but demanded that he examine their spiritual condition first.

Craft resented the lack of hierarchical support, writing in 1897, "Catholics alone seem bitterly hostile to the poor Sisters. If the Sisters were white, you know how quickly they would find friends, even in less need. Well, I am in the fight to stay. If the Sisters must be destroyed, I must go first. If the Church don't want them it don't want me" (in ibid., 358). He quit the Indian Service and left the active priesthood, and with the remaining four female followers (there had been as many as twenty in the 1890s), he volunteered for service in the Spanish-American War in Cuba—they as nurses, he as a hospital steward. One died there (and received a military burial in honor of her service); two others defected in 1900, after they were expelled from Cuba. The last one closed the history of the Native order when she quit in 1903. As for Craft, he served eighteen uneventful years as a parish priest in Pennsylvania and never again returned to Indian country. His experiment with an Indian sisterhood had not only failed, but had also soured other churchmen from similar dreams. Father Craft's debacle delayed other American attempts at establishing an Indian sisterhood until the 1930s.

The early twentieth century witnessed the vows of several American Indian sisters. Sister Mary Olivia (Nellie Taylor), O.S.F., a Choctaw-Chickasaw who taught on the Osage Reservation in Oklahoma, was perhaps the most prominent. In 1932, Rev. John P. Fox, S.J., established Our Lady of the Snow sisterhood, a new religious congregation of Eskimo and Indian women in Alaska. The novices were to serve as catechists and "domestic helpers" (*The Indian Sentinel,* 13, no. 1, Winter 1932–1933: 8) for the Jesuit missionaries. They performed spiritual exercises under a director, wore habits, but their vows were to be renewed year by year. They were to be devoted to the care of their own people. At least five women served in this way in the 1930s, but the order faded, only to be renewed in the 1950s, fostered by Ursulines.

In 1935 at St. Paul's Mission among the Yankton Sioux in Marty, South Dakota, Father Sylvester Eisenman, O.S.B., responded to the request of seven Indian high school girls who wished to become postulants, by creating the Oblate Sisters of the Blessed Sacrament. This religious community of Indian women would serve their own people, with the financial support of Mother Katharine Drexel, S.B.S. Over the decades this order has trained several dozen Indian women, and in the 1960s it took in non-Indians, too. It remains an active congregation, which advertises for vocations among Catholic Indian populations: "Is God calling YOU to a Life of Service for Christ?" (Fargo, August 5, 1989). Among the sisters of this congregation is Sister Inez Teresa Jetty, O.S.B.S., from Devil's Lake Sioux Reservation in North Dakota. She took her final vows in 1954, and in 1991 she was selected for a four-year term to the national advisory council to the U.S. Catholic Bishops' Conference.

At the same time, Indian women have joined a variety of other congregations, especially after the Second World War, when racial prohibitions began to be lifted in Catholic orders. Sister Kateri Cooper became the first Pima sister in 1949, a member of the Franciscan Sisters of Christian Charity; Sister Lucia Antone, the first Papago nun, took the veil in the same year in the same order. Both returned to their Native communities in Arizona to serve as teachers and translators. The Ojibway and Sioux sent several women to the convent in the post-war years.

In the years after Vatican II the numbers of Indian sisters increased, including Navajos, Pueblos, Apaches, and Iroquois among the numbers. For the most part they have chosen lives of service among Indian peoples, as teachers, counselors, catechists, and administrators, especially in educational settings. Like Indian men, they have often experienced difficulty in adjusting to life away from their people in novitiates, and although they rarely speak in public of mistreatment by their orders, their primary loyalties to their Indian communities have sometimes tugged against their religious vows. A common refrain in their testimonies, however, is that their tribal upbringing prepared them for the spirituality and life of service in the convent.

Sister Gloria Ann Davis, S.B.S., has an M.A. in pastoral counseling from Loyola University; she has been a Sister of the Blessed Sacrament for over forty years and has taught for many of those years at St. Catherine's Indian School in Santa Fe. Her mother was a Mississippi Choctaw, her father a Navajo. Her mother's side of the family is Southern Baptist; however, she was raised as a Catholic on the Navajo Reservation, where traditional Navajo culture flourished side by side with Catholic faith.

Her earliest recollections are of her Navajo grandfather and his gentle reverence toward the world, his love of its beauty. He wanted his family to respect all things, even food: "Never stab any food; we cut it with reverence," he would say (in Wintz 1975: 34). Sister Gloria reports, ". . . this is where I got a real appreciation of God, our Creator" (ibid., 35). From her Navajo family she learned a religiousness, a respectful attitude toward the cosmos, that has formed the basis of her Catholic faith. Her father became a peyote road chief, and she attended prayer meetings with him; on Sundays they went to mass. The peyote meetings were ecumenical times for intense prayer. Members of different tribes, participants in different traditional and Christian orientations, all prayed together. Those from Catholic backgrounds said the Hail Mary, the Our Father, or made the sign of the cross, in the midst of the peyote services. The common ingredient of prayer impressed her—"This is where I learned spontaneous prayer" (ibid.)— and today she finds the same type of heartfelt conversation with God at Catholic charismatic circles. The peyote prayer meetings helped in her Catholic religious formation. Because her spirituality was formed in traditional Navajo and Native American Church contexts, Sister Gloria emphasizes the continuity between Catholicism and Indian religiousness. She says, "The Church would be placing before us a terrible block if it denied us the right to continue to treasure what was taught us by our ancestors" (ibid.). She is grateful that her upbringing took place among the Navajos, whose religious traditions are still strong, rather than among the Baptist Choctaws, whose aboriginal faith has disintegrated.

Sister Gloria has brought her Navajo sensibilities to her many years of teaching Native Americans. At St. Catherine's she has aimed to train Indians for leadership in their communities and in the Church, instilling in them a pride in their own traditions. Throughout the 1980s she has worked through the Tekakwitha Conference to make Catholic Indians comfortable with Native spirituality. She has been disappointed, however, that St. Catherine's, for all of its public image of training Indian leadership, has never hired Indians for its own primary leadership positions. Like the Tekakwitha Conference itself and the Diocese of Gallup, where Bishop Pelotte rules sternly, the Indian school has maintained a hierarchy tilted toward clergy and religious, and toward Whites, and away from Indian laypersons. In 1992 she said (Davis, August 7, 1992) that she was glad to be leaving St. Catherine's after so many years there, in order to perform pastoral work among her father's people, the Navajos.

Like Sister Gloria, Sister Kateri Mitchell, S.S.A., grew up Catholic in a dynamic Indian cultural context, the Mohawk St. Regis Reservation. Her people have been celebrating Catholic liturgy in Mohawk for centuries, combining Mohawk religious culture in Catholic service, and hence she is comfortable in both overlapping circles. She is named after Kateri Tekakwitha, and she grew up in a culture of devotion to the Mohawk maiden. To her, the physical symbolism of water, fire, and incense make sense to both her Catholic and Mohawk identity—which is one identity to her. She is as comfortable reciting the traditional Iroquois thanksgiving address as she is in Catholic liturgy, or in the songs she has composed in honor of the Venerable Kateri Tekakwitha.

The struggles between Longhouse and Church at St. Regis belie her own sense of ease between traditionalism and Catholicism, and she has felt the sting of criticism among her own people. Hence, she has served for a good part of the last decade in British Columbia, attempting to "empower" (Mitchell, August 7, 1986) isolated Native villages by encouraging local Catholic leadership; in Alberta, where she worked at the Kisemanito Center, the training ground for Canadian Catholic ministries, teaching prospective Indian leaders in the ways of Cursillo, youth groups, Marriage Encounters, and home visitations; in Alaska, and now in northern Manitoba, where she is providing diocesan outreach to Native populations. As a Native American catechist, she has tried to encourage other Indians to discover "one's personal truth as learned and re-enforced by our parents, grandparents, aunts and uncles," and to appreciate "our creation truths as we have listened to our legends and tribal stories" (Mitchell, May 1987: 5). As a self-aware Mohawk, she knows that tribes have always borrowed concepts and rituals from one another, and she is not against pan-Indian borrowing in the realm of religion. At Tekakwitha conferences she has often led activities of intertribal sharing, in which members of one tribe make public their traditional and Christian practices, to be appreciated by members of other tribes. She encourages the religious forms to "rub off—a good rubbing off" (Mitchell, August 7, 1986), in order to produce a more ecumenical, "deeper interior life." For a Mohawk to perform a Christian sacrament or a Seminole dance does not make her or him less of a Mohawk, she argues. In 1998 Sister Kateri Mitchell was named Executive Director of the Tekakwitha Conference.

Sister José Hobday's mother was a Seneca from New York; her father was of Seminole background. She grew up in the Southwest, "among Indians" such as the Utes and Navajos. She has emphasized pan-Indian spirituality in her work for the Tekakwitha Conference and in making liturgical and catechetical presentations throughout the United States for the past three decades. She travels hundreds of thousands of miles each year, to parishes, conferences, retreats, and especially to Indian communities, talking about Indian spirituality and Catholic worship. This Franciscan also teaches a course on Native American spirituality at the Center for Creation Spirituality in California.

Sister José is all for intercultural borrowing. She says of her own last name that her father was looking for work in the South, and his Native name was getting in the way of finding jobs. Prejudiced Whites recognized his name as Seminole and didn't want to hire him. So, he walked around an upper-class white neighborhood, spying at names on mailboxes. "Hobday" sounded vaguely like his Seminole name, so he took it as his own. He figured, "They stole our land. I'll steal their name" (Hobday, August 8, 1986). His daughter has stitched Catholic and various Indian patches into a single quilt of spirituality that she calls her own.

She even encourages non-Indian American Catholics to learn from the religious forms of Native Americans, reminding them of something Thomas Merton once said, that all American religiousness will be alien, not at home, until it incorporates the spirit of Native Americans. "There is a spirit of this land," she says, "whether Catholics realize it or not, that helps form our spiritual life." She adds that modern American Catholic spirituality, in its emphasis on individualism, personalism, pluralism, and spontaneity, is approaching a kind of Indian ethic. Especially since Vatican II, she argues, American Catholicism has been "Indianized," and that is why "American Catholicism is distinctive from European Catholicism" (ibid.).

For these liberal views Sister José has come under sanction from conservative Catholics in the 1990s. Her speaking engagement at the Johannes Hofinger Catechetical Conference at New Orleans in 1991 was cancelled because of pressure from a "conservative watchdog group," the League of St. Michael of Baton Rouge. The president of the organization called Sister José "a proponent of New Age philosophy" and an adherent to the "creation theory of Matthew Fox" (in *Tekakwitha Conference Newsletter,* December 1990: 12). The Indian sister responds, "I've been speaking for 28 years and no one has ever questioned my Catholicism until now. . . . Suddenly I'm supposed to be strange and unorthodox" (in ibid.).

To non-Indian Catholics the liturgical practices of Catholic Native Americans, including Indian sisters, may seem liberal or unorthodox; however, to the Franciscan Sister Juanita Little, born and bred among the Mescalero Apaches, her people are conservatives in terms of their loyalty to the pope and in their moral lives. Her father was taken in by Apaches, and she considers herself an Apache. She has no problem reconciling her Apache and Catholic values as she serves her home community. Nevertheless, after taking her vows and making a decision "to return to my people," she had to choose consciously against importing her "Midwest ideas" learned in the novitiate. Instead, she tried to "learn to become one of the people again" (Fargo, August 3, 1989). The Apaches were suspicious—"they watched me," she says, to see "how non-Indian I had become"—and even she wondered, "Could I be Catholic? Could I be Indian? Could I integrate the two?" Yet, the community accepted her back, and she learned once again to live like them, without foregoing her Catholic faith. She reports, "I became a whole person again" (ibid.), loyal to the Church and loyal to the Mescalero Apaches.

In the same way, Sister Genevieve Cuny, O.S.F., and Sister Geraldine Clifford, O.S.F., both of them Pine Ridge Oglala Lakotas from long-standing Catholic families, have attempted to serve their own people as Catholic sisters. Sister Genevieve has worked among the Sioux for almost forty years, and most recently she has been director of Native catechetics for the Diocese of Rapid City. Sister Geraldine served her religious congregation for many years before returning to Pine Ridge to stay. In principle, neither sees a conflict between Catholic and Lakota loyalties, but in the practical matters of time and space, they have had to make choices to serve at home. Both of them credit their families for their Catholic faith, and both of them see their Catholicism as an outpouring of Lakota kinship values.

Sister Genevieve believes that Catholic tradition offers the fullest type of spirituality: "Catholicism is what I know; it is what I was brought up in. Maybe I'm prejudiced, but I think it has the most to offer Indian people," she remarks (Cuny, August 8, 1986). Nevertheless, she will not make negative judgments about Indian or Protestant modes of religious life. As a leader in Native religious formation, she attempts a "cross-cultural approach" (Cuny, May 1987: 6), in which she recognizes the particular realities of Lakota faith on their own terms, as valid forms of religiousness, which Catholicism must face squarely if it is to become inculturated among Lakota people. "A lot of our people have been baptized," she says, "but few have been evangelized. . . . We need to get these baptized Catholics excited about their faith so they will practice it every day" (in Walsh 1990b: 10–11).

MARIE THEREſE ARCHAMBAULT, O.ſ.F.

Marie Therese Archambault, O.S.F., a Hunkpapa Lakota from Standing Rock, South Dakota, is a splendid and complex model of contemporary Catholic Indian leadership. A Franciscan sister, she has worked at mission schools among the Lakotas. She holds a B.A. from Regis University in Denver, and three different master's degrees—from St. Mary's University, St. Louis University, and the University of Colorado. After studying for seven years in Rome and receiving advanced degrees in theology (a Baccalaureate from Gregorian University and a Licentiate from the Pontifical Biblical Institute, both in Rome), she has ministered to Indians in Denver, while developing a nationwide strategy of urban ministry as Native urban outreach facilitator for the National Tekakwitha Conference. She returns to Standing Rock regularly to reintegrate "in the family circle" (Archambault, August 5, 1989), but like Sister Geraldine Clifford, she finds that her siblings have nothing to do with Catholicism; the Church is "lost" on them (Archambault and Clifford, August 7, 1993). She says that she is the "only Catholic left" (Archambault, June 14, 1997) in her family, and she is often put in the position of having to defend the Church against attacks by her relatives who have left the faith with contempt. Her kin were "nominal Catholics" who never practiced the Catholic faith seriously. She and her siblings attended Catholic boarding schools, not because of a familial commitment to Catholicism, but rather because her parents "could not afford to keep us at home" (Archambault 1996: 136). In contrast to her kin, Catholic faith took root in her, and her life is devoted to her Catholicism, for all of its ambivalence and irony as a force in the lives of Indian peoples.

Her reflection upon Indian Catholicism and her role within it has been tempered—moderated but also hardened—by her many years of study in Rome. She says that being away, a woman among men, an Indian among non-Indians, gave her perspectival "distance" from whatever Native hurts she felt, and made her strong. While in Denver she completed a master's degree in Religious Studies at the University of Colorado at Boulder, focusing upon the interface between Jesuits and Lakotas (see Archambault 1995), partially under the tutelage of her fellow Hunkpapa, and famously militant author, Vine Deloria, Jr. Like many of her relatives, Deloria has no patience with Christianity; Archambault is not sympathetic to his atheism or his association with AIM. Nonetheless, they get along as fellow Sioux as she balances her Catholic training with an academic understanding of Native spirituality.

As a catechist and counselor to Indian peoples, Archambault states that Native Americans must read the good news of Christianity from their own ethnic perspective:

> We must learn to subtract the chauvinism and the cultural superiority with which this Gospel was often presented to our people. We must, as one author says, "de-colonize" this Gospel, which said we must become European in order to be Christian. We have to go beyond the *white gospel* in order to perceive its truth. (In Hall 1992: 23)

She points with hope at the "rising" but "fragile" development of Indian Catholicism since the Second Vatican Council, the "bi-cultural religious reality" (Archambault 1991: 3) for Catholic Indians that she finds prevalent at Tekakwitha conferences. She writes that this expression is a "*self-chosen* native identification with catholicism," but also a response to the encouragement by priests and other Church leaders for Indians to demonstrate "their culture *within* the Roman catholic sacramental rituals *[sic]* . . ." (ibid.). "It is akin," she notes, "to the experience of the *unloved ones* being told that now they are loved. This is a new experience; it feels awkward and many are still 'trying this new awareness on for size'" (ibid., emphases hers).

The issue of traditional Indian expression within Catholicism is especially vexing for her because she grew up in mission schools, apart from Sioux culture; her time in Rome placed her even further from Indian ways. Since her return she has tried to enter the realm of Indian spirituality, and she admits that she is still in the process of learning. She acknowledges that she will never be able to be "spontaneously Indian" (Archambault, August 5, 1989) again; she has too much theological education. At the same time, she does not feel alienated from her people because of her Western analytical training. Instead, she feels "methodically, self-consciously Indian" (ibid.).

When she observes her cohorts—the Indian priests and sisters she meets at retreats and Tekakwitha conferences—she suspects that they are "trying out" Indian spirituality, self-consciously experimenting with syncretism. They are "looking at themselves" (ibid.) as they perform sweats and smudges, and she doesn't find their expressions completely

comfortable or wholly artless. On the other hand, she recalls how seeing a young Native American priest in jeans, tee-shirt, and ponytail revealed to her how "the Catholic Church could take on the look of us,
Native people" (Archambault 1996: 137). On another occasion she
watched a Papago man pick up a Bible and offer it to the four directions
and proceed to dance with it. His gesture was "the most natural" co-
joining of Catholic and Native spirituality she had ever seen (Archambault, August 5, 1989). Finally, her reading of *Black Elk Speaks* (Neihardt
1932) and *The Sacred Pipe* (Brown 1953) "evangelized" her as she realized
that Black Elk's vision of the "Jesus Christ as a Lakota man" was a
means by which "these two worlds—Catholic and Native—came together within me" (Archambault 1996: 137). She herself joins in Indian
rituals, including sweats, especially among the Association of Native
Religious and Clergy, and she wishes that she could feel more at home
in them. Perhaps someday she will, but they seem artificial to her as yet.

For her the questions of bicultural Indian Catholicism are still "un-
settling" (Archambault 1991: 4): Can an Indian Catholic like herself
practice Native and Catholic religiousness simultaneously? When the
two roads meet, do they become a single thoroughfare? Does she really want to follow the ways of Native religion? Does she truly wish to
be identified with Catholicism, considering the Church's role in destroying the integrity of Indian cultures? She recognizes that there are
Indian traditions that are ways to the Sacred—a sense of relatedness to
all beings, a sense of humor, a value placed on generosity—but there
are also obstacles to evangelization and inculturation, mainly the patterns of "Native codependency" (by this she means drug and alcohol
abuse) and "paternalism" (Archambault 1996: 145–148). Indians have
accepted Church and governmental paternalism for so long that they
have difficulty breaking the patterns of passivity and rage. They are so
defensive about their cultural self-worth that they have trouble criticizing themselves prophetically. Hence, she acknowledges that both sides
of Indian-Catholic religion have need of reformulation. Combining
the two traditions without critical self-awareness, she says, is not a sat-
isfactory spiritual solution to the fragmented identity of many
Catholic Indians.

Studying theology in Rome honed Sister Archambault's feminist
perspective on the Church and increased her insight regarding Indian
Catholicism from that vantage. She still regards the Church's refusal to

have women priests as a "taboo" (Archambault, August 5, 1989) over-laid with rationalization; however, she also suggests that Americans are such "nontraditional" people that they have the capacity to em-brace progressive goals that other corners of the globe have yet to con-sider seriously. She tells how one Roman priest remarked that he couldn't understand American women, so different were they from their European counterparts. An African priest told about how he took sides with the women who were beaten by their African husbands (as tradition allowed); he alienated all the men in the process. By hear-ing these stories, Sister Archambault saw how far ahead American Catholic women are ("we talk about women priests!"). She has confi-dence that the American Church will change, and she has patience born of this perspective, even when she is snubbed by male Church of-ficials who are unable to take her theological training seriously and treat her in a "patronizing" manner (Archambault, June 14, 1997).

Her perspective has made her look at the women in her own tradi-tion, and helped her realize that Indian women have a strong voice in tribal affairs. In her own family her father left when she was young, and her mother brought the family up alone, as in many other Lakota families. The men, she says, have been hardest hit by the changes in In-dian culture over the century; they have been devastated by modern life. As a result, the Lakotas have a kind of "matriarchy" (ibid.) today. In Catholic services, she notes, Indian women predominate, and it makes sense that they should be leaders in the Catholic Indian com-munities.

Sister Archambault attended the WomanChurch conference in New Mexico in Spring 1993. She has sympathy with the goals of the organizers, since as a woman she has felt denigrated by the Church. She was frightened a bit by the lesbians' butch appearance and their anger toward the Church and toward men. Her main objection, how-ever, was to the use of Indian designs—on bowls, jewelry, and other art objects—by non-Indian women who have adopted Indian spiritu-ality for themselves and are wealthy enough to purchase Indian crafts. She finds it ironic that the WomanChurch participants appropriated the Indian designs and forms of Indian spirituality without any real understanding of their meanings. As a feminist as well as a Catholic, she cannot but view the world from an Indian perspective. Her pri-mary loyalty, and her primary ministry, is to Indian peoples.

In her ministry Sister Archambault attempts to heal the hurts of her fellow Indian Catholics. She asks them to meditate upon Kateri Tekakwitha, the girl marred by smallpox but spiritually pure, as a meditational device that reminds them of their own beauty amidst their scars, but also of the salvific power of the divine which Venerable Kateri shares. By focusing upon Kateri, as in meditating upon Jesus Himself, Indian people can envision and experience their own suffering and the means of overcoming that pain. "Our Indian peoples' lives are fragmented, scarred," she says; "they are in great need of healing" (Archambault, August 5, 1989). She attempts to provide that healing.

In Denver and around the United States she has met regularly with the Catholic Indian communities. Most of these Catholic Indian people are disaffected from the Church, and so the numbers who attend Catholic services are small. In establishing her own ministry, nationally as well as locally, she has often been frustrated in reaching alienated Indian Catholics. On the one hand, Native American Catholics are often reluctant to accept invitations from the institutional Church. More significantly, she has experienced a lack of support from Church authorities for her inculturative projects. Often she has felt at loggerheads with what she calls "hardcore patriarchy" (ibid.) in the Church. There are some priests in Indian ministry, she says, who are able to reevaluate their roles and loosen the reins of their authority; others, however, think of themselves as the embodiments of Catholicism. They try to control every aspect of liturgy and community organization, thereby "stifling all Indian initiative." Sister Archambault sometimes threatens this clerical hegemony by encouraging greater Indian leadership and coordination. At times she has been disparaged as an "aggressive" Sioux, as opposed to the "peaceful" Indians of the Southwest, and therefore a fomenter of factions among the Indian Catholics in Denver and elsewhere. When faced with Sister's plan for lay leadership, one priest said, "It will fail. I have seen this before. Indians aren't ready for leadership" (ibid.). It has been against these odds that she has conducted her ministry in Denver, while at the same time lobbying for a national urban ministry board of the Tekakwitha Conference in order to coordinate ministries for Catholic Indians living in cities, fallen away from the Church, anonymous in non-Indian parishes, and disinclined to join in with Whites in their parishes. In her disagreement with deeply held paternalistic attitudes, Archambault has received criticism from her aged Lakota mother, who tells her that she is too "uppity." Her mother says to her that priests are "elders" who have inherent authority. "We were brought up and taught to respect and obey the priest," and even though he may treat Indians "like children," there is the expectation of obedience and loyalty. So the elder Archambault walks the road of obedience, while her daughter cuts her own path.

Sister Archambault ponders these ironies in attempting to understand her role as a Catholic Indian leader in a Church in which Indian Catholics hardly have an effective voice. She finds that the ironies are deep as well as multiple, going to the heart of her identity. She learned in the many schools she has attended to "act like a white person" (Archambault, June 14, 1997), and although she has received praise and reinforcement from Whites for that behavior, she still questions that part of her being. She says, "As a native Catholic the very faith you embrace is one that was used to destroy you, that collaborated with the government in cultural genocide. . . . This is the terrible irony of being Native American and Catholic" (in Walsh, August 17, 1992).

CONCLUSION

These ironies are not lost on Indian sisters, any more than they are on Indian priests, deacons, catechists, or other lay persons. The ambivalence of serving a position of leadership and service in the Catholic Church contributes to the small number of vocations, in the sisterhoods as well as the male domains. For many, the price of the ticket to Catholic respectability is too great. A sister, like a priest, has to separate herself somewhat from her people to associate with an institution with which she does not sympathize thoroughly. The loyalty and obedience expected of a sister are too great to be accomplished easily.

Yet, there are Indian women who are attempting in the present day to create Indian sisterhoods in order to develop female leadership. Sister Eva Solomon, C.S.J., an Ojibway in Ontario, has a handful of members in a Native sisterhood, Companions of Kateri Tekakwitha, after five years of efforts. Her hope is that these Indian sisters will have fewer problems of adjustment than those who have tried to achieve "cultural adaption" (*Tekakwitha Conference Newsletter*, November 1989: 11) in non-Indian orders. In her view, the strongest Catholic faith among Native peoples has been among those who were able to build upon the foundation of their indigenous faith. A Native American sisterhood, she thinks, will best preserve traditional religiousness while training Indian women for Church and community leadership.

The Mohawks at St. Regis Reserve have also considered forming a Native sisterhood under Kateri Tekakwitha's banner, with the purpose of serving Native American Catholic parishes. Kateri appeared, they say, to a Mohawk man, calling him to "help, pray, and elevate." The community took this to mean that Mohawk women already engaged in Kateri circles should consider forming a sisterhood. The red tape (or "white tape," as the Indians call it) in establishing such an organization is daunting, and many Mohawks have been content to pray for further guidance. One Mohawk woman, Julie Daniels, has been unhappy with the delay: "I feel very strongly that Kateri wanted more. Otherwise, she wouldn't have asked for more" (Fonda, July 15, 1989). Unlike Sister Eva Solomon's effort, which has received diocesan encouragement, the Mohawk plans are still contained within the Indian community. At the same time, the Diocese of Sault Ste. Marie has formed an order of women—lay women, rather than nuns—to encourage female leadership among Native Americans.

We have seen that in the period following Vatican II those of the Church committed to Indian ministry have encouraged Indian Catholic leadership. As Father Gilbert Hemauer wrote (Hemauer 1982: vi), "If the story of Jesus and the Catholic way are to take flesh in each culture, the native people themselves must be the storytellers. . . ." At the same time, those Indian Catholics who have become authoritative leaders—priests, deacons, and sisters—are few, and their difficulties have been many. In order to provide a support group for those leaders, Navajo Brother Lorenzo Martin, O.F.M. (now married and a deacon), and Sister Gloria Ann Davis, S.B.S. (Navajo-Choctaw), organized the National Association of Native Religious (NANR). In recent years the group changed its name to the Association of Native Religious and Clergy (ANRC).

For two decades this organization has had as its goal "to help native religious appreciate their Indian heritage and identity, and to find ways of spreading Christ's message more effectively" (Wintz 1975: 35). The assumption of the organizers was that Indian leaders are most effective when they are comfortable with themselves as Native people; they are most spiritual as Catholics when their Indian spirituality is encouraged and supported. Every year, usually in coordination with the Tekakwitha convocation, about a score of Indian religious out of an ANRC membership numbering around a hundred have met in order to share their goals, commiserate about their struggles both in the Church and in their communities, and to assuage each other's pains. Their discussion focuses upon the continuing problematic of being Indian Catholic religious leaders at this moment in time, a half millennium since the first encounter of Native Americans and Christendom. There are still many adjustments to be made, and this support group helps formulate strategies in an atmosphere of prayer. Often the members hold a sweat ritual, and every full moon they pray for one another when they are apart. Finally, they act as a pressure group within the Church to support theological, liturgical, and administrative goals of Native Catholics, sometimes, for instance at the Tekakwitha assembly in Orono, Maine, in 1992, in sharp opposition to other circles of Church hierarchy. The history of Catholic Indian leadership has often featured such contention, and today is no exception.

Rev. Francis Craft is flanked by four American Indian sisters in Cuba, 1898.
Photograph by Harmon and Shaw.

Catechist William Eagle Thunder instructs a Sioux family,
Rosebud, South Dakota, c. 1912.
Used by permission of Special Collections, Marquette University Memorial Library.

Rev. Philip Gordon (Ojibway) receives a visit from Dr. Carlos
Montezuma (Yavapai), Reserve, Wisconsin, 1919.
Used by permission of Special Collections, Marquette University Memorial Library.

Urban Indians and Church personnel mark the opening
of St. Valerian Center, Gallup, New Mexico, 1947.
Used by permission of Special Collections, Marquette University Memorial Library.

Sr. Lucia, O.S.F. (Vera Antone, Papago) commemorates
her vows with her parents and sisters, 1949.
Used by permission of Special Collections, Marquette University Memorial Library.

Haskell Indian Junior College students celebrate
their confirmation, Lawrence, Kansas, 1960.
Used by permission of Special Collections, Marquette University Memorial Library.

Rev. John Hascall, O.F.M. Cap. (Ojibway) offers the pipe
among the Association of Native Religious and Clergy,
Bandolier Cliffs, New Mexico, 1981.
Used by permission of Special Collections, Marquette University Memorial Library.

Bishop Donald E. Pelotte, S.S.S. (left, Abenaki), Burton
Pretty-on-Top (Crow), and Bishop Charles Chaput, O.F.M. Cap.
(Potawatomi) prepare for a powwow at the annual Tekakwitha
Conference, Fargo, North Dakota, 1989.
Used by permission of photographer Catherine Walsh.

Deacon Edwin D. Poulin (left, Apache, Tarahumara, Iroquois) and Rev. Ed Cook carry the banner of the Milwaukee parish, Congregation of the Great Spirit, at the annual Tekakwitha Conference, Orono, Maine, 1992.

Used by permission of photographer Catherine Walsh.

Passamaquoddies display a tribal monstrance and cross at
the annual Tekakwitha Conference, Orono, Maine, 1992.
Used by permission of photographer Catherine Walsh.

✳ IV ✳

Two Traditions, Meeting

INTERFAITH DIALOGUE

Through most of their half millennium of history together, little trace of interfaith dialogue has been recorded between Roman Catholic authorities and American Indians. When Euroamerican Catholics traveled, traded, or courted with Indians, surely conversations took place concerning religious matters; however, the historical record is bare in this regard. We know in great detail what missionaries have said to Native Americans: what the priests and their helpers have tried to teach Indians about God, humanity, sin, salvation, sacrament, grace, Church, and morality. Until recently, however, the Indians have remained mute to us in their non-literacy.

Only on occasion have the evangelizers written down their versions of Indian responses to catechesis. In 1564 Bernardino de Sahagún composed fictional debates between Franciscans and Nahua nobles and priests of Mexico. In these *Colloquies* (Burkhart 1996: 68) the Natives defended their aboriginal customs eloquently, but in the end were persuaded, according to a logic Sahagún found convincing, of Christianity's higher authority. We know that a far more substantial and slippery dialogue took place throughout the colonial era, both in the Spanish and French empires, as Catholics translated their concepts into indigenous languages and Indians learned the lingo of the Church (see Burkhart 1989). In the seventeenth century French Jesuits put into writing (see Thwaites 1896–1901, 6 and 7; cf. Harrod 1984 and Ronda 1977) a series of debates between themselves and an intrepid Montagnais named Carigonan, in which the Indian laid out his people's reasons for not accepting Christianity as their own faith. The same arguments were repeated between Jesuits and Ojibways in Ontario in the 1840s (see Cadieux 1973; cf. Delâge and Tanner 1994). In volumes 1 and 2 of *American Indian Catholics* we have observed the nature of these disputations.

As interesting as these palavers are, they are limited in scope—not only because they constitute the written record of the missionaries (and thus are one-sided, even when two voices interact), but also because they so exemplify the spirit of argument rather than dialogue. When the two religious ways have met, Indians and Catholics have tried surely to negate one another's worldview. Missionaries have listened to the religious ideas of the Indians, primarily with a mind to prove them untenable. In return, Indians have been more open-minded about the Christian message (in most cases they have *had* to be, by force of circumstance), but only in recent decades do we have neutrally recorded examples of mutual religious deliberation between Indians and Catholics (e.g., Anishinabe Spiritual Centre, October 12–14, 1990).

Through the centuries of Catholic interaction with American Indians, Church authorities have assumed the exclusivity of their theological claims, and they have assumed an attitude of confidence that, eventually, all Native Americans would be christianized. In such a context, religious dialogue—interfaith discussion carried out on an individual level in a spirit of cooperation and with a mutual openness to spiritual growth—was hardly necessary. Indeed, to listen seriously to the theological propositions of other religionists, especially those considered primitive or inferior, seemed a contradiction to the evangelical impulse. Missionizing in the New World took place with the expectation that American Indians would convert, whereas sincere dialogue would require on the part of missionaries a willingness themselves to change.

Only since the Second Vatican Council has the Church encouraged a new relationship of dialogue between Catholicism and other religions. Pope Paul VI founded the Secretariat for Non-Christians in 1964 (now called the Pontifical Council for Interreligious Dialogue), and he issued a 1975 document, *Evangelii Nuntiandi,* which raised the questions of continuing relations between a missionizing Church and the non-Christian peoples of the world. In 1984 the Secretariat for Non-Christians published "The Attitude of the Church toward the Followers of Other Religions," in which it discussed and encouraged four types of interfaith dialogue: 1. dialogue of life (Christians and others living in a neighborly spirit); 2. dialogue of action (working together toward liberation of people); 3. dialogue of theological exchange (deliberating together by experts); and 4. dialogue of religious experience (sharing prayer, contemplation, and faith). To further these goals Pope John Paul II founded the Pontifical Council for Culture in 1991, which he charged to pay especial attention to traditional tribal religions. As a result, it has been said, the Church "seems ready to recognize the authenticity and the legitimacy of the traditional African, Asian, and Amerindian religions among which she is, in fact, recruiting the majority of her new members." This is a substantive move forward, since "at the time of Vatican II, these religions were still referred to as paganism and animism" (Peelman 1995: 152).

Pan-Indian organizations like the American Indian Ecumenical Conference, begun on the Assiniboin reserve in Alberta in the early 1970s, have fostered interfaith dialogue among Indians of various Christian (and even anti-Christian) persuasions (see Snow 1977: 142–149; cf. Peelman 1995: 157–158). Institutes like the Anishinabe Centre in Ontario and the Kisemanito Centre in Alberta have engaged in the sharing of theological and experiential points of view. The National Tekakwitha Conference has tried to engender all four types of dialogue in an ecumenical spirit; in the next chapter we shall examine its programs.

MEDICINE MEN AND CLERGY MEETINGS

The most sustained (and most thoroughly documented) example of theological dialogue, the Medicine Men and Clergy Meetings, took place on the Lakota Rosebud Reservation between 1973 and 1979, orchestrated by Father William F. Stolzman, S.J., of St. Francis Mission. Carl Starkloff calls these conversations, dozens of which were tape-recorded and transcribed (Stolzman 1973–1978), a "great breakthrough in Christian-Indian dialogue" (Starkloff, October 12, 1990). The participants included Jesuits, Lakota medicine men, Episcopalian priests, and other interested and knowledgeable parties. The subject matter was everything relevant to religious life. A scholar in religious studies writes that the spirit was often indicative of a willingness to listen, disagree, and to change (Grim 1991a: 19–21), although the Lakota Sister Marie Therese Archambault, O.S.F., suspects that Stolzman "manipulated" the discussions by setting the agenda, defining the categories, and determining the content (Archambault, June 14, 1997).

As we have seen in our review of Pine Ridge, William Stolzman began his ministry among the Lakotas in 1966, first at Holy Rosary and then at St. Francis. Even before he was ordained in 1971, Stolzman was already immersed in a study of "acculturation theology," with the guiding question, "What truth and virtue can be found in the traditional Lakota religion?" (Stolzman 1969: 2). He consulted first with his fellow Jesuits possessing long experience among the Lakotas; then he began to question Lakotas regarding their faith. His first, tentative speculation consisted of a comparison between Catholic and Lakota religious systems, particularly their theological, sacramental, and moral aspects. He sought the ways in which they were like each other, and he found the likenesses especially in their rituals. He wondered how the Lakota sweat lodge resembles a Catholic baptism, and how a vision quest is like confirmation. He perceived the centrality of the pipe ceremony to all Lakota religious practice. He compared the Sun Dance to Easter services, and the conjuring ritual of Yuwipi to the mass, and postponed other comparisons pending future investigations.

Two years after his ordination, while stationed at Rosebud, Stolzman began to write position papers (Stolzman 1973–1975), which he circulated among the missionaries of the area. How do we balance the universality of our Church, he asked, with the diversity of the world's peoples? How can we conduct evangelization and still affirm American Indian religious freedom? His grounding principle was that God reveals Himself to various peoples according to their own culture. In this way He prepares them for the coming of Christianity. Stolzman concluded that God's revelation to the Lakotas was not to be disparaged, even though Christ is the fully divine unveiling.

In his first position paper, Stolzman upheld the Church's duty to preach the gospel in order to bring salvation; however, those who have yet to hear the word are not damned, nor are those who reject it. On the other hand, he wrote, there are "heresies on the reservation" (September 11, 1973) in which Indians claim that all peoples are God's relatives, and that any prayer (e.g., the sweat bath, the vision quest, the Yuwipi and Lowanpi rites, the tobacco offerings of the pipe) is as good as any other (i.e., Catholic praxis). Despite his earlier comparisons, Stolzman was still asserting the uniqueness of Christianity, yet he was already engaged in dialogue with Lakota medicine men, comparing their prayers to his.

In hindsight (Stolzman 1986b: 13), Stolzman formulated the context for the conversations in this way: For decades Christian churches had regularly condemned Indian religious practice. In the 1970s militant Indians returned the favor and denounced Christianity in all its aspects. Yet some Indians continued to "embrace Christianity" while continuing to "perform ancestral religious ceremonies," while certain Christian authorities, liberated by Vatican II, were beginning to appreciate (and even participate in) Indian ritualism. Given that complex situation, Stolzman hoped to establish a means by which Lakota and Catholic religious leaders could seek a common ground, where their two roads might meet in mutuality, where the pipe and Christ might coincide.

What follows is an account, in roughly chronological order, of the conversations which took place at Rosebud under Stolzman's instigation and guidance. This surely will not be the definitive study of these dialogues; indeed, scholars fluent in Lakota should be encouraged to analyze the original tape recordings in order to provide the most insightful analysis which these rich documents deserve. One expects to encounter many interpretations of the Medicine Men and Clergy Meetings in the years to come.

Father Stolzman began the first meeting (February 13, 1973) with a comment on its purpose: "to talk about the things of God. This is a holy assembly . . . ," he added, stating that "God has spoken to all peoples . . . in different ways" throughout history, revealing Himself through Lakota as well as Christian symbols. Following a short prayer which underscored the premise of humanity's pitiful condition (a common element in Lakota as well as Catholic piety), he asked the Lakota medicine men to speak about their religious traditions and the ways in which they have learned about God.

What followed was six years of intermittent conversation. At first Father Stolzman invited a small number of Lakota religious specialists whom he knew and trusted, all of whom had some connection to Catholicism. Moses Big Crow, a medicine man from a lineage of medicine men, an officer in the Rosebud Medicine Men Association, and a knowledgeable Catholic layman, played an important role throughout. Not only did he mediate disputes and translate between Lakota and English, but after many meetings he analyzed the proceedings with Stolzman and set the agenda for the dialogues to come. The Catholic leader and medicine man Arthur Running Horse also played a prominent role in the discussions. Charles Kills Enemy, George Eagle Elk and his son Joseph, Frank Picket Pin, Benjamin Black Bear, Sr., and his namesake son (now a Catholic deacon) were all active in the conversations. Benjamin Black Bear, Jr., often supplemented Moses Big Crow as translator.

Late in 1974 Father Stolzman opened up the meetings to other Lakota medicine men and beginning in 1975 he paid each person $5 (and later more, thanks to funding from the Jesuit Council of Theological Reflections in Milwaukee) to cover costs to attend each gathering. Over the years Bill (Chief Eagle Feather) Schweigman, Gilbert Yellow Hawk, Rudy Runs Above, Norbert Running, Robert Stead, Willie Good Voice, Francis Lies Down, and Joseph Black Tomahawk all joined the discussions. On occasion non-Christian spokesmen like John (Lame Deer) Fire and Wallace Black Elk held forth about their own religious and political agendas. In 1976 and 1977 Leonard Crow Dog, an important spiritual leader of the American Indian Movement, was serving time in prison for his role in the Wounded Knee standoff of 1973. The medicine men and priests prayed for his health and for his speedy release, and they welcomed him back upon his return to Sioux country.

There were also Lakota women who participated: Iva Black Bear
(the senior Black Bear's wife), Julie Walking Eagle, Lucille Running
Horse (Arthur's spouse), Jane Marshall (daughter of Moses Big
Crow), Ellis Head, Elizabeth Clifford, Laura Black Tomahawk
(Joseph's wife), Marie Two Charges, Myrtle Swift Eagle, and others.
Some of the numerous Lakotas had Catholic affiliation; others were
decidedly non-Christians.

Over a dozen Jesuits—Stolzman most prominently but also Fathers
Robert Demeyer, Bernard Fagan, George Haas, Kenneth Walleman,
Harry Zerner, and Robert J. Hilbert—represented Christianity during
the talks, as well as a few other priests, sisters, and ministers on occasion. Sometimes the Lakotas asked that a greater variety of Christian
pastors be invited; however, Stolzman kept mostly to a small cast of Jesuits and thereby avoided interdenominational disagreements and
maintained Jesuit authority. At times there were as many as forty in attendance, including eight of the twelve most prominent Rosebud medicine men and seven of the eleven Catholic priests on the reservation.

In the first meeting Charles Kills Enemy described how he became
a medicine man and how he upholds that tradition in the present day.
Big Crow compared the process of becoming a medicine man to that
of priestly formation, and he found them similar: "That's just like you
priests that you study years and years—this is the same way with these
medicine men. They fast and they go through a lot of hardship" (February 13, 1973). In this way the Lakotas validated their religious specializations in the company of priests who constituted a competing organization of spiritual authority on the reservation.

Arthur Running Horse said that because of this competition Lakota
spiritual life has been destroyed; there are no more holy men among
his people as there were in his grandfathers' generation. Still, he was
happy to be talking about the old ways. Benjamin Black Bear, Sr., recalled that his great-grandfather was a Catholic, but he also "did
dream—dream in the old manner of medicine man." He was not supposed to, because he was Catholic; however, "you just can't—you
know—throw away your Indianness . . ." (February 13, 1973). He himself acknowledged that he still believed in the power of the pipe and
prayed with it, even in Catholic church services. Moses Big Crow
noted: "I am a Catholic. I've been a Catholic all my life. So when I feel
like a non-Indian I go to church." This evoked laughter from the participants, reaffirming as it did the notion that Catholicism is a non-Indian

religion. "And when I feel like an Indian," he concluded, "I go to the sweat bath and go to the ceremonies" (February 13, 1973).

At the outset some of the Catholic Lakotas worried about their people's engagement in traditional ritualism, especially if it meant turning away from the Catholic faith. Charles Kills Enemy wondered what happened to the souls of Lakotas who lived before the coming of Christ's saving grace in the visible Church. And what about the people who are attracted to the pipe today and turn away from the "white man's church?" They may "get themselves in the wrong direction," he mused (February 13, 1973).

From the beginning the discussants wrestled with comparisons between their religions. Arthur Running Horse likened both Yuwipi and the pipe ceremony to the Catholic mass, calling them all prayers for eternal life. Stolzman pressed the distinction between Christ and the pipe. He asked the medicine men if the pipe is "primarily for health and help while the person is here on earth but is not the means by which a person saves his soul . . . , the means by which he reaches his eternal reward." He went on to say that God gave means of prayer to all peoples but only with the coming of Jesus Christ was there a clear, sure means of "salvation," of reaching "a kingdom after death . . . through the work of God in His Son Jesus Christ" (February 13, 1973).

Moses Big Crow noted that in the "non-Indian religion," the sacramental elements (and particularly the mass) function to "save our souls." He wondered, too, whether the Lakota pipe functions in that way, to help Indians "to be with God" after death. He did not think so, although if Whites had not "come over" into Lakota life, the pipe would function "the same way" as the mass does today (February 13, 1973). Charles Kills Enemy asserted that his teachers "told me that this pipe will save no soul" (February 13, 1973), that it does not play a role in eternal salvation. Stolzman asked if the pipe was ever used in the past for war. Moses Big Crow said yes, the pipe and the Sun Dance were means to gain power over enemies through divine aid. These were instruments of "survival in the old days." Stolzman replied, "Yes But today war is not of survival" (February 13, 1973). Arthur Running Horse attributed sacred tasks to the pipe, but he demurred, "It cannot save a soul." George Eagle Elk interpreted the question differently, saying that if Lakotas were to use the pipe correctly, "that this *will save* a soul" (February 13, 1973). Benjamin Black Bear, Sr., tried to mediate, avowing that "the pipe and the Catholic faith are both alike . . . , that regardless of which religion, the Catholic faith or the peace pipe way of religion, if he does it right and lives accordingly, when he dies, . . . his soul will be saved" (February 13, 1973).

Stolzman carried the question further, asking if Lakotas pray with the pipe for the dead. Are those prayers to "quiet the soul? or does it actually help the soul?" The medicine men said that Lakota beliefs about the afterlife were less graphic than Catholic notions. Lakota prayers were made to quiet the souls of the dead and living relatives, to maintain their bonds of kinship.

Thus there were differences of opinion between the priests and medicine men, and even among the Lakotas, about crucial soteriological questions, even from the first day of discussion. Two years later the discussants were still wrestling with the issue of the pipe's purposes, and Arthur Running Horse was saying definitively that "the pipe cannot save a soul. They pray for a man while he's alive so that he would have a long life. The pipe cannot save a soul" (February 11, 1975). In 1977 and 1978 the same issue still occupied the minds of the discussants, as we shall see.

When the topic moved to the sweat lodge, the various Lakotas spoke of its healing properties and powers of purification, as well as its ability to strengthen the body. But Stolzman wanted to know if the sweat possessed the potency to heal the soul as well. The Indians affirmed that the sweat lodge could help a soul, but not save it. Lakotas take sweats, they said, to ask help from God with their problems, but the ritual itself was not salvific in the way that the Jesuits claimed the Church is. Then, do Lakotas "ever see a vision of God" in the sweat lodge? Not in the main, the Lakotas, responded, "they do not see God, but He gives them power. Meaning He answers their prayers I guess," said Arthur Running Horse.

George Eagle Elk rejoined, asking the Catholic priests, after all their years of training, "Do they see God?" The Lakotas laughed at the question. After a while one of the Catholic priests, John McCurack, responded that Jesus is God and whoever sees Jesus sees God directly.

Stolzman asked if a man ever receives help directly from God, or does help always arrive through spirits placed in the world by *Wakantanka*. Charles Kills Enemy replied that eagles, spiders, and other beings help the Lakotas pray to "the Almighty" (February 13, 1973). What ensued was a discussion of the terminology for aspects of the *wakan* realm, during which Moses Big Crow made it clear that Christian missionaries had already influenced the way in which Lakotas referred to the sacred by conflating the concepts of "God" and *Wakantanka*. Any theological dialogue in the present day would have to recognize the seepage that had already occurred between the Lakota and Christian systems of thought and nomenclature. In general, however, the Lakotas affirmed their continuing belief in spirits apart from a single, personal deity.

One gets the impression that Stolzman and the other Jesuits were using the early sessions to quiz the Lakotas about their religious beliefs. The Indians retorted with queries of their own, but in general they found themselves having to explain their religious worldview to priests who had assumed religious authority on the reservation. The medicine men tended to avoid direct answers about their religious specializations, and to joke in order to relieve potential tension between the two groups. And on occasion they expressed relief if their answers were not challenged by their Jesuit examiners. "Boy, I got out of that one," sighed Moses Big Crow after trying to untie a theological knot.

In some situations we find Stolzman attempting to deconstruct an aspect of Lakota religion, for example, the claim that spirits make sparks as they gather around a medicine man within a sweat lodge, or rather, in Yuwipi performances. Stolzman asked if the sparks were not made by a medicine man rather than by spirits. "I wonder if the answer . . . is not something similar to the mass," he said, "that through the power of God, by the power of God, the priest changes the bread and wine into the body and blood of Christ. . . . That is the holy man, by the power of the spirit, makes the sparks" (February 13, 1973). Charles Kills Enemy replied that the spirits make the sparks. Then Moses Big Crow acknowledged that some people accuse the medicine men of legerdemain, like causing the sparks with cigarette lighters; however, he still believed in the possibility of the miraculous, in which the spiritual realm revealed its presence with visible signs. Benjamin Black Bear, Jr., averred that when you start analyzing the miraculous, you eventually come to the "conclusion that there is no such thing. . . . You don't see God, you don't see anything miraculous" (February 13, 1973).

Stolzman persisted: Are the sparks caused by spirits, or are they a sleight of hand perpetrated by bad medicine men? Arthur Running Horse refused to say. A medicine man would not accuse a fellow practitioner of trickery, he demurred, "In plain words, he minds his own business. . . . He does not nosey around him" (February 13, 1973).

Stolzman again: there are charlatans, and we need to discern the difference between flimflam and miracles, "truly supernatural phenomena. We see miracles, we witness cures. . . . We also know that God can use men as his instruments to do these things" (February 13, 1973).

Father McCurack reminded Stolzman that the priests must steer clear of approving Indian performances like the sweat lodge or Yuwipi, not only because they contain imposture, but also because they can be vehicles for evil. This comment caused a general disruption among the Lakotas, during which Iva Black Bear exclaimed, "I even say my Lord's prayer in there." Charles Kills Enemy added, laughing: "Maybe what you are thinking of is demons." George Eagle Elk concluded, with some seriousness, "If these non-Indians didn't come across with the devil, then we'd be all right" (February 13, 1973). The room crackled with Lakota laughter.

Stolzman tried to explain his question. In the past the priests forbade Yuwipi practice among Catholic Lakotas, because of "bad prayermen," he said (February 13, 1973). He was asking his question because he wanted to know what priests should do: allow or prohibit Catholic Lakota participation in Yuwipi.

This explanation caused more nervous laughter among the Lakotas, which Moses Big Crow interpreted for the priests. The medicine men, he said, cannot justify themselves in front of the Jesuits—calling themselves upright and honest in their spiritual practice—because they should always be humble. On the other hand, the priests should trust the integrity of medicine men of high repute. If the Lakotas say that a particular Yuwipi service is honorable, the Jesuits ought to accept that judgment.

This led the priests to recall that in the early twentieth century the Jesuits had allowed a certain catechist to continue in his vocation as a medicine man, so long as he did not perform Yuwipi ceremonies. As far as the clerics had been concerned, an Indian could conduct healing services, employing herbs and prayers. Yuwipi, however, continued to arouse the priests' suspicions because of its claim to invoke Lakota spirits and signal their existence with magical evidence. In 1973, as the dialogue revealed, Yuwipi remained a challenge to Catholic evangelization.

All of this took place in the first dialogue. Father McCurack concluded the first meeting with a reminder that this discussion was an expression of everyone's good will. He also avowed that "we all pray to the same God. There is only one God," an assertion unchallenged at the moment but which already had been made problematic by the preceding discussion. Arthur Running Horse closed with a brief prayer, a translation into Lakota from a Jesuit prayer book.

Later in February 1973 Henry Crow Dog addressed the Jesuits at a special gathering, in order to describe the Native American Church, particularly the branch which uses the symbolism of the cross. Father Stolzman wanted to know if the cross represented Christ; Crow Dog said that it also symbolized the four directions of the Lakota universe. Is Jesus present in peyote? Stolzman asked. Yes, said the Lakota religious leader, especially in the visions produced by the cactus. Crow Dog extolled the virtues of peyote ritualism and rued the day that the Jesuits ordered him out of St. Francis because of his peyotism, even though he was praying to Christ and the Great Spirit in church. He claimed that a child of his died as a result of his expulsion from the Church. "After that," he said, "I quit the Catholic Church and no more" (February 20, 1973).

THE PIPE AND CHRIST

The third meeting of the medicine men and pastors consisted of a long discussion of the Lakota sacred pipe, brought in legend by the White Buffalo Calf Woman. Father Robert Demeyer, S.J., began by asking the Indians, "Do you or do you know of anyone who says this pipe is Christ . . . that this pipe represents Jesus Christ?" (February 20, 1973). Charles Kills Enemy replied, "Yes, it is Christ in the Indian way" (February 20, 1973). This led Stolzman to a comparison of Lakota pipes and Christian crosses: how there are innumerable versions of each with which a person can pray, yet there is a true pipe and a true cross.

The Jesuit then asked the medicine men to compare the pipe to Christ. Here Benjamin Black Bear, Sr., commented that before Christians came into Sioux country, the Lakotas had prayed to God according to the rule of the pipe. The Indians accepted Christian elements and the rules of the Bible into their prayers, and even in the Sun Dance. They combined these elements, he said, because both religions are "true" (March 20, 1973). In the early days of the Catholic mission, he reported, the priests used Lakota language and taught the Indians prayers in Lakota language. An old-timer like himself could understand that kind of Christianity, through the medium of his own language. However, in more recent decades, as the priests abandoned Lakota language, Catholicism became less comprehensible. "When we go to mass and the priest says prayers and since we don't understand it we also pray in a different way and in confession we cannot express" (March 20, 1973). Thus, he continued to pray to God with the pipe, to state his religiousness in his own language and in a form that made sense to him.

Father Stolzman presented a lengthy lecture on the theology of mediation, in order to depict the place of the pipe in Lakota religion. He said that in ancient times angels mediated between God and humans, but Christ superseded them, becoming the prime mediator of Christianity. Was there a similar sequence, he suggested, with the coming of the pipe? Formerly the Lakotas had prayed through various spirits, the powers of the world. But, he argued, "God sent his pipe. . . . So as Jesus Christ was placed above the angels, was not the pipe placed above the [spirits]. Is this a valid statement?" (March 20, 1973). He even wanted to know which was stronger: spirits or the pipe?

The Lakotas did not accept this line of questioning. They agreed that the pipe was given by the divine as a means of prayer, but not in order to supersede the spirits. Indeed, given their history in relation to Christian missions, they were bemused by the idea of one religious form replacing another. Arthur Running Horse stated:

> The non-Indians came across and they introduced the religion and dis-
> carded the other one. The life of the people was destroyed through this
> change and so they weren't as strong and they didn't live the good life
> because of this change and perhaps we should go back to the pipe to
> bring ourselves back. (March 20, 1973)

The Lakotas saw a virtue in prayer with the pipe, because it enabled them to pray "from the heart. If you pray from a book," they posited, "your whole mind may not be there" (March 20, 1973).

Charles Kills Enemy concluded with a personal memoir. He re-called that he was excommunicated from the Church for twenty-five years, during which time he continued to attend Catholic services, while also praying with the pipe and peyote. "Some day I will go back on the right road, the Catholic way," he had told himself, "and I pray that way with the pipe, too." Now he was married in the Catholic Church and was on the "right track." He was a good Catholic, or at least tried to be. At the same time, he attested, he was also on "my medicine road. . . . I have a belief and I have a pipe. I believe in the pipe and my Catholic Church too." Finally, he offered the hope that Christian and Lakota religious forms would soon "combine," or at least "cooperate," and in this new age, he said, "the pipe is going to be stronger again" (March 20, 1973).

At the end of October the conferees reconvened, this time with an agenda to discuss "the experience of spirits" (October 30, 1973). The Jesuits were trained in the practice of discerning spirits, Stolzman said, and so in the past they made judgments about Lakota spirits. Lacking an understanding of them, the priests were "fearful" and tried to "sup-press" them. Today, he said, we wish to understand these better. Espe-cially in light of the Catholic pentecostal movement, in which Catholics are opening themselves to the possibility of experiential spir-ituality, the Jesuits were asking the medicine men to "share" their per-sonal experience of spirits.

Moses Big Crow made it clear in response that these medicine men were not allowed to converse about the spirits they encountered in visions or employed in curing. These men did not want even to be referred to as "medicine men," since to do so amounted to "bragging" about spiritual experiences and prowess. Thus, even though Father Robert Demeyer, S.J., offered the possibility of "working to bring the two religions together . . . serving the same God" (October 30, 1973), the medicine men felt cultural sanctions against revealing their personal experience of spirits. Instead of talking about their experiences, they invited the priests to the Lakota ceremonies they were conducting—sweat lodges and the like—so that the Jesuits might experience firsthand the spiritual presences in Lakota religion.

On occasion the dialogues served as an opportunity for the Lakotas to vent their resentment at past treatment by Church authorities. One of the Lakota men told how as an altar boy in his youth a Jesuit asked him to fetch a bench for some latecomers at mass. The boy got the bench from the vest room, but it fell over as the people approached. The Jesuit slapped the boy for interrupting mass, and the boy left crying. As the old man told it, the people were so horrified at the idea of a holy man striking a child, that they left the church and never returned to it. And afterwards, whenever he saw priests, he was frightened of them. "I don't want nothing to do with them," he recalled. "Now I am getting over it and that is why I am here" (October 30, 1973).

At the fifth meeting, a year after the first, Father Stolzman recognized that so far the priests had been asking the questions, and he hoped that the Lakotas would take more initiative in raising topics for conversation. At the same time Moses Big Crow reminded all present that the purpose of the meetings was to share religious ideas and experiences; it was not for criticizing one another. The medicine men were encountering "turmoil" enough within their own association, and they were reticent to speak for their tradition when, as one of them admitted, "we don't understand each other among ourselves" (January 29, 1974).

At that meeting, however, the medicine men took an active stand against the introduction of pipe ceremonies into the context of the Catholic mass, which several Jesuits (most notably, Paul B. Steinmetz) had been doing among the Lakotas for several years. The medicine men argued that priests take years before they are ordained and are permitted by the Church to say the mass. Should the same not be true for the pipe, they asked? They stipulated that a priest cannot merely pick up a pipe and pray with it, because he does not have the training or the authority to do so. Perhaps a pipe can be placed on an altar, as a permanent fixture like a crucifix, but the use of pipes should be circumscribed to Lakotas with the requisite training.

To the question raised by the Jesuits—can the cross and the pipe go together?—some of the Lakotas like Frank Picket Pin replied, "If you want to be Christian, give the pipe up" (January 29, 1974). Other medicine men allowed that Lakotas could engage in pipe rituals as well as Catholic mass; however, the two should be kept separate from one another. "Our peace pipe is not ready to go into the church," they exclaimed. "Keep them apart and . . . try to find a way to make them work together" (January 29, 1974).

Even with such cooperation in mind, however, the medicine men were sure that "it is going to take years" (January 29, 1974) before the two religious systems could work in mutual understanding and harmony, and even then, their goal was not for amalgamation of the pipe and the cross, but rather parallel participation. One Lakota warned against the Jesuits' attempt to co-opt the pipe in order to increase attendance at mass. "I disagree," he said, "[with] taking the peace pipe into the church. The church law and our Indian culture are two different things. However," he added, "we are praying to one person, almighty God" (January 29, 1974).

While the medicine men and clergy continued to meet every month in 1974, Father Stolzman was conducting separate interviews with Lakotas about their traditional religion. His most immediate concern was the phenomenology of the Lakota pipe. At the April 30, 1974, meeting he presented a position paper, "On the Pipe" (Stolzman 1973–1975), in which he discussed its great antiquity and cosmic symbolism among the Lakotas. "The pipe is a gift from God," he wrote, recognizing that in Lakota legend it is the White Buffalo Calf Woman who brought the sacred pipe to the Indians. During the conversation that ensued, he and the Lakotas debated the truth content of the legend. Whether the event was historically true, or the stuff of vision or dream, did not matter, according to Stolzman, since the narrative carried religious truth about the nature of humans and the divine.

A month later Stolzman's fellow priests strongly criticized his attempt to correlate the mythic and ritual aspects of the pipe with biblical imagery, especially in the "Book of Revelation." Using technical language of the Church regarding covenant, conscience, prophecy, numerology, and biblical interpretation, they told the Jesuit that he had gone too far in equating Lakota and Christian symbolism regarding, respectively, the pipe and Christ. The Lakotas listened in bewilderment to the jesuitical "jawbreakers," as they called the theological terminology. One Lakota conceded that he did not "understand any of it. It ain't really on my terms," he confessed (May 29, 1974).

Stolzman redrafted his study of the pipe, removing the biblical references; then he hoped to present it to the entire membership of the Rosebud Medicine Men Association. Not all the medicine men arrived to hear his presentation, nor were they all invited; however, the meetings which took place during the last few months of 1974 and into 1975 witnessed an outpouring of reflection upon the sacred pipe in Lakota religious culture. Some of the discussion was oddly skewed, e.g., when one Lakota tried to fit the coming of the White Buffalo Calf Woman into the biblical history he had learned from Mormons (September 24, 1974), and at times Father Stolzman seemed more interested in his position papers than the testimony of the Lakotas (October 8, 1974).

Stolzman (1973–1975: October 15, 1974) traced the use of pipes among North American Indians back four thousand years, whereas the calf leg pipe appeared, he suggested, in the late seventeenth century. For him the sacrality of Lakota pipe use lay in its focusing human attention on God. At the same time, he mused, it joins Lakotas to their natural and cosmic environment (especially the buffalo and the four directions) and evokes spirits. Stolzman was careful to say that pipes can be misused with evil intent; however, he concluded that the pipe has functions parallel to those of Christ on the cross and can be utilized in Christian worship. Indeed, he said, the pipe was already in Catholic Lakota liturgy, at funerals, Sioux Catholic Congresses, at the ordination of catechists, and at church dedications. In his opinion pipes were appropriate to Christian ceremony, if and when Indian people wanted them there.

While Stolzman was developing his view of the pipe, one Lakota medicine man after another narrated his version of the sacred pipe's origin. In great detail they provided a rich layering of images and interpretations concerning its meaning to Lakota culture and its revelation of the divine realm. At times they disagreed with one another about ritual and mythic details, or they allowed that variations were acceptable in praxis and belief. When the Jesuits challenged the truth content of the legend, they countered with questions of their own.

"Can you prove," Arthur Running Horse asked the clergy, "that your prayers for the dead really work?" (September 24, 1974).

More than one Lakota was encouraged by Stolzman's comments about the suitable place of pipes in Catholic worship. One medicine man asked if he could bring his medicine bundles to church and perform rituals there. At this the Jesuit applied caution, responding that these meetings were designed to answer such questions, "but we feel we should not act or do something until we understand" the particular religious practice at hand. We Catholics, he said, write down our theological meanings for observation. We want to do the same for Lakota religion, and when we have compared, contrasted, understood, and evaluated a certain rite, then we shall know what is appropriate for its usage (January 14, 1975).

Having probed the contours of pipe ceremonialism, Stolzman turned his attention in his writings after 1974 to other Lakota rituals in order to discern their religious content and their relationship to Catholic sacraments. While he concentrated on questions about Lakota rituals, e.g., "What are some of the main advantages of having a sweat-bath" (January 28, 1975), and while he highlighted the role of rituals in relating Lakotas to God and cosmos, the growing number of Lakota participants—especially the women—emphasized their concern with holding their community together. The sweat bath might be good for individual doctoring, but its primary importance to them was to help people to "walk the red path" (January 28, 1975) of kinship responsibility. Stolzman might argue that the real meaning of baptism is how it binds us to Jesus, but for the Lakotas its primary function is to introduce infants to the obligations of their human relatives (September 30–November 25, 1975). The Lakotas wanted to know what *relationship* a priest has to the child he baptizes: does he really look after the child until he is an adult, or "does he just go through the motions?" (January 6, 1976). Stolzman replied that all priests represent Jesus Christ and it is the relationship to Christ that is crucial for the child. Father Fagan realized that the Lakotas were thinking of baptism as the making of relatives, so he acknowledged the importance of godparents, who are really supposed to look after the child they have sponsored.

Throughout Stolzman pushed the conversation toward ceremonialism and the divine; the Lakotas spoke recurringly of their people's dissolution and need for societal recovery and unity through religion. One evening Arthur Running Horse explained

> why we have hardship in our life. Everyone in the reservation drinks beer, bar none. They have a baby-sitter for their children. The man and woman work. They open a can of food and say to their children, "We are going over here." And they leave. They leave the children again. They come back late at night. The young people drive around in cars all night. They come home in the morning and they sleep all day.

This is reservation life, he said, and talk of rituals, ghosts, and priests does not change the physical, social realities. "These are the things we should straighten out before we talk about these other things" (October 28, 1976).

Since religion was important to Lakota social cohesion, the Indians continued to fret over their religious loyalty and participation. Should they give up Catholicism and engage only in their Lakota rituals, or should they leave behind their traditions for the Catholic faith? In either half of this equation the premise held that there were two roads, parallel to one another, and a person must choose one or the other. Another option was that the two traditions fulfilled one another; hence, a person could believe in the pipe *and* in Christ without split loyalty or spiritual contradiction. Father Bernard Fagan asked the Lakota conferees which position they held (March 25, 1975). What he heard was mixed opinion. Some medicine men prayed to the Christian God when performing their cures; some kept their traditions separate. Still others, as reported by Moses Big Crow in their absence, would have nothing to do with dialogue or syncretism. They "practice this pipe religion," he stated, and want nothing to do with "this other religion," Christianity (March 25, 1975).

Big Crow noted, ironically, that these nativist medicine men would not be able to avoid Christianity totally, however, because they would be buried in a Christian cemetery when they died. Medicine men do not have their own burial ground. Then he noted,

> Since we the Indian people have our pipe, we pray with it. But still we are supposed to be civilized, how can we go native? Our buffalos are gone. We wear the white man's clothes, we eat their food, we spend [their] money. . . . the two religions are different. You cannot practice both of them because they can not run together. (March 25, 1975)

It would appear that Big Crow was opting for participation only in Christian institutions, which he associated with other aspects of white culture. He would walk the Catholic road rather than that of the pipe. On the other hand, on another occasion he formulated his religious loyalties differently. "I think the world of my Indian religion and I was baptized a Catholic," he commented, "so I believe in that. But for some reason if the Catholic church kicked me out I would never go to another church. But my Indian religion, I can always go there" (May 14, 1976).

Wallace Black Elk chose his Native path not only because it constituted the way of his ancestors, but also because the trail of white intrusion into Lakota country was littered with betrayal, destruction, and death. For him the way of the pipe was sacred; Christianity was the religion of immoralists. He could not even appreciate interfaith dialogue; to him it smacked of telling holy secrets to one's enemy (March 25, 1975). Father Stolzman retorted that sacrality exists in places other than the pipe, and that Indians should keep an open mind to Christian spirituality. Furthermore, he argued, sin is not the exclusive domain of Whites; Lakotas have their own history of bloodshed. He hoped that his audience would judge a religion by its holy men, not by its sinners (March 25, 1975).

Father Stolzman wished to move beyond such confrontations because he was becoming convinced of a common ground between Lakota and Catholic religions. Beyond "some surface differences," he said, the two religions had similar goals and methods; "in both religions we pray to the same God." He told the discussants that, as far as he was concerned, a person can believe in Lakota and Christian religions, or one can believe in one or the other; however, if a Lakota prayed with both Lakota and Christian beliefs, "his prayer will be so much stronger" (April 22, 1975). In Stolzman's view, the meeting of the two roads produced a sturdier thoroughfare of prayer. Throughout the spring of 1975 he and his fellow Jesuits enjoined the Lakotas to examine the levels of their prayer, so that a rich tradition of Lakota Catholic prayerfulness might be established.

The quest for commonality did not prevent the clergy from criticizing aspects of Lakota religious practice. In particular, Father Demeyer prodded the medicine men to justify the exclusion of mixed-bloods from the ranks of Lakota religious specialists. The medicine men explained that they needed to be pure; was it not the same with priests? Did the Church not discriminate on some basis before allowing a man to handle the Eucharist? Demeyer answered that to receive communion a person must be pure; therefore, the Church encourages people to make confessions before receiving the body and blood of Christ. Sweat baths perform the same function in Lakota religion, he said, to purify Indians with sage and steam, so that a person can engage in other rituals with a clean heart. But why, he asked, are mixed-blood Lakotas not allowed to purify their hearts and become medicine men? The Lakotas responded that full-bloods should be the ones who exemplify and express the Indian way of life (April 8, 1975).

As the discussions continued, it became clear that Lakotas had concerns which arose directly from their culture—the ritual difference between full- and mixed-bloods, or the presence of menstruating women during pipe ceremonies at church—which struck the priests as unreasonable, or at least easily resolvable. Couldn't medicine men perform pipe services in the sanctuary of the altar, Stolzman asked, and therefore consider themselves shielded from menstruating women? Why not place such women behind a rail, at a distance from the pipe, just as they are isolated at Sun Dances? (May 27, 1975). The Lakotas listened to these recommendations with civility. Only on occasion did they remind the priests that the Catholic Church has its own traditional taboos, e.g., racial and sexual restrictions regarding the taking of holy orders. "Just like in your religion," chided John Fire, "I don't think I've seen one of the sisters taking a priest's place behind the altar, have you?" (January 20, 1976). Neither did the Lakotas retreat from their own cultural predilections.

The Indians continued to worry over the co-joining of the pipe and the Church. In several instances, on Lakota reservations and in Rapid City, pipes were being hung in church settings, and some Indians objected to their being treated as ornaments. Pipes should be used by trained practitioners, then put away, not left out to decorate a non-Indian space (March 23, 1976). John Fire asked Stolzman what he would think about bringing a crucifix and other church paraphernalia into a sweat lodge. Would it be appropriate? Would he leave them there? Stolzman replied that the crucifix fits "in many places," including a sweat lodge. The priest imagined Jesus, stripped of his clothing, reminding the devotees in the sweat of their own nakedness. Jesus suffered as an Indian does in the hot steam of the lodge. And Jesus is related to all persons, Stolzman noted, in the way that is recalled in the ejaculation, "all my relations," which Lakotas exclaim as they leave the lodge. "I find great meaning with the cross in there," Stolzman said (April 6, 1976). Where some of the medicine men were reticent to place Lakota and Catholic religion side by side, Stolzman was eager to experiment with syncretism. Thus, he opened one meeting with breathless urgency: "We will be praying with the pipe. We will be praying with Christ. Really showing how the two are coming closer and closer together" (September 7, 1976).

Stolzman was proposing syncretism on Catholic terms. The Jesuits insisted upon a concept of universal human sinfulness, even when Lakotas told them that they lacked such a notion in their traditional religion (September 16, 1975). Was it really the case, Father Demeyer queried, that Indians had no aboriginal concept of sin? The Indians were nonplussed as they tried to unravel the distinctions between present and past Lakota beliefs on the one hand, and on the other between a concept of sinning (as an offense to beings to whom we are related) as opposed to the notion of inherent human sinfulness. Finally they conceded, "Yes they knew what sin was" (January 20, 1976). For a month running in 1976 (January 20; February 3, 24), Fathers Stolzman and Fagan held forth on the differences between sinful guilt and societal shame—concepts employed in the anthropological literature of the day to distinguish between Western and tribal ethical sanctions—and Stolzman lectured at length to silent Lakotas about sinning against God (in essence, saying "no" to Him), temporal punishment, and atonement for sin, as if he were conducting catechesis (March 9, 1976).

Subsequently (May 4, 1976) Stolzman delivered a homily on the topic of responsibility for Jesus' death. "So who killed Jesus?" he asked. "Every person who sinned. Which includes me." Moses Big Crow followed: "You are talking the Christian way, right? Or does this include Indian religion? It includes every one of us?" The Indians took the position that "the killing of Jesus . . . happened across the ocean, . . . and not in Indian country. Therefore," they contended, "the white spirit and the Indian spirit cannot communicate," because Whites are struck by their own sinfulness and guilt, and Indians are not. Stolzman refused to accept such a principle because, "if I understand you right . . . Wakantanka is only for this country. Therefore my God is a different God and I don't believe that. Is my God Wakantanka? All right, therefore we have the same God."

The Lakotas disagreed in a cacophonous outburst. Their medicine men held to the idea that their spirits are different entities than the Christian God, whereas the Jesuits maintained a theological syncretism which missionaries had developed during a century of contact with the Sioux. Arriving with the idea that there must be one God, the evangelizers had adapted the Lakota term, *Wakantanka*—which referred to a class of spirits—to carry the monotheistic connotations of Christianity. Now in 1976 Stolzman remonstrated the Indians: your *Wakantanka* and our God are one and the same, and he did so ostensibly in the spirit of ecumenism. The medicine men demurred on this point. They still believed in a variety of spirits.

Moreover, they refused to accept a second, long-standing principle of Christian catechesis, that all humans are participants in the fall of Adam and Eve and share in an inherent human sinfulness (and therefore are in need of salvific grace). The Lakota medicine men would not take responsibility for the fall, or for the death of Jesus. These were events which took place across the ocean, in another time and place and to another people. They remained geographical, societal, and theological particularists in the face of Father Stolzman's syncretic universalism.

In 1975 (February 25) the conferees discussed their concepts of human metaphysics: souls, ghosts, afterlife, and reincarnation. Both medicine men and priests believed firmly in the spiritual dimension of humanity; however, the priests held firmly to Christian beliefs about the afterlife (heaven, hell, limbo), whereas the Indians entertained concepts of reincarnation and traveling souls of the dead. Both sets of religious specialists could report on their encounters with ghosts. The medicine men dealt with such spirits in Yuwipi rites, at funerals, and in visions. The Jesuits claimed to have chased away ghosts who were bothering Lakotas; sometimes, Stolzman said, ghosts come to us as messengers from God to inform or reassure us.

A year later (May 4, 1976), Fathers Stolzman and Fagan asked for clarification regarding Lakota metaphysics: Do the Indians believe in reincarnation? Is it a traditional belief, or something adopted in recent years? Fagan expressed especial skepticism when the Lakotas affirmed reincarnation as part of their worldview. He contended that such notions were merely metaphors, e.g., when so-and-so is the spitting image of his grandfather. Julie Walking Eagle disagreed. In her (Lakota) view, human spirits can reincarnate and carry memory from one life to its regeneration.

Fagan: "I cannot remember a thing before 1928. Nothing." Walking Eagle: "That says nothing for you, because you are a white man." She proceeded to tell of a Lakota girl who was born with a scar, exactly the same scar as her dead grandmother's. And she shared many other characteristics, too. Stolzman brushed off the claim that this anecdote proved the reality of reincarnation. Two plants can look the same, he argued, but they are not proof of reincarnation. Julie Walking Eagle took offense at the priest's rebuff: "I didn't want to tell you this but I did and I am sorry that I did." Moses Big Crow added that reincarnation is a topic in Lakota metaphysics which "we are not supposed to reveal. . . . I was wondering why Mrs. Walking Eagle opened up" to the priests.

Still, the Jesuits pushed for more information about Lakota beliefs regarding the afterlife. Is there reward or punishment after death? Does reincarnation occur in all cases? One of the medicine men allowed that the Lakotas held different, uncodified ideas about the destiny of human souls: Some go to the place that Whites refer to as the happy hunting grounds; some are reincarnated; some spirits get stuck between worlds in a kind of limbo; and some appear on earth as ghosts. Medicine men speculate about these possibilities, he said, but they do not know for certain—at least not with the certainty with which the Jesuits come to the question of human mortality and fate.

At a later meeting (September 21, 1976), Arthur Running Horse tested the priests' knowledge about the destiny of souls, and he discovered in their responses a range of opinions, colored by their varied experiences. Father George Haas commented that this was a fruitful development, in that the Indians were doing the questioning for a change, and the responses were open-ended rather than dogmatic.

This exchange led, several weeks later (October 12, 1976), to a cross-cultural sharing of spiritual affairs. A Lakota man asked the priests and medicine men if they can talk with ghosts. Arthur Running Horse answered yes, he speaks with deceased Lakota holy men whose ghosts can fly to places where they are needed or summoned. There are many of these ghosts, he said. Where they live is a mystery; however, you can ask them questions, such as when a person is going to die—not to curse but only to inform. Just a few nights previous, Running Horse's daughter had put up such a ceremony and a ghost arrived. The medicine man commented that he did not like talking about ghosts; nevertheless, he had encountered them many times. Moses Big Crow corroborated this testimony, and reported that in general these ghosts are living happy lives, in community with the ghosts of Lakota kinsmen. They are able to carry messages between the worlds of the living and the dead. Some ghosts, however, are lost; others are hungry for tobacco smoke.

Father Kenneth Walleman countered this deposition with a summary of Catholic beliefs about heaven, hell, purgatory, and limbo. He emphasized the community of saints in heaven: Mary, Joseph, certain angels, martyrs, and other saints canonized by the Church. He even avowed that his mother and father were in heaven with Jesus, although he acknowledged that the Church does not know for certain who, or how many, have attained their celestial reward.

Mention of heaven led the Lakotas to ask, with some anxiety, what happened to Lakotas who were buried *in* and *outside* the boundaries of the Catholic cemetery at St. Francis Mission. Priests had always told them that to go to heaven one must be buried in the cemetery of the Church. Denying an Indian the right to a Catholic burial was a powerful sanction, and these Lakotas were worried about relatives who failed to gain admittance to the churchyard. At an earlier meeting one Lakota had even wondered out loud if baptized Lakota Catholics would be permitted into heaven: "Paradise. It seems that we don't even fit there. The question is do we go to the same place as they do" (September 7, 1976). Now Father Haas tried to allay their concerns, not altogether successfully, for they continued to press this point in later dialogues. Moses Big Crow was able to alleviate some tension, however, by joking: "You say that heaven is in that [cemetery]. Now I know why those guys go there to drink. I guess I will have to join them. No wonder they are so happy there" (October 12, 1976).

In discussing their experiences of the spirit world, the medicine men and the priests engaged one another as religious practitioners. They validated their professional status by sharing episodes of their specialization in the realm of the invisible, powerful spirits. All the Lakotas had experiences of ghosts and spirits—in visions, Yuwipi, and other rites. The Jesuits had fewer adventures with the spiritual world; however, they possessed training in the discernment of spirits and were very intererested in the topic. Despite their being heirs of the Enlightenment—embracing rationalism, eschewing superstition in principle—the priests believed in ghosts and spirits, and thus achieved significant common interest with their Lakota counterparts.

Two weeks later the discussants compared their traditions' methods for communicating with spirits. The Lakotas described "tobacco ties" (October 28, 1976)—wrapping of tobacco in colored cloths (the colors matching the symbolic directions of the cosmos) and leaving them as offerings in graveyards as prayers to the dead. Rudy Runs Above said that the participants in the 1890 Ghost Dance employed tobacco ties in the days before they were massacred by U.S. troops at Wounded Knee; today such offerings are to be found at the gravesite of the slaughtered ghost dancers. The priests compared this Lakota tradition to the Catholic practice of lighting votive candles in church as remembrances of the dead, and also to attract good spirits and keep away the bad.

Several days later Moses Big Crow commented privately (November 2, 1976) to Stolzman that the recent meetings had emboldened the medicine men to brag about their contacts with the spirit world, and he worried that they would be spurred on to compete with each other for reputation at future meetings. Rather than boosting cooperation with the fathers and with one another, Big Crow stewed, the gatherings were becoming potentially divisive.

Some days later the Lakota conferees once again were recounting in great detail their personal experiences of ghosts and other spiritual entities, and in so doing was the implication that their powers were appropriate to the religious milieu of Sioux country. From this Big Crow inferred a rejection of the Catholic priests and he felt impelled to come to their defense.

Their duty, he stated, was to "come across to us, . . . to pass their religion unto us." His fellow Lakotas, he remarked, "all say 'across. They belong over there, they don't belong here, they belong over there.'" But Big Crow stood up for the priests' evangelizing duty. A hundred years ago, he exhorted, the Lakotas were like the Jews worshipping the golden calf. Jesus sent his missionaries to all corners of the earth, and that is why the Jesuits are where they are today. We should appreciate their honest interest in our religion today. Then turning to the Jesuits, Big Crow said that the more they learned of Lakota religious belief and practice, "the more and better you can preach to the Indian people" (November 9, 1976). For Big Crow the dialogues were useful as evangelical tools. Other medicine men, however, wished to use the meetings to rekindle the fires of Lakota traditionalism.

Big Crow reminded his listeners of the days when Father Eugene Buechel and other Jesuits used to ferret out baptized Lakotas in their sweat lodges. When the priests found them, "they kicked them right out of the church." Even in recent years Father Fagan has done that, Big Crow said, and today he still avoids the sweats because "that's on his conscience" (November 9, 1976). Therefore, Big Crow concluded, the Lakotas should take advantage of the Jesuits' change of heart, now that they are trying sincerely to learn about us. For Big Crow the dialogues were an opportunity to gain increased status for Lakota religiousness, even while enhancing Catholic missionizing goals.

Stolzman joined in, telling the Lakotas why the priests have been reluctant to attend Lakota ceremonies. First, they remember their past policies and feel strange attending services they once forbade. Secondly, they aren't sure that all the ghosts and spirits are good and so they seek informed discernment. That is why these meetings are so important, he said, so that the Jesuits' fears can be put to rest. Indeed, he reported, the priests had met on their own after the recent dialogues about ghosts. "I think," he said, "that the fathers have come to really accept the ghosts. . . . [They now] know how the ghosts fit into purgatory, and the passage from this world to the next" (November 9, 1976).

In the closing months of 1976 the Lakota medicine men had further opportunity to discuss their knowledge of ghosts, when the State of South Dakota Mental Association invited several of them to a conference with Dr. Elizabeth Kübler-Ross regarding out-of-body, at-death experiences (November 30, 1976). Then when John Fire died, the pastors and medicine men spent their evening (December 14, 1976) "feeding the mourners" with the solidarity of their interfaith prayers. Months before, several Lakotas had complained that "there is nothing that we have accomplished. I think there is a connection," one said, "between talking about something . . . real deep and doing something about it" (September 7, 1976). By the end of the year the participants were engaged together in the experience of common, prayerful mourning for a man beloved by all.

COMMONALITY?

At the meeting on December 14, 1976, Stolzman raised questions of mutual interest to the participants. What is the common vocation of medicine men and priests? What should they be doing for the Lakota people? Two weeks later (December 28, 1976) the discussants were revealing what they had learned from each other about their roles as religious specialists. Arthur Running Horse remarked that he came to understand the good red road of medicine men by meditating upon the Road Picture catechism promulgated by the Jesuits. Two Lakota women acknowledged the Catholic priests' selfless comforting of the sick as an ideal worthy of emulation. Father Haas avowed that he was learning how to be a good priest by listening to the medicine men. The first lesson he gained was that each man must follow his own vision—his inspiration from the divine, his unchanging reference point—acting toward everyone so as to fulfill that ideal. "There were times when I left the meetings," Father Haas recalled, "and I felt down inside that I wished that I had a vision" (December 28, 1976). Haas allowed that perhaps he *did* possess a vision, in a white man's way. Jesus was his model of the good priest: kind, available, generous, humble, uninterested in personal gain or fortune. These were values Haas had heard extolled by the medicine men; therefore, he felt a common bond with them and they reinforced his vocational paradigm.

Father Stolzman commenced the new year of 1977 by posing what he called a "mountaintop question" (January 10, 1977), built upon four years of ascending trust among the medicine men and priests. Why, he asked, do the pastors distrust Yuwipi and its sister ceremony, Lowanpi (a healing sing conducted in unison by many medicine men)? Why won't they attend these ceremonies when they have no trouble with pipe rituals, even at mass?

He suggested four reasons for priestly concern. First, the Jesuits fear that hexing takes place at these two rituals. Stolzman attested to his belief in evil spirits, and his suspicion that people utilize them against each other. He recalled how he was hexed once in Sioux country, and how he had to exorcize the evil spirits set upon him. Casting spells, he said, is not peculiar to Lakota religion—it can occur in Christian contexts, too—but the Jesuits suspected that Yuwipi and Lowanpi are sometimes vehicles for Lakota sorcery.

Second, Stolzman reported, the Jesuits are apprehensive that Yuwipi practitioners engage in false prophecy, claiming to foretell future events with supernatural aid. Third, the pastors charge the Yuwipi men with the hocus-pocus of tricks during their performances. The Lakotas use a rubber ball with an eagle whistle attached to make the sound of an eagle spirit's cry; they employ cigarette lighters to make mystical sparks; and so forth. They claim their legerdemain to be signs of the divine. Finally, the priests have heard that Lakota medicine men make sacrifices to the spirits (and particularly to Iktomi, the spider divinity whom Stolzman regarded as a devil, much to the consternation of Moses Big Crow, May 14, 1976), in order to increase the vital force of a patient.

Father Fagan reiterated Stolzman's concerns and wanted to know from the Lakotas whether these four aspects are essential parts of Yuwipi, or whether they take place only when the ritual is appropriated by evil practitioners. The Jesuits weren't about to condone (or much less validate by their presence or participation) Lakota ceremonies which feature black arts, false prophecy, sleight of hand, and sacrifice—ceremonies which the Jesuits had tried to stamp out for almost a century.

During two meetings the Lakotas tried to convince the Jesuits that Yuwipi and Lowanpi are primarily prayer services, calling upon the divine for the commonweal of the community. Father Haas replied to these explanations by exclaiming:

> Today, what I feel here is that we are getting to the point now where maybe Christ can really become incarnated in an Indian way. What [d]o I mean by that? Well, I am personally not worried about Lowanpi and Yuwipi ceremony when I know the men who are performing the ceremony. These are good Christian men who I know, like me, are trying to live the way Christ taught us to live. (January 24, 1977)

Gilbert Yellow Hawk was not to be appeased by kind jesuitical words. He called the priests "two-faced . . . politicians" (January 24, 1977) who were not about to sanction Lakota ritualism on its own terms. He claimed to prefer the priests who are blunt in their misgivings about Lakota religion, who "want nothing to do with us" and stay away from Indian ceremonialism. Yellow Hawk even said of Father Fagan that "he is the one that is hexing," not the Yuwipi artists.

The Lakota medicine men tried to allay the Jesuit apprehensions about Yuwipi and Lowanpi; however, in private Moses Big Crow admitted that hexing, contacting evil spirits, and capturing souls were all parts of Lakota ritualism. He cautioned Stolzman against a sanguine appreciation for all Lakota religious cult. At the same time he expressed impatience at several Jesuits for "dragging their feet" in accommodating Lakota religious forms like pipe ceremonies and sweat lodges. He said of one conservative Jesuit, Robert Demeyer: "I would like to get him in a sweat bath." Stolzman replied, "Now, that is what I am hoping for and that is what I am aiming at" (January 2[5], 1977). (A month later Big Crow put Father Fagan through a sweat to help heal a minor ailment. The priest endured the heat "like a statue." When he emerged, he asked if he could put his clothes back on. Big Crow reported laughingly, "I had just wanted to say, you have to stand out there for twenty minutes naked. I couldn't do it." February 28, 1977.)

At the next meeting the medicine men were more forthcoming, recounting episodes of Lakota magic: a woman who asked that her cheating husband be hexed; a politician who requested a ritual to ensure his election; a grandfather who taught his grandson the trick (an herbal salve) of placing his arm, unharmed, in boiling water, and so forth. The medicine men denied that *they* would do such things, and *certainly* they would never attempt magic with the pipe. "Does that make you pastors feel easier?" Big Crow crooned. Then he added for effect, recalling the accusation of hexing made against one priest, "If it does, don't tell Father Fagan" (February 14, 1977).

Father Stolzman suggested that Lakota sorcery—like black masses and curses—are carried out in secrecy, apart from the normative rituals of the faith. Thus, you don't find hexing at mass, or at a pipe ceremonial or a public Yuwipi, the "regular Indian ceremonies" (February 14, 1977). He recalled Lakotas who came to him seeking protection from witchcraft (yes, he was willing to offer prayers to aid them), and politicians seeking electoral victory (no, he would not pray for that end). Stolzman's main message was that God's will is supreme, and that Christians are to accept that will as a religious duty, rather than asserting their own desires through magic.

Two weeks later Moses Big Crow returned in a jocular fashion to the distinction between human desires and God's will. He asked why it is that St. Francis School's basketball team wins its games? Is it because Father Fagan puts hexes on the opposing teams? No, he said (more seriously), it is a matter of God's will and the team's abilities, and we should not pray for our team to win, but rather that God bless the players and that they "be physically fit" (February 28, 1977).

In light of these comments the medicine men and priests tried to define their role in healing people. What happens when a family asks a priest to anoint a sick person with oils? Do they expect that he will use those oils to cure the illness? Do the oils actually have such power? Does the priest? Should the priest raise or douse expectations about spiritual healing? Stolzman reiterated his message, "We do not perform magic," yet he did not rule out the possibility of miraculous curing. "Our healing," he said, "requires faith in God and faith in the spirits" (February 28, 1977).

Arthur Running Horse was less circumspect in this regard. He said that he always has coals in the stove at home, ready to light a pipe. When people come to him for healing—and here he reported on two recent cases—the spirits tell him what medicine to use. By smoking the pipe he can ascertain whether the person will recover, at least temporarily.

Father Haas perceived a difference between the presentations of Stolzman and Running Horse. The latter, expressing his Lakota tradition, considered spiritual healing and communication with spirits a more-or-less normal aspect of his vocation, whereas Catholic priests are less certain what they should do when faced with requests for curing. Haas reminded everyone that Jesus was a healer who inspired people's faith through his cures; therefore, the Christian tradition was no less involved than the Lakota with healing. Indeed, at the start of many of the meetings the medicine men and priests prayed together for various patients' recovery.

There still remained a question in Stolzman's mind about "truthfulness and . . . deception" (March 21, 1977) in the professional lives of medicine men and priests. Do they claim to speak for the spirits or Christ, when they are really expressing their own ideas and feelings? To what degree is their self-interest wrapped up in their vocation? Benjamin Black Bear, Jr., replied that he knew no word in Lakota for "proof. . . . From the Lakota point of view," he said, "there is no proof, evidence. . . . Whether the thing is really happening or not. Although the idea is there" (March 21, 1977). George Eagle Elk added that Lakota medicine men "perform in the darkness" (March 21, 1977), a fitting expression for a culture that tends more toward faith than doubt in its religious life. Stolzman understood this point, that the Indians are "silent" (April 18, 1977) in religious matters, waiting for understanding to come to them, whereas Christians go about their religious lives by asking questions. The medicine men resented the priests' suspicions about Lakota religious practice; Stolzman suggested that suspicion was merely part of white culture rather than a particular judgment about the Indians. Moses Big Crow added as evidence, in his habitual good humor, that "[when Father Stolzman comes to my house], he checks my rosary to see if it is used" (April 18, 1977).

Stolzman proceeded to compare Lowanpi and the Catholic mass as rituals which emphasize sacramental kinship and group worship of the divine in their respective traditions. When he was finished, Father Demeyer attacked the parallels drawn by his fellow Jesuit. Football and basketball can be so structurally and functionally described, he argued, that they might be called the same game, "and I don't believe it" (April 18, 1977). He denounced the likening of Lowanpi and the mass as a tactic to "convert" him to believing in the Lakota religion. He was willing to "understand" it but he would never "believe in it. . . . Maybe I am throwing a bombshell into this thing and making a lot of enemies," he stated, but his faith rested in the divine, not the man-made; Jesus, not the White Buffalo Calf Woman.

The various Lakotas attempted to calm Demeyer. We aren't trying to convert you, they avowed. We are saying in these dialogues that we believe in one God and we believe that God reveals Himself through Catholicism and also through Lakota traditions. We believe in both and we follow both. Charlie Little Eagle appended to this his own testimony: "Just one God. . . . I believe in the Catholic Church. . . . I believe in the peace pipe." And, "there is another religion that I believe too, because I receive my help from them. The Native American Church, peyote" (April 18, 1977).

Father Hilbert replied that as a priest he was of two minds. He enjoyed learning about Lakota religion, which he respected, and he acknowledged that God reveals Himself to different peoples in different ways. At the same time his priestly duty was to administer Catholic sacraments and he did not consider Lowanpi an equivalent of the central sacrament of Catholicism, the mass.

Here was the rub, as Moses Big Crow articulated quite well during his postmortem with Stolzman. He had tried to soften the impact of the Lowanpi-mass discussion with several quips. First, "After the Lowanpi is over, Father Fagan and I are going to get drunker [than]

hell and he is going to furnish the vodka." Then, after Stolzman's comparison, he had reminded everyone of the two elements most held in
common by the two ceremonies: "whispering" and "gossiping" (April
18, 1977). This badinage had not prevented Father Demeyer's upset,
and Big Crow knew why, because it is one thing for a priest to "recognize" or "understand" the importance of an Indian ritual; it is quite
another matter to "believe" or "accept" that ritual. What made Demeyer "really hot," Big Crow surmised, was that Stolzman's comparison made Yowanpi parallel to the mass without saying that the
Catholic ritual is "true" or "best" (April 18, 1977). Stolzman concurred
with Big Crow's assessment; still he thought it had been a good meeting. "There was a misunderstanding," he said, "and we worked it out"
(April 18, 1977).

In May 1977 the discussants returned to questions about human
souls: what is their condition during life and their fate after death, and
what impact does religious ritual have upon them? Moses Big Crow
reiterated a long-standing agreement, that the religion surrounding
the Lakota pipe does not "save souls" in the sense of providing the
grace necessary to merit a heavenly reward; however, Lakota spirits
traditionally were thought to guide the souls of the dead to the "happy
hunting grounds" through the intercession of prayers (May 9, 1977).
Stolzman remarked that in the early mission days Lakotas were drawn
to Catholicism because its exponents claimed its power to "save souls,"
that is, to gain individuals entry to heaven. He noted the continuing
emphasis among the Lakotas on the place where you were buried—in
the Catholic cemetery or not. Today, however, Lakotas talk about saving souls in a more this-worldly way, as Stolzman perceived in the dialogues. Salvation means helping the Lakota community face its problems. Given this shift in focus—perhaps a reversion to aboriginal
Lakota values, away from Christian other-worldliness—what is the
purpose of Lowanpi and the mass? the Jesuit asked (May 9, 1977). Indeed, what are the purposes of religious traditions? And might different religions have differing purposes?

Stolzman and Big Crow spent hours on their own, ruminating over
this conundrum, and when the group reconvened, the question still
confronted them. Charlie Little Eagle disclosed his uncertainty about
"the pipe and the cross. I live in a confusing balance," he declared.
"Where is this soul going, . . . through the pipe or through the . . .
cross and Christ? This is the way I feel" (May 23, 1977). Is Catholi-

cism's purpose to save souls in the afterlife? Is Lakota religion's goal to provide bodily health here and now? For all the talk about praying to the same God, do the two religious systems have separate (albeit complementary and partially overlapping) ends? If that is true, does it make them distinct types of religion, one spiritual and the other materialist in orientation?

Arthur Running Horse recalled Father Haas's lecture about Jesus the healer. For the Jews of Jesus' time there was no soul-body dichotomy. Jesus came to earth to serve and save the whole person: by healing, edifying, forgiving, and offering God's grace. The Greeks, said Running Horse, had introduced the soul-body dichotomy into the Christian discourse, and with this language we can make distinctions between spiritual and material life. For Lakota Catholics, however, the distinction does not make convincing sense. In Running Horse's view, the goal of religion, Lakota or Catholic, should be to save the integral human in all ways imaginable.

To this proposition the discussants gave their assent.

The Rosebud Medicine Men and Clergy Meetings carried on for another two years. At times the conversations expressed the pastoral concern for Lakota youths seemingly lost to the hopeless abandon of drugs and alcohol (September 12, 1977). At other times theological constructs—what role do the good works of humans play in achieving salvation? to what degree is Jesus man and God? (October 10, 1977) — loomed large. Sometimes they shared eerie tales of preternaturalism (October 24, 1977). From time to time the conversations seemed to devolve into generalities about manners and respect (November 21, 1977).

More than once the Jesuits found themselves apologizing to the Lakotas for the disciplinary violence institutionalized at the Catholic boarding schools like St. Francis and Holy Rosary. Stolzman admitted privately to Big Crow that the Jesuit trainees (scholastics) at the mission schools were told by their superiors to "swat" the Lakota students in order to maintain control. "Every scholastic that I've come across was taught how to do swats," he confided, and this system of corporal punishment constituted "a very great injustice" to Indians who were accustomed to a less aggressive training based upon familial responsibility. All that Stolzman could muster in apology was that there were too many children and not enough teachers, and the latter had no way of invoking the Lakota system of relational duties (December 5, 1977).

Father Stolzman continued to rely heavily on Moses Big Crow, as translator, mediator, and guide to the Lakota language and worldview. Their private conversations honed the contours of the larger gatherings and set the future agenda. So, only after confidential discussions about the meaning of Lakota affective verbs did Stolzman introduce the group to a continuing symposium on the various forms of "love" and the conceptual bases of ethical codes (December 12, 1977–January 16, 1978).

Some disputes, like the mutual accusations of hexing (e.g., May 8, 1978), appeared to find resolution, only to unravel and fray the bonds of mutual respect. Other paradoxes, including the question of the appropriate relationship between Lakota and Catholic religious authority, tradition, and loyalty, defied conclusion and consensus. On many occasions the Lakotas continued to express "anger against the Church for their suppression of traditional religion for so many years" (Stolzman 1986b: 18).

Through the seventy-eight meetings for which transcripts exist, and apparently in every gathering to the very end, Father Stolzman proposed a comparison between two religious systems, not as an intellectual exercise, but as a means of reconciling Lakota and Catholic religions. His solutions were not everyone's, whether medicine men or pastors, nor did they result in any easy melding of Lakota and Catholic ritualism. Perhaps it is true, as Benjamin Black Bear, Jr., has remarked (Black Bear, August 4, 1988), that Stolzman overemphasized antiquated aspects of Lakota religious culture and promoted parallels between the religious systems which other conferees found implausible. Nonetheless, the priest provided a forum for interfaith dialogue unknown in Indian country before (and perhaps since) his tenure. Medicine men could take comfort in the appreciation expressed by the priests, however slanted, for their traditional values, beliefs, and practices.

Based upon the Rosebud Medicine Men and Clergy Meetings, Stolzman formulated (1982, 1986a, 1986b) his squaring of the two religious systems. At great length he compared their rituals (including Yuwipi, Lowanpi, and the mass), their spirituality, and their narrative traditions. In the end he sought the most appropriate way to say how Lakota and Christian religions are related. He articulated four potential answers (see Stolzman 1986b: 206–210).

First, we can blur the distinctions between the two and state that Lakota and Catholic religionists all pray to the same God. From that proposition the two camps can determine not to argue with one another about theological or ritual matters.

Second, we can conclude that the two religious systems are incompatible, and that one is better than the other. With that judgment in hand, we can decide not to relate the two in any significant manner.

Third, we can recognize similarities and differences between the two religions. Having achieved this understanding, we ought to keep the two separate in practice, even though they share similar (or even identical) functions.

Fourth, we can realize the differences between Lakota and Christian traditions, but appreciate the similarities enough to fit them together, where appropriate. This would be Stolzman's path, given the opportunity.

Throughout Christian history, Stolzman argued, non-Christian cultures and religions have enriched Church liturgy, theology, and philosophy. Catholicism has grown in its catholicity by incorporating elements once foreign into its sacramentalism. From his point of view the Church should be willing to bring Lakota phenomena into Lakota Catholicism.

However, he averred, Lakota medicine men do not want to transport formal Christian elements into Lakota religion, even though many of them are Catholics. As persons they accept Christian praxis but they want their Lakota religious system to be pure of external contamination. For his own part Stolzman would have preferred more syncretism rather than less. He wished to see the two roads meet and become a single path for Lakota Catholics. Nevertheless, he heard the opinions of the Lakota medicine men over six years of dialogue. Their preference was to compartmentalize the two religions for the most part, at least formally but even conceptually, allowing individuals to shift from one to the other depending on situation and need (see ibid., 213–215).

From his dialogical experience Stolzman was willing to acknowledge that such a "paradigm shift" (ibid., 215) was neither impossible nor hypocritical. Indeed, it seemed in large part to be the Lakota Catholic way.

Some years later Father Stolzman left Rosebud and the Indian ministry. He eventually left the Society of Jesus, though not the Catholic priesthood. Other priests at Rosebud have taken up the questions he addressed and Lakota-Catholic dialogue has continued, albeit in less sustained and documented fashion (Archambault 1995: 162). Catholic Lakotas a generation later still refer to the discussions of 1973–1979 between their medicine men and their pastors (ibid., 24–25). Sometimes in amusement, sometimes in appreciation, the interfaith dialogue has become a famous aspect of Lakota oral heritage.

THE INTERNAL DIALOGUE

As consciousness has been raised within Catholic circles in recent decades regarding the need for dialogue between Indians and Church officials, a realization has developed that a most important "internal dialogue" (Grim 1991b: 2) must also take place. Native American Catholics in their communities, and within themselves as individuals, embody a double identity which stands in need of reconciliation.

For those who identify themselves both as Indian and Catholic—the aged shaman whose medicinal knowledge was gained from his Catholic grandparents (ibid., 4–5); the sister for whom "traditionalist" and "Christian" are synonymous expressions of God's command to love (Mitchell, August 7, 1986); the teenage girl whose tribal rite of passage into puberty is blessed by the local Catholic priest and attained for the community "with the help of Jesus Christ" as a means to "become stronger Christians" (*Tekakwitha Conference Newsletter,* 9, no. 4, December 1990: 18); the peyotists who "make no distinction between Catholicism and the Native American Church" (Glenmary Research Center 1978: 4), and many more—there are choices to be made about how to comport themselves spiritually and live their lives in general. When Indian Catholics are married to peyotists or traditionalists (Monahan, September 18, 1988), or when they are married to Whites (Huhndorf and Huhndorf, August 5, 1992), they need to keep in balance the dictates of two faiths or ethnicities in an intimate setting.

Some observers (e.g., Jennings 1977) contend that the Christian and Native "ethos" are at odds with each other. Conversion from one to the other system means not only a theological shift, but also a transformation of values, worldview, and psychology. Over the centuries many Catholic missionaries have held such a position and worked strenuously to rid Indians of their indigenous traits in order for the Natives to achieve a Catholic identity. But, as the Flathead spiritual leader, Johny Arlee, has said, "It's a different Church nowadays" (Bozeman, August 7, 1986), one in which Indian religious tenets and practices are no longer deemed irreconcilable with Catholicism. Arlee adds, "Today we have freedom. We're all new. We're all young."

Father William Stolzman once asked of Lakota Catholics, "Can a single individual practice both religions authentically without any real conflicts or contradictions?" (Stolzman 1986b: 13). No one denies the difficulties, whether in harmonizing two contrasting attitudes toward nature (Wintz, July 1975: 39), practicing two separate sets of sacramental rites (St. Hilaire 1976), or squaring a Creation theology to the Christian doctrine of original sin (McDonnell, July 1987: 22). Even while the American Indian bishop, Charles Chaput, argues that "God was here before the Church was here. . . . We can be Native American, and we can be Christian. There is no contradiction," he reminds his fellow Indians that "the Gospel purifies our tradition" by judging and transforming it (in Cosgrove, March 1992: 10). Father Gilbert Hemauer, then chief executive of the National Tekakwitha Conference, once said that a person can be simultaneously Indian and Catholic, an "Indian enfleshing of Christianity," if he or she is committed to the "base values and teachings of the gospel, without compromising Catholic or native essentials. Of course," he acknowledged, there is ambiguity about what is "essential" to each tradition, and there is a constant give and take between the two, making for an "ongoing process of adjustment and growth" (Hemauer, August 9, 1986).

In truth, the two-fold condition of being an Indian and a Catholic contains no small inner tension. If Indian identity were merely a matter of ethnicity and Catholic identity simply one of religion, an individual could say, "I am an Indian Catholic" (or "Catholic Indian") with no psychological turmoil. There would be no felt need to compartmentalize (or to syncretize) elements of the two categories, alternating as adjective and noun; there would be no conflicting loyalties. However, both ethnicity and religion are matters of cultural identity. A person is culturally (ethnically, religiously) an Indian, and the same is true for a Catholic, and it is not easy to live out the ethos of two different cultures simultaneously.

The contemporary Catholic Church has embraced the project of inculturation; to name it as a project implies obstacles to be overcome, a problematic to be worked through. American Indian Catholics perceive that conundrum inside themselves, not only because "Catholic" and "Indian" are manifest as two separate categories of being, but also because of the contentious history of missionizing, including the present evangelical insistence upon inculturating.

A priest writes in the St. Paul–Minneapolis Archdiocese, Office of Indian Ministry *Newsletter* (December 1989: n.p.) that there is sharply felt concern among Native Catholics about the Church's teachings on "cultural understandings, practices and faith." Part of this concern, he states, "involves reconciling negative past experiences with the current openness to traditional practices. There is confusion and bitterness among some of the older people. Likewise the past and its moralizing tone [have] set a framework of negative self understanding *[sic]*." The Indians ask, "How can this be reconciled to create a more holistic and healthy self respect?" As one Catholic observer (Cosgrove 1992: 11) sees the situation, Catholic Indians today feel the deep hurts of their ancestors, hurts sometimes inflicted by the Church. These feelings make it difficult for contemporary Church officials to heal those hurts, since they are standing in the tradition of the hurters.

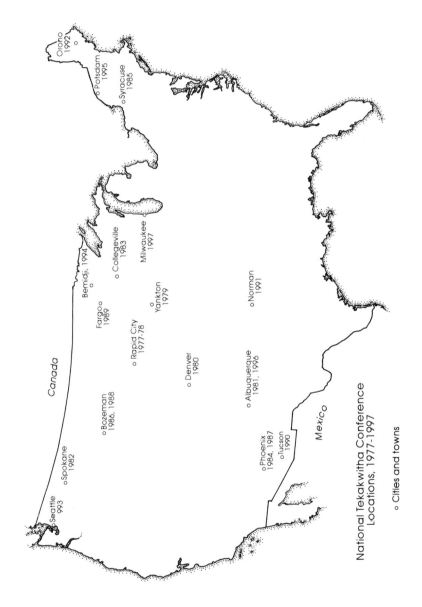

Orono
1992

Potsdam
1995

Syracuse
1985

Bemidji, 1994

Collegeville
1983

Milwaukee
1997

Norman
1991

Fargo
1989

Yankton
1979

Rapid City
1977-78

Canada

Denver
1980

Albuquerque
1981, 1996

Bozeman
1986, 1988

Mexico

Phoenix
1984, 1987

Tucson
1990

Spokane
1982

Seattle
993

National Tekakwitha Conference
Locations, 1977–1997

o Cities and towns

National Tekakwitha Conference Locations, 1977–1997

THE NATIONAL TEKAKWITHA CONFERENCE

Over the past two decades the National Tekakwitha Conference has provided a forum for Native American Catholic dialogue and inculturation. Named for the saintly seventeenth-century Mohawk convert to Catholicism (see Chauchetière 1887, *The Positio* . . . 1940, and volume 2 of *American Indian Catholics*), the organization grew in the late 1970s from a small missionary support group (founded in 1939) to an assembly for American Indian Catholics with membership in the thousands and participation at national, regional, and local levels.

For the Indian Catholics who revitalized its aims and have formed its ranks, the Tekakwitha Conference has provided the hope of an opportunity to choose a direction for their double-sided spiritual lifeway, with the blessed Kateri as an inspiration and model. As such, the conference has held the potential to give Catholic Indians a voice, to marshall their cultural and spiritual energies, and to make them feel at harmony with a Church which has alienated as well as enriched them. At the same time, the Tekakwitha Conference has constituted an institution, like the Bureau of Catholic Indian Missions, controlled by the Church hierarchy with the spiritual interests of Indian Catholics in mind. The organizers—a collectivity of clergy and laity, Indians and Whites—defined their group as a mediator between the ways of Indians and Catholic structures:

> an agency relating to the national Church and to international bodies, sensitizing them to the varieties of Indian peoples and cultures, and to the commonality of religious and societal concerns, lobbying before these bodies about Indian needs and acting as an agency by which these bodies can act responsibly to their commitment. (In Starkloff 1982: n.p.)

Carl Starkloff, S.J., expressed a more populist hope, that the Tekakwitha Conference was a "movement (at least it is an organization that is beginning to take on the characteristics of a movement) that promises to alter the face of the Roman Catholic Church among the Amerindian people" (ibid., n.p.).

Whose organization is it? There are estimates that as many as 50,000 Indians in the United States and Canada are involved in the Tekakwitha movement in general (Kozak 1991: 41)—praying in their local Kateri Circles, supporting the drive for Kateri Tekakwitha's canonization, attending area liturgies and catechetical workshops, and receiving encouragement for inculturative initiatives—although only 10,000 in the U.S. pay dues to the organization (and under a thousand in Canada), and some of these are non-Indians (*Tekakwitha Conference Newsletter,* 11, December–January 1992–1993: 4). At the annual meetings Indian Catholics come from all across North America, numbering about 2,000 each year, although in 1987 when Pope John Paul II joined the conference in Phoenix, there were as many as 10,000 in attendance, many of them non-Indians (Walsh 1989: 30–31).

With these figures in mind one can envision the Tekakwitha Conference as an organization of Indian Catholics with a Native program. When the non-Indian priest Gilbert Hemauer, O.F.M. Cap., was chief executive, he vowed that the Conference would be a "grass-roots" movement. "The Indian people have to evangelize each other," he stated, "without patronizing or manipulation from above" (Hemauer, August 9, 1986). Every year for more than a decade, he offered to resign from Tekakwitha control, but Indian Catholics in the movement trusted him and kept him on (Leute, August 7, 1986). Through the 1980s the annual meetings reflected his commitment to Indian leadership and initiative. Indians led the various public sessions; the Tekakwitha staff became predominantly Indian; the agenda reflected the concerns of Indian communities; the liturgies fostered inculturation. This was "not mere tokenism" in the eyes of observers (Fox, December 24–31, 1988: 542), and Indians within the Conference structures expressed hope in the organization's future. "As Native Catholics," read the Vision Statement of the 1988 meeting, "we are encouraged by the recognition of our Native cultures, traditions, and languages in the Roman Catholic Church. The beginnings of liturgical inculturation are nourishing our spiritual lives" (*Tekakwitha Conference Newsletter,* 8, no. 2, 1988: 1).

As much as the Tekakwitha Conference has become a movement for *and of* Native Catholics—and there have been dozens of Indians who have served on the elected board of directors and as executives, as we have seen in our survey of Indian Catholic leadership—the managership has also felt clerical and non-Indian influence, with a resulting tension in style and direction. Monsignor Paul A. Lenz of the Bureau of Catholic Indian Missions has maintained a role on the steering committee, and while encouraging Indian creativity, he also makes it clear who bankrolls the Conference. Each year, he says, the BCIM provides as much as $100,000 (Lenz, August 7, 1993). Bishop Donald E. Pelotte, S.S.S., adds that the American Board of Catholic Missions, the Extension Society, and the BCIM pay as much as 80 percent of the Tekakwitha budget. "Without funding from these groups," he declares, "the Tekakwitha Conference would collapse" (in Walsh, October 31, 1992: 330). More than once Msgr. Lenz has threatened to "jump ship" (Thiel, January 22, 1992) when displeased by the direction or indirection of the Tekakwitha Conference. This monetary pressure symbolizes the tensions within the Tekakwitha Conference. Is it a movement of Catholic Indians or an agency of the Church? Is it lay or clerical? These tensions have erupted in the 1990s and continue to mark its existence.

The Indian clientele who attend the annual Tekakwitha meetings are a "pietistic bunch" (Starkloff, August 7, 1986) of Catholics from all across America, devoted to Kateri, and by and large apolitical, searching for a way to express their Indianness alongside their Catholicism, and hungry for an experience of social solidarity with other Indians from their communities and around the country. One of the joys of attending the conferences, says the Mohawk Sarah Hassenplug (Fargo, August 3, 1989), who has portrayed Kateri in pageants over the years, is to catch up on old business and old gossip with intertribal acquaintances from far away. She and her fellow Mohawks rent a bus and travel cross-country every August, enjoying a fellowship of common faith and identity. Along the way they play bingo, see the countryside, sing hymns (in Mohawk and English), and catch up on their sleep, while taking a vacation from their reservation. No wonder that some Indians refer jokingly to the Tekakwitha gatherings as "Take-a-week-off" (Bucko, September 29, 1991). For many Natives the conference is like an old-time powwow, a holiday, a spiritual celebration, with public displays of story-telling, song, and dance, an elaborate feast of indigenous victuals, and an opportunity for sharing concern and emotional catharsis, all under the banner of Catholic authority.

Each year the national Tekakwitha meeting takes place in a different locale—from Montana to Arizona to North Dakota; Oklahoma to Maine to Washington; Minnesota to New York to Wisconsin. The Indians who attend must have the wherewithal to cover travel and housing costs. It is apparent, for instance at the Northeast regional Tekakwitha conference (Fonda, July 14–16, 1989), that the Native participants are far from impoverished. They arrive in late model vehicles,

dressed in conventional mainstream attire. The BCIM and other sponsors provide some funding in order to boost participation, and local
dioceses sometimes hire buses to carry the Tekakwitha devotees to the
conferences, making it possible for the poor as well as the middle class
to take part. The Navajo Nation Transit Authority bus is a common
sight at Tekakwitha gatherings. Sisters and priests pack the parish van
or organize caravans to make the cross-country pilgrimage. Other con-
tingents book group airfares; they share their flights with bishops and
other dignitaries who provide an annual presence.

Hundreds of Whites assemble, mostly Church personnel with an
Indian ministry, but also non-Indians who share an urban parish (e.g.,
St. Lucy's in Syracuse, New York) with Native Americans, or who
have an especial attachment to Kateri's cause. One priest, Dan Madlon
("Dan, Dan, the Congress Man") attended almost every Tekakwitha
conference from its inception in 1939 until his death in 1998, and was
described as the "walking history" of the organization. "I remember
during World War II," he said, "when there were only five priests who
met. Now look at this grand assembly" (Fargo, August 6, 1989). Many
of the white priests wear ribbon shirts or other sartorial signals of their
solidarity with Indians. The white sisters sometimes hover about their
Native flocks, shepherding them to liturgies and meals and hedging
them from reporters and others who might distract them from their
devotions.

To a stranger the Indians are a friendly, even open-hearted and vulnerable lot, eager to make new acquaintances and willing to share
pieties, confidences, and concerns. They show an unknown white man
a polite deference usually reserved for priests; maybe they assume that
any white man at a Tekakwitha conference *must* be a priest. Although
most Indians arrive at the gathering in a tribal unit, and the proceedings begin with a parade of parish and mission banners, with each
group marching in a display of localism, the Tekakwitha conference
emphasizes inter-tribal sharing and pan-Indian liturgy. Father
Hemauer installed a formula by which Indians can display their tribal
colors — especially the local hosts, like the O'odham in Tucson, the
Penobscots in Orono, the Coast Salish in Seattle, or the Mohawks in
their home territory—but they are to worship "side by side, sharing
their gifts" (Hemauer, August 9, 1986), as a model of catholicity. The
Southwest and the northern plains clusters have sometimes vied for
primacy at the conference—whose liturgies should be performed?

whose spokespersons should hold forth?—but the shifting of annual sites has given each region a chance to shine with a resultant muting of intertribal competition.

If anything, the conference presents an image of self-focused sameness. Here are Indian Catholics talking among themselves about issues of common interest. Some of the participants have traveled around the world, to the "Day of Prayer" in Italy in 1986, or the "Shinto International Workshop on Global Survival" in Japan in 1990. They are visited by papal delegates, members of the Vatican curia, influential U.S. bishops, members of the national media, and other outsiders. Nonetheless, they conduct their business on a parochial, almost familial, level. They declare, among themselves in public without challenge, that Indians are the most spiritual people in the world; that they share a common religiousness; and that Catholic faith can combine with their Native grace and strengthen it (Fargo, August 2–6, 1989). These assertions appear almost axiomatic at Tekakwitha conferences.

ALCOHOLIJM AND HEALING

The other side of this enunciated godly confidence is the confessional expression of self-inflicted wounds and the intensely felt need of healing. A small example: An agitated Indian man approaches a stranger in the bleachers (Fargo, August 5, 1989), beseeching a "reconciliation" to his daughter, who sent him to prison on a sex charge three years ago — falsely, he avers. As a result, his wife has deserted him and he wishes to win her back. The stranger directs the distraught man to a priest for counsel. It is not unknown at the meetings to be told, sometimes by a bishop or monsignor, about *that* woman who shot a priest who had been her lover (Orono, August 6, 1992), or *that* Native religious who has been accused of sexual wrongdoing back home (Seattle, August 7, 1993).

More typical, indeed almost universal, is the acknowledged devastation wrought by alcoholism. Partially because Father Hemauer is a recovering alcoholic—when he left the Tekakwitha Conference in 1989 he helped form a Catholic organization, Pathways for Peace, committed to combating substance abuse—but more importantly because of alcoholism's prevalence in Native American communities, the Conference has tried to address this plague. An Indian sister active in the Tekakwitha movement declares that she has never encountered an Indian family spared by this pervasive disease, this lethal outpouring of Indian self-hatred in desperate need of healing (Archambault, August 5, 1989); indeed, she claims that many members of the Tekakwitha board of directors are recovering alcoholics (Walsh, August 30, 1992). The Tekakwitha "Vision Statement" states that "addiction to alcohol and drugs is destroying many of our native people. We need to develop awareness and recovery programs adapted to our native communities" (in *Tekakwitha Conference Newsletter*, 8, no. 2, 1988· 1).

One can apprehend the immediate impact of alcohol abuse by listening to regional youth caucus reports at the conference. A Southwest teenager describes his growing up among alcoholic relatives, "when the loving is just not there"; a northern plains representative tells about a Church-sponsored project which encourages youngsters to tell their seniors that "it isn't Indian to be drunk." Indian youths thank the Tekakwitha Conference for its anti-drug and anti-alcohol ministry and pray that the various programs sponsored by the Conference will take effect in their communities (Fargo, August 4, 1989). A Papago man who has designed the official brochures and banners for the year's gathering under the theme, "Walking the Sacred Circle with Jesus Christ," confides publicly how his artwork used to reflect his alcoholism: cruelty, sadness, and beseeching. Now that he has controlled his drinking with the help of Kateri Tekakwitha, he works with peaceful motifs (ibid.). When a prominent tribal chairman announces at a plenary session that he has eschewed liquor for twenty-four years, with the help of God, he receives an immediate and booming applause (Seattle, Swinomish, and Lummi, August 5, 1993). In a less formal setting a St. Regis Mohawk identifies himself as an alcoholic. The story of Indians today, he declares, is one of confusion, disorientation, drinking, and drugs. Why? "Because we don't know what to believe anymore. The world we live in isn't our own." He attests that coming to the Tekakwitha meeting provides him the opportunity to think clearly about his situation and focus on God, through Kateri's example. By sharing his experiences with other Indian alcoholics like himself, including those who have kept themselves sober, he see that he is not alone, and that gives him hope. A fellow Mohawk comforts him. "Just have faith," she soothes. "God will give you all the help you need" (Fargo, August 6, 1989).

At regional Tekakwitha convocations (Fonda, July 15, 1989), the same testimony prevails concerning alcohol and drugs. One Mohawk tells of his cocaine addiction: how he once spent all of his dead brother's $3,000 insurance policy on a binge; how he drove his car "like a madman" while under the influence; and how he quit drugs with spiritual help at St. Regis, after two of his friends died in a drug-related head-on car collision. Another Mohawk, a college graduate, terms herself a "recovering alcoholic" whose first drunk occurred at age five, and who became a "suicidal maniac" in her teens. Now "nine years sober," she states that Indian people are genetically, chemically predisposed to alcoholism, and its effects batter everyone surrounding the alcoholic. "It is a family disease," she says, which leads directly to familial violence, abandonment, poverty, reprisal, and guilt. No condition of contemporary Indian life delivers as much ruin; no condition is more distinctively Indian. Alcoholism is not a "moral" issue to be sermonized against, she concludes, but rather a physical condition to be treated and a social pattern to be broken. A third Mohawk suggests that his wife's novenas provided him the grace to stop drinking; now he remains sober with the help of a "charismatic . . . family spirituality" and a "community support system. You have a bad day, you make some phone calls, and you have the whole community with you," he proclaims, and "There's no Christian here who can survive on his own."

As we have seen, the Tekakwitha Conference constitutes but one setting for treating Indian alcoholism. Blackfoot representatives have spoken about the Pilgrimage at Tekakwitha assemblies (e.g., Fargo, August 5, 1989), inviting Catholic Indians from around the country to partake of this treatment. And many Indians are members of Alcoholics Anonymous.

Tekakwitha conferees ponder the relation between A.A. and their own organization. At a session regarding alcoholism a Passamaquoddy man notes that "there is a spirituality in Alcoholics Anonymous. As more and more Indians get sober through A.A., they pick up this 'higher power, twelve steps' spirituality and they bring it to their religious lives. The question," he asks, "is how can we merge this movement with our Catholicism?" (Fargo, August 3, 1989). A Mohawk woman suggests that after A.A. sobers you up, you have the mental capacity to ask who you are and what you should be doing. Now that you are asking these questions, you are ready to look for God. You are ready for the Church. Perhaps this is a model, she says, for joining A.A. to the Church. In response a priest comments that "very few who go through A.A. go back to Church; they are satisfied with an unspecified 'higher power.'" A Northern Cheyenne adds that the "higher power" is for people who are "turned off to organized religion," but still have a spirituality that can help them sober up. A.A. is the "magic bridge" between their spirituality and successful sobriety. A.A. is "not a religion," he declares, and "there is a substantial gulf" separating A.A. from the Church. When he has spoken of the Catholic spirituality of the Tekakwitha movement to Indian alcoholics in Washington, D.C., it "spooked them." They are afraid of religion, he posits, with its connotations of doctrinal rigidity and moral condemnation, but interested in spirituality.

If Catholic missionizing of the past has often tended toward the dogmatic assertion of human sinfulness, trying forcefully to convince Indians of their inborn iniquity and need of salvific grace, the Tekakwitha Conference ministry has steered another course. With a clientele suffering in large number from alcoholism and its concomitant depression of self-esteem, the Tekakwitha ministry has emphasized themes of hope and healing. Father John Hascall has been the most vocal exponent of the charismatic Creation theology at the gatherings, but a more general liturgy of healing has suffused the proceedings and seems to stand side by side with the mass and other Tridentine rites.

Healing is promoted on several levels. A Crow speaker exhorts his tribesmen to make peace with their former enemies, the Sioux: "We're Christian now; we're one," he intones, delivering a sermon of social and political healing (Bozeman, August 9, 1986). There is also a call for the healing of the individual soul. With upraised hands the Mohawks pray that God will bridge the inner breech caused by intoxication (Fonda, July 14, 1989). Healing services also treat physical ailments, in a style more generally associated with Protestant faith curers.

While an Indian band strums guitars and croons Alleluia hymns, the officiant at a healing liturgy calls out to "a lady in a blue shirt and black slacks, who has had a liver problem: the lord is healing you now." Hands upraised, clapping hands and swaying to the music, the Indians attest to the mending, soothing power of God. "Jesus has touched me," one cries. Another, a man with a cast on his right leg, is told, "You are feeling pins and needles. Accept this pain." Acceptance is part of the remedy. "It is time to rejoice and be glad," the leader exclaims. "This is the day that the Lord has made. Let us rejoice." Together the congregation hollers, "Praise the Lord!" (Fargo, August 5, 1989).

John Hascall maintains (Bozeman, August 9, 1986) that many Indians journey to the Tekakwitha sessions because of the healing services. They appreciate other liturgies; they enjoy the socializing; they pay attention to certain political issues germane to their Native communities. Above all, however, they cherish the ceremonials of medicinal spirituality.

The Tekakwitha organizers sometimes take up matters of social justice, including the desecration of traditional Indians' holy grounds and the hemming in of Native American religious freedoms; the disharmony among racial groups in America; and the mistreatment of Indians in Latin America (Fargo, August 3–4, 1989). However, in general the board avoids politics and tries to keep prayer at the center of the conferences, much to the liking of the attendees, who are largely apolitical. Even when the board has raised ecclesiological questions related to Native Catholic history, such as the potential canonization of Junipero Serra, most conferees have paid little attention.

The moral and political questions surrounding abortion rarely get raised as agenda items, even though some Indian Catholics have taken strong public stands, for example, at the National Pro-Life Rally held at the Washington Monument in April 1990, or in the Native Californian anti-abortion agency, Indians for Life. The Northern Cheyenne Mort Dreamer informs one Tekakwitha session that whenever he has $50 to spare—the money needed to bail himself out of jail—he pickets an abortion clinic in the D.C. area. He feels the same kind of passion about abortion as he does about racism (Fargo, August 4, 1989). Joseph Savilla of Isleta reports that the Puebloans, like most Native Catholic people, detest abortion. They aren't about to kill off their population. If white women want to do so in an America that permits them the license, so be it; the Indians will inherit the earth (Savilla, August 6, 1993). On occasion one hears an angry Indian voice railing against the legalized practice of "killing babies" in America (Seattle, August 7, 1993), and some Indians (Orono, August 5, 1992) would like the Tekakwitha Conference to place its spiritual weight against abortions by holding pro-life prayer sessions at the annual convocation. For the most part, however, such issues are tangential to the business of the Tekakwitha movement.

LITURGICAL INCULTURATION

The business is inculturation and the format is liturgical. Every Tekak-witha assembly is a planned opportunity for Indians to express their Catholicism in a ritual manner deemed appropriate to their cultural heritage. "We are a sacramental people," states an Indian Catholic from the northern plains. "Everything talks to us about God" (Fargo, August 4, 1989). Through the Tekakwitha conference the Church tries to bind its own sacramental system to indigenous forms of ritualism.

On various reservations Native Catholics have established local modes of inculturation. Mohawks, Micmacs, Navajos, Choctaws, and Lakotas have arranged with the Vatican's Congregation for Divine Worship to conduct liturgy in their own languages. Puebloans have synchronized their aboriginal calendars with the feast days of the saints. Pipes, processions, sweats, and smudgings all take place in homegrown Catholic contexts. The task of the Tekakwitha organizers is to celebrate these regional patterns. When meeting in Albuquerque, invite the sacred clowns and earth spirits at Santo Domingo to celebrate St. Dominic's day with dance and chant. When in Seattle, have the Swinomish singers intone their power songs at mass. These ritual displays may inspire other Indians to seek similar accommodations and the project of inculturation will thereby be furthered.

The Tewa Dolores Rousseau says (Rousseau, August 6, 1992) that at the Tekakwitha meetings she learns "other ways" beyond those of her Tewa relatives, whose "protocol" she already knows. She observes a pipe ceremony and recognizes it as the way of her husband's people, the Sioux. She observes Apache dancers and gains respect for their ritual idiom. Through the Tekakwitha assemblies she gains a greater understanding of not only Catholicism but also Native American culture.

A danger of such displays is that Indians look upon them as entertainment rather than liturgy. It is common at the Tekakwitha conferences for an audience to applaud a dance, a pipe ritual, or even prayer in an Indian language. The Indians seem to be expressing their appreciation of a performance well executed, a valued cultural outpouring, a work of theatrical art. Their applause distances them from the event, establishing themselves as onlookers rather than participants, and identifying the exhibition as something other than religious. At the least, the large numbers in attendance at Tekakwitha convocations turn most people into spectators, even if they identify with the ceremony taking place.

Another danger is that Indians of one tribe are left indifferent to the liturgy just performed, either because they cannot understand the words that were spoken in a foreign tongue, or because they are jealous of their own tribal prerogatives. They want to celebrate their own liturgies rather than serve as spectators at someone else's show. This was especially true one year in Tucson, where the O'odham recited numerous prayers and songs, to the distraction of other Indians, who complained that the local Indians "sing and sing and sing and sing. . . . A song or two would be enough. . . . Why can't there be English as in our parishes?" (in Lenz, November 19, 1993).

On the other hand, there are many reservations where "very little inculturation" takes place, where "many of the elders gave up Indianism to become Catholics and can't integrate the two" (in Bastien, August 20, 1992: 4). The Tekakwitha coordinators are interested in promoting an internal dialogue among these Indians, and therefore formulating liturgies in which all American Indian Catholics can participate. They search for ritual motifs common to most Indians—the pipe, the sweat, the sunrise observance, the procession—in the hope of establishing a pan-Indian Catholic liturgy which can be termed "traditional" (Bucko, September 29, 1991). This is no small endeavor, and one fraught with its own dangers. Some Indian Catholics deplore the invention of a manipulated commonality (Ojibway, November 23, 1992; Savilla, August 6, 1993). They are perhaps no more at home in a sunrise sacramental or a smudging than their ancestors were centuries ago in the Tridentine Latin rite. And they may experience a prayer to the six directions with an eagle wing (to the tune of "He Will Raise You up on Eagle's Wings") as an act of cultural imposition rather than a statement of their own cultural identity.

The desire not to offend any tribal group's tradition of inculturation sometimes leads the Tekakwitha handlers to incorporate many diverse rites into a single ceremonial: an Ojibway prayer, a Salish pageant, a Corpus Christi processional, a Crow smudging, a Pueblo penitential observance, all surrounding a mass in a congery which Father Carl Starkloff refers to as "a carnival." He adds, "Perhaps it's what they need at this time but it seems overwrought" (Bozeman, August 10, 1986).

What makes for the right inculturative balance between diverse ritual elements? Among the different tribal ways? Between Indian and Catholic traditions? Should the Tekakwitha Conference leave the matter of inculturation to individual Indian communities, or should it establish ground rules for Native inculturation in general? Should inculturation consist of various means "to enhance the mass" (Lenz, November 19, 1993) with peripheral Native decorations, leaving normative liturgy intact? Or, should Indian rituals, like sweats, take on a sacramental character which might enhance the spiritual life of not only Native American Catholics but also many others throughout the universal Church?

It will not be simple to achieve agreement within the Church or within American Indian communities regarding these questions. Beyond these circles there is criticism of Tekakwitha's project of "guided syncretism" (in Kozak 1991: 6). In anthropologist David Kozak's view, the Catholic hierarchy has concocted a movement coated superficially with pan-Indian spiritual elements, whose goals are to massage Native hurts and to manage safe modes of Native worship. The hierarchy has chosen Kateri as the saint-to-be. It has chosen the ritual core, the organizational structure, the tenets of faith, all meant to gather Indians more tightly into the Catholic fold. Kozak sees this as a "homogenization process" (5) by which particular tribes become less distinctly themselves as they come to identify with a "master symbol" created by the Church. The Tekakwitha Conference seems to grant Indian Catholics a voice and allows for a nostalgic romanticizing of selected aspects of old Indian culture; however, its purpose is to complete the religious acculturation of nominally Catholic Indians. In Kozak's vision, the Tekakwitha campaign is a mopping-up action after several centuries of evangelical combat.

Kozak's language will strike some as unnecessarily accusatory; however, he is not the only one to observe that the Tekakwitha endeavor of inculturation exists at an ironic crossroad. At the horizon of the twentieth century the aboriginal forms of Native American religiousness are often moribund, especially in those communities where Catholic faith took hold a long time ago and acculturation has been a mode of survival for generations. "Very little of the native religion remains," one observer comments, "and then it is practiced in only a few families. Since tribal peoples are notoriously conservative," the commentator suggests, "they are often scandalized today by missionaries' efforts to reintroduce old Indian customs into Catholic liturgy" (St. Hilaire 1976: 186). Why should the Tekakwitha Conference be intent upon reviving ancient rituals already abandoned or teaching one Indian group the traditional practices of another? Is it because Indian culture today is so little different from mainstream American ways that it is safe to glorify its past? Would Tekakwitha spokespersons be encouraging the revival of old Indian customs if Natives were still torturing, enslaving, or devouring their enemies, or if they posed a military threat to the United States, or if they practiced polygamy, or if they engaged in the sacrifice of dogs—that is, if Native American culture still constituted a modality dangerously different from Catholic American civilization?

A generation ago it would have been unthinkable for an American Indian priest like John Hascall to conduct a sweat like the ones he led in Maine in the summer of 1992 (Orono, August 7–8, 1992). For this event white clergy in the Indian ministry placed themselves under the ritual leadership of the Ojibway "medicine priest." Two Indian bishops took part, neither of whom had engaged in such ritualism in his formative years (and neither of whom, incidentally, completed the steaming rounds of prayer). Most of the people in the sweats were strangers to this form of Native ceremonialism, including Choctaws and Houmas from the rural Southeast and urban Indians from the Northeast.

Hascall's sweat was part of the inculturative program of the Tekakwitha Conference. No bishop or priest was heard to utter a protest to this liturgy at a Catholic assembly. Bishop Donald Pelotte found it "touching, although exhausting" (ibid., August 8). Others were impressed by the Native spirituality it expressed. Some of the Houmas were bemused. Why had the Bureau of Catholic Indian Missions paid their way from Louisiana to Maine to participate in a non-Catholic ritual they had never even heard of? They had attended the Tekakwitha meeting in order to get in touch with other Catholic Indians; in this they were not disappointed. But they also hoped to deepen their Catholic faith, and they were hard-pressed to say how a sweat lodge functioned toward that end (ibid.).

Other Indian Catholics have questioned Tekakwitha-sponsored syncretism, even under the mission of inculturation. The late Sioux deacon Francis Hairychin complained before his death that the Conference was "going too far with Indian liturgy" (Fargo, August 3, 1989), "placing the medicine man on the pedestal" (Condon, August 5, 1992). He may not have meant this as an explicit criticism of John Hascall; nevertheless, he worried for the integrity of Catholic faith when coupled with Indian ceremonialism.

A papal representative also raised alarm over the use of terms like "Great Spirit" and "Grandfather" in prayers enunciated at Tekakwitha gatherings. He asked Msgr. Paul Lenz if Catholic Indians mean "God the Father" when they employ these appellations. Lenz tried to allay his concern with a lengthy missive, but the delegate was "not totally satisfied." As for the BCIM's sponsoring Tekakwitha sweats attended by Indians for whom the ritual is a cultural novelty, Lenz replies that it is an ironic religious development; however, "As a *cultural happening* I see no problem with the sweat lodges. Many of the Catholic people enter the sweat lodges" (Lenz, November 19, 1993).

DYNAMICS OF CHANGE

From the late 1970s, when Indians commandeered the clerical Tekak-witha gathering and created a Church-sponsored movement for Native Catholics, to the late 1990s, the Tekakwitha Conference has undergone an evolution. The stated goals—dialogue and inculturation— may have remained the same, but the tone has shifted several times in the past generation. Following the angry confrontations of the first years, the annual meetings achieved a well-controlled harmony through the 1980s, only to erupt once again into acrimony in the early 1990s. The past several conferences have been more carefully super-vised by the board of directors; dissidents have defected and the pro-ceedings have been relatively subdued. If we take several looks at the Conference proceedings over the past decade, we can observe the un-folding of the Tekakwitha movement to the present day.

Bozeman, August 6–10, 1986: The conference prominently features a series of paintings called "An Indian Jesus" by Dick West, a Southern Cheyenne artist. West portrays biblical scenes of Christ's life, using Cheyenne imagery. The angel Gabriel appears to Mary with eagle wings; he wears a headdress and carries a flute. An American turtle dove appears in several scenes, symbolizing the Holy Spirit, rather than a white dove, which denotes sorrow to the Cheyennes. The baby Jesus lies in a plains cradleboard under an arbor, surrounded by horses. Mary is costumed in red face paint and a beadwork blouse. The Last Supper takes place in a tipi, where Christ uses sign language for a forked tongue to reveal Judas's betrayal. The doomed apostle holds a pouch full of valuable elk's teeth, the price he has received for his mas-ter's death. In the garden of Gethsemane Jesus again employs sign ges-tures to say that his heart is ready. At his crucifixion a centurion is de-picted as a Pawnee, a traditional Cheyenne foe

West's paintings illustrate Pope John Paul II's inculturative ideal of the Amerindian Christ. Here is Jesus enacting the scenes of salvation, and he has an Indian body. His mother, his clothing, his gestures, his enemies, his entire cultural context—all are Indian. At the same time the paintings are foursquare, biblically Christian. The 1986 Tekakwitha conclave at Bozeman tries to strike the same inculturative, inclusive balance. Here are masses, graced by eagle feathers and the smoke of sage and cedar. Here are homilies extolling the virtues of familial values, illustrated by tribal rites of passage. Here are charismatic liturgies for healing; the wounds are those felt most deeply by Native Americans, pierced by the arrows of racism, poverty, and alcoholism. To make a point about God's all-encompassing infinitude, a Tlingit speaker uses his own language, in which divinity is termed "the spirit of everything."

In "the spirit of everything," a harmony of expression is encouraged between Native and Catholic cultures. A Pueblo man with prep school and Ivy League education speaks in one breath of "the gift of our Native religions, the gift of Christianity." He says that "there are more similarities than there are differences between the two." A Blackfoot couple acknowledges "a difference" between Indian and Catholic ways of worship, "but there is no reason for conflict between the two. They are both works of God and complement each other."

The Second Vatican Council, explains a bishop, has placed a value on cultural freedom and cultural diversity. "God speaks through cultures," he declares. "Individuals achieve their humanity through culture," and thus "the Church embraces all cultures." In America, he comments, we used to brag about the "melting pot." But, "thanks be to God, today we speak of the stew pot, where each culture flavors all while maintaining its own identity." He exhorts his Indian audience to convey their cultural heritage through their Catholicism.

Why, at a time when the pope is wary of American Catholic heterodoxy, is the Church fostering Native Catholic cultural freedom? A Lakota sister in the Tekakwitha hierarchy suggests (Cuny, August 8, 1986) that experiments in inculturation pose no danger to authority as long as Indian Catholics maintain doctrinal and moral orthodoxy and loyalty to the papacy. She adds that a contemporary Indian ministry needs to indulge cultural articulation in order to reverse the many years of hurtful condemnation of Indian ways by a missionizing Church. Now is the time for pastoral compassion, affirmation rather than conversion, ministration to Native needs rather than missionary rigidity.

At the Tekakwitha meetings of the late 1970s the Indians vented their anger at the centuries of evangelical imperialism, as they saw it. Now, says Msgr. Lenz of the BCIM, "the criticism that the Church doesn't care about Indians . . . is far in the past." Father Hemauer

(August 9, 1986) agrees that for those involved in the Tekakwitha Conference the process of "reconciliation" with the Church is well under way—although this is certainly not the case for all Indians, and not even for all Catholic Indians. Nonetheless, those at the gathering recognize the past wrongs perpetrated upon Native Americans by the Church. At Tekakwitha dialogues churchmen have sought and received Indians' "forgiveness." Now it is time to further the healing project of inculturation and address the contemporary needs of the Catholic Indian community.

Hemauer suggests that the Tekakwitha clientele is satisfied with the liturgical contours of the Bozeman conference. In large part he is correct, yet two Indian men express their wishes for some additional modes of worship. An Anishinabe from Michigan finds it "kinda weird" to be encircled by Native Catholic ritualism without holding a sweat lodge. "I wish that some of the Indians here at Bozeman had organized a sweat. But I really don't think it would be right for the Conference to advocate one." A South Dakota Sioux complains that the Conference pays too little attention to the Blessed Virgin. While handing out rosaries and devotional literature about Fatima, he scolds the Tekakwitha organizers for downplaying Mary's special place in Catholic faith. "If a woman can get to heaven," he pronounces, "we all can."

Phoenix, September 12–14, 1987: At last year's Tekakwitha congress an Arizona Apache proposed that Pope John Paul II meet with the 1987 conclave in Phoenix. He uttered a determination to "use this papal visit to stimulate and strengthen our . . . Indian Catholicism" (Bozeman, August 9, 1986). Now thousands of Catholic adherents in Veterans Memorial Coliseum are awaiting the pope's arrival. Two nights ago they witnessed a moonlit performance by masked Apache dancers at the Heard Museum. Yesterday they participated in Tekakwitha liturgies, including John Hascall's healing prayers and a pageant of songs and speeches by Kateri's Mohawk devotees. Indians socialized and snapped each other's pictures, readying themselves for the historic papal visitation.

There is an outpouring of excitement as the pontiff enters the coliseum, escorted by an honor guard. He walks to the center stage and stands before an enormous throne made by regional Indian artisans. A Pima man, Emmett White, blesses Pope John Paul II with an eagle feather and incense, and then gives him the feather as a gift.

Bishop Donald Pelotte rises and receives a standing ovation from the audience. He welcomes the pope, thanking him for Kateri's beatification. He says that he looks forward to her canonization—another standing ovation. Then he closes by telling John Paul, "We love you very much."

A planned dialogue ensues. First, Alfretta Antone, Vice President of the Salt River Pima Tribe, provides a substantive statement for the pope to ponder. She recalls fifty thousand years of North American Indian history in a land eventually "invaded" by Europeans. She speaks of Euroamerican "plundering" and "abuse" in what is now the United States—policies and patterns of behavior which have left Native Americans poor and vulnerable. "We want to keep alive all our cultural and traditional ways of life," she declares, "our legends, our dances, our languages," and she asks the pope to help "us" Indians in the struggle to uphold treaty rights, lands, and natural resources. She reminds the pope that, "Until recent times, many of our people turned away from the Church." But now she is "encouraged" by the Church's "support" for the "beauty and value of our traditional prayers and ceremonies. . . . We seek a fuller participation in the universal Catholic Church," including positions of leadership. Like Bishop Pelotte, she calls for Kateri's canonization—to another standing ovation—and for a greater incorporation of Indian culture in Catholic sacraments.

Pope John Paul II enjoins the issues Vice President Antone has raised. He praises aboriginal Indians for their long-standing encounter with the Creator, which led to their deep respect for the world around them. He exhorts the audience to "work for reconciliation" between Indians and Euroamericans, all members of "one human family." At the same time he encourages Indians to "keep alive your cultures, songs, customs, that have served you well in the past." Mentioning alcoholism and chemical dependency, he states, "You have endured much . . . and your difficulties are not at an end." He then calls Indians to a "new life in Jesus Christ," imploring his listeners to live in the spirit of caring for all living beings, "from the unborn to the aged," including the earth itself.

The pope states that Kateri Tekakwitha was an "outstanding example of Christian life"; however, he does not announce her canonization, to the disappointment of all. Nonetheless, John Paul says that he is gratified by the participation of Indians in the life of the Church today. He repeats what he said to Canadian Indians in 1984, that Indians have enriched Catholic tradition in the past, and that today they can be culturally at home within the Church. "The gospel has not destroyed what is best in you. It has enriched . . . your cultures," he avows. "Our Catholic faith is capable of flourishing in all cultures and nations, without being captive to any."

Fargo, August 2–6, 1989: The heady papal visit is now a matter of memory and the Tekakwitha Conference is trying to implement continuing dialogue and inculturation in an atmosphere of countervailing voices. Father John Hascall is leaving the agency; so is Gilbert Hemauer, replaced by Fred Buckles, a Catholic Indian with few ties to Tekakwitha stalwarts. With these changes there is concern about the future unity of the organization.

Bishop Chaput (August 3, 1989) is saying privately that the Conference is only "a cosmetic" that fails to address the most important spiritual and material questions of contemporary Indian life. In his view the organization seems to avoid asking hard questions so as not to exacerbate potential factionalism. The bishop remarks that Tekakwitha holds several thousand Catholic Indians together for several days at their lowest denominator of commonality without lasting effect. Chaput wants the congress to become "more interesting," with increased and more free-wheeling debate, even though public disagreement may lead to a "crisis." Let it be, he says. Let those from various tribal backgrounds and regions disagree. Let those with different liturgical preferences enact their visions of Catholic Indian ritual. Let political discussion occur. He reminds his listener that "crisis" can be an "opportunity."

In another locale Father Carl Starkloff is confiding that factions are already struggling for control of the Tekakwitha Conference. Now that Hemauer is leaving there is already a "crisis" in the corporation. The main point of contention, he says, is the matter of inculturation. The Navajo deacon, Daniel Nez Martin, sits in a noisy university cafeteria, eloquently complaining that the Conference is about to "snuff out" traditional Indian spirituality. He raises the specter of Black American Catholics led by Father George Stallings of Washington, D.C., struggling against the Catholic hierarchy for the right to perform an African mass. He wonders aloud if the same kind of "crisis" might take place in Native American communities, and at the Tekakwitha meetings themselves, in the near future.

Perhaps a crisis is already at hand. In the public report of the Southwest caucus, the Isleta Joseph Savilla is giving voice to Indian anger. "We are hurt today," he declares. "We are crying within ourselves. . . .

It is time to come forward . . . to be heard." He is reluctant to utter words of dissent; however, the caucus (including non-Indian religious), whose members rise to support him, must be heard. In their judgment the Tekakwitha Conference has lost its way. Savilla utters several recommendations for returning to the proper path. These include retaining John Hascall; appointing more lay Indians to the board of directors; consulting Native communities about each year's agenda; increasing the devotions to Kateri; serving as ombudsman between Catholic Indians and insensitive local bishops. Savilla pronounces a demand that Tekakwitha financial records be open to auditing. "We pray that you do your job for our people," Savilla says to the board; however, the implications of his speech are anything but prayerful.

Savilla states, "Our Church stymies us." The hierarchical leadership gives Indians mixed signals, saying on one hand that we should express our traditional spirituality, and then prohibiting pipe ceremonialism during mass. "From our two Native bishops we get nothing," he asserts, even when they and other Tekakwitha board members are asked to intercede with non-Indian clergy who have turned a deaf ear to Native concerns. In one case, he charges, the Church is destroying an Indian burial ground to build an institutional edifice. In another the Church has closed an Indian church and "embezzled" the Native community's recent donations.

Savilla's impassioned speech sets the assembly buzzing. Board member Vivian Juan tells a reporter that she is concerned about his "confrontational" claims, which she says do not represent the Southwest caucus's point of view. Sister Kateri Mitchell characterizes his behavior as "passive aggression." But the public furor passes without rebuttal or reconciliation.

On the next day the gymnasium convocation witnesses the ordination of Sioux John L. Cavanaugh as permanent deacon in the Diocese of Fargo. He and his bishop, the Most Rev. James Sullivan, receive a blessing with a pipe. The deacon prostrates himself on a star quilt laid out by four elderly Sioux women, while his friends and family, dressed in suits and dresses, sing the Kyrie to the accompaniment of an organ. Following Cavanaugh's vows Sioux drummers sing an honoring song for him and quilts are distributed to honored guests.

The ordination service, a balance of Catholic and Sioux elements, is the prelude to a powwow of exultant communal spirit. Even as the rite is in progress, the gym is filling with Native-costumed revelers, arriving for "The People of God Powwow." They parade in—lay and clergy, Red, White, and Black, the communion of visible saints and sinners— in an impressive display of regalia: fur turbans, beaded leggings, breastplates, bells, moccasins, jingle dresses, lace shawls, bandoliers, porcupine roaches, eagle feathers, as well as a scattering of Roman collars. To the beat of Indian drummers they perform a choreography of unity: a round dance, an honoring dance for the papal delegate, a grass dance (albeit on the indoor tarmac), men's and women's dances, competitive fancy dances, and other Indian steps. Kyrie Elation! If we were to look at photographs of the event, we might ask: Is that an Indian sister, fetching in her fitted, fringed buckskin dress? Is that a BCIM archivist, high-prancing in fancy dance attire? Which one is the priest and which the lay catechist? Which the missionary, which the Indian? It is hard to locate everyone's place in the Catholic hierarchy out on the dance floor; however, you would not have to guess where in the jubilant crowd to find the members of the Church's body. They are everywhere and they are moving together to the music.

For all the high spirit energy of celebration at the powwow, the 1989 Tekakwitha meeting reveals itself to be a tenuous balancing act. The representatives of the Vatican and the U.S. Bishops' Conference are trying to steer the organization and the Indian Catholics it represents toward normative Catholicism. At the closing mass, the Nigerian cardinal, Francis Arinze, president of the Vatican's Council for Interreligious Dialogue, warns the congregation that "anyone who criticizes Mother Church in public *does not love* the mother." He and the other princes of Catholicism want Native American Catholics—by implication, the children of the Church—to love their ecclesial mother.

Some of the Indians, however, are on the verge of disaffection from the Church they are exhorted to love. These are hurt people who have been raised on the spirit of hurt, who have inherited hurt, who parade their hurt. They are insecure, jealous for attention, resentful of the Church which has adopted them. Sometimes they feel the unworthiness of their culture; sometimes they overcompensate by romanticizing themselves. They align themselves in geographic, tribal, liturgical factions. They are a difficult people to unify in the spirit of love.

A third constituency of the Tekakwitha Conference are those in direct ministry to Indians. Some of these are Whites, some Indians. They do not all love the powers that be, but they all depend on the moneys that be. They are ambivalent about Indians because they know painfully well how dissipated Indian culture is today; because they know "their people" intimately; because they care desperately to save these folks from ruin, but cannot convince themselves that Church programs are widely effective; because they are loyal to a hierarchy that they often feel at odds with but also grateful to.

The Tekakwitha board tries to keep these three groups in balance; indeed, the board is made up of these three groups. The categories get mixed when the hierarchy is Pelotte or Chaput, or the missionary is Hascall or Cuny. Will Fred Buckles tilt the balance one way or another? He is a layman, an Indian, but he is not all powerful, and he is subject to pressures, not least of all monetary.

And it isn't even as though any one of these constituencies has the answers to Indian problems, like the hell-on-earth alcoholism that daily drowns their spirit.

Two contentious Tekakwitha gatherings have passed. In Tucson, Arizona, in 1990 the incipient structural tensions were smothered under the magnitude of O'odham piety. Fathers John Hascall and Ed Savilla performed a mass which combined Indian and Catholic symbolic gestures to a degree that disturbed the more conservative clergy and bishops, and even some Indians. The Native priests wore no priestly vestments and sat barefoot on the floor, praying in their indigenous languages. Msgr. Lenz found the liturgy almost unrecognizable as a mass. He walked out; however, the assembly avoided an extended public controversy. In private Hascall was told "never again" (Lenz, November 19, 1993) to repeat his liturgical experiment at a Tekakwitha gathering. Bishop Pelotte made it clear that inculturation is fine, so long as it doesn't disrupt the sacrosanct centrality of the Eucharist. Regarding the central rite of Catholicism there can be little variation from liturgical rules, he warned (Walsh, August 17, 1992).

The following year in Norman, Oklahoma, Hascall refused to say a mass at all, given the strictures placed upon him. To Hascall and many of his followers the doors seemed to be closing to liberal inculturation; "some said they felt they were being told not to be Indian" (Walsh, August 17, 1992; see Grim 1991a). Joseph Savilla and his allies once again took the floor and complained of a Tekakwitha Conference dominated by retrograde clergy. They demanded a public forum to air grievances, and so the board members sat on the dais and engaged in a "stormy debate" (Walsh, October 31, 1992: 330) over liturgical inculturation and other complaints, most of which recalled the issues raised in 1989 at Fargo. The dialogue failed to reconcile the disputing parties, however, and the conference at Orono approaches in a mood of anxious embattlement.

The year 1992 marks the quincentenary of Columbus's appearance in the New World—a half millennium of star-crossed contacts between white invaders and Native Americans. Indians throughout the Americas are observing the anniversary in a critical mood, mindful of the ruinous impact of Western expansion across their lands. Euroamerican institutions, including the missionizing Christian churches, are feeling the effects of long-standing Native resentments, piqued by the Columbian remembrance. Bishop Pelotte has been active in Catholic circles, trying to temper his Church's triumphalist tendencies with a call, more or less successful, for sober reflection upon the history of Indian-Christian relations. Still, Catholicism is a visible and perhaps appropriate target for the arrows of Indian umbrage. The Tekakwitha congress provides a potential setting for faultfinding.

Closer to home, the Tekakwitha Conference board has provoked the ire of some members by firing Fred Buckles from his directorship. Joseph Savilla, the most vocal critic of the board over the last several years, predicts an eruption of anger in Orono. "They may try to clam me up," he declares; however, he and his affiliates are "quite upset" by "political maneuvering" by the board and they plan to speak publicly (Savilla, July 7, 1992).

Waiting for the proceedings to commence, Savilla and his wife Peggy discuss (Savilla and Savilla, August 5, 1992) the issues that have concerned them over the past several years. Their disgruntlement with the Conference, he says, is a matter of "wanting to be recognized, . . . trying to find a voice" in the Church. "It's paternalism," she concurs, "being treated like kids, . . . not being heard." They are tired of Tekakwitha's being controlled by clerics and by non-Indians. "Even our two Indian bishops have failed us," they charge. "The fact is, they didn't become Indians until they became bishops."

What rankles them especially is the firing of Fred Buckles. The board of directors claimed that the chief executive needed more "theological" know-how, but the "truth of the matter" is that the clerics on the board fired Buckles "in retaliation" for the public complaints at the last several conferences. The Savillas accuse Gilbert Hemauer of taking Tekakwitha funds in order to found Pathways for Peace, a nonprofit agency for Indian alcohol rehabilitation. "They caught up with him" at the 1989 Fargo congress and supposedly Hemauer returned the money; however, there is no record of the reimbursement. When Joseph Savilla blew the whistle on this financial imbroglio in Fargo, the board blamed Buckles for "leaking" the potential scandal, even as he was being hired. Then came the discord, two years running, over inculturation. "Fred hadn't kept us quiet in Tucson or Oklahoma. He and John Hascall were not part of the team" on the board—"so, they're gone." When Buckles was fired, Joseph tried to get the American bishops to investigate the board, but to no avail. He is sure that bishops Chaput and Pelotte quashed his grievance.

The Lakota deacon Harold Condon corroborates the Savillas' charges regarding the missing money. A trained accountant who used to be the treasurer for the Cheyenne River Sioux, he could find "no receipt or audit trail" (Condon, August 5, 1992) for the funds supposedly returned by Father Hemauer. He resents the fund-raising tactics of Church officials "in the Indian business," maintaining their own "luxury" while advertising "our poverty, our children, our suicides, our alcoholism." Whether this diatribe is directed at Father Hemauer or others is left unclear.

Condon was part of the movement which revolutionized the Tekakwitha Conference in the late 1970s. Now he is feeling left out of the decision making and without recourse. When his wife Geraldine tried to put herself forward for election to the Tekakwitha board, she was shunted from the ballot, in a process which Condon calls "a farce." When he has complained to the board, he has received no response, except that his bishop, Charles Chaput, has asked Condon if he belongs "to some group of dissidents." The deacon replies that he is simply a "concerned Catholic Indian," concerned about the future of Native spirituality for Indian Catholics and lay control of the Conference, concerned that the board has "reneged" on everything promised in the late 1970s.

According to the Savillas the board is now "breaking all its promises, like the United States and its treaties" (Savilla and Savilla, August 5, 1992). Father Hemauer had pledged that when he stepped down from Tekakwitha leadership, lay Indians would gain in authority, "but it was just words that kept us coming back, hoping." Now Msgr. Lenz and other priests are saying that "we are not ready." The present board, the Savillas say, arranges the annual congress in advance, hoping to prevent lay Indians from voicing their criticisms and exerting their will. "They have us going on sightseeing trips," Joseph states, "rather than holding public workshops and business meetings." He wonders if this might be the last annual congress, and if the Tekakwitha movement might be better served if the National Conference were abandoned. Native Catholics could still honor Kateri on their own without having to deal with yet another bureaucratic institution within the Church.

Could this be the last Tekakwitha convocation? Sister Marie Therese Archambault calls it a "critical" conference, perhaps the final one if "gloomy predictions" hold true. Whatever happens, she says, it is an "interesting" time, "like the Chinese curse, 'May you live in interesting times.'" The issue that is vexing the Tekakwitha Conference, she explains, is not so much Fred Buckles's dismissal—"Indian or not, Fred was incompetent as an administrator"—but rather the more general question of "lay Indian control." It is an issue that needs to be resolved, she declares (Archambault, August 5, 1992).

The Ohlone priest Michael Galvan agrees that the organization is undergoing difficulty; however, he locates the source of contention elsewhere. He has been given the assignment of conducting Conference business until a new executive director can be named, and for him the question of lay authority is a "mask" for deeper problems, primarily liturgical and psychological. All the Church agencies he belongs to—his parish in California, the Tekakwitha Conference, etc.—make decisions with substantial lay participation and even power. He is in favor of inclusive decision making and he says that most priests share that view. There is no major hiatus between Tekakwitha clergy and laity, he avers, and Fred Buckles was fired "for business reasons," nothing more.

Liturgy has been the bone of contention the last several years, Galvan says, not because of a basic disagreement over the course of inculturation, but rather because the Tekakwitha Conference is meant to be the medium through which the details get worked out. Galvan is not opposed to disagreement at the annual meetings over liturgical experimentation; indeed, he invites debate about inculturation because that is what the congress is for. "Misunderstandings" will occur. "Anger" will be expressed. The Conference will be a "target for complaints." All of these are part of the long and difficult process of establishing the most appropriate liturgical forms for American Indian Catholics.

Father Galvan theorizes about a "psychological dimension" to the anger he has witnessed in the recent past. No group of Americans feels "completely at home" with the Church, he says; but for Indians the Church has always been felt as a foreign force, prodding them to change their indigenous ways. They have often felt bullied by the Church, even as they have joined it. Today they continue to identify with their "ethnic folk community" and label all institutions beyond that community as "not them" and "the oppressor." Many Indian

Catholics regard the Tekakwitha Conference as an organization alien to themselves, even as it is intended as a vehicle for their will. Galvan doesn't see this situation as ironic. For him it makes sense that the Conference serve as a lightning rod for discontent, because the organization is designed as an instrument of change, and change is always a painful process. Through the Tekakwitha organization Indian Catholics will locate themselves within the Church, Galvan states, but they will not always appreciate the Conference along the way (Galvan, August 5, 1992).

As the Orono congress begins on the campus of the University of Maine, one can sense undertones of ill will. Even as the Native Catholics march beneath their parish and mission banners; even as the Knights of Columbus and Daughters of Isabella, both Indian and White, serve an enormous feast to two thousand guests on the Penobscot Reservation at Old Town; even as healing rituals, pipe ceremonies, sunrise services, and masked dances fill the need for spiritual expression; even during mass, there are continuing hints of hurt feelings and spite. Rumors circulate that the Native religious will bolt the proceedings. Rump caucuses withdraw from public view to plan strategy. A band of young California Indians spread rumors about Bishops Pelotte and Chaput's alleged disinterest in Native inculturation. The Association of Native Religious and Clergy (ANRC) hands out a mimeographed statement in support of Fred Buckles. The proceedings have become factionalized. Where the two roads meet, fear and loathing are on the rise.

Rev. James M. Dixon, S.J., observes the swelling sourness. Having conducted Native ministry for most of his career, he finds the situation sadly typical of tribal politics nationwide. The questions of "forgiveness and resentment" are being played out at the Tekakwitha congress, he says, just as they are on reservations rich and poor. The fact here, he says, is that Indian Catholics are a "church within a Church." They need to develop their spiritual autonomy to some degree, and develop their own forms of worship. But the Church also has authority, rules, and liturgical standards which need to be upheld. There will always be tension between these two impulses, and the Tekakwitha Conference is where the tensions need to be worked out. Like Father Galvan, Dixon does not expect an outpouring of appreciation here from Native Catholics, especially not in this year of the Columbian quincentenary (Dixon, August 7, 1992).

Considering the large sums of money contributed by the Bureau of Catholic Indian Missions to the Tekakwitha gathering, it is both paradoxical and predictable that its director, Msgr. Lenz, is one of the least, as well as most, appreciated mortals in attendance at Orono. He has attended every meeting since 1977 and he is widely recognized in Catholic Indian circles. Mark Thiel, an archivist at Marquette University and keeper of the BCIM historical records, remarks (Orono, August 5–8, 1992) that Lenz is known privately as a generous, kindhearted man who uses his wherewithal for the good of Catholic Indians and Blacks throughout the United States. (He also heads the Catholic Negro-American Mission Board and the Black and Indian Mission Office, formerly the Commission for Catholic Missions among the Colored People and the Indians.) Still, or maybe as a result, he is a target for animosity. Critics say that the BCIM is "his own little kingdom" which he conducts "like a ruler." One hears the accusation that he "runs a spoils system," distributing money to those who will kowtow to him and withholding support from those who deign to criticize him in public. He uses his assets, they say, to sway decisions of the Tekakwitha board, threatening to "withdraw his support" as a form of "blackmail" when things don't go his way. And he lets it be known that Native priests require his endorsement if they wish to become bishops (ibid.). Whether or not these accusations have any substance, they indicate the kind of resentment an influential, well-endowed, white priest elicits among Catholic Indians at a time of heightened tensions. For them, he represents the Church that is not theirs. When the monsignor and his entourage climb into his big white Cadillac following mass, you can hear a grumble from the crowd of onlookers (ibid., August 8, 1992).

In the various workshops the activity of the Conference continues. Don Yellow, a Lakota employed by the Office of Native Concerns in the Diocese of Rapid City, conducts a fruitful discussion regarding Native Catholic liturgy, where one hears a wide range of ideas about inculturation (Yellow, August 7, 1992). Father Hascall conducts a series of memorable sweats. Newcomers to the conference enjoy the comradeship of their fellow Native Americans. At the same time, a "showdown" (Walsh, October 31, 1992: 328) is brooding on the padres' trail, on the path of Kateri's kin.

The Southwest contingent, including the Savillas, has been calling for a public explanation of Fred Buckles's dismissal. Asserting that

"Saint Kateri has given us a new vision," and charging that the "hierar-chical, ecclesiastical structures no longer hear the people's concerns nor meet their needs," the ANRC has threatened to withdraw support for the Conference and form a new "National Native Catholic Confer-ence" (Orono, August 8, 1992), unless the board holds a public forum.

In order to establish a tenor of good will for the proceedings, Bur-ton Pretty-on-Top arranges a collection of eagle feather "sacramentals" (Bastien, August 13, 1992) in the university hockey stadium. He also provides a relic of Kateri; anyone who wishes to hold forth must clasp the relic, and therefore speak words of truth and love.

Neither the board nor Buckles, who is in the audience, is able to dis-cuss his sacking in any detail, because he is threatening a lawsuit against the Tekakwitha Conference. Consequently, several hours of speechmak-ing before an impassive audience of hundreds focus on more general concerns regarding Native inculturation and lay leadership. It is diffi-cult to hear as the words echo around the rink; however, it is clear that the Southwest caucus has grown impatient with the abstract issues. Its members turn to more inflammatory rhetoric, calling the board mem-bers "liars" and calling for "no more lies" (Orono, August 8, 1992). At least one person demands the board's resignation. Finally Fred Buckles gets his say, depicting himself as an innocent sufferer of biblical propor-tions. His lawyer has advised him not to discuss his firing; however, he announces that God has spoken to him and justified him in his indigna-tion. In the end he accuses the Tekakwitha board of malfeasance, to some applause.

As he speaks, hundreds of participants are entering the arena for a solemn high mass, the liturgical centerpiece of the conference. They are dressed in buckskins, beads, feathers, ribbons, all the finery of their In-dianness. They are visibly unsettled by the scene before them. Follow-ing Buckles's remarks, members of the board get up to speak. Pretty-on-Top gathers up his ineffective, profaned paraphernalia and quits the Conference. "I've done the best I can," he maintains. Later he says he feels he has been "crucified by my own people" (in Walsh, October 31, 1992: 329), but withdraws his resignation. Eva Solomon utters, "We are killing ourselves" (Orono, August 8, 1992), as she and Vivian Juan weep openly. Deacon Merlin Williams resigns; so does a non-Indian ordinary who explains, "Bishops are supposed to be agents of unity." Bishop Pelotte can barely contain his anger. "I've never heard such vilification," he declares, and warns that he will never again tolerate such a destructive meeting. He is scheduled to be chief celebrant at mass but it takes the cajoling of a fellow bishop, John Kinney of North Dakota, to turn him toward his task. He leaves the stadium to don his vestments.

Now the facility is filled with conferees seeking liturgical uplift, and it feels to them like a battleground. The congregants hear that the Conference is at a point of dissolving and many are dismayed. Some of them approach board members, begging them not to disband. "We need you," one Ojibway Indian says to a white bishop. Others call out for Bishop Pelotte to say mass and offer him their applause. Then Vivian Juan controls her tears and announces that the procession of co-celebrants is already on its way into the arena; there can be no more disputation. The parish priest from Old Town calls upon the assembled to cleanse themselves of ire, greet strangers with Christian affection, and prepare for mass.

Within minutes the liturgy has begun. Acolytes bless the crowd with feathers and smoke. Eagle dancers and drummers parade in, followed by dozens of clerics in their robes. When Bishop Pelotte enters, the audience cheers him with its greeting. Before celebrating the mass, Pelotte delivers a brief homily about the Eucharist, a symbol for unity and "brokenness . . . in the life of Jesus and in our own lives" (in Bastien, August 13, 1992). He hopes that the core sacrament of Catholicism will be a source of strength in this time of brokenness.

Neither Burton Pretty-on-Top's eagle feathers nor Kateri's relic have proven sufficient to maintain harmony. The Eucharist's powers are also tested, as one of Bishop Pelotte's most churlish young defamers slouches and smirks in front of the altar throughout the mass, waving his eagle feather as a means of defiance and distraction. When it is time to distribute communion, however, it is obvious that the longest line of devotees is waiting to receive the body and blood of Christ from the bishop. Many of them offer him exclamations of endearment and encouragement.

AFTERMATH

As the meeting comes to a close, Indians are offering their assessments of predictions. Chet Eagleman, Crow urban activist, remarks that he is unconcerned about the "growing pains" (Eagleman, August 9, 1992) of the Conference. He has seen grass-roots organizations undergo turmoil before; it is in the nature of such dynamic, democratic institutions to engender public disagreement. He is confident that the annual congress will continue, for the needs are too great for it to disappear. He himself will work with Tekakwitha to develop a more active urban ministry to Native Americans. Harold Condon is certain that board members who "quit" (Condon, August 9, 1992) will return, at least to plan for the future. He expects reforms to occur, as a result of the Orono brouhaha.

Rev. C. P. Jordan is less sanguine about the organization and its troubles. He prefers his Sioux Catholic Congresses back in the Dakotas; based on his Orono experience, he finds the conference only "passable, liturgically and socially." And politically? He comments, ruefully, "Politics in a religious organization poisons the whole being. I learned that in the old country, as the German priests used to say" (Jordan, August 8, 1992).

Several Passamaquoddy women who attended the Orono gathering express dismay at the meanspiritedness they witnessed. Joan Dana thinks of the Tekakwitha Conference as part of her spiritual network. Having participated in eight straight annual convocations, she states that the Conference "touches me very deeply, just to know how much work Indian people are doing to help one another." She was involved in the planning for Orono and feels close to those who put the congress together. With this degree of investment, she says, "it hurts a lot" to see the public fighting that took place this time (Dana, August 23, 1992). Joan Paul is dismayed by the Orono fracas. It reminds her too much of factional disputes on her own reservation—"It happens here, too"—but she hopes that the conference will continue (Paul, August 21, 1992). M. Grace Roderick is less concerned by the infighting than she is impatient about Kateri's canonization. "Why is it taking so long to make her a saint," she queries, "when we have already experienced miracles enough?" (Roderick, August 21, 1992).

In his *Bureau of Catholic Indian Missions Newsletter* (11, no. 7, September 1992), Msgr. Lenz states his determination not to allow a "very small group" of discontents, making "false accusations" and "maligning the duly elected members of the Board," to bring the Conference to a close. He reminds his readers that "the Bureau of Catholic Indian Missions has been very supportive of the Conference," and he asks Indian Catholics to communicate their concerns directly to the Tekakwitha board.

In an interview (Lenz, November 19, 1993) the monsignor seeks to set the record straight on several fronts. First, he insists that Father Gilbert Hemauer paid back all the money ($39,000) he had used from the Tekakwitha stockpile in order to start up his Pathways for Peace. There was surely no financial malfeasance on Hemauer's part, nor on the part of any Conference board member. More important, Lenz reassures Tekakwitha critics that the Conference is still committed to dialogue and inculturation, as well as to lay Indian decision making. The BCIM director regrets the acrimony aimed at himself by the Savillas and their cohorts. He suggests that Joseph Savilla became bitter when he was not reelected to the Tekakwitha board, and has blamed Lenz for it. Lenz has tried to mollify him, saying, "Why don't you be one with us?" but his words have had no effect. In the meantime, Lenz adds, the new bishop of Santa Fe has "got rid of" the Savillas from their Native Ministries post. Of course they are still welcome at Tekakwitha gatherings, and Lenz hopes that the anger aroused in Orono will subside at future meetings. He is confident that "the 'never come back' feelings" will be overcome in time.

Seattle, Swinomish, Lummi, August 4–8, 1993: Some funding sources have withheld support for the Tekakwitha Conference, on the heels of the Orono disruptions. Msgr. Lenz's Bureau is bankrolling this year's meeting, even though he and Bishop Pelotte preferred not to assemble this year. Lenz feels that last year the board members looked like "dunces," unable to speak their minds due to their lawyers' sanctions. Vivian Juan convinced the board that the annual congress should take place; however, the monsignor says bluntly that he will not finance future meetings if they are to be plied to tear down the Church.

This year the board has arranged the agenda so as to avoid public occasions for confrontation. There are no regional caucuses, few workshops, and no open forums. In this way, Lenz declares, the organizers aim to keep the conference "quiet" (Lenz, August 7, 1993). Bishop Pelotte adds that the board has made certain to keep microphones out of the hands of the "disgruntleds. That's how you keep control, by controlling the mike," he states (Pelotte, August 6, 1993).

The conferees notice the "calm" this year, at least contrasted with last year's open animus. The Mohawk Elaine Cook recalls that in Orono "people would walk past you in the halls and not say hello." This year most of the dissidents have stayed away—Fathers John Hascall, Ed Savilla, etc.—and the ambiance is friendlier (Cook, August 7, 1993). Rev. Paul Ojibway is not sure that the calm and smaller numbers are good omens for the Conference. He says that people seem "depressed," reticent to speak their feelings; and he wonders what future relevancy the organization has, to urban Indians and to youths, if it appeals primarily to "old ladies from the reservations" (Ojibway, August 6, 1993).

Msgr. Lenz is "extremely uplifted" by what he sees this year. "Our unity," he says, "will lead to more influence among the American bishops" and win back financial backers (Lenz, August 7, 1993). He points out an Indian man from California who is attending his first Tekakwitha congress because he wants it to be know that "one or two troublemakers" don't represent the Indians of his region. Vivian Juan and other speakers who control the microphones acclaim the revivification of the Conference.

The Indians of the Puget Sound display their hospitality to the thousand or so Tekakwitha congregants. At Swinomish, Native singers perform traditional spirit power songs; at Lummi, costumed dancers welcome the visitors with a lively exhibition in honor of Indian war veterans. At St. James Cathedral in Seattle, the region's Native Americans form an impressive choir at mass to chant their sacred indigenous melodies.

The cathedral liturgy blends Native and Catholic rites; however, not to the satisfaction of many congregants. In a vigorous discussion afterward, one Indian woman complains that the liturgy had "no Indian content." It was "too highly clerical, . . . too Roman." Another woman declares of the Conference's efforts at inculturation, "We're going backwards. Several years ago we had far more Indian content to liturgy; now it is disappearing and the priests are taking over again." A third woman says that she felt honored that so many priests were present to co-celebrate mass. To which a fourth woman replies that she used to feel that way but she is tired of the male, priestly dominance in liturgy. "We are all the Church," she attests. A Pueblo woman from New Mexico comments that Archbishop Sanchez always lets the Indians "take over" the services in his cathedral. She invites the discussants to attend the Santa Fe Indian Mass in several weeks.

Vivian Juan speaks in defense of the cathedral mass, explaining that it was planned by the local Indians as an expression of their cultural heritage and offered as a gift to Catholic Indians from across America. Two male respondents are unimpressed, noting that the Indian content was limited to the "periphery" of the ritual—the entrance and exit processions, the regalia, the hymnody—whereas the "core" of the mass, the Eucharist, remained purely Roman. One of the male critics is the Californian who came to Seattle to show his support for the Conference. The other is Joseph Savilla.

Joseph and Peggy Savilla still hope to reform the Conference; at the same time they intimate the possibility of a new movement of Native American Catholics, clear of white and clerical control. The Savillas have already resigned their position as liaisons to the Indian population around Santa Fe, in order, Joseph says (Savilla, August 6, 1993), to have the freedom to speak candidly nationwide without fear of "embarrassing the chancery." In Seattle Joseph vocalizes his discouragement and spleen. "The Tekakwitha Conference was a good, spiritual movement," he vents to Vivian Juan and other board members, "but now you guys are tearing it apart." He reserves his strongest outrage for Msgr. Lenz, whom he claims to have "blackballed" him. "Monsignor Lenz says, 'Joe's a troublemaker; he's part of the disgruntled group,' just because we won't kiss his you-know-what." Savilla concludes his tirade by exhorting the board to "listen to your people" (Seattle, August 7, 1993).

Vivian Juan replies that the Tekakwitha board deserves more respect. "I feel we are moving forward," she says, "we can't stay at the same place." Savilla and the board are at an impasse with little opportunity for reconciliation in sight. At the conference-closing powwow, Msgr. Lenz appears fed up with Joseph Savilla, saying, "I hear he took my name in vain today" (Lenz, August 7, 1993). Savilla later reports (Savilla, August 7, 1993) that the monsignor "cornered" him and accused him of "ruining" the conference once again.

The Tekakwitha Conference possesses significance beyond any personal tiff between Paul Lenz and Joseph Savilla, although their dispute symbolizes important tensions within the organization's structure, constituency, and goals. Bishop Pelotte perceives correctly (Pelotte, August 6, 1993) that the Conference is greater than any set of individuals who attend its meetings or set its agenda, and that the Conference is less important to American Indian Catholics than the greater issue of contemporary inculturation.

The process of inculturation, he states, is the most "frightening and exciting" prospect for him as a Native Catholic bishop, and for Indian Catholics in general. The Vatican II goals regarding cultural autonomy are lofty but dangerous, because to make Christianity at home in every culture is to examine every facet of every culture, to determine compatibility with the Catholic faith. Who controls that process? he asks, who makes the decisions? There are so many sensibilities—of Catholics, of Natives—that have to be addressed, in order to resolve which aspects of culture are appropriate and which to be excluded.

It was among the African Masai, "nomadic, in first evangelization," that Pelotte really faced a people following Jesus, but according to their own cultural meanings. This was a real problem of inculturation, he declares. Pelotte learned in Kenya to be "not uncomfortable with unanswered questions," like what should be done with Masai polygamy, which was not going away in any hurry. Pelotte decided, "I'm not going to be the one who decides" exactly how they must live as Masai Christians. There has to be "ongoing dialogue," he figured, "with necessary tensions." Inculturation, he discovered, is a long, thorny, problematic road to travel.

Here at the Tekakwitha congresses we are not accomplishing inculturation in any profound sense, the bishop acknowledges. That must be done in home communities with tremendous care. At the annual conference "the stuff we do is baby stuff," having only to do with liturgical expressions. But even with these ritual accommodations "we need to be patient." We cannot offend particular tribal customs or usurp the prerogatives of community authority. We also have to respect Catholic as well as tribal ways, Pelotte declares; there is propriety to recognize on both sides of the Catholic Indian road. He reflects upon those who disrupted the Orono conference, those who were bent upon defiling the mass and desecrating Burton Pretty-on-Top's circle of peace. He cannot help but think that they were "evil personified," profoundly disrespectful of both Catholic and Native spirituality. Pelotte concludes that the Conference has a long set of tasks ahead of it: "to instill good catechesis, good ecclesiology, good inculturation." It must also mend the hurts of its own making.

The Tekakwitha Conference continues to hold annual meetings of Catholic Indians, in Minnesota, New York, New Mexico, and Wisconsin. The banners of Indian communities continue to drape the university arenas which serve as congress settings: Blessed Kateri Tekakwitha Parish, in Tucson, Arizona; St. Michael's Tekakwitha Circle, Pechanga Reservation, Temecula, California; Congregation of the Great Spirit, Milwaukee, Wisconsin; Isleta Pueblo, St. Augustine, New Mexico; St. Paul's Church, Swinomish, Washington; Our Lady of the Snows, Prairie Band Potawatomi Tribe, Mayetta, Kansas; St. Anthony Parish, O'odham Nation, Arizona; St. Augustine's Mission, Winnebago & Omaha Tribes, Nebraska; St. Mary's Mission, Red Lake, Minnesota; the list goes on, a panorama of Indian Catholic geography (Potsdam, August 2–6, 1995). The number of participants has leveled at about a thousand, a figure considerably lower than in the days before Orono.

The conference agenda (*Tekakwitha Conference Newsletter,* 16, no. 2, June–July 1997: 1) still focuses attention on inculturation, deacon formation, ecumenism, liturgy, urban ministry, intertribal sharing, special needs of youths, storytelling and scripture, Native language choirs and hymns, family values, powwows, and Marian devotions, as well as treating the wounds caused by boarding schools, and contemplating the relation of Indians to indigenous peoples worldwide.

The board of directors includes lay and clerical Native Americans, some old, some new, from diverse tribes, as well as the ubiquitous Msgr. Lenz. They are still sensitive to criticism—about the agendas they have arranged, their personal finances, their tribal politics and spiritual leanings—but they carry on the Tekakwitha mission with dedicated zeal. "We are all healing," says board member Gerald Tuckwin, a Potawatomi from Kansas (Potsdam, August 5, 1995). Other Tekakwitha officials admit that the Conference still has not recovered from the Orono schism. "It was like a drunken family brawl," observes Sister Marie Therese Archambault (ibid.)

Like all internecine skirmishes, Orono has left inner scars—one more layer of wounded tissue on the thin skins and damaged psyches of American Indian Catholics. The Tekakwitha Conference is meant to be a balm; at times it has been an abrasive. Ironically, the Conference has tempered its ardor for healing services, leaving some conferees burning for the kind of emotional charisms once provided by Father Hascall. Deacon Tony MacDonald, a Sioux from Devil's Lake Reservation, North Dakota, wants the annual meetings to place "more emphasis on healing, more spirituality, more prayer" (ibid.).

In 1992 the Ojibway Joan Staples-Baum declared that ten years of attending the Tekakwitha meetings had healed a great wound in her. "Now I can be proud of who I am as an Indian and as a Catholic" (in Walsh, August 9, 1992). Sister Archambault says now that there is "so much grief" (Potsdam, August 5, 1995) among her people, including the sorrows of Tekakwitha conclaves past, that the Conference has much mending still to do.

POSTSCRIPT: TWO MEN, MEETING

Through three volumes we have observed the history of relations between North American Indians and Roman Catholics, a record spanning five hundred years and comprehending millions of men and women. In the Native American homelands which became French, Spanish, and American domains; through invasion, warfare, trade, disease, intermarriage, evangelism, syncretism, resistance, conversion; in reductions and reservations, cities and countrysides; across the centuries, we have witnessed the complex, diverse unfolding of American Indian Catholicism.

Although we have fixed our attention primarily on the Native Americans influenced by Catholicism, we have tried not to ignore the motives and methods of the Church's Euroamerican evangelists. Often, however, we have viewed them—as in the Navajo pictorial weaving of a priest flanked by traditional deities (*On the Padres' Trail*, cover)—through the eyes of Indians. At the same time, our reliance on historical records of non-Indian origin, at least until recent decades, has necessitated our seeing Indian Catholics from the perspectives of others. Witness, for instance, the earliest known painting of Kateri Tekakwitha, attributed to Rev. Claude Chauchetière, S.J. (*The Paths of Kateri's Kin*, cover). The Navajo weaver's depiction of the priest and the French Jesuit's portrayal of Kateri both color their subjects with their own cultural cast.

Whenever possible, however, I have tried to employ the testimony of missionaries and Indians about themselves, allowing them the latitude to define themselves in their own words. The heft of these three tomes has been due, in part, to my unwillingness to leave out any professions of faith I had gathered from Indians and Whites alike. The reader, thus, has the opportunity to hear diverse voices, speaking firsthand of their experiences.

Throughout the three volumes there has also been sufficient occasion for more objective, distanced discernment. As with the photograph on the cover of this book, we often have surveyed the vivid scene of Natives and Catholics, meeting. Where the two traditions have met, in person, there has sometimes been confrontation, sometimes dialogue, sometimes silence, but always effect.

It is my design to conclude the series with portraits of two contemporary men who know each other well: one a priest engaged in fulltime ministry to Native Americans in California, the other a Hoopa Indian on his spiritual journey. Neither Rev. Ralph John Monteiro, O.S.A., nor Hilton Hostler is meant in these sketches to be typical (and certainly not stereotypical); however, together they present a probing picture of American Indian Catholics in relation to the Church.

In 1988 the president of the National Tekakwitha Conference, the Ojibway priest John Hascall, characterized contemporary Indians' "levels of participation" in Catholic and Native ways:

> Traditionalists only—no participation in Catholic Way.
> Traditionalists who participate at functions here and there.
> Traditionalists who fully live the Catholic/Native Way.
> Christian peoples who fully live the Catholic/Native Way.
> Christian peoples who participate at functions here and there.
> Christian peoples who reject the Traditional Way.
> Those who gave up everything Christian or Native.
> Those who have left the Catholic Church and joined another
>   Christian sect. (In *Tekakwitha Conference Newsletter,* 7, no. 4,
>   1988: 13; cf. Kinlicheeny, December 1972: 45)

Father Hascall provided a thumbnail geographical survey of Catholic Indians in the United States: from the Northeast and Southwest, where there is a deep history of Catholicism, combined or compartmentalized with traditional religion; through the North and Northwest, where the influence of Catholicism is only a century or so long and where Indian medicine ways are still strong; in the Southeast, where the degree of Catholic-Indian contact is still small; to the West Coast, that is, the state of California, where the pious remnants of the Mission Indians contrast with the multitudes of largely unchurched urban Native Americans in the Los Angeles area.

Hascall concluded his overview with a reference to the Hoopa Indians of northernmost California, who have received only desultory missionizing over the years and among whom Catholicism has never taken hold. Occupying a twelve-mile square reservation (established in 1864 following the violently invasive gold rush, only a small portion of their aboriginal holdings) in a mountainous valley within the Diocese of Santa Rosa, the four thousand Hoopas have maintained their tribal ritualism while trying on the garb of several Christian denominations. In the 1940s several Catholic women, including the Papago Lucille Sanderson, moved to the Hoopa Valley Reservation and introduced the Roman faith. A priest built a church on the reservation in the 1950s and visited intermittently; however, in 1979 there were only 160 Catholic Indians living in the area (Beaver 1979: 157), few of them full-blood Hoopas.

In the 1980s the bishop of Santa Rosa, Mark J. Hurley, wished to initiate a more active Native ministry in his diocese to the more populous Pomos (several thousand of whom had Catholic ties) as well as to the Hoopas. Among the latter he found particular resistance. "It is of course questionable whether they can ever disassociate themselves from the cruelty of the white settlers," he wrote (DCRAA, January 14, 1985); therefore, he brought in a priest from India, "from, of course, another culture. They are really pleased." The priest was recalled home almost immediately, to everyone's dismay; however, Bishop Hurley was determined to develop religious education among the Hoopas and to integrate them into the life of the Church. He hired Rev. Ralph John Monteiro, an Augustinian of Portuguese descent from New York City with strong credentials of commitment to civil rights and ethnic diversity.

Monteiro's was the first full-time clerical ministry to Native peoples in the diocese. When he arrived on the reservation in 1986, he found a Hoopa population which he describes as "anti-Catholic." Some of them had been "begging for a priest," but "they didn't know what to do with me," since the vast majority of them had "never been Catholic" (Monteiro, September 1, 1992).

Among the more catholicized Pomos to the south, whose experiences had embittered them toward the Church, he received a vituperative greeting. One woman yelled at him about beatings her parents and grandparents had gotten in their youth from priests and nuns. He felt offended, but he suspected that the charges were true. He asked what he could do to make up for these hurts. The woman said, "Nothing. I'll watch you" (Monteiro, November 19, 1992). A year later she apologized publicly for blaming him for the actions of others. He has maintained cordial relations with the Pomos ever since, visiting them at their far-flung "rancherias" and offering Catholic services (Monteiro 1990–1992).

To the north of Hoopa two small Native American communities were involved in a dispute with the United States government over the construction of a wilderness road through their off-reservation prayer grounds. Father Monteiro became immediately involved as an advocate for the Indians, hoping in part that his supportive stance would be a "healing presence" (Monteiro, November 18, 1992), a symbol of fence-mending between the diocese and disaffected Native Americans. He was surprised that the Hoopas had no interest in their Indian neighbors' cause, even though they possessed sacred sites which were similarly threatened by developers. He found among the Hoopas a very "provincial" view of the world, a "tribal" consciousness which cared little for people beyond their kin group. "They're only a hundred years out of the Stone Age," Monteiro avers; "that's not a condemnation but a fact, pure and simple" (Monteiro, November 19, 1992).

Father Monteiro lives on the Hoopa reservation. The Church of Blessed Kateri Tekakwitha, of which he is pastor, is also on the reservation. It is the only Catholic church in a fifty-mile radius, and so he also ministers to non-Indian Catholics in the area. Nonetheless, his main task is to serve as Liaison for Native American Affairs for the Diocese of Santa Rosa. He describes his ministry as "unique, distinct. I'm not welcome unless the Indians need me. I don't work unless I'm asked" (Monteiro, September 1, 1992).

For the most part the Hoopa Indians keep him at a distance. They resisted his attempts to learn their language. They objected to Monteiro's attempt to purchase an acre of land next to the church in order to construct a CCD hall. They do not especially like the visitations of Whites to weekly masses. Lucille Sanderson's offspring—the Papago woman married a string of three Hoopa men—constitute almost the whole of Monteiro's Indian community at church. He does not seek conversions among the Hoopas, and although he attends public meetings on the reservation and "speaks my mind" (Monteiro, November 19, 1992), he tries to stay out of the tribe's business.

Monteiro tells of a priest he knows who worked on an Indian reservation for thirty years. When the cleric asked to be buried there, the Indians said no. Monteiro wondered of his friend, "Didn't he know that he didn't belong there? I've been a priest for twenty-six years; I've been here for seven years and I feel as if I were just starting" (ibid.). Monteiro reminds himself daily that he is a white man who will always be an outsider to the Hoopas. In his first years among them he would decide three times a day to quit. Now he thinks he has committed himself to live the rest of his life here, except when he realizes how "bored" he becomes, waiting for the Hoopas to proffer invitations that rarely come. He is not going to force his ministry on unwilling Native Americans; he is not going to reenact the aggressive missionizing of an earlier epoch. As a result, he is in little demand and his hopes for healing in the Indian community still lie in the future.

Ministering to Catholic Indians has its "emotional ups and downs," Monteiro says (November 18, 1992). One Native family tried to run him over in their car following a funeral which dissatisfied them. Some have thrown things at him, or scolded him, or snubbed him as if didn't exist. Even the Sanderson clan has been a trial for him. "I've been through hell with that family," he states (November 19, 1992), characterizing them as "dysfunctional" in their patterns of drinking, bearing children out of wedlock, divorcing, and feuding. "They tormented me" at first, he declares, although he has come to terms with them, and they with him. Before her death in 1993 Lucille Sanderson served as liturgical leader at the Tekakwitha church services, guiding Whites as well as Indians in prayer. Her family members became mainstays in the pews, and when Monteiro "cured" her grandson of a life-threatening infection in his foot—by touching it to a picture of Kateri Tekakwitha—a special bond was cemented between the family and the priest.

The pastor wishes that his ties to the Hoopa community were stronger. He admits that Sister Pat Carson, R.S.M., who performs the social services for the parish at Hoopa, has greater rapport than he with the Indians. She counsels many people; she has contacts beyond the small Catholic circle; she is not hedged by a clerical role. "By my position I am their elder," he says (ibid.), and he takes seriously his duty to engage in "fraternal correction" among the congregation when he sees fit. "I'm in charge" of the parish, he asserts, "and I'm not fooled by their Indian games. They say, 'We're Indians. We don't plan. We don't lead.'" Monteiro prods them toward greater responsibility as a matter of "human development." He has goaded the Indians to contribute money to the homeless, building their self-esteem by realizing that there are people worse off economically than they are. He has coaxed them to think seriously about the dangers of AIDS on the reservation. He has also formed numerous parish committees and trained Indians to play a role in Catholic ceremony. In general, however, he has had to "adjust—that is, lower" his expectations for Native initiative, in the realms of social awareness, ecclesiastical autonomy, and liturgical vitality. "They haven't learned to lead yet," he avers. Nor has he ceded his authority among them.

To encourage greater liturgical experimentation and enhanced catechesis among his flock, Monteiro sponsors attendance at National Tekakwitha Conference gatherings. Several Hoopas have gone to these meetings and returned enthused about the Tekakwitha program. At home he performs a novena each year in honor of Kateri, leading up to her feast day celebration. Indians identify with the Lily of the Mohawks, and they look forward impatiently to her elevation by the Church. The priest thinks that the pope "blew it" (ibid.) by not canonizing Kateri in Phoenix, or at least in time for the Columbian quincentenary conference in Orono. Monteiro fears that there is not enough money behind her cause, and that Msgr. Paul Lenz is the only powerful non-Indian cleric in the United States lobbying the Vatican effectively for her sainthood. Nonetheless, Monteiro continues to urge devotions to Kateri as an aspect of Hoopa inculturation.

Father Monteiro refers to himself as "charismatic" (ibid.); he brings to his Native ministry the notion that "genuine spirituality is genuine, wherever it is." He has served so many types of communities—youths, the aged, Blacks, gays, the urban and rural poor, etc.—and he has gone through so many movements in the Church, he says, that he views spirituality as a single human activity that takes many forms. "It's me and God," he avows, "that's spirituality." His task as pastor is to make spirituality possible. Hence, he is "open to the spirit" of Indian dances, the twelve-step program of Alcoholics Anonymous, the Eucharist—whatever will engage his congregation's spiritual instincts.

If it were not for a priest, he says, no Catholic life would take place among the Indians of Santa Rosa diocese. Indeed, there would be far less Native spirituality, because he expresses and encourages it. The Hoopas have always kept up their semiannual White Deerskin and Jump Dances (for renewal, healing, fertility, and thanksgiving); Monteiro has sponsored sweats (conducted by John Hascall) and other Native prayer services. He himself seems truly influenced by Indian spirituality. He prays to the four directions at mass; he smudges with sage. His church, his home, his car are all decorated with Indian-style amulets. Wherever he goes in Indian Country he beseeches local spirits for protection. He attempts to have Indians experience the Christian liturgical year "as Indians": Children dress in Indian regalia at Christmas pageants; an Indian infant plays the role of Jesus; the wise men come dressed as Native dancers, etc. He refers to the "Creator" rather than "God the Father" when addressing an Indian audience in prayer. "I'm not trying to play Indian," Monteiro says (ibid.); instead, he is replicating the gestures he has learned at Tekakwitha congresses and from visiting Indian liturgists like Father Hascall. "I imitate him," Monteiro states; "if he can do them, so can I."

It is not clear that the Indians appreciate his attempt to appropriate Native spirituality. Some tell him that the four directions constitute a power that is dangerous to evoke. He replies, holding up the Eucharist, that "no power is stronger than the power I'm holding in my hand" (ibid.). Some complain about his smudging; he tells them that the practice is just like the Catholic use of incense. His fellow churchmen do not criticize his liturgies; indeed, he has received nothing but support from his bishops. However, the Indians are "held back" by "old-fashioned" notions of ritual. "They're into the rosary but they don't know what the sacraments are." They do not think that they can integrate traditional and Catholic liturgies. They have a passive attitude toward liturgical participation, especially the women, who are used to being observers rather than actors at Hoopa dances. Monteiro acknowledges that he used to get as many as thirty congregants for daily liturgies but now almost no one comes. He does not understand why and no one will tell him what, if anything, he is doing wrong.

Despite discouragements Father Monteiro remains hopeful in his vocation. There are not many in the Church, he says, who will serve the needs of Indians today. Native ministry "is drying up because people are not spiritual enough," and because "too many of us treat others as *them*." In Christianity, he avows, "there is no *them*" (ibid.).

One of Monteiro's Hoopa parishioners is Hilton Hostler, dwelling an hour from the reservation in a coastal city with his white wife, Jackie, and their two teenage children. He also has two grown children from a previous marriage who live nearby. Hostler is a student at Humboldt State College, who possesses an inquiring mind and a "great potential for leadership" in his community (ibid.). His pastor sponsored Hostler's attendance at Tekakwitha assemblies and expresses "tremendous frustration" at his leaving the reservation, just when his "charisma" might have had salutary effect among his landsmen.

Hostler describes himself as a "recovering alcoholic" (Hostler, November 19, 1992) who hasn't taken liquor or drugs since 1985. His reclamation from alcoholism was part of the same process that brought him spiritual renewal and conversion to Catholicism. Baptized Presbyterian as an infant, he says, "I don't consider myself a Christian. I consider myself as a spiritual person on a spiritual journey." He is enrolled in a college course about world religions; his reading of books such as Huston Smith's *The Religions of Man* (1958) leads him to declare that "everyone prays to one God, one higher power, only by different names." Like Father Monteiro he is more committed to "spirituality" than to any of its particular manifestations.

As a youth on the Hoopa reservation, Hostler had little Presbyterian training. He hated going to church, preferring to stay home and watch football on television. Christianity had a bad name among the Hoopas then because missionaries had forced children into boarding schools and a military regimen at home. Christian agents had tried to quash traditional Hoopa religious practices and discredit dance leaders. What little Protestant culture he gained was imbued with "anti-Catholic" imputations: Catholics pray to statues; they worship Mary; they encourage you to sin because you can always go to a priest and confess, and so forth. He heard these remarks but was always curious about Catholicism, though only from a distance.

He describes his Hoopa upbringing as "a matter of survival, with no affection." His parents were divorced. He lived with his father, who gave him little advice, except to be tough in the face of white racism. As he reads Colin Turnbull's anthropological account in *The Mountain People* (1972) of the Ik tribe of Africa—a hunting people dispossessed, forced onto a reservation, where their societal bonds fell apart and they turned violent upon one another—Hostler recognizes his own kinfolk's cultural predicament. "Our affection was with the land," Hostler remarks, "not with one another."

He attended Hoopa rituals but never became an active participant in them. He never took part in a sweat lodge ceremony. He did not learn Hoopa creation stories or legends about the origin of his people. He preferred softball to traditional lore. He hunted deer once, at the age of eighteen, but was disturbed by the tender eyes of his prey and could never again pick up a gun. His family moved back and forth between the city and Hoopa Valley.

In 1979 Hostler's brother was murdered. Within a year five relatives of his died. This spate of deaths precipitated a crisis, which was resolved only after years of anger and "dysfunction." His young white wife, who had come to Hoopa as a runaway from her stepmother (a "Cinderella situation"), was a baptized Catholic. Their two children received Catholic christening, and Hilton began to attend Sunday mass with his family. He was curious about the rite of communion; however, he remained an observer.

The Hostlers were living in the city, where his wife began to attend a Bible study course. When she came home "full of spirit," Hostler became "jealous" about the instructor, an Assemblies of God preacher. So, Hilton invited the class to meet at his home, where he could keep an eye on the proceedings. Soon he found himself scrutinizing the lessons. The minister emphasized the biblical book of *Revelation*, focusing on the end of the world. Hostler thought, "I don't want to hear about that. I don't want to be forced to religion by terror of the last days."

At the same time he found himself yearning for redemption from his immediate, earthly ills: his desire for vengeance; his use of drugs and alcohol. He wanted to forgive his brother's killer; he wanted to cure his own addiction. The only way to these ends, he thought, was to "accept the Lord as my savior"; therefore, he adopted the preacher as his "spiritual leader." Simultaneously he began to receive Catholic instruction. "I wanted, I craved, to be part of a Catholic family," he declares, and by 1985 he became a Catholic communicant. It was this "two-pronged movement," he assesses, a combination of Protestant and Catholic instruction, which began to heal his soul.

The Hostlers moved back to Hoopa Valley, where Hilton met Father Monteiro in 1986. The question still worrying the Indian was to what degree he could live his life as a renewed Christian and still attend his Native rituals on the reservation. The priest sponsored his attendance at the 1986 Tekakwitha congress in Bozeman, where he observed a pipe ceremony and watched other Indian Catholics combining Native and Catholic spirituality. "This brought it together for me," Hostler states, and he took a refreshed interest in his tribal religion.

When he got home from Bozeman, he asked his grandparents whom they pray to in their Hoopa rituals. They said, "'The one the white man calls God.'" They told him that the Great Spirit and God are the same; indeed, his grandfather suggested that the Jump Dance is performed at least partially "'in honor of Jesus.'" Hostler saw then that he did not have to give up attending the aboriginal ceremonies, unless the leaders of these rituals would exclude a committed Christian like himself, which they did not.

Hostler thinks his people's dances are wonderful. He observes them several times a year but he does not take an active part. "You only dance when your heart is right," he says, and even after years of abstinence from alcohol and drugs, he does not consider himself "worthy" enough to perform Hoopa rituals. You have to be "100 percent pure," he declares, because what you do in the ceremonies determines patterns in the community for the next two years. You are praying for all and the responsibility is enormous. It upsets him to see other Hoopas, users of drugs and alcohol, dancing just for show. "It's a mockery when it's not from the heart," he maintains.

He and his family go to Catholic mass each Sunday in town. His most consistent liturgical activity is prayer at home: before meals, joining hands, sharing a common spirituality. Hostler intimates that his children have grown accustomed to an atmosphere of prayer in the house, which has drawn them closer to him, "thanks to the Holy Spirit. . . . I thank God every morning for protecting my family." Sometimes Hostler prays with Father Monteiro, sometimes with the Assemblies of God minister, sometimes together with both.

Hostler would rather live on his reservation; however, he brought his family to town for better financial and educational opportunities. The adjustment has not been easy for him, leading to bouts with the blues. When the dark moods come, he finds it difficult to pray, but he finds that "prayer brings me back from depression." Father Monteiro misses his helpful presence at Tekakwitha Church but maintains a close relationship with him, counseling Hostler through his emotional struggles.

Hostler finds in Monteiro the "verbal" guidance generally missing in his indigenous religious tradition, for all its sacrality to him. He is thankful for the Bible, which offers him moral advisement along his spiritual journey. He is grateful for the mass and the other liturgies of the Church. Christianity offers him a means toward a life of forgiveness which he experiences as a godsend. "I'm more adapted to the Catholic ways right now, on a daily basis" he says, "than to my Native ways."

Still, Hostler is glad to have "two home bases—the Catholic Church and my own people"—where he can pray. He will not, *he need not,* choose one set of sacred ways over the other. As an American Indian Catholic he discerns two roads of spirituality available to him and appropriate to him. Sometimes, he says, these roads appear "parallel," separate but leading in the same direction. Sometimes they seem to "diverge," at least in their manifest forms. Sometimes, where his spirituality most deeply dwells, the two roads meet.

BIBLIOGRAPHY

ARCHIVAL SOURCES

Kansas City   Chancery Archives, Archdiocese of Kansas City in Kansas

Marquette   Department of Special Collections, Marquette University Memorial Library, Milwaukee, Wisconsin. Files include: BCIM (Bureau of Catholic Indian Missions); DCRAA (Diocesan Correspondence, Reports, and Applications for Aid); HRMR (Holy Rosary Mission Records); JINNAM (Jesuits in Native North American Ministry); SFMR (St. Francis Mission Records); TCA (Tekakwitha Conference Archives).

Notre Dame   The Archives of the University of Notre Dame, Notre Dame, Indiana

Ogdensburg   Chancery Archives, Diocese of Ogdensburg, New York

Santa Fe   Records Center, Archdiocese of Santa Fe, New Mexico

Santa Rosa   Office of the Diocesan Native American Liaison, Hoopa, Santa Rosa, California

St. Regis   St. Regis Church Archives, St. Regis, Quebec

Wisconsin   The State Historical Society of Wisconsin, Manuscripts, Madison, Wisconsin

REFERENCES

Abbott, (Rev.) Walter M., S.J., ed. 1966. *The Documents of Vatican II.* New York: Guild Press.

Alcoholics Anonymous, Inc. 1976. *Alcoholics Anonymous.* New York: Alcoholics Anonymous World Services, Inc. Original publication 1939.

Anawin Center. 1989. *Anawin Center News* (newsletter).

Angrosino, Michael V. 1994. "The Culture Concept and the Mission of the Roman Catholic Church." *American Anthropologist* 96, no. 4:824–832.

Anishinabe Spiritual Centre, Anderson Lake, Espanola, Ontario. October 12–14, 1990. Author's fieldnotes.

Archambault, (Sister) Marie Therese, O.S.F. August 5, 1989. Interview by author, Fargo, North Dakota.

———. 1991. "The Time for Turning Around." Unpublished manuscript in author's possession.

———. August 5, 1992. Interview by author, Orono, Maine.

——. 1995. "'Back to Back': Roman Catholicism among the Brule at St. Francis Mission, South Dakota." M.A. thesis, University of Colorado.

——. 1996. "Native Americans and Evangelism." In *Native and Christian: Indigenous Voices on Religious Identity in the United States and Canada,* ed. James Treat, 132–153. New York: Routledge.

——. June 14, 1997. Interview by author, Washington, D.C.

——. 1998. *A Retreat with Black Elk: Living in the Sacred Hoop.* Cincinnati: St. Anthony Messenger Press.

Archambault, (Sister) Marie Therese, O.S.F., and (Sister) Geraldine Clifford, O.S.F. August 7, 1993. Interview by author, Seattle, Washington.

Ballew, Jeff. August 9, 1986. Interview by author, Bozeman, Montana.

Bancroft, Dick. Autumn 1985. Personal communication with author.

Baraga, (Rev.) Frederic. 1831–1868. Correspondence, Notre Dame.

——. 1973. *A Dictionary of the Otchipwe Language, Explained in English.* Minneapolis: Ross & Haines. Original publication 1878.

Barry, Lawrence E. Post-1965. "The Trapping Season." Mimeograph, TCA, Marquette.

Bartholomew, Marianna. February 1990. "A Legacy of Faith." *Extension* 84:14–17.

——. September–October 1992. "Blue Thunder Walks the Good Road." *Extension* 87:8–17.

Bastien, Claire M. August 13, 1992. "Be Strong for Each Other." *Church World,* p. 7.

——. August 20, 1992. "Tekakwitha Conference." *Church World*, pp. 4–5.

Beaver, R. Pierce, ed. 1979. *The Native American Christian Community: A Directory of Indian, Aleut, and Eskimo Churches.* Monrovia, Calif.: Missions Advanced Research and Communication Center.

Berg, (Sister) Carol, O.S.B. 1981. "Climbing Learners' Hill: Benedictines at White Earth, 1878–1945." Ph.D. dissertation, University of Minnesota.

Berkemeier, Elizabeth. August 6, 1988. Interview by author, Pine Ridge, South Dakota.

Birmingham, Mary Louise. 1976. "Introduction: Native American Wisdom, Ritual, and Vision." *Cross Currents* 26, no. 4:129–131.

Black Bear, Ben, Jr. August 4, 1988. "Dialogue between Medicine Men and Priests." Two Roads Conference.

Black Elk, Charlotte. August 2, 1988. "Oral History and Traditional Religion." Two Roads Conference.

Black Elk, Wallace H., and William S. Lyon. 1990. *Black Elk: The Sacred Ways of a Lakota.* San Francisco: Harper & Row.

Blackbird, Andrew J. 1887. *History of the Ottawa and Chippewa Indians of Michigan, and Grammar of Their Language.* Ypsilanti, Mich.: Ypsilantian Job Printing House.

Boudreaux, Eva Pierre, and Joseph Norris Boudreaux. November 21, 1990. Interview by author, Grand Caillou, Louisiana.

Boudreaux, (Msgr.) Roland J. November 17–23, 1990. Interviews by author, Louisiana.

Bowden, Henry Warner. 1981. *American Indians and Christian Missions: Studies in Cultural Conflict.* Chicago: University of Chicago Press.

Boyer, Ron. August 11, 1986. Interview by author, Bozeman, Montana.

———. October 14, 1990. Interview by author, Anderson Lake, Espanola, Ontario.

Bozeman, Montana. August 6–10, 1986. Author's fieldnotes, Tekakwitha Conference.

Braden, Charles S. 1930. *Religious Aspects of the Conquest of Mexico.* Durham, N.C.: Duke University Press.

Brokenleg, Martin. August 3, 1988. "Use of the Lakota Language in the Missionary Process." Two Roads Conference.

Brown, (Rev.) John J. 1947–1948. Correspondence, Indian Affairs, Santa Fe.

Brown, Joseph Epes. 1953. *The Sacred Pipe.* Norman: University of Oklahoma Press.

Bryde, (Rev.) John F., S.J. 1949, 1951, 1953, n.d. Correspondence, HRMR, Marquette.

———. 1966. "The Sioux Indian Student: A Study of Scholastic Failure and Personality Conflict." HRMR, Marquette.

———. 1967. "Acculturational Psychology or Modern Indian Psychology." HRMR, Marquette.

Bucko, (Rev.) Raymond, S.J. September 29, 1991. Interview by author, Madison, New York.

———. 1992. "*Inipi:* Historical Transformation and Contemporary Significance of the Sweat Lodge in Lakota Religious Practice." Ph.D. dissertation, University of Chicago.

Buechel, (Rev.) Eugene, S.J. 1917. "A Retreat for Our Indian Children." HRMR, Marquette.

Bull Bear, Leona. August 4, 1988. Interview by author, Pine Ridge, South Dakota.

Bunoz, (Most Rev.) E. M. 1942. "Bishop Durieu's System." *Études Oblates* 1, no. 4:193–209.

Bureau of Catholic Indian Missions Newsletter. 1981–1998.

Burkhart, Louise M. 1989. *The Slippery Earth: Nahua-Christian Moral Dialogue in Sixteenth-Century Mexico.* Tucson: University of Arizona Press.

———. 1996. *Holy Wednesday: A Nahua Drama from Early Colonial Mexico.* Philadelphia: University of Pennsylvania Press.

Burns, John F. September 20, 1987. "For Arctic Indians, a Papal Promise." *New York Times,* p. 30.

———. September 21, 1987. "Pope Ends Trip at Mass beneath Arctic Rainbow." *New York Times,* p. B12.

Burns, (Rev.) Robert Ignatius, S.J. 1988. "Roman Catholic Missions in the Northwest." In *Handbook of North American Indians,* vol. 4, *History of Indian-White Relations,* ed. Wilcomb E. Washburn, 494–500. Washington, D.C.: Smithsonian Institution.

Cadieux, Lorenzo, ed. 1973. *Lettres des Nouvelles Missions du Canada, 1843–1852.* Montreal: Les Éditions Bellarmin.

Cadot, (Rev.) J. C., S.J. 1920. "Bruce County and Work among the Indians." *Ontario Historical Society Papers and Records* 18:22.

Campion, Owen F. October 8, 1989. "Alaska: 'The Church in The Great Land.'" *Our Sunday Visitor,* pp. 6–7.

Carson, Mary Eisenman. 1989. *Blackrobe for the Yankton Sioux: Fr. Sylvester Eisenman, O.S.B., 1891–1948.* Chamberlain, S.D.: Tipi Press.

Catholic Sioux Congress. 1920–1988. Minutes, HRMR, Marquette.

Cavagnaro, (Rev.) Camillus, O.F.M. August 3–6, 1988. Interviews by author, Pine Ridge, South Dakota.

Chaput, (Most Rev.) Charles, O.F.M. Cap. 1988. "The Church's Teachings on Inculturation." *Tekakwitha Conference Newsletter* 8, no. 2:6–7.

———. August 3, 1989. Interview by author, Fargo, North Dakota.

Chauchetière, (Rev.) Claude, S.J. 1887. *La Vie de la B. Catherine Tegakoüita Dite a Present la Saincte Sauvagesse.* Albany: Fils de Feu Joel Munsell.

Chittenden, Hiram Martin, and Alfred Talbot Richardson, eds. 1905. *Life, Letters and Travels of Father Pierre-Jean de Smet, S.J., 1801–1873.* 4 vols. New York: Francis P. Harper.

Clifford, (Sister) Geraldine, O.S.F. October 16, 1991. Telephone interview by author.

———. August 9, 1992. Interview by author, Orono, Maine.

Cloud-Morgan, Larry. October 16–19, 1990. Interviews by author, Madison, New York.

———. July 19–21, 1991. Interviews by author, Ball Club, Minnesota.

———. January 26–28, 1992. Interviews by author, Hamilton, New York.

———. October 15–16, 1995. Interviews by author, Burlington, Vermont.

Cole, D. C. March 23, 1987. Interview by author, Hamilton, New York.

Collins, Dabney Otis. 1969. "A Happening at Oglala." *American West* 6, no. 2:15–19.

Condon, Harold. August 5–9, 1992. Interviews by author, Orono, Maine.

Cook, Elaine. August 7, 1993. Interview by author, Seattle, Washington.

Cook, Katsi. Midwinter 1988. "'Through the Women's Door.'" *Daybreak* 2:12–13.

Cooper, (Rev.) Leo. November 26, 1991. Interview by author, Kansas City, Kansas.

Cosgrove, James. March 1992. "Caught between Two Worlds." *Extension* 86:8–15.

Cousins, (Rev.) John, O.F.M. Cap. November 29, 1991. Interview by author, Lawrence, Kansas.

[Craft, Francis]. June 1897. "Native Indian Vocations." *Catholic World Magazine* 65:343–355.

Crossette, Barbara. January 20, 1990. "Christians Revel in Conversion Back to Indianness." *New York Times,* p. A4.

Cuny, (Sister) Genevieve, O.S.F. August 8, 1986. Interview by author, Bozeman, Montana.

———. May 1987. "Leadership and Professional Development in the Light of the Native American Experience." *Tekakwitha Conference Newsletter* 6:6–8.

————. July 11, 1987. "Oral Autobiography." Audiotape, Siggenauk Center Spiritual Day, Wisconsin Indian Cultural Center, Milwaukee, Marquette.

Curry-Roper, Janel, and Greg Bowman. 1982. *The Houma People of Louisiana: A Story of Indian Survival.* Houma, La.: United Houma Nation.

Dana, Joan. August 23, 1992. Interview by author, Grand Lake Stream, Maine.

Davis, (Sister) Gloria. July 7, 1992. Telephone interview by author.

————. August 7, 1992. Interview by author, Orono, Maine.

Degand, Mercedes, Cheryl Gillespie, and Donna Holstein. November 24, 1991. Interview by author, Potawatomi Reservation, Kansas.

Delâge, Denys, and Helen Hornbeck Tanner. 1994. "The Ojibwa-Jesuit Debate at Walpole Island, 1844." *Ethnohistory* 41:295–321.

Delfeld, Paula. 1977. *The Indian Priest, Father Philip B. Gordon 1885–1948.* Chicago: Franciscan Herald Press.

Deloria, Vine, Jr. 1970. *Custer Died for Your Sins: An Indian Manifesto.* New York: Avon.

DeMallie, Raymond J., ed. 1984. *The Sixth Grandfather: Black Elk's Teachings Given to John G. Neihardt.* Lincoln: University of Nebraska Press.

Digmann, (Rev.) P. Florentine, S.J. c. 1922. "History of St. Francis Mission 1886–1922." HRMR, Marquette.

Diocesan Correspondence, Reports, and Applications for Aid (DCRAA). 1976–1986. Marquette.

Diocesan Permanent Diaconate Program. 1970–1976. Records, HRMR, Marquette.

Dionne, E. J., Jr. July 5, 1986. "Pope, Backing Indians, Wins Colombia Cheers." *New York Times,* p. 3.

Dixon, (Rev.) James M., S.J. August 7, 1992. Interview by author, Orono, Maine.

Doll, (Rev.) Don, S.J. 1994. *Vision Quest: Men, Women and Sacred Sites of the Sioux Nation.* New York: Crown Publishers.

Duratschek, (Sister) M[ary] Claudia, O.S.B. 1943. *The Beginnings of Catholicism in South Dakota.* Washington, D.C.: Catholic University of America Press.

————. 1947. *Crusading along Sioux Trails: A History of the Catholic Indian Missions of South Dakota.* Yankton, S.Dak.: Benedictine Convent of the Sacred Heart.

————. 1971. *Under the Shadow of His Wings: History of Sacred Heart Convent of Benedictine Sisters, Yankton, South Dakota 1880–1970.* Aberdeen, S.D.: North Plains Press.

Eagleman, Chet. August 9, 1992. Interview by author, Orono, Maine.

Eberschweiler, (Rev.) Frederic, S.J. September 1897. "An Indian Clergy Impossible." *Catholic World* 65:815–824.

Egan, (Rev.) Thomas F., S.J. July 8–10, 1989. Interviews by author, St. Regis, Quebec.

————. June 5, 1991. Telephone interview by author.

Egan, Timothy. March 19, 1988. "Despairing Indians Looking to Tradition to Combat Suicides." *New York Times*, pp. 1, 54.

Enochs, Ross. September 20, 1992. Telephone interview by author.

——. 1993. "Lakota Mission: Jesuit Mission Method and the Lakota Sioux 1885–1945." Ph.D. dissertation, University of Virginia.

——. 1996. *The Jesuit Mission to the Lakota Sioux: Pastoral Theology and Ministry, 1886–1945.* Kansas City: Sheed & Ward.

Ewens, (Sister) Mary, O.P. 1988. "The Native Order: A Brief and Strange History." In *Scattered Steeples. The Fargo Diocese: A Written Celebration of Its Centennial,* eds. Jerome D. Lamb, et al., 10–23. Fargo, N.Dak.: Burch, Londergan and Lynch.

Fagan, (Rev.) Bernard, S.J. August 4, 1995. Interview by author, Kahnawake, Quebec.

Fargo, North Dakota. August 2–6, 1989. Author's fieldnotes, Tekakwitha Conference.

Farrell, Timothy W. September 3, 1989. "People Reflect on Faith in Jubilee Essay Contest." *Voice of the Southwest*, pp. 1–2. Publication of the Diocese of Gallup, New Mexico.

"Father White to Note 25th Anniversary in Priesthood with 10:30 Mass Sunday." June 2, 1970. *Massena Observer,* p. 11.

Feraca, Stephen E. 1963. *Wakinyan: Contemporary Teton Dakota Religion.* Browning, Mont.: Bureau of Indian Affairs Blackfeet Agency.

Fisher, Ann. 1968. "History and Current Status of the Houma Indians." In *The American Indian Today,* ed. Stuart Levine and Nancy Oestreich Lurie, 133–147. Deland, Fla.: Everett/Edwards.

Fiske, Edward B. August 23, 1972. "Indians Reviving Religious Heritage." *New York Times,* p. 43.

Fittipaldi, Silvio E. Spring 1978. "The Catholic Church and the American Indians." *Horizons* 5:73–75.

Flanagan, Thomas. 1979. *Louis 'David' Riel: 'Prophet of the New World.'* Toronto: University of Toronto Press.

Foley, Thomas W. 1997. "Hovering Eagle: The Life, Letters and Journals of Francis M. Craft, Sioux Missionary." Unpublished manuscript in author's possession.

Fonda, New York. July 14–16, 1989. Author's fieldnotes, Northeastern Tekakwitha Conference.

Fox, (Rev.) Robert J. Paul. December 24–31, 1988. "Catholic Native Americans: A Church in Renewal." *America* 159:541–543.

Fox, Thomas C. March 1, 1985. "'Silo Pruning Hooks' Found Guilty in K.C." *National Catholic Reporter,* p. 4.

Foy, (Rev.) Felician A., O.F.M., and Rose M. Avato, eds. 1989–1995. *Catholic Almanac.* Huntington, Ind.: Our Sunday Visitor.

Francis, John. November 21, 1990. Interview by author, Grand Caillou, Louisiana.

Francis, Shirley, and Simon Francis. August 6, 1992. Interview by author, Orono, Maine.

Fritz, Henry E. 1963. *The Movement for Indian Assimilation, 1860–1890.* Philadelphia: University of Pennsylvania Press.

Fruth, (Rev.) Alban. 1958. *A Century of Missionary Work among the Red Lake Chippewa Indians, 1858–1958*. Redlake, Minn.: St. Mary's Mission.

Galvan, (Rev.) P. Michael. May 1987. "Native Catechesis and the Ministry of the Word." *Tekakwitha Conference Newsletter* 6:1–3.

——. August 5, 1992. Interview by author, Orono, Maine.

George-Kanentiio, Doug. March 4, 1998. Personal communication with author.

Giago, Tim A., Jr. 1978. *The Aboriginal Sin*. San Francisco: Indian Historian Press.

——. 1984. *Notes from Indian Country*. Vol. 1. Pierre, S.Dak.: Keith Cochran.

Glenmary Research Center. 1978. *Parishes of the Diocese of Gallup: Accomplishments and Challenges*. Washington, D.C.: Glenmary Home Missioners.

Goll, (Rev.) Louis J., S. J. 1940. *Jesuit Missions among the Sioux*. Saint Francis, S.Dak.: Saint Francis Mission.

Gordon, (Rev.) Philip B. 1909–1932. Papers, BCIM, Marquette.

——. 1916. "Two Needs for Real Indian Progress." *Report of the Thirty-Fourth Annual Lake Mohonk Conference*, pp. 83–87.

"The Gospel and American Indians." October 4, 1984. *Origins* 4, no. 16: 230–232.

Goulet, (Rev.) Jean-Guy, O.M.I. Fall 1982. "Religious Dualism among Athabascan Catholics." *Canadian Journal of Anthropology* 3:1–18.

——. 1984. "Liberation Theology and Missions in Canada." *Église et Théologie* 15:293–319.

——. 1987. "The Church and Aboriginal Self-Government." *Kerygma* 21:207–224.

Goulet, (Rev.) Jean-Guy, O.M.I., and (Rev.) Achiel Peelman, O.M.I. 1983. *The Amerindian Reality and the Catholic Church in Canada*. Bulletin 93. Brussels: Pro Mundi Vita.

Grant, John Webster. 1985. *Moon of Wintertime: Missionaries and the Indians of Canada in Encounter since 1534*. Toronto: University of Toronto Press.

Graves, Rachel. January 11, 1997. "Catholic Churches Bring Indian Traditions into Their Worship." *Greenfield, Mass. Recorder*, p. H3.

Green, (Rev.) Jim, S.J. August 4, 1988. Interview by author, Pine Ridge, South Dakota.

Gregoire, Mary, Lydia Gregoire Duthu, and Ted Duthu, Sr. November 20, 1990. Interview by author, Dulac, Louisiana.

Grim, John A. 1991a. "From Conversion to Inculturation: 'New Evangelization' in the Dialogue of Native American and Catholic Spiritualities." Unpublished manuscript in author's possession.

——. 1991b. "Relations between Native American Religions and Roman Catholicism." Unpublished manuscript in author's possession.

Grotegeers, (Rev.) Henry, S.J. 1931. "Instruction by Means of the Two Roads." HRMR, Marquette.

Gschwend, (Rev.) Joseph, S.J. June 20, 1931. "Catholic Sioux Indians in Council." *America*, pp. 253–254.

Gualtieri, Antonio R. 1980a. "Canadian Missionary Perceptions of Indian and Inuit Culture and Religious Tradition." *Studies in Religion* 9, no. 3:299–314.

——. 1980b. "Indigenization of Christianity and Syncretism among the Indians and Inuit of the Western Arctic." *Canadian Ethnic Studies* 12, no. 1:47–57.

——. 1984. *Christianity and Native Traditions: Indigenization and Syncretism among the Inuit and Dene of the Western Arctic.* The Church and the World 2. Notre Dame, Ind.: Cross Cultural Publications.

Gutiérrez, Ramón A. 1991. *When Jesus Came, the Corn Mothers Went Away: Marriage, Sexuality, and Power in New Mexico, 1500–1846.* Stanford, Calif.: Stanford University Press.

Hall, (Sister) Suzanne, S.N.D., ed. 1992. *The People: Reflections of Native Peoples on the Catholic Experience in North America.* Washington, D.C.: National Catholic Educational Association.

Hann, John H., and Bonnie G. McEwan. 1998. *The Apalachee Indians and Mission San Luis.* Gainesville: University Press of Florida.

Harrod, Howard L. 1984. "Missionary Life-World and Native Response: Jesuits in New France." *Studies in Religion* 13, no. 2:179–192.

Hascall, (Rev.) John, O.F.M. Cap. 1980. "Prayer Service with Homily on Healing and Forgiveness." Audiotape, Marquette.

——. 1984. "Healing and the Family." Audiotape, Marquette.

——. July 19, 1986. "Day of Native Spirituality." Archbishop Cousins Catholic Center, Milwaukee, Wisconsin.

——. August 9, 1986. Interview by author, Bozeman, Montana.

——. Fall 1986. "Keynote Address 1986 Annual Tekakwitha Conference." *Tekakwitha Conference Newsletter* 6:6–8.

——. 1988. "President's Letter." *Tekakwitha Conference Newsletter* 8, no. 1:13–16.

——. 1996. "The Sacred Circle: Native American Liturgy." In *Native and Christian: Indigenous Voices on Religious Identity in the United States and Canada,* ed. James Treat, 179–183. New York: Routledge.

Hatcher, (Rev.) John E., S.J. 1987. "Paul VI's *Evangelization in the Modern World* and the Mission to the Sioux Indians of South Dakota: Theory and Praxis." Sacred Theology Licentiate thesis, Regis College, Marquette.

——. 1996/1997. "An Inculturated Church." *Tekakwitha Conference Newsletter* 15, no. 4: 12–14.

Hatcher, (Rev.) John E., S.J., and (Rev.) Patrick M. McCorkell, S.J. 1975–1976. *Builders of the New Earth: The Formation of Permanent Deacons.* 3 vols. Rapid City, S.Dak.: Diocese of Rapid City.

——. 1986. *Builders of the New Earth: The Formation of Deacons and Lay Ministers.* Vol. 1. Rev. ed. Rapid City, S.Dak.: Diocese of Rapid City.

Hemauer, (Rev.) Gilbert F., O.F.M. Cap. 1976. "An Approach to Religion Education with Native Americans." Typescript, Marquette.

——. Spring 1977. "A Cross-Cultural Approach to Catechesis among Native Americans." *The Living Light* 16:132–137.

——. 1982. *The Story and Faith Journey of Seventeen Native Catechists.* Great Falls, Mont.: Tekakwitha Conference National Center.

——. August 9, 1986. Interview by author, Bozeman, Montana.

Henderson, James Youngblood. 1997. *The Mikmaw Concordat.* Halifax: Fernwood Publishing.

Hernou, (Rev.) Paul. 1987. "Missionary among the Cree of Northern Alberta: The Challenge of Inculturation." *Kerygma* 21:233–244.

Hettich, (Rev.) Leo, O.S.B. 1966. "The Problem of Indian Vocations." Mimeograph, TCA, Marquette.

Hilbert, (Rev.) Robert, S.J. 1975a. "Possible Injustice of Church in Relationship to the Sioux People." SFMR, Marquette.

———. 1975b. "The Impact of American Culture on Church Personnel." Typescript, Marquette.

———. 1987. "Contemporary Catholic Mission Work among the Sioux." In *Sioux Indian Religion: Tradition and Innovation,* ed. Raymond J. DeMallie and Douglas R. Parks, 139–147. Norman: University of Oklahoma Press.

Hilger, (Sister) M. Agnes, O.S.B. 1963. *The First Sioux Nun: Sister Marie-Josephine Nebraska, S.G.M. 1859–1894.* Milwaukee: Bruce Publishing Company.

Hillman, Eugene. November 15, 1980. "From Tribal Religions to a Catholic Church." *America,* pp. 303–305.

Hobday, (Sister) José. Summer 1976. "Forced Assimilation and the Native American Dance." *Cross Currents* 26:189–194.

———. August 8, 1986. Interview by author, Bozeman, Montana.

Hoffman, Matthias M. July 1930. "The Winnebago Mission; A Cause Célèbre." *Mid-America* 13:26–52.

Hofinger, (Rev.) Johannes, S.J., ed. 1960. *Liturgy and the Missions: The Nijmegen Papers.* New York: P. J. Kennedy & Sons.

Holler, Clyde. 1983. "Black Elk's Relationship to Christianity." Paper presented at the American Academy of Religion annual meeting, Dallas, Texas.

———. 1984. "Lakota Religion and Tragedy: The Theology of *Black Elk Speaks.*" *Journal of the American Academy of Religion* 52, no. 1:19–45.

———. November 23, 1986. Interview by author, Atlanta, Georgia.

———. Late 1980s. "Contemporary Lakota Religion: Black Elk's Legacy." Unpublished manuscript in author's possession.

———. 1995. *Black Elk's Religion: The Sun Dance and Lakota Catholicism.* Syracuse: Syracuse University Press.

Holy Rosary Mission. 1972–1979. Restricted Correspondence, HRMR, Marquette.

Hostler, Hilton. November 19, 1992. Interview by author, Arcata, California.

Hottinger, (Rev.) Ted. June 13, 1988. Interview by author, Milwaukee, Wisconsin.

Houma Indian Communities, Louisiana. November 18–22, 1990. Author's fieldnotes.

Huel, Raymond J. A. 1996. *Proclaiming the Gospel to the Indians and the Métis.* Edmonton, Alberta: University of Alberta Press and Western Canadian Publishers.

Huhndorf, Max, and Beverly Huhndorf. August 5, 1992. Interview by author, Orono, Maine.

Indian Sentinel, The. 1902–1962.

"Indian to Become a Catholic Priest." July 12, 1976. *New York Times,* n.p.

"Indian Unit Names Three Top Enemies." June 18, 1975. *New York Times,* n.p.

Inter-Mission Board. 1966–1976. Records, HRMR, Marquette.

International Theological Commission. May 4, 1989. "Faith and Inculturation." *Origins* 18, no. 47:800–807.

Jacko, Ursula. October 12–14, 1990. Interviews by author, Toronto-Anderson
Lake, Ontario.

Jacobs, (Rev.) Michael, S.J., and (Rev.) Thomas Egan, S.J. 1973, 1989. "The St.
Regis Reserve . . . Baptisms, Marriages, Deaths . . . ," St. Regis.

Jaenen, Cornelius J. 1976. *Friend and Foe: Aspects of French-Amerindian Cultural Contact in the Sixteenth and Seventeenth Centuries.* New York: Columbia University Press.

Jelovich, Eileen Tibbits. August 5, 1988. Interview by author, Pine Ridge,
South Dakota.

Jennings, George J. 1977. "The American Indian Ethos: A Key for Christian
Missions?" *Missiology 5,* no. 4:487–498.

Jesuit Papers. N.d. Records, HRMR, Marquette.

Jesuits in Native North American Ministry (JINNAM). 1983–1988. Letter exchange, Marquette.

Johnson, (Rev.) Jacques, O.M.I. 1982. "Native Spirituality and the Catholic
Faith." *Kerygma* 16:123–132.

Johnson, Tim. Midwinter 1988. "The Second Coming: The Pope's New Move
towards Indians." *Daybreak* 2:14–17.

Jordan, (Rev.) C. P. August 8, 1992. Interview by author, Orono, Maine.

Juan, Vivian. August 8, 1986. Interview by author, Bozeman, Montana.

Jumping Bull, Calvin. August 2, 1988. "Traditional Lakota Religion." Two
Roads Conference.

Jutz, (Rev.) John B., S.J. 1918a. "Historic Data on the Causes of the Dissatisfaction among the Sioux Indians in 1890. The Ghost Dance Religion."
Woodstock Letters 47:313–327.

———. 1918b. "Recollections of an Old Indian Missionary." *Canisius Monthly,*
pp. 16–24, 63–68, 143–149.

Kemnitzer, Luis. August 3, 1988. "Contemporary Religion of the Lakotas."
Two Roads Conference.

Kerygma (Mission: Journal of Mission Studies). 1967–1996.

Kilborn, Peter T. September 20, 1992. "Sad Distinction for the Sioux: Home-
land Is No. 1 in Poverty." *New York Times,* pp. 1, 32.

Killoren, (Rev.) John J., S.J. 1994. *"Come, Blackrobe": De Smet and the Indian
Tragedy.* Norman: University of Oklahoma Press.

Kinlicheeny, Jeannette. December 1972. "Indian." *Momentum* 3:44–46.

Kozak, David. 1991. "Ecumenical Indianism: Kateri and the Invented Tradition." Unpublished manuscript in author's possession.

Krieger, Carlo. 1993. "The Micmac and the Question of Discourse." In *Re-
Discoveries of America,* ed. Johan Callens, 87–101. Brussels: VUBPress.

Lakota Times, The. August 2, 1988. *Holy Rosary Special Centennial Edition,
1888–1988.*

Lang, (Sister) Joan, C.S.J. July 8, 1992. Telephone interview by author.

Langhans, (Rev.) Victor E. 1986. *The Pilgrimage.* Browning, Mont.: Church of the Little Flower.

Lenz, (Msgr.) Paul A. 1979a. "American Indian Catholic Missions." *New Catholic Encyclopedia* 17:19–20.

———. 1979b. "Bureau of Catholic Indian Missions." *New Catholic Encyclopedia* 17:60.

———. August 7, 1986. Interview by author, Bozeman, Montana.

———. August 7, 1993. Interview by author, Seattle, Washington.

———. November 19, 1993. Interview by author, Washington, D.C.

———. N.d. *Bureau of Catholic Indian Missions* (brochure).

Lequin, (Rev.) Thomas. August 22, 1992. Interview by author, Indian Township, Maine.

Leute, (Rev.) Charles, O.P. 1975. Papers, BCIM, Marquette.

———. August 7, 1986. Interview by author, Bozeman, Montana.

Linton, Ralph, ed. 1940. *Acculturation in Seven American Indian Tribes.* New York: D. Appleton-Century.

Little Sky, Edsel. August 5, 1988. Interview by author, Pine Ridge, South Dakota.

Local Sodalities. 1909–1986. Records, HRMR, Marquette.

Lucero, Sam M. April 26, 1990. "Spruce Returns to Faith, Reservation after Absence." *Catholic Herald*, p. 3.

Lunstrom, Richard H. 1973. "A Hard Look at American Catholic Folklore: Mohawks, Martyrs, and Myths," and "'For If the Indian Peoples Die, Who among Us Deserve to Live?'" *Akwesasne Notes,* reprints, Marquette.

Luzbetak, (Rev.) Louis J. 1961. "Toward an Applied Missionary Anthropology." *Anthropological Quarterly* 34, no. 4:165–176.

———. 1967. "Adaptation, Missionary." *New Catholic Encyclopedia* 1:120–122.

———. 1979. "Missiology." *New Catholic Encyclopedia* 17:416–419.

MacGregor, Gordon. 1951. *Warriors without Weapons: A Study of the Society and Personality Development of the Pine Ridge Sioux.* Chicago: University of Chicago Press.

Mails, Thomas E. 1979. *Fools Crow.* New York: Avon Books.

Markowitz, Harvey. 1987. "Catholic Mission and the Sioux: A Crisis in the Early Paradigm." In *Sioux Indian Religion: Tradition and Innovation*, ed. Raymond J. DeMallie and Douglas R. Parks, 113–137. Norman: University of Oklahoma Press.

———. 1994. "'But Great Father, You Promised Us Blackrobes': The Origin Narrative of Saint Francis Mission." In *The Artist & the Missionary: A Native-American & Euro-American Cultural Exchange.* Proceedings of the 1992 Plains Indian Seminar, pp. 11–21. Cody,Wyo.: Buffalo Bill Historical Center.

Martin, Douglas. September 16, 1984. "Pope Urges Indians and 'Newcomers' to Reconcile." *New York Times,* p. 16.

Marzal, Manuel M., et al. 1996. *The Indian Face of God in Latin America.* Maryknoll, N.Y.: Orbis Books.

Masters, (Sister) Lorraine, O.L.V.M. August 6, 1992. Interview by author, Orono, Maine.

Mathes, Valerie Sherer. Fall 1980. "American Indian Women and the Catholic Church." *North Dakota History* 47:20–25.

Mathieu, (Rev.) Georges P. 1937–1987. Miscellaneous, Marquette.

———. September 14, 1987. Interview by author, Phoenix, Arizona.

McCarthy, Martha. 1995. *From the Great River to the Ends of the Earth: Oblate Missions to the Dene, 1847–1921.* Edmonton, Alberta: University of Alberta Press and Western Canadian Publishers.

McDonnell, Claudia. July 1987. "Kateri Tekakwitha: Native Americans' Gift to the Church." *St. Anthony Messenger* 95:19–23.

McGloin, (Rev.) John Bernard, S.J. 1950. *Eloquent Indian: The Life of James Bouchard, California Jesuit.* Stanford, Calif.: Stanford University Press.

McMullen, (Rev.) John, O.S.B., M.S.L.S. 1969. *A Guide to the Christian Indians of the Upper Plains (An Annotated, Selective Bibliography).* Marvin, S.Dak.: Blue Cloud Abbey.

McNally, Michael David. 1996. "Ojibwa Singers: Evangelical Hymns and a Native Culture in Motion." Ph.D. dissertation, Harvard University.

"A Meeting with Native Americans." October 8, 1987. *Origins* 17, no. 17:295–298.

"Memorandum from a Consultation on Mission." 1982. *The Secretariat for Promoting Christian Unity (Vatican City), Information Service* 4, no. 50:138–149.

Merton, Thomas. 1976. *Ishi Means Man.* Greensboro, N.C.: Unicorn Press.

Merz, Nancy. 1994. "The First Native-American Priest in the United States." *Jesuit Bulletin* 73, no. 1:16–17.

Michalowski, Francis. 1949. Correspondence, HRMR, Marquette.

Miller, Elmer S. 1970. "The Christian Missionary, Agent of Secularization." *Anthropological Quarterly* 41, no. 1:14–22.

Miller, Jay. 1989. "The Early Years of Watomika (James Bouchard): Delaware and Jesuit." *American Indian Quarterly* 13, no. 2:165–188.

Minamiki, (Rev.) George, S.J. 1985. *The Chinese Rites Controversy from Its Beginning to Modern Times.* Chicago: Loyola University Press.

Mitchell, (Sister) Kateri, S.S.A. August 7, 1986. Interview by author, Bozeman, Montana.

———. May 1987. "Program Development and Native Catechesis." *Tekakwitha Conference Newsletter* 6:3–5.

———. 1996. "Program Development and Native American Catechesis." In *Native and Christian: Indigenous Voices on Religious Identity in the United States and Canada,* ed. James Treat, 170–178. New York: Routledge.

Mittelstadt, (Rev.) John, O.F.M. January 18, 1987. Interview by author, St. Michael's Mission, Arizona.

Monahan, David. September 18, 1988. "Traditional Tribal Religion Continues among Kiowa." *The Sooner Catholic,* n.p.

Monteiro, (Rev.) Ralph John, O.S.A. 1990–1992. Correspondence, Santa Rosa.

———. September 1, 1992. Telephone interview by author.

————. November 18–20, 1992. Interviews by author, Hoopa, California.

————. May 13, 1998. Telephone interview by author.

Mooney, James. 1973. *The Ghost-Dance Religion and Wounded Knee.* New York: Dover Publications. Original publication 1896.

Moorman, (Rev.) Otto J., S.J. 1924a. "A Lily of the Sioux." HRMR, Marquette.

————. 1924b. "The Rose of the Sioux." HRMR, Marquette.

Morales, (Rev.) Francisco, O.F.M. 1973. *Ethnic and Social Background of the Franciscan Friars in Seventeenth-Century Mexico.* Washington, D.C.: Academy of American Franciscan History.

Morrison, Kenneth M. 1985. "Discourse and the Accommodation of Values: Toward a Revision of Mission History." *Journal of the American Academy of Religion* 53, no. 3:365–382.

Naquin, (Rev.) Roch R. November 18, 20, 1990. Interviews by author, Grand Caillou, Louisiana.

Native American Catholics: People of the Spirit. 1986. TeleKETICS, Franciscan Communications. Videocassette.

"Native American Parishes Promote Spiritual Heritage." February 1990. *West River Catholic,* p. 21.

Negahnquet, (Rev.) Albert. 1903–1920. Papers, BCIM, Marquette.

Neihardt, John G. 1932. *Black Elk Speaks.* New York: William Morrow and Company.

O'Brien, (Rev.) James F., S.J. August 8, 1992. Interview by author, Orono, Maine.

Official Catholic Directory, The. 1991. Wilmette, Ill.: P. J. Kenedy & Sons.

Ojibway, (Rev.) Paul, S.A. November 23, 1992. Interview by author, San Francisco, California.

————. August 6, 1993. Interview by author, Seattle, Washington.

Oktavec, Eileen. 1996. *Answered Prayers: Miracles and Milagros along the Border.* Tucson: University of Arizona Press.

Orono, Maine. August 5–9, 1992. Author's fieldnotes, Tekakwitha Conference.

Ortiz, Alfonso. January 23, 1987. Interview by author, San Ildefonso Pueblo, New Mexico.

Our Negro and Indian Missions. 1926–1976.

Painter, Muriel Thayer. 1986. *With Good Heart: Yaqui Beliefs and Ceremonies in Pascua Village.* Tucson: University of Arizona Press.

Palladino, (Rev.) Lawrence B., S.J. 1922. *Indian and White in the Northwest: A History of Catholicity in Montana, 1831–1891.* Lancaster, Penn.: Wickersham Publishing Company.

Palm, (Sister) Charles. N.d. *Confirmation Preparation.* [Marvin, S.Dak.: American Indian Culture Research Center].

————. 1985. *Stories That Jesus Told.* [Marvin, S.Dak.: American Indian Culture Research Center].

Partida, (Rev.) Raphael. August 7, 1992. "Appreciating Our Native American Spirituality." Lecture, Orono, Maine.

——. August 8, 1992. Interview by author, Orono, Maine.

Pates, (Rev.) Richard, S.J. August 5, 1988. Interview by author, Pine Ridge, South Dakota.

Paul, Joan. August 21, 1992. Interview by author, Pleasant Point, Maine.

Peelman, (Rev.) Achiel, O.M.I. 1995. *Christ Is a Native American*. Ottawa: Novalis-Saint Paul University.

Pelotte, (Most Rev.) Donald E., S.S.S. 1976. *John Courtney Murray: Theologian in Conflict*. New York: Paulist Press.

——. August 7, 1986. Interview by author, Bozeman, Montana.

——. August 11, 1986. Interview by author, Billings, Montana.

——. August 6, 1992. Interview by author, Indian Island, Maine.

——. August 6, 1993. Interview by author, Seattle, Washington.

Perrig, (Rev.) Emil M., S.J. 1886–1909. "Diary." SFMR, Marquette.

Peterson, Iver. May 7, 1986. "American Indian Is Ordained as a Catholic Bishop." *New York Times*, p. A20.

Phoenix, Arizona. September 12–14, 1987. Author's fieldnotes, Tekakwitha Conference.

Pine Ridge Educational Society. 1910–1949. Records, HRMR, Marquette.

Pine Ridge, South Dakota. August 4–7, 1988. Author's fieldnotes, Holy Rosary, Red Cloud Indian School Centennial.

Pizzorusso, Giovanni. 1990. "Roman Ecclesiastical Archives and the History of the Native Peoples of Canada." *European Review of Native American Studies* 4, no. 2:21–26.

Placilla, (Sister) Mary Hugh, I.H.M., and (Sister) Therese Culhane, I.H.M. August 5, 1992. Interview by author, Orono, Maine.

"Plowshares Hit Silo near Missouri Base." November 23, 1984. *National Catholic Reporter* 21:1.

The Positio of the Historical Section of the Sacred Congregation of Rites on the Introduction of the Cause for Beatification and Canonization and on the Virtues of the Servant of God, Katherine Tekakwitha, the Lily of the Mohawks. 1940. New York: Fordham University Press.

Potsdam, New York. August 2–6, 1995. Author's fieldnotes, Tekakwitha Conference.

Pouliot, (Rev.) Léon, S.J. 1967. "American Indian Missions (Canada)." *New Catholic Encyclopedia* 1:401–402.

Powell, (Rev.) Peter J. September 24, 1970. Letter to (Rev.) Thomas A. Hillenbrand, O.S.B. TCA, Marquette.

Powers, Marla N. 1986. *Oglala Women: Myth, Ritual, and Reality*. Chicago: University of Chicago Press.

——. August 3, 1988. "The Boarding School: A Photoethnography." Two Roads Conference.

Powers, William K. 1987. *Beyond the Vision: Essays on American Indian Culture*. Norman: University of Oklahoma Press.

——. August 2, 1988. "Dual Religious Participation: Traditional Religion vs. Christianity." Two Roads Conference.

——. 1990. "When Black Elk Speaks, Everybody Listens." In *Religion in Na-*

tive North America, ed. Christopher Vecsey, 136–151. Moscow: University of Idaho Press.

Pretty-on-Top, Burton. 1991. "Dignity in Prayer: A Crow Indian's Journey to Assisi," ed. John Grim. Unpublished manuscript in author's possession.

Provincial's Visitations. 1888–1962. Records, HRMR, Marquette.

Prucha, (Rev.) Francis Paul, S.J. 1979. *The Churches and the Indian Schools, 1888–1912.* Lincoln: University of Nebraska Press.

——. July 21, 1986. Interview by author, Milwaukee, Wisconsin.

——. 1988. "Two Roads to Conversion: Protestant and Catholic Missionaries in the Pacific Northwest." *Pacific Northwest Quarterly* 79, no. 4:130–137.

Puckkee, Jane, and Sarah Patterson. November 24, 1991. Interview by author, Potawatomi Reservation, Kansas.

Quilty, (Sister) Mary Ellen, S.B.S. 1979. *An Historical Narrative of the Catholic Sioux Indian Congress 1890–1978.* [Washington, D.C.: Bureau of Catholic Indian Missions].

Rahill, Peter J. 1953. *The Catholic Indian Missions and Grant's Peace Policy, 1870–1884.* Washington, D.C.: Catholic University of America Press.

Ramsey, Jarold. 1977. "The Bible in Western Indian Mythology." *Journal of American Folklore* 90:442–454.

Red Cloud Indian School. 1869–1988. Records, HRMR, Marquette.

——. 1978. Workshop/Seminar, audiotapes, HRMR, Marquette.

Red Owl, (Rev.) Edward. M., O.S.B. 1967. "A Study and Commentary of the Culturally Disadvantaged Student." HRMR, Marquette.

——. c. 1970 "The Concept of Tribal Politic." HRMR, Marquette.

Reddy, Marlita A., ed. 1993. *Statistical Record of Native North Americans.* Detroit: Gale Research.

Reilly, L. W. 1890. "Why Is There No Indian Priest?" *American Ecclesiastical Review* 4: 267–280.

Reilly, Robert T. February 1979. "Indian Catholics: Bringing Prayer Back Down to Earth." *U.S. Catholic,* pp. 25–30.

"A Report on the Meeting of the Indian Missionaries of the Oregon Province." June 7–10, 1960. BCIM, Marquette.

Resendes, Daniel F. March 2, 1993. Telephone interview by author.

Rhodes, Willard. 1960. "The Christian Hymnology of the North American Indians." In *Men and Cultures,* ed. Anthony F. C. Wallace, 324–331. Philadelphia: University of Pennsylvania Press.

Ricard, Robert. 1966. *The Spiritual Conquest of Mexico.* Berkeley: University of California Press.

Riel, Louis. 1976. *The Diaries of Louis Riel.* Ed. Thomas Glanagan. Edmonton, Alberta: Hurtig Publishers.

Rigel, (Sister) Teresa, C.S.J. August 6, 1988. Interview by author, Pine Ridge, South Dakota.

Riggs, (Sister) Francis Mary, S.B.S. 1967. *Attitudes of Missionary Sisters toward American Indian Acculturation.* Washington, D.C.: Catholic University of America.

"The Rights of Native Americans." May 1, 1975. *Origins* 4, no. 45:719–720.

Rivera, Luis N. 1992. *A Violent Evangelism: The Political and Religious Conquest of the Americas.* Louisville, Ky.: Westminster/John Knox Press.

Roderick, M. Grace. August 21, 1992. Interview by author, Pleasant Point, Maine.

Rodríguez, Sylvia. 1996. *The Matachines Dance: Ritual Symbolism and Interethnic Relations in the Upper Río Grande Valley.* Albuquerque: University of New Mexico Press.

Ronda, James P. 1977. "'We Are Well as We Are': An Indian Critique of Seventeenth-Century Christian Missions." *William and Mary Quarterly* 34, no. 1:66–82.

Ronnander, Chad. July 10, 1991. Interview by author, Milwaukee, Wisconsin.

Rosaldo, Renato. 1989. *Culture and Truth.* Boston: Beacon Press.

Rosen, (Rev.) Peter. 1895. *A Catholic Can Not Consistently Be a Member of Secret Societies Because They Are Religious Organizations.* Heidelberg, Minn.: Peter Rosen.

Rostkowski, Joëlle. 1998. *La Conversion Inachavée. Les Indiens et le Christianisme.* Paris: Albin Michel.

Rousseau, Dolores. August 6, 1992. Interview by author, Orono, Maine.

Salvo, Dana, Ramón A. Gutiérrez, Salvatore Scalora, and William H. Breezley. 1997. *Home Altars of Mexico.* Albuquerque: University of New Mexico Press.

Savilla, Joseph. July 7, 1992. Telephone interview by author.

———. August 6–7, 1993. Interviews by author, Seattle, Washington.

Savilla, Joseph, and Peggy (Cornelius) Savilla. August 5, 1992. Interview by author, Orono, Maine.

Schieber, (Rev.) Joachim, O.S.B. 1984. "Centennial Sacramental Presence." Marquette.

Schmidlin, Joseph. 1931. *Catholic Mission Theory.* Techny, Ill.: Mission Press, S.V.D.

Schmidt, David L., and Murdena Marshall, eds. and trans. 1995. *Mi'kmaq Hieroglyphic Prayers: Readings in North America's First Indigenous Script.* Halifax, Nova Scotia: Nimbus Publishing.

Schmidt, W. 1933. *High Gods in North America.* Oxford: Clarendon Press.

Scott, (Rev.) John M., S.J. 1963. *High Eagle and His Sioux.* St. Louis: n.p.

Seattle, Swinomish, and Lummi, Washington. August 4–8, 1993. Author's fieldnotes, Tekakwitha Conference.

Shields, (Rev.) David, S.J. August 4, 1988. Interview by author, Pine Ridge, South Dakota.

Shillinger, Sarah. August 5–6, 1993. Interviews by author, Swinomish, Seattle, Washington.

Sialm, (Rev.) Placidus F., S.J. 1912–1915, n.d. "Ethnological Notes." HRMR, Marquette.

———. 1930s a. "Camp Churches." HRMR, Marquette.

———. 1930s b. "The History of Holy Rosary Mission, Pine Ridge, South Dakota, 1888–1932." HRMR, Marquette.

———. 1930–1932, n.d. "Retreat Notes." HRMR, Marquette.

Siggenauk Center. 1974–1989. Records, Marquette.

Simon, (Brother) C. M., S.J. August 3, 1988. "History of Holy Rosary Mission." Two Roads Conference.

Simons, Marlise. January 23, 1991. "Pope Urges a Convert Drive, Even Where Muslims Ban It." *New York Times*, p. A2.

"Sioux for Christ." 1963–1980. Audiotapes of weekly sermons, SFMR, Marquette.

Sisters of St. Francis. 1888–1969. Chronicles, HRMR, Marquette.

Smith, Huston. 1958. *The Religions of Man*. New York: Harper.

Smith, Jeanne. 1985. *Teaching on the Reservation: Reflections on the Period between the Wars*. Kyle, S.Dak.: Oglala Lakota College.

Snow, John. 1977. *These Mountains Are Our Sacred Places*. Toronto: Samuel Stevens.

Southall, (Sister) M. Florence, O.S.F. 1964. "The Work of the Jesuit Fathers and the Franciscan Sisters among the Teton-Sioux of South Dakota." HRMR, Marquette.

Spicer, Edward H. 1940. *Pascua: A Yaqui Village in Arizona*. Chicago: University of Chicago Press.

"Spirit in the Wind." 1988. Videotape, Archdiocese of Oklahoma City.

Ste.-Anne-de-Beaupré, Quebec. July 26, 1990. Author's fieldnotes.

St. Hilaire, George P. 1976. "Indian Sacraments: A Sanpoil Model." *Cross Currents* 26, no. 2:172–188.

St. Lucy's Church, Syracuse, New York. November 6, 1993. Author's fieldnotes.

St. Paul and Minneapolis, Archdiocese of, Office of Indian Ministry. 1989–1992. *Newsletter*.

Starkloff, (Rev.) Carl F., S.J. 1971. "American Indian Religion and Christianity: Confrontation and Dialogue." *Journal of Ecumenical Studies* 8, no. 2:317–340.

———. 1972. "American Indian Religion and Christianity: Confrontation and Dialogue." In *New Theology no. 9*, ed. Martin E. Marty and Dean Peerman, 121–150. New York: Macmillan.

———. 1974. *The People of the Center: American Indian Religion and Christianity*. New York: Seabury Press.

———. November 1974. "Evangelization and Native Americans." *Jesuit Missionary News* 34:1–6.

———. 1975. "'Evangelization' and Native Americans." *Studies in the International Apostalate* 4, no. 1:1–37.

———. 1977. "Mission Method and the American Indian." *Theological Studies* 38, no. 4:621–653.

———. 1978. "Oppression, Death and Liberation: Thoughts in a Context." *Review for Religious* 37, no. 6:801–808.

———. 1979. "Cultural Problems in Mission Catechesis among Native Americans." *Occasional Bulletin of Missionary Research* 3:138–140.

———. May 1979. "Ministry in 'Another America.'" *Pastoral Life*, pp. 15–21.

———. 1980. "Sacred Space: The Project of Tribal Catechesis." *The Living Light* 17, no. 1:20–26.

———. 1981. "A Reflection on 'The Catholic Church and the American Indian.'" *Horizons*, pp. 255–258.

———. 1982. *A Theological Reflection: The Recent Revitalization of the Tekakwitha Conference*. Great Falls, Mont.: Tekakwitha Conference National Center.

———. 1983. "God as Oppressor? Changing God's Name among Contemporary Arapaho." *Kerygma* 17:165–174.

———. 1985a. "Religious Renewal in Native North America: The Contemporary Call to Mission." *Missiology* 13, no. 1:81–101.

———. 1985b. "The Anishinabe Ministry Training Project: Scriptural-Theological Formation." *Kerygma* 19:71–81.

———. March 18, 1985. Personal communication with author.

———. August 7, 1986. Interview by author, Bozeman, Montana.

———. 1989. "Keepers of Tradition: The Symbol Power of Indigenous Ministry." *Kerygma* 52:3–120.

———. August 24, 1990. Personal communication with author.

———. October 11–14, 1990. Interviews by author, Toronto-Anderson Lake, Ontario.

———. 1991. "'Good Fences Make Good Neighbors' or 'The Meeting of the Two Rivers.'" Unpublished manuscript in author's possession.

———. 1993. "The Problems of Syncretism: Why We Have to Keep Talking — and Doing." Paper presented at the American Academy of Religion annual meeting, Washington, D.C.

———. 1995. "'Good Fences Make Good Neighbors' or 'The Meeting of the Rivers.'" *Studia Missionalia* 44:367–388.

Statement of U.S. Catholic Bishops on American Indians. 1977. United States Catholic Bishops' Conference, Washington, D.C.

Steinfels, Peter. July 4, 1988. "Founder of Order in U.S. Is Canonized." *New York Times*, p. 26.

———. January 29, 1991. "Spreading the Faith, and the Debate." *New York Times*, p. A19.

Steinmetz, (Rev.) Paul B., S.J. 1969. "Explanation of the Sacred Pipe as a Prayer Instrument." *Pine Ridge Research Bulletin*, no. 10:20–25.

———. May 1970. "The Relationship between Plains Indian Religion and Christianity: A Priest's Viewpoint." *Plains Anthropologist* 15:83–86.

———. 1980. *Pipe, Bible and Peyote among the Oglala Lakota*. Stockholm: Almqvist & Wiksell International.

———. 1984. *Meditations with Native Americans: Lakota Spirituality*. Santa Fe: Bear & Company.

———. 1986. "A Native American Christian Spirituality." *Leadership Conference of Women Religious, Occasional Papers* 13, no. 3:7–8.

Steltenkamp, (Rev.) Michael F., S.J. 1976. "Green Grass Visitation Notes." HRMR, Marquette.

———. 1982. *The Sacred Vision: Native American Religion and Its Practice Today*. New York: Paulist Press.

———. 1987. "No More Screech Owl: Lakota Adaptation to Change as Profiled in the Life of Black Elk." HRMR, Marquette.

———. August 5, 1989. Interview by author, Fargo, North Dakota.

————. August 7–9, 1992. Interviews by author, Orono, Maine.

————. 1993. *Black Elk: Holy Man of the Oglala*. Norman: University of Oklahoma Press.

Stewart, Omer C. May 1982. Review of *Pipe, Bible and Peyote among the Oglala Dakota*, by Paul B. Steinmetz. *Plains Anthropologist* 27:180–181.

Stipe, Claude E. 1980. "Anthropologists versus Missionaries: The Influence of Presuppositions." *Current Anthropology* 21, no. 2:165–179.

Stolzman, (Rev.) William F., S.J. 1969. "Lakota Christian Theology: A Beginning." HRMR, Marquette.

————. 1973–1975. "Position Papers." SFMR, Marquette.

————. 1973–1978. "Transcript: Medicine Men and Clergy Meetings." SFMR, Marquette.

————. 1975, 1982. "Monograph: The Pipe and Christ." SFMR, Marquette.

————. 1986a. *How to Take Part in Lakota Ceremonies*. Pine Ridge, S.Dak.: William Stolzman.

————. 1986b. *The Pipe and Christ*. Pine Ridge, S.Dak.: Red Cloud Indian School.

Stuart, Paul. 1981. "The Christian Church and Indian Community Life." *Journal of Ethnic Studies* 9, no. 3:47–55.

Suro, Roberto. November 23, 1986. "Maoris Want Pope to Appoint Bishop." *New York Times*, p. 5.

Tac, Pablo. 1958. *Indian Life and Customs at Mission San Luis Rey*. Ed. and trans. Minna Hewes and Gordon Hewes. San Luis Rey, Calif.: Old Mission.

Tekakwitha Conference Newsletter (Cross and Feather News). 1981–1998.

Tekakwitha Missionary Conference. 1956. Minutes, annual meeting, "Social Order and the Indian," Chamberlain, South Dakota. TCA, Marquette.

————. 1957. Minutes, annual meeting, Rapid City, South Dakota. TCA, Marquette.

————. 1958. Minutes, annual meeting, Stephan, South Dakota. TCA, Marquette.

————. 1962. Minutes, annual meeting, St. Michael, North Dakota. TCA, Marquette.

————. 1970. "Tekakwitha Missionary Conference Proposal for Acceptance of Native Clergy." TCA, Marquette.

Tennelly, (Rev.) J. B. 1967a. "American Indian, Education of." *New Catholic Encyclopedia* 1:400–401.

————. 1967b. "American Indian Missions (U.S.)." *New Catholic Encyclopedia* 1:402–408.

Thiel, Mark G. 1983. "The Omaha Dance in Oglala and Sicangu Sioux History, 1883–1923." Marquette.

————. July 21, 1986. Interview by author, Milwaukee, Wisconsin.

————. June 4, 1987. Personal communication with author.

————. June 14, 1988. Interview by author, Milwaukee, Wisconsin.

————. July 26, 1989–August 1, 1989. Interviews by author, Milwaukee, Wisconsin.

————. 1989. "Catholic Sodalities among the Sioux, 1882–1910." Unpublished manuscript in author's possession.

——. July 9, 1991. Interview by author, Milwaukee, Wisconsin.

——. December 3, 1991. Telephone interview by author.

——. January 22, 1992. Telephone interview by author.

——. July 22, 1992. Interview by author, Milwaukee, Wisconsin.

——. May 17, 1994. Personal communication with author.

Thomas, Robert K. 1967. "The Role of the Church in Indian Adjustment." *Kansas Journal of Sociology* 3, no. 1:20–28.

——. N.d. "Encouraging Indians to Relate Realistically to the Total Cultural Enterprise in the Present World." Unpublished manuscript, Marquette.

Thompson, Donald R. 1953. "A History of Holy Rosary Indian Mission from Its Beginnings to the Present." M.A. thesis, University of Denver.

Thwaites, Reuben Gold, ed. 1896–1901. *The Jesuit Relations and Allied Documents.* 73 vols. Cleveland: Burrows Brothers Company.

Tiffin, (Rev.) Brian, S.J. 1985. "Memories and Anticipations: The Native Apostolate—Then and Now." *Kerygma* 19:179–184.

Tinker, George. 1993. *Missionary Conquest: The Gospel and Native American Cultural Genocide.* Minneapolis: Fortress Press.

Treat, James, ed. 1996. *Native and Christian: Indigenous Voices on Religious Identity in the United States and Canada.* New York: Routledge.

Troy, (Sister) Margaret, S.S.M. August 3, 1989. Interview by author, Fargo, North Dakota.

——. August 5, 1993. Interview by author, Swinomish, Washington.

Turnbull, Colin M. 1972. *The Mountain People.* New York: Simon and Schuster.

Turner, Harold W. 1973. "Old and New Religions among North American Indians: Missiological Impressions and Reflections." *Missiology* 1, no. 2:47–66.

Two Bulls, (Rev.) Robert. August 4, 1988. "The Preference of Episcopalianism by Full Blood Lakotas." Two Roads Conference.

Two Roads Conference: A Century of Christian Missions among the Lakota. August 2–4, 1988. Holy Rosary Mission, Pine Ridge, South Dakota.

Twohy, (Rev.) Patrick J., S.J. 1984. *Finding a Way Home: Indian and Catholic Spiritual Paths of the Plateau Tribes.* Inchelium, Wash.: St. Michaels [sic] Mission.

Urban Catholic Indian Ministries. 1989–1992. *Kateri Urban Circles* (newsletter).

"Vatican Issues New Regulations That Provide Gradual Initiation." February 18, 1972. *New York Times,* p. 8.

Verret, Kirby. November 18–22, 1990. Interviews by author, Grand Caillou, Dulac, Louisiana.

"A Visit to Canada's Native Peoples." October 15, 1987. *Origins* 17, no. 18: 334–335.

Walker, James R. 1991. *Lakota Belief and Ritual.* Ed. Raymond J. DeMallie and Elaine A. Jahner. Lincoln: University of Nebraska Press.

Walsh, Catherine. December 1987. "Donald Pelotte: First Native American Bishop." *St. Anthony Messenger* 95:16–23.

———. April 1989. "Native Catholics." *St. Anthony Messenger* 96:28–36.

———. February 1990a. "Making Native Americans at Home in the Church." *Extension* 84:20–21.

———. February 1990b. "Walking the Sacred Circle with Christ." *Extension* 84:8–13, 22–23.

———. August 5, 1992. Interview by author, Orono, Maine.

———. August 9, 1992. "Catholicism and Tradition in a Meeting of Indians." *New York Times,* n.p.

———. August 17, 1992. "Catholic Indians Try to Reconcile 2 Traditions." *New York Times,* p. A16.

———. August 30, 1992. Telephone interview by author.

———. October 31, 1992. "Native American Catholics at a Crossroads." *America* 167:328–331.

———. July 19, 1993. Telephone interview by author.

———. August 7, 1993. Interview by author, Seattle, Washington.

———. N.d. "The Eucharist and the Sweat Lodge: A Lakota Sioux Speaks Out on His Journey." Unpublished manuscript in author's possession.

Waugh, Earle H. 1996. *Dissonant Worlds: Roger Vandersteene among the Cree.* Waterloo, Ontario: Wilfrid Laurier University Press.

Weiser, (Rev.) Francis X., S.J. 1972. *Kateri Tekakwitha.* Montreal: Kateri Center.

Westropp, (Rev.) Henry Ign., S.J. c. 1910. *In the Land of the Wigwam.* Pine Ridge, S.Dak.: Holy Rosary Mission.

———. c. 1918. "Bits of Missionary Life among the Sioux." HRMR, Marquette.

———. N.d. "In the Land of the Wigwam: Children's Lecture on the Jesuit Missions in S. Dakota." HRMR, Marquette.

White, Elizabeth L. 1996. "Worlds in Collision: Jesuit Missionaries and Salish Indians on the Columbia Plateau, 1841–1850." *Oregon Historical Quarterly* 97, no. 1:26–45.

White, (Rev.) George M., O.M.I. August 5, 1995. Interview by author, St. Regis, Quebec.

White, James D. 1997. *Getting Sense: The Osages and Their Missionaries.* Tulsa, Okla.: Sarto Press.

White, (Rev.) Robert A., S.J. February 1959. "The Indian Comes to Town." *Reign of the Sacred Heart,* pp. 15–18.

———. 1960. "The Urbanization of the Dakota Indians." M.A. thesis, St. Louis University.

———. 1965. "Christianity on the Reservations." HRMR, Marquette.

———. November 17, 1968. "Transcript of speech, Mother Butler Center, Rapid City." HRMR, Marquette.

———. August 1969. "Church-Imposed Uniformity," *Great Plains Observer,* pp. 13–14.

———. 1970. "The Lower-Class 'Culture of Excitement' among the Contemporary Sioux." In *The Modern Sioux: Social Systems and Reservation Culture,* ed. Ethel Nurge, 175–197. Lincoln: University of Nebraska Press.

———. c. 1973. Untitled manuscript, HRMR, Marquette.

———. N.d. "The Crisis among the Sioux Today." HRMR, Marquette.

Whitehead, Margaret. 1981. *The Cariboo Mission: A History of the Oblates.* Victoria, B.C.: Sono Nis Press.

———. 1988. *They Call Me Father: Memoirs of Father Nicolas Coccola.* Vancouver: University of British Columbia Press.

Wind River Rendezvous, The. May–June 1979.

Wintz, (Rev.) Jack, O.F.M. July 1975. "Respect Our Values." *St. Anthony Messenger,* pp. 34–40.

Wolcott, John. July 1, 1990. "Appreciating the Gifts of Native Americans." *Our Sunday Visitor,* p. 10.

Works Progress Administration. 1936–1940, 1942. *Chippewa Indian Historical Project Records.* 2 reels microfilm, Wisconsin.

Wren, Christopher S. March 10, 1985. "Pope's Cancelled Visit Makes Mark in Canada." *New York Times,* p. 20.

Wynne, (Rev.) John J., S.J. September 22, 1929. "Indian Missions Past and Present." *The Catholic Mind* 27:341–347.

Yellow, Don. August 7, 1992. "Diocesan Concerns/Native American Ministry." Lecture, Orono, Maine.

Zeilinger, Ron. 1984. *Lakota Life.* Chamberlain, S.Dak.: St. Joseph's Indian School.

———. 1985. *The Way of the Cross: Tree of Life.* Chamberlain, S.Dak.: St. Joseph's Indian School.

———. 1986. *Sacred Ground: Reflections on Lakota Spirituality and the Gospel.* Chamberlain, S.Dak.: Tipi Press.

Zens, (Sister) M. Serena, O.S.B. 1936. "The Educational Work of the Catholic Church among the Indians of South Dakota." M.A. thesis, University of South Dakota.

Zimmer, (Rev.) Ronald P., O.M.I. October–December 1973. "Early Oblate Attempts for Indian and Metis Priests in Canada." *Études Oblates* 32: 276–291.

Zuern, (Rev.) Ted. S.J. N.d. *Indian Nations, American Citizens.* Washington, D.C.: Bureau of Catholic Indian Missions.

———. March 18, 1987. Telephone interview by author.

———. 1991. *Bread and Freedom.* Chamberlain, S.Dak.: St. Joseph's Indian School.

———. August 4, 1995. Interview by author, Kahnawake, Quebec.

INDEX

A

Abeita, Marcelino, 239

Abenaki Indians, 217

abortion, 81, 338

Abraham, 15

accommodationism, 7, 90, 110, 117, 119, 123, 125, 133, 135, 243–244, 317, 339

acculturation, 27, 51, 71, 73, 91, 98, 290, 341

Acoma Indians, 218, 220, 238

Act of Contrition, 14, 236

Adam and Eve, 15, 123, 310

afterlife, 17, 19, 68, 133, 295, 310–311, 321

AIDS, 220, 371

Akwesasne, Quebec, 188, 191, 249

alcohol use, 17, 22, 31, 46, 49, 75, 79, 81, 115, 124, 128–129, 139, 145, 150, 152, 160–162, 190–191, 201, 206–209, 215, 219–220, 224, 235, 245–246, 261, 278, 312, 321, 334–337, 345, 347, 351, 353–354, 365, 371–376

Alcoholics Anonymous (AA), 139, 160–161, 209, 336, 372

Algonkian Indians, 76, 175, 234, 265

Allouez, Claude, 7

altar boys, 25

altars, xiii, 25, 53, 67, 154, 159, 181–182, 191, 206, 210, 236, 254, 301–302, 308, 359

American Indian Leadership Council, 58, 63

American Indian Movement (AIM), 19, 57, 59, 65–66, 108, 205, 244, 277

Amiotte, Arthur, 21

ancestors, 75, 90, 103, 120, 123, 133, 137, 193, 229, 236, 245, 255, 271, 291, 306, 327, 340

angels, 24, 255, 299, 312, 344

Anishinabe Indians, 128, 130, 156, 182, 346. *See also* Ojibway Indians, Ottawa Indians, Potawatomi Indians

Anishinabe Spiritual Centre, Ontario, 128, 130, 132, 242, 244, 289

Antone, Alfretta, 270, 347

Apache Indians, 89, 99, 155, 159, 179, 215, 218, 220, 225, 244, 270, 274, 339, 346

Apostles' Creed, 152

Apple, John, 13

Arapaho Indians, 38, 77, 80, 89, 98, 100, 127, 129–130, 132–133

Archambault, Marie Therese, xiv, 42, 78, 81, 155, 245, 276–281, 290, 324, 355, 365–366

Archambault, Theresa, 78

· 401 ·

Sisters of St. Joseph, 182

Sitting Bull, 10

Skanudharoura, Geneviève-
Agnes, 265

Skylstad, William S., 117

Skyworld Woman, 123

Smet, Pierre Jean de, 7–8, 86, 90,
175

Smith, Huston, 374

sodalities, 15, 20, 24–26, 30–33,
36, 186

Solomon, Eva, 282, 358

souls, 17, 188, 209, 249, 294–295,
310–311, 317, 320–321

Spears, John, 244, 252

spirituality, 5, 23–24, 28, 33, 36,
40, 52, 55, 63–64, 72, 75, 78–79,
81, 97, 108, 111, 113, 115, 120–
121, 123–124, 127, 130–133, 137,
139, 149–151, 155–156, 160, 168–
169, 175, 179, 187, 197, 204–205,
207, 209–212, 215–216, 220,
227–228, 230, 240, 244–245,
252, 254, 260–261, 267, 270–
271, 273, 275, 277–279, 283,
300, 307, 322, 336–337, 342,
348–349, 354, 365–366, 372–377

Spokane Indians, 89

Spotted Eagle, Grace, 65

Spotted Tail, 8, 78

Spring Hill Academy, Michigan,
85

St. Agnes Church, South Dakota,
42, 66

St. Aloysius Church, Washington,
155

St. Aloysius Mission, South
Dakota, 238

St. Anthony Church, Arizona, 365

St. Augustine Church, New Mexico, 365

St. Augustine Mission, Nebraska,
365

St. Barbara Church, South
Dakota, 13

St. Benedict Joseph Labre's Mission, Montana, 77, 93

St. Catherine's Indian School,
New Mexico, 271–272

St. Cecelia's Church, South
Dakota, 13

St. Eloi Church, Louisiana, 198

St. Francis Home for Children,
South Dakota, 72

St. Francis Mission, South
Dakota, 8, 18, 37, 50, 55, 77–78,
156, 290, 298, 312, 317, 321

St. Francis Seminary, Wisconsin,
177

St. Francis Xavier Church,
Michigan, 156

St. James Cathedral,
Washington, 362

St. John's Abbey, Minnesota,
252

St. Joseph and St. Mary
Societies, 30, 32, 35, 57, 76, 125,
268

St. Joseph's Seminary, Louisiana,
198

St. Louis University, 276

St. Lucy's, New York, 155, 250,
332

St. Mary's Mission, Minnesota,
365

St. Mary's Mission School,
Wisconsin, 177

St. Mary's University, 276